(46-8751)   10-14-03   Sparks

FOLLOWING THE INDIAN WARS

The Story of the Newspaper Correspondents
Among the Indian Campaigners

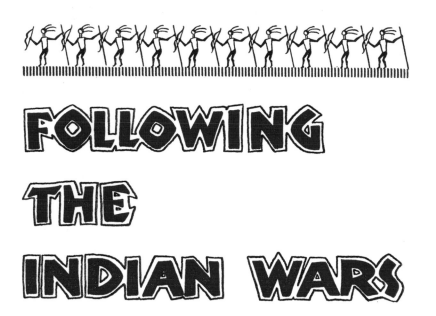

FOLLOWING THE INDIAN WARS

The Story of the Newspaper Correspondents
Among the Indian Campaigners

by OLIVER KNIGHT

UNIVERSITY OF OKLAHOMA PRESS : NORMAN

By OLIVER KNIGHT

Fort Worth: Outpost on the Trinity (Norman, 1953)
*Following the Indian Wars: The Story of the Newspaper Corre-
spondents Among the Indian Campaigners* (Norman, 1960)

LIBRARY OF CONGRESS CATALOG CARD NUMBER: 60–8751

For Mike and Skipper

PREFACE

A NEWSPAPER REPORTER is an interesting sort of guy, no matter under what circumstances you find him. And when you find him out fighting Indians, he becomes downright fascinating. It's so out of character.

However, the men discussed in this book were not really out of character. They constitute a group of war correspondents who have been rather generally ignored both by frontier historians and by historians of journalism. They don't deserve to be ignored.

These men were in truth war correspondents, and emphasis has been placed upon them as such in these pages, but a number of other factors intruded from the very beginning of my research which need a word of explanation here.

To begin with, this account is confined to accredited newspaper correspondents who reported various campaigns of the United States Army against hostile Indians in the trans-Mississippi West between 1866 and 1891. An accredited correspondent is defined as one representing a given newspaper on assignment, although in today's parlance the term usually means that a reporter has received credentials from a proper agency, such as the Department of Defense. The restriction to accredited correspondents means leaving out a number of other writers, such as army officers and free-lancers, but their inclusion would have necessitated a study of how the American press generally handled news of Indian campaigns, and that is not the point at all.

The point, rather, is to take a look at a group of war correspondents in a specialized war, with the realization that they —and other war correspondents as well—are reporters first and war correspondents second. Unfortunately, their place either as reporters or as war correspondents cannot be fixed with any assurance, because the larger history of war correspondence has not been thoroughly explored and because adequate historical studies of the newspaper reporter have not been made. This fact, however, does not prevent us from looking at this group both as war correspondents and as reporters and finding some good adventure stories in the bargain.

One other exclusion should be noted and explained here. An important element of all war reporting since the Civil War has been the pictorial angle. An artist-correspondent, William Simpson of the *London Illustrated News,* was the only staff man of a foreign publication on any Indian campaign. Other pictorial journalists also appeared—the young photographer Ridgeway Glover, killed by an Arapaho in 1866; T. R. Davis on the Hancock expedition of 1867; and possibly one or two artists who joined Crook in August, 1876. These artist-correspondents have been excluded from this account because they represented a specialized and differentiated reporting function, which it is not my purpose to examine and assess.

Perhaps one reason why the work of the newspaper reporter has been neglected is the difficulty of identification of his work. Until relatively recent years, the newspaper was much more impersonal even than it is now, and seldom was the identity of a reporter disclosed through by-line or initials at the end of the story. Consequently, in many instances, the identity of the reporter has been lost forever. On other occasions, fortunately, participants identified certain reporters in reminiscences written in after years. It was through the latter process that many of these correspondents were identified initially, although some had to be identified by other means.

When it came to identifying a given story as having been written by a certain reporter, I was often forced to resort to association—that is, a given reporter is known to have represented a certain newspaper on a given campaign, and in the absence of evidence to the contrary, all stories in that newspaper from that campaign were assumed to have been written by that correspondent. This method was used in every instance in connection with *New York Herald* correspondents, for example. There was, of course, no problem when newspapers used signed stories; however, only the *Chicago Times* followed that practice consistently.

The day-by-day life of men on an Indian campaign has been described in order to present accurately the conditions under which the reporters lived and worked. Only in that manner, it was felt, could even a near approach to verisimilitude be made. The atmosphere, the attitudes, the habits, the dress, the food, and the daily routine of officers and men must be understood before the work of the reporter in their company can be understood.

The reporter's experiences and stories have been considered chronologically, in the belief that such treatment affords the means of answering certain crucial questions: What did the reporter know? When did he get his information? From whom did he get it? Under what circumstances? How much did he get from personal experience? How reliably did he report what he knew? What did he not know?

The circumstances under which a man receives information or comes to an understanding of some incident or condition—whether in intense excitement, in peril, in anger, or in the quiet of a lazy Sunday in camp—will affect the manner in which he communicates that awareness to others. Whenever possible, then, those circumstances have been described. Examples can be found in the account of how the *New York Herald* correspondent with Sheridan first learned of Custer's battle on the Washita and of the slow realization that Sitting Bull was not the war leader of the Sioux in 1876.

Attention has also been given to the personal history of each correspondent, especially his background before he reported an Indian campaign, although no effort at all has been made to make an encyclopedic study of every correspondent in the field.

Obviously, a book like this could never have been written

without the aid of many individuals in locating the basic information. In the course of both research and writing, I have incurred obligations to persons and institutions for their generous assistance and kind consideration. In particular, I wish to acknowledge the assistance of the following persons and institutions: the Graduate School of Indiana University for a faculty research grant; Professor Vernon Carstensen, University of Wisconsin; Professor John E. Stempel, Indiana University; Miss Barbara Brand of the Interlibrary Loan Department of Indiana University Library; Mr. Stanley Pargellis, Newberry Library; Mr. Allan R. Ottley, California section librarian of the California State Library; Wisconsin State Historical Society Library; New York Public Library; Mr. Willoughby M. Babcock, curator of newspapers of the Minnesota Historical Society; Mr. Donald F. Danker, archivist of the Nebraska State Historical Society; Mr. Victor Gondos, Jr., archivist in charge, Civil War Branch, National Archives and Records Service; Miss Reta Ridings, head of Research Services, Wyoming State Archives and Historical Department; State Historical Society of Colorado; Mr. Matthew Redding, reference librarian, *New York World-Telegram and Sun;* Mrs. Helen H. Bretnor, reference librarian, Bancroft Library, University of California; the British Museum; San Francisco Public Library; Mrs. Edythe L. George, South Dakota Historical Society; Mr. Richard G. Elliott, librarian, Strahorn Memorial Library, the College of Idaho; United States Military Academy Library; Miss Margaret Rose, librarian, State Historical Society of North Dakota; and the Office of the Chief of Military History, Department of the Army.

Other contributions are recognized in the footnotes, but one source should be singled out here. The late Elmo Scott Watson, of the Medill School of Journalism in Northwestern University, was the first person to dig into this subject, and he compiled the biographical information for many of the correspondents discussed in this volume. Through the courtesy of the Newberry Library, I examined the Watson Papers and found there biographical information which otherwise would have required protracted research.

OLIVER KNIGHT

Bloomington, Indiana
April 23, 1960

CONTENTS

ILLUSTRATIONS AND MAPS

FOLLOWING
THE INDIAN WARS

The Story of the Newspaper Correspondents
Among the Indian Campaigners

Precede

1♦ INDIAN FIGHTING
IS HARDEST KIND OF WAR

> *Let no easy-going journalist suppose
> that an Indian campaign is a picnic. If
> he goes out on such business he must
> go prepared to ride his forty or fifty
> miles a day, go sometimes on half ra-
> tions, sleep on the ground with small
> covering, roast, sweat, freeze, and
> make the acquaintance of such vermin
> or reptiles as may flourish in the vi-
> cinity of his couch; and, finally, be
> ready to fight Sitting Bull or Satan
> when the trouble begins, for God and
> the United States hate non-combatants.*
>
> JOHN F. FINERTY[1]

EXPLOITATION of the continent made more fighting inevitable as soon as the American people were released from the
demands of the Civil War. They had first realized a sense of
continent in the 1840's, had been deflected from this interest
by the Civil War, and returned to it with vigor once that war
was over. Frenziedly compensating for the lost years of violence, they beat upon the treasure house of the mountains,
forced their unthinking way on to the plains, and demanded
for themselves all of whatever the desert might hold. They
had to fight for it, just as the settlers on the eastern frontiers
had fought, but with several significant differences.

Coming to the Great Plains as woodland pedestrians, they
met the shock force of mounted Plains Indians, red Cossacks
of the inland. Only by systematic warfare could those war-
riors-by-birth be forced aside. Because the challenge was too

---

[1] John F. Finerty, *War-Path and Bivouac*, 120. Troops seldom traveled as
far as "forty or fifty miles" in a day.

3

much for the guerrilla-settler type who had fought his way through eastern forests, the task of fighting western Indians devolved upon the Regular Army. The nature of the military obstacle required the services of the army, to be sure, but another factor also was involved: the federal government was expected to provide far more services than during the more individualistic period of frontier advance east of the Mississippi River.

In course of time the Regular Army became in part an organization of professional Indian fighters. In 1866 it was, in almost every respect, a new army, but out of its services in the West it gained such distinctiveness that in after years it was spoken of as the "Old Army." It fought a new war that often proved too much for its habit-bound organization, but finally won that war—perhaps more through logistics than skill of arms. The war, which lasted for twenty-five years, from 1866 to 1891, is comparable to nothing else in the frontier experience.

Ordinarily, this phase of the moving frontier is known as that of Indian *wars,* in the plural. However, the continuous fighting over a twenty-five year period appears in perspective as one general western war, involving many campaigns in various theaters. The "Western War" can be likened somewhat to the Hundred Years' War or the Thirty Years' War in Europe in that hostilities extended over many years, including periods of both active warfare and quiescence.

Upon the western warfare American newspapers turned their newly acquired technique of war reporting. War correspondence had bloomed into a specialized journalistic function during the Civil War, and thereafter the war correspondent took his place as a singular figure in both journalism and adventure. But the Civil War correspondents had earned their ease—most of them—and left war to others. Just as a new army went into the West, so a fresh corps of war correspondents went with it. The nature of western warfare made the Indian war correspondent just as different from his fellows as it made the Indian-fighting West Pointer, in campaign hat

4

and buckskin jacket, a sort of guerrilla fighter in comparison with gold-braided traditionalists.

The Western War correspondent was compelled to ride to the charge and to do his share of the fighting when occasion demanded, a requirement that set him off from correspondents in other wars. True, war correspondents have fought in other wars, but not because they had to, except in isolated instances. In the West, the war correspondent's first requirements were a weapon, a mount, and a courier with courage enough to take the story back through a country picketed by savages. As a member of the expedition—itself a privileged new position for the war correspondent generally—he accompanied an undermanned army in search of a foe superior in numbers, to fight battles, each of which was a "forlorn hope," as General Phil Sheridan expressed it.[2] He had to live, and dare to die, on even terms with the rough-and-ready men of the Old Army—a fighting corps adjudged by the British commander-in-chief as the finest in the world, man for man.[3]

General William Tecumseh Sherman called Indian fighting the "hardest kind of war,"[4] and an analogy might be extended to Indian war coverage. An army column, cut loose from its base of supplies, became an unsupported military element far advanced into hostile territory. Usually, the column had no clear idea exactly where the enemy force might be encountered, but the enemy less frequently was ignorant of the whereabouts of the army. Surrounded by wilderness, the correspondent was one with the soldier—a white man, one to be slain, not a noncombatant bearing credentials. He had also to meet the soldier's test of rugged endurance—long hours and days in an unaccustomed saddle, sometimes months in the field, marching through dust or scorching heat or driving snow or sub-zero temperatures, miles from a roof, facing instant death and mutilation upon straying from the column, subsisting on hardtack, bacon, and coffee, and sometimes vile

[2] Secretary of War, *Report, 1878*, I, 38.
[3] Fairfax Downey, *Indian-Fighting Army*, 309.
[4] 41 Cong., 2 sess., *House Ex. Doc. 240*, 177.

5

water. Worse yet, communications facilities were as far removed from the reporter as civilization from wilderness. Only at great personal risk could a courier get the dispatches back to a telegraph operator.

Front-line coverage was the only kind known by staff men who went into the field. There, too, the distinctive nature of western warfare made its impress upon the coverage. Most war coverage has come from the rear echelon or, in earlier years, from a point of vantage. There was no rear echelon in Indian fighting, and anyone on a near-by point of vantage might never have another haircut. The reporter either went all the way or stayed at home.

Accredited correspondents of daily newspapers—that is, either staff men or reporters hired specifically to represent a given newspaper during a campaign, as distinct from part-time correspondents—went with army expeditions into the three theaters of the Western War of 1866–91—the plains, the mountains, and the desert.

It was essentially a war of races—a paradoxically imperialistic war fought on America's own back stoop, imperialistic in the sense that a powerful civilized government took land which a primitive people regarded as their own. Two causes of the war—or, more accurately, the causes of two phases of the war—presented themselves to General Sheridan, an opinionated direct-actionist who, strangely, could be reflective. Having exercised command through the hardest part of the fighting, he looked back in 1878 and decided that the first cause was the collision of races—the Indians were happy in the mastery of an abundant land when "along came the nineteenth-century progress, or whatever it may be called, to disturb their happy condition." He explained: "In other words, we took away their country and their means of support, broke up their mode of living, their habits of life, introduced disease and decay among them, and it was for this and against this that they made war. Could anyone expect less?" He said the second cause appeared when the Indian, cooped up on an unaccustomed reservation, sickened because of the change,

6

went hungry when the government provided insufficient food, became generally dissatisfied, and broke out in an effort to regain himself. Sheridan viewed the first cause as inevitable "in accordance with our ideas of progress," but thought "second wars are within our control, and we are responsible for them." He maintained that the government was obligated to give the reservation Indian the kind, firm, and just treatment which he had not theretofore received from that source.[5]

Most of the resulting fighting occurred on the Great Plains, the area formerly regarded as the permanent home of the American Indian. Once the Great Plains had bridled the advance of a westward-moving people. To a woods and sea people the Great Plains were lonely in their immensity, frightening in their treelessness, confounding in their aridity. Often the plains evoked a comparison with the ocean. Early explorers left Americans with the idea that the plains constituted the "Great American Desert," of no possible use to a civilized people; but in time that image vanished. Until after the Civil War, however, the plains were important only as an avenue of travel, on a few restricted routes, to the West Coast.

When the plains land came into demand after the Civil War, population pressed against the Indian lands from both East and West. The one-directional westward movement of the frontier became a two-directional movement, because of miners moving eastward from the Pacific Coast and others moving westward.

At first, the land of the plains was not in great demand for settlement. Rather, it was wanted for immense grazing preserves during the days of the cattlemen's frontier. More importantly, United States citizens demanded free and safe transit across the Indian lands. The demands of the transportation frontier in turn were twofold—to reach the West Coast and to reach the mountain communities that had appeared on the mining frontier. The first transcontinental railroad was completed through the Indians' hunting grounds on the plains during the 1860's. Others were built in the

[5] Secretary of War, *Report, 1878*, I, 34–38.

course of years, and along the railroads towns were built. From the railroad towns, freight and stage routes connected with the mining settlements in the mountains.

As the years progressed, farmers moved westward to the plains, cautiously at first, willing to try only the more fertile valleys, huddling around communities on established transportation routes. Invited by the Homestead Act, which made western land cheap, and by the allure of railroad advertising, more and more settlers took up land on the plains.

The swiftness of the resulting demographic change on the plains suggests the strength of white pressure on the interior lands. At the end of the Civil War the nomadic Plains Indian lived well by his standards. The grassland fattened his commissary—two huge herds of buffalo, known as the northern and southern herds, each numbering from two to three million animals. The entire region pastured his large pony herds, required for hunting, transportation, and war. Trapping gave him furs in addition to buffalo robes for barter to white traders. He went when and where he pleased within the dominion of his own tribal area. But within thirteen years all that was changed. Looking back in 1878, General Sherman, who had seen it all come to pass from a position of command, said: "This vast region has undergone in the past ten years a more violent and radical change than any like space of the earth's surface during any previous fifty years."[6]

A long prelude to the Western War began with the first white competition for the lands in question. The miners' invasion of the mountains brought intermittent warfare with the Snake, Bannock, and Ute Indians, who were forced on to reservations or circumscribed within restricted areas. Hard fighting in the Southwest brought the Navahos under control during the Civil War, but Apache resistance continued until the 1870's. On the plains, a treaty concluded at Fort Laramie in 1851 assigned definite areas for all the Plains tribes north of Indian Territory; but the discovery of gold in the Pikes Peak region in 1858 brought a new crisis with an effort to

[6] *Ibid.*, 4–5.

8

restrict the Southern Cheyennes and Arapahos still further. In retaliation Cheyenne warriors went on the warpath for the three years of 1861–63. Then, in 1864, J. M. Chivington, erstwhile minister of the gospel, led a group of Colorado militia who massacred more than four hundred Indians at Sand Creek in eastern Colorado. Infuriated Indians retaliated through the winter of 1864–65 with raiding parties through the Platte Valley. A peace commission in 1865 forced the Cheyennes and Arapahos to accept a smaller reservation and the Kiowas and Comanches to give up claims to central Texas, western Kansas and eastern New Mexico in return for a hunting ground in the region of the Texas Panhandle. Farther north, the Sioux served notice in 1865 that they would not permit white men to travel the Bozeman Trail through their hunting ground to the Montana mining settlements.

Still the white man encroached upon the western lands, and to defend those lands, the Indians struck at settlements and transportation routes. The army struck back in turn. The net result was a war which occupied the army for twenty-five years. The warfare centered on the plains, from the Canadian border to the Río Grande, but the army pursued hostile Indians even into Mexico. The Plains Indian commanded the attention of two-thirds of the U. S. Army during the Western War, while Apaches, Snakes, Bannocks, Utes, and Nez Percés engaged troops in other episodes.

An army record shows 1,065 engagements with Indians between 1866 and 1891.[7] Statistically the compilation is not consistent in that it includes engagements between civilians and Indians as well as between troops and Indians; nor does the record purport to count all encounters with Indians.

Of the total engagements recorded, 930 were fights between soldiers and Indians; 592 were fought by small bodies of troops—a company, a detachment, or an escort. Thus, small units fought 63 per cent of the army's western engagements. Only 70 engagements, or 7 per cent, were fought by five com-

[7] *Chronological List of Actions, &c., with Indians, from January 1, 1866, to January, 1891* (Office Memoranda, Adjutant General's Office), 2–56.

panies or more. On the basis of the 1,065 fights, the white man averaged 37 warring encounters a year with Indians.

/ The peak of the fighting came in the three fighting seasons of 1867–69. In 1868, the army recorded 140 engagements, the greatest number for any one year. However, the number of engagements does not always accurately reflect the true situation in any one year. For example, the hardest fighting and campaigning occurred in 1876 when but 41 engagements were recorded. After the subjugation of Southern Plains Indians in 1874, the number of fights dropped substantially. And after the final submission of the Sioux in 1881, the number of engagements each year dribbled down to one, two, seven, and eleven.

The Western War went through three general phases. What can be identified for want of a better term as the phase of reversal came immediately after the Civil War, signalized by the government's abandonment of forts protecting the Bozeman Trail at the insistence of the Sioux. The military recognized the critical situation existing between 1867 and 1869, for in 1867, General Sherman, then commanding the Military Division of the Missouri, said he thought that year would be the year of crisis on the plains. Actually, the entire three-year period was one of crisis, in which the army adjusted to the conditions of plains fighting and began the relentless warfare in which it lost many of the battles except the last. The phase of decision came in the 1870's, especially in the middle of that decade. Then, well-organized columns sought out the irreconcilables of the Southern Plains Indians in the fastnesses of the Staked Plains and defeated them. Others broke up the Sioux and Northern Cheyennes, forcing the remnants into Canada. Troopers crushed the military power of the Apaches. The army also re-subdued the Modocs, Bannocks, and Utes who rebelled against reservation conditions or treaty violations, and then met long frustration at the hands of the Nez Percés, who made one of the most brilliant military movements of history. The phase of mopping-up, to use a military expression, came during the 1880's when

10

small outlaw bands of Apaches had to be hunted down like so many wild animals. Then came the *finis* in a few days of the winter of 1890–91, when the once-proud Sioux fought for the last time at Wounded Knee against overpowering odds.

Practically all the fighting was confined to the plains and desert. Only one campaign of consequence was fought on the Pacific Coast—the Modoc War of 1873. Three were in the mountains—the Ute, Bannock, and Nez Percé campaigns.

The fighting included twelve major campaigns between 1866 and 1891—campaigns in a general war for which the army belatedly awarded the Indian Campaign Badge in 1905. These were:

1. In southern Oregon and Idaho and northern California and Nevada, 1865–68.

2. Against the Southern Plains Indians in Kansas, Colorado, and Indian Territory, 1867–69.

3. The Modoc War in northern California in 1873.

4. Against Arizona Apaches in 1873.

5. Against Southern Plains Indians in Kansas, Colorado, Texas, Indian Territory, and New Mexico in 1874–75.

6. The Sioux-Cheyenne campaign of 1876–77.

7. Nez Percé campaign of 1877.

8. Bannock campaign of 1878.

9. Against Northern Cheyennes in 1878–79.

10. Against the Utes in Colorado and Utah in 1879–80.

11. Against the Apaches in Arizona and New Mexico in 1885–86.

12. Against the Sioux in South Dakota in 1890–91.[8]

The army's record shows 932 officers and enlisted men killed and 1,061 wounded during the twenty-five year period.[9] The total may not seem overly large when spread over twenty-five years, but the percentage of casualties is arresting in at least one instance. General Sheridan reported that the

[8] *Compilations of General Orders, Circulars and Bulletins . . . 1881 . . . 1915,* 163–64.
[9] *Chronological List of Actions.*

proportion of casualties to troops engaged on the Great Plains in 1876–77 exceeded those of the Civil War or the Russo-Turkish War then in progress.[10] His computation included the heavy loss suffered in Custer's defeat on the Little Big Horn; ordinarily, the casualty rate was much lower. The army's record also showed 461 civilians killed and 116 wounded, making a total of 2,571 white casualties during the twenty-five years. The same record shows 5,519 Indians killed and wounded.

The army estimate of Indian casualties must be accepted with reserve, however, even though it was based on reports from combat commanders. Soldiers seldom saw dead or wounded warriors; the Indian's code of honor compelled him to take his dead and wounded from the field. After an engagement, therefore, the military could only guess at the number of Indians slain. Even though the Indian fought only when he had superiority of numbers or when surprised, soldier estimates were apt to be exaggerated because of the confusion of battle and the fact that many troopers were rookies.

Indian estimates of dead and wounded, on the other hand, have received considerable credence by some white investigators, who have considered the Indian a valid source of information because his standing in the tribe depended in part upon his deeds in war. He thus had to watch the other warriors to avoid being outranked through falsehood. Indian accounts of battles, then, included not only the number of dead and wounded but the names of the fallen. Sioux accounts of twelve battles between 1865 and 1876 turned up only 69 warriors killed and 102 wounded.[11]

It must be remembered, however, that Indian accounts were of what any one warrior saw, and that there was no compilation of reports at the time. Thus, in spite of the credence which some investigators have given to Indian reports, any word-of-mouth account must be regarded with reserve, at best, especially when given long after the event. What it

[10] Secretary of War, *Report, 1877*, I, 58.
[11] Stanley Vestal, *New Sources of Indian History*, 131–36.

comes down to is that the historian does not have a trust-worthy guide to Indian casualties. As a matter of fact, one suspects at times that army casualty figures may have been masked.

The twenty-five years of fighting drained much treasure, in addition to much blood, from the United States. In 1882, Secretary of War Robert T. Lincoln estimated that Indian campaigning between 1872 and 1882 had cost $223,891,264. He based the estimate on the fact that three-fourths of the army was west of the Mississippi during those years and that fighting Indians was the chief occupation of the western army. An accurate estimate proved impossible for military administrators, however. General expenses of the army, such as food, forage, and transportation, could not be broken down exactly to show what was spent for actual campaigning and what for general maintenance of the military establishment.

Although fighting the Plains Indians would alone have been sufficient to make it a distinctly new war for the army, new military thought and technology, as well as an enlarged military responsibility, also stamped the Western War as different from anything preceding it. Much of the change must be attributed to the traumatic experience of the Civil War, which marks a break in the western military frontier as clearly as in politics.

The principal difference between the ante and post bellum missions of the army is implicit rather than explicit. It would appear that the army maintained an essentially defensive posture in the West before the Civil War, but pressed offensive operations after the Civil War. Before the Civil War, the army served a triple function in the West—defending settlements, maintaining peace among western tribes, and protecting the Indian against white intruders.[12] After the war, the army defended the advancing tide of civilization by nulli-

[12] For illustrations of the defensive posture, see Henry Putney Beers, *The Western Military Frontier, 1815–1846*, v, 50, 67, 70–71, 78, 98–99, 173, and Louis Pelzer, *Marches of the Dragoons in the Mississippi Valley*, 8, 37, 78, 81, 97.

fying the Indian's war power and forcing him to submit to Indian Bureau supervision on a reservation.

The changed concept is dramatized in the contrasting statements made by two officers of the different periods, showing an entirely different tenor and temper. In 1834, a Dragoon expedition approached Pawnee Pict and Toyash villages on the plains to establish either a friendly understanding or war—"officers and men on the alert, as if in the atmosphere of war."[13] There was no uncertainty of any sort, however, when Sherman said in 1867, "The more we can kill this year, the less will have to be killed the next war, for the more I see of these Indians the more convinced I am that they all have to be killed or be maintained as a species of paupers."[14]

Technology made the later fighting different, too. Muzzle-loaders of the pre–Civil War plains soldier gave way to repeating weapons, and the saber disappeared from the sword knot because its clanking heralded the approach of troops. The railroad and the telegraph speeded the concentration of troops in meeting the demands of war. The change can be seen in campaigns on the Texas plains. When Major Philip St. George Cooke led a small detachment from Fort Mason against warring Lipan Apaches in 1852, the troops had but two pistol bullets per man because the fort had contained no more. Twenty-two years later, soldiers unloosed the repeating fire of a Gatling gun against the Comanche Indians on the Staked Plains.

Territorial involvement also distinguished the Western War. Held to a strength of about 25,000 men through most of the period, the army fought throughout the West, from the Mississippi to the Pacific, from Canada and into Mexico. Never before and not again until World War II did the United States Army fight over such extensive terrain, nor has it ever fought for so long a time. In the plains area the army was stretched so thin that it averaged one man per 120 square

[13] Pelzer, *Marches of the Dragoons*, 37.
[14] Robert G. Athearn, *William Tecumseh Sherman and the Settlement of the West*, 223.

miles in Texas and one to 75 square miles farther north. The situation on the plains is illustrated by a typically caustic Sheridan comment in 1878:

No other nation in the world would have attempted the reduction of these wild tribes and occupation of their country with less than 60,000 or 70,000 men, while the whole force employed and scattered over the enormous region described never numbered over 14,000, and nearly one-third of this force has been confined to the line of the Río Grande to protect the Mexican frontier. The consequence was that every engagement was a forlorn hope, and was attended with a loss of life unparalleled in warfare. No quarter was given by the savages, and the officers and men had to enter on their duties with the most barbarous cruelties staring them in the face in case of defeat.[15]

Continuity of command further characterized the Western War. At no other time have American military forces been engaged for so long under the same commanders. Immediately after the Civil War, Sherman commanded the Military Division of the Missouri, embracing the Great Plains, with Sheridan as one of his department commanders later on. Sherman later was advanced to the post of General of the Army, and Sheridan succeeded him, first in command of the division and then of the entire army. Between them they directed military operations against western Indians during most of the period.

Military men repeatedly remarked upon the newness, to them, of the kind of fighting involved in the Western War. Almost invariably, that comment came from men who served against the Plains Indian. One officer, who came as a subaltern to the Fourth Cavalry, said the regimental commander —Colonel Ranald S. Mackenzie, a Civil War general at twenty-five—had to learn "a perfectly new game" when he took the field against Indians. "It differed so greatly from what we old Civil War veterans had seen, and so little was known of it that it proved to be an absolutely new kind of warfare, and the experience we had to gain, and that quickly—as we had

[15] Secretary of War, *Report, 1878*, I, 33, 36.

no time in which to study or any books from which to gain it —was to everybody in that command of a kind we had never seen or encountered."[16]

A similar comment, with a trace of bitterness, came from a young lieutenant with General Alfred Terry's Yellowstone Expedition after the Custer disaster. He mentioned in his diary of August, 1876, that newspapers had reached the command. "Some severe criticisms emanate from the press of many who know nothing of Indian warfare," he wrote. "They seem to think the same grand tactics are employed in it that is used in 'civilized' warfare, or battles."[17]

The mobility, tactics, arms, and training of the Plains Indian helped to make the Western War distinctive. The horse and the buffalo enabled him to hold out as long as he did, checking the advance of both the Spaniard and the Anglo-Saxon for a longer period than any other American aborigine was able to retard European invaders in the temperate zone. Because the Plains Indian lived in a horse culture, he was the only American Indian who was always mounted. Depending almost entirely upon the buffalo for commissary, he migrated much as the herds migrated, and was released from the necessity of developing even a rudimentary agriculture which made most of the eastern Indians at least partially sedentary. In addition, he has been characterized as among the most formidable fighters met during the entire frontier experience. Three reasons have been advanced to explain his ability to maintain an effective barrier against the whites: He was a nomad, without a settled village which could be made the target of attack; by nature he was more cruel, ferocious, and implacable than any other Indian; and he was a good horseman.[18]

However, the Plains Indian's barrier might not have lasted so long if his homeland had been as much in demand as were the lands east of the Mississippi. The military frontier was

[16] Capt. R. G. Carter, *On the Border with Mackenzie*, 535–36.
[17] *The Field Diary of Lt. Edward Settle Godfrey*, 31.
[18] Walter Prescott Webb, *The Great Plains*, 48, 53, 58–60, 61.

farther advanced in the West—generally speaking—than it had been in the East. In Pennsylvania and the Old Northwest, moreover, settlers moved in and occupied the land as soon as it had been wrested from the Indian. There was no one to move in and hold the land on the plains in quite the same manner as in the East. This in itself, of course, further contributes to the distinctiveness of the Western War.

Mobile warfare, fought by a mobile civilization, enabled the Plains Indian to frustrate even veterans who had learned something about mobility in the Civil War. For example, the Sioux could travel with his family at the rate of fifty miles a day, living on the country, moving through a region he knew intimately without the aid of maps. Even while moving at fifty miles a day, the Sioux Indians could—according to an army commander—keep scouts advanced at distances of twenty to fifty miles in all directions, know the number and movements of troops operating against them, know the army column's capabilities, and—above all—choose their own time and place of battle.[19] That may have been, and probably was, true of the Sioux campaign in the summer of 1876, but it was not always so. Although the militaristic Plains Indian did post scouts to warn of danger or to report buffalo, the organization of his society made any systematic espionage system impossible. On the other hand, hostile Indians often could learn of army movements through the agencies. Only to a limited degree could the Indian choose the time and place of battle. During the spring and summer, when his ponies were fat and lively, he could do so on some occasions, but when the army found and surprised a village, the shoe was on the other foot. Army officers as a group—judging from the popular writing and official reports of many of them—seem to have understood and appreciated the Indian. At the same time, they also showed a tendency to credit him with superior wisdom and intelligence, as frontiersmen often did, too. Both the soldier and the frontiersman thus subscribed at times to the myth of the Indian as concocted by romanticists.

[19] Gen. George Crook's report, in the Secretary of War's *Report, 1876,* I, 500.

In battle the Plains Indian used a new weapon which distinguished him from the Plains Indian the army had known before the Civil War—the breech-loading rifle with metallic cartridges. In the 1850's the Indian seldom used the rifle, but when he did, his muzzle-loader gave scant pause to soldiers. With saber alone the troops charged Indians. Then, in the 1850's, soldiers received Colt revolvers, with which they put Indians to rout. After the Civil War the Plains Indian had both the revolver and breech-loading rifle—sometimes given him by the same government which then asked its soldiers to fight him.

Not all Indians had rifles, but enough had modern arms to make a difference in the fighting after 1866. An army officer of long experience remarked that the breech-loading rifle and metallic cartridges transformed "the Plains Indian from an insignificant, scarcely dangerous adversary into as magnificent a soldier as the world can show."[20]

General George Crook observed that the breech-loader and metallic cartridge made the Plains Indian "ten thousand times more formidable."[21] He also said that with "the great improvement in arms in the hands of the savages, the perils of conflicts with them have immensely increased since the close of the rebellion, as our ghastly list of killed and wounded officers and soldiers will certify."[22] General O. O. Howard, the one-armed Quaker who was outgeneraled by Nez Percé chiefs, remarked poignantly: "In times gone by, when we have been better mounted and better armed than the Indians, and as well trained as they, we have beaten them in our conflicts."[23]

Considerable difference of opinion existed about how good the Indian was with a rifle. Crook placed a high value upon the Indian's marksmanship, using the hunt as an example of superior shooting. Shooting an animal, however, differed

[20] Col. Richard Irving Dodge, *Our Wild Indians: Thirty-three Years' Personal Experience Among the Red Men of the Great West*, 449–51.
[21] Secretary of War, *Report*, 1876, I, 500.
[22] *Ibid.*, 1880, I, 80.
[23] O. O. Howard, *Nez Perce Joseph*, 108.

quite a bit from firing at someone who could shoot back, and the judgment of Colonel Richard I. Dodge appears better balanced, justifying quotation in full:

> Compared with the white hunter of the plains, the Indian is a wretched shot. He is about equal to the United States soldier, being deficient for the same reason—lack of practice. The Government and the Indian are each too poor to afford to waste more than ten cartridges a month on drill, and no man ever became an expert marksman on that allowance. The Indian is really much more dangerous with the bow than with the pistol; but the latter gives a longer range, and the Indian does not like close fighting any better than other people.[24]

Certain it was that the soldier received precious little target practice. In 1874, for example, the Secretary of War pointed out that but 120 cartridges per year could be issued to each soldier for target practice because of the cost.

Whether armed with a Sharps rifle or with bow and lance, the Plains Indian employed tactics based upon slashing attacks made with lightning speed, followed by kaleidoscopic movement on the field. No orthodox tactic of white warfare could quite match the Indian's.

Fighting on horseback like the Mongol and Cossack, the Plains Indian went into battle, "charging at the enemy in extended order, then, if the foe did not stampede, circling rapidly around him."[25] Having once encircled the enemy, the Plains Indian, especially the Comanche, used his galloping pony as a shield. Hanging by one foot, the warrior dropped down on the side of his animal and fired under its neck at troops who thus could not get a clear shot at him. Again, Dodge gives the clearest picture of Indian tactics:

> The strength of the Indian is in surprises or ambuscades, and I have heard of no single instance of his acceptance of battle in the open field, except as preliminary to some huge trap, or when

[24] Richard Irving Dodge, *The Plains of the Great West and Their Inhabitants*, 331.
[25] Maj. Gen. John K. Herr and Edward S. Wallace, *The Story of the U. S. Cavalry, 1775–1942*, 149–50.

relying on an overwhelming preponderance of force. His tactics are always the same; never to receive a charge, but by constantly breaking, to separate the enemy into detached fragments; then suddenly concentrating to overwhelm them in detail. Having no trains or impediments of any kind, he is always able to avoid battle if the ground or opportunity does not suit him. The heavier slowly-moving troops, encumbered with trains of supplies, must attack when they can, and therefore almost always at disadvantage. Since the common use of breech-loaders by both combatants, I know of no single instance where troops have gained any signal advantage over Indians in open fight, and this for the reason that the moment they gain even a slight advantage, the Indians disappear with a celerity that defies pursuit. On the other hand, if the Indians gain the advantage, they press it with a most masterful vigor, and there results a massacre, which, like that of Custer's command, for a moment appals the country.[26]

The Indian had one great weakness, wherein the soldier found his own great strength. The savage intellect could see only the immediate gain or loss in warfare. He could not look ahead. Had he seen the importance of following up a victory, he might have lasted much longer than he did.

The white soldier's second wind and persistence allowed him to carry out a strategy which took advantage of another Indian weakness. The Indian fought voluntarily only when the grass greened; in winter he was a slugabed who liked his warm buffalo robes. To him it was senseless to go raiding in winter. But the army learned to fight the year round. Instead of waiting to meet depredations from a defensive posture, the army developed the practice of carrying the war to the Indian camp in winter, against the advice of plainsmen, as the one stroke of tactics which demoralized the enemy. The real problem was to find the village, but once the village was found, a surprise attack by troops could leave a band or tribe destitute and unable to fight any longer. When the soldiers had destroyed the buffalo-skin lodges and their contents and

[26] Dodge, *Our Wild Indians*, 490–92.

20

rounded up the pony herd which always was a prime objective in plains warfare, the Indians had nothing left. Strangely, at that most crucial of moments for him, the Indian fought at his worst. "No people who fight at all, fight so badly when surprised" as the Indian, Dodge said.[27]

The anomaly of a peacetime war also characterized the Western War. The presidents' annual messages said the country was at peace, but "within our own borders war was never ceasing; that for acrimony and deviltry on the part of the Indians, and of hardships, suffering and privations on the part of the troops engaged in it, was absolutely unknown in a war of any other character."[28]

Another and almost incredible factor distinguished the Western War. It was the one war in which the government told the army to fight, on the one hand, and on the other sometimes fed and sheltered the enemy. The army from time to time found that the enemy took refuge with another branch of the government—the Interior Department—whose Bureau of Indian Affairs supervised the reservations and issued annuities, including guns, to the Indians. Cries of indignation from eastern humanitarians also caused western commanders literally to fight on two fronts—to carry out government policy and then defend themselves against humanitarians.[29] The army, which had administered Indian affairs until they were transferred to the Interior Department in 1849, regularly criticized the civilian Indian agents, many of whom were self-seeking political appointees. On the other hand, Indian agents sometimes accused the army of responsibility for Indian outbreaks and of persecution of the Indian. Once again Dodge summed up the situation:

It is doubtful if there be a people on earth concerning whom there is so wide a difference of opinion as the North American Indians.

[27] Dodge, *Plains of the Great West,* 308.
[28] Maj. W. R. Parnell, "The Battle of White Bird Canyon," in Cyrus Townsend Brady's *Northwestern Fights and Fighters,* 91–92.
[29] Carl Coke Rister, *Border Command: General Phil Sheridan in the West,* vii.

21

Eastern people, educated, by reading Cooper's and other similar novels, to a romantic admiration for the "red man"; misled by the travellers' tales of enthusiastic missionaries, or the more interested statements of agents and professional humanitarians; and indulging in a philanthropy safe because distant, and sincere because ignorant, are ready to believe all impossible good, and nothing bad, of the "noble savage."

The western frontier people who come in contact with him, who suffer from his depredations, and whose life is made a nightmare by his vicinity, have no words to express their detestation of his duplicity, cruelty and barbarism. No amount of reason, no statement of facts, will ever change the opinion of either eastern or western people on this subject.[30]

Made unique by its composition and service, the Old Army reflected in its beginnings the dislocation of the Civil War. The older Regular Army disappeared during the Civil War, and out of the polyglot of regulars, volunteers, and draftees of the war the government fashioned a new military arm. The change can be seen most clearly in the officers of two cavalry regiments organized for western duty, one in each period. In 1855, Secretary of War Jefferson Davis created the Second Cavalry, an elite corps to serve in the West. Officered by many of the best men, its staff and line included Robert E. Lee, Johnston, Thomas, Van Dorn, Kirby Smith, Stoneman, Fitzhugh Lee, and Hood. Out of twenty-five officers, twelve became Confederate generals and several others became Union generals. Only eleven years later, the army formed the Seventh Cavalry, also for western duty—Custer's regiment. It was officered by three West Pointers, a Frenchman, a Prussian, a former member of Congress, a mixed-blood Indian, a former judge, a former papal Zouave, and a grandson of Alexander Hamilton. An extreme example, granted; yet those two regiments, unusual as each was, exemplify the difference between old and new in the type of officers available at regimental and lower levels. In the one case, professional officers were available; in the other, a hodgepodge of backgrounds

---

[30] *Plains of the Great West*, 255.

brought together as a result of a war which had called for more officers than West Point could supply.

During the twenty-five years of fighting the Old Army became an entity with a sharp beginning and an almost as sharp ending, fading as it did into the modern army that began taking shape in the late 1890's and early 1900's. Its ranks at first were filled by seasoned veterans of the Civil War, with a growing number of new recruits and new junior officers fresh from the Academy.

In mixture of nationalities, it was a foreign legion—Americans, Irish, Germans, French, British, Scandinavians, Italians, and Russians. The Eighth Infantry band in Montana during the 1880's reputedly had been imported as a unit from Italy. Many former Confederates were in its ranks, including some former Southern officers barred from holding commissions in the new United States Army. Another new element was the Negro—two cavalry regiments in the West were composed solely of Negro troopers, known to the Indians as "buffalo soldiers" because of their kinky hair.

The soldier of the Old Army came to be classed as a guerrilla type by European militarists. The forage cap gave way to the campaign hat, similar to the cowboy's adaptation to plains weather. The soldier adapted his clothing to the circumstances—stripped to a shirt under an Arizona sun, wore buckskin on the plains, bundled up in buffalo garments during a Montana winter.

Development of the Old Army began in 1866, when the last volunteers were withdrawn from the West. The presence of Civil War volunteers on the frontier helps to mark the change from the ante bellum to the post bellum army. The army suffered doubly when volunteers were substituted for regulars early in the Civil War. Withdrawal of the regulars meant weakness in Indian eyes, which led to more daring on the part of savages. Even though the volunteers wore army uniforms, they were relatively ineffective in the West, because they were not willing to fight Indians. In 1865, for example, three hundred deserted from General Connor's Powder River expedition. After the Civil War the government began dispersing the ballooned wartime army. Volunteers were discharged, and the government began the difficult task of rebuilding a Regular Army.

The Regular Army had numbered but 16,000 in 1860, and carried only 26,000 on its muster rolls during the Civil War. Heavy casualties, plus the Southern service of many able officers, left command positions open. Some of the command positions fell to volunteer officers who elected to remain in the army after the Civil War. In fact, volunteers filled the ranks of the new Regular Army from general to private. But in the sudden telescoping in size, inevitable demotions swiftly placed the officers in new ranks. Regimental commanders directed platoons; brigade commanders took their places at the head of cavalry troops. A young second lieutenant reporting to his first station in 1876 found in his company of enlisted men a former lieutenant colonel of New York volunteers, a Confederate captain then serving as bugler, and a major of volunteers.

Officer selection became a problem, soon solved. At first, the lieutenants of the new Regular Army came entirely from the wartime volunteers; higher officers came in equal numbers from the Regular Army and the volunteers, distributed geographically according to the number of troops furnished by each region. The grab-bag system made it difficult to cull out the proper officers from the hundreds who would have made the army a vocation. Within three years the army met the problem of officer selection with a "Benzine Board," which in 1869 cleansed the army of incompetent and unfit officers.

The quality of the men serving in the Regular Army seems to have been good, especially during the 1870's when the army fought through the decade of decision in the Western War. Major General J. M. Schofield, commanding the Military Division of the Pacific (the West Coast) in 1875, remarked on the contrast between the army officer and government civilian officers in the West. The army officer, he said, holds a commission for life. "It embodies all he has or hopes for. All his official acts undergo constant supervision; and, wherever he may be, a court-martial is always ready to inflict disgrace and imprisonment for any breach of honor." But, he said, the civil agent—referring to the Indian agent—holds his appointment for a few years at most and cannot be punished beyond loss of his "almost worthless" office. The civil agent, the General noted, could make more "out of one little 'job'" than his whole annual salary.[31] In the same year—the year of exposures and scandal in the Grant administration—Sheridan said he thought "the moral standing of the officers and men in the service higher at the present time than at any period within my knowledge."[32]

Although such comparisons probably were true for a majority of the army officers, it must not be thought that the army was simon-pure, either. The scandal involving Secretary of War W. W. Belknap with the sale of post traderships is an example of corruption in Washington. That such corruption may have extended to officers at the regimental level is indicated by a story told by Captain Frederick W. Benteen which connects Major General George Armstrong Custer with an attempted "shakedown" of at least one post trader. As Benteen related the story, Custer marched the Seventh Cavalry back to Camp Supply, in present Oklahoma, in 1869, and then hustled it off at daylight the day after arrival, even though the paymaster had waited for the regiment with orders to pay the men there. Upon reaching Camp Supply, according to the story, Custer allowed his men to visit the post only with passes issued by himself. He had sent an officer to the post trader with a message that if the trader would give him $3,500 in exchange for a bill of sale for an ambulance and four mules and horses, Custer would pay his men there, where they could spend their money with the trader. Otherwise, Custer would leave at daybreak and pay his men at Fort Hays, Kansas. The trader refused, and Custer marched at daylight. Benteen obtained the details, he said, from a man

[31] Secretary of War, *Report, 1875,* I, 123.
[32] *Ibid.,* 58.

who had been the trader's bookkeeper, but Benteen had also been with the regiment at the time and remembered leaving the day after arrival. In this connection it must be remembered that Benteen was an inveterate enemy of Custer.[33]

Pay of the army received much criticism, and it certainly enforced impecunious living upon officers who faced a life of austerity at most frontier posts, anyway. Yet the Secretary of War said in 1886 that officer pay through all grades was higher than that of any other army except the Anglo-Indian army.

Pay of enlisted men was cited frequently as a cause of desertions—a plague which tormented many western commanders. Causes of desertion varied. The enlisted soldier's pay, beginning at $13.00 a month for privates, was one factor. Economic opportunity in the West also contributed to the desertion rate. An enlisted man found in the West a demand for mechanics and laborers which offered him greater income than did the army paymaster. Retribution followed capture, but capture did not always follow desertion.

The army in the West accomplished much during the years of the Western War. Since its mission was primarily military, the military accomplishment must be ranked first. By wresting control of the Great Plains from the Indian, the army cleared the way for white settlement. The soldier also brought law and order to the frontier. Sheridan's enumeration of the army's duties in the West shows further what the military believed to be its contribution to the development of western America: protecting frontier citizens against Indians and Mexicans, exploring unknown territory, escorting railroad surveyors and scientific parties, assisting and guarding railroads and other lines of travel, helping to enforce the law in remote places, and ". . . to do generally all that is constantly required of our Army in the way of helping and urging forward everything which tends to develop and increase civilization upon the border."[34]

[33] Letter from Benteen to Theodore W. Goldin, Feb. 12, 1896, in Col. W. A. Graham's *The Custer Myth*, 203.
[34] Secretary of War, *Report, 1873*, I, 40.

The army's role in systematically recording knowledge of the West often is overlooked in the attention given to the Mountain Man. But the wanderer's knowledge of the West died with him, whereas the knowledge of land gained on army scouting trips was recorded as part of the permanent available knowledge of the country. Engineer officers attached to division and departmental headquarters systematically collected geographical and topographical information with the assistance of field commanders. Their work sparked an interest on the part of line soldiers, perhaps as a relief from the tedium of long scouts. Line officers and enlisted men kept journals and made sketches. Thus journals and sketches described 23,000 miles of country in the Department of Missouri in 1874, in contrast to 9,000 miles the year before.[35] As specific examples, the explorations in West Texas revealed well-watered and extensive grazing lands as well as mineral lands in the trans-Pecos region. In other departments, army expeditions found a new wagon route from the Union Pacific Railroad to Yellowstone Park, built a new wagon road from Santa Fe to Taos, and surveyed part of the Black Hills in 1874. Not the least of military accomplishments was the construction of army telegraph lines in the Southwest and into Indian Territory, which helped speed the conquest of the Indian.

When the Western War began, United States newspapers had become accustomed to war news written by staff correspondents. Introduced to war correspondence in the Mexican War, the newspapers had gained much experience with it during the Civil War. They kept the function alive in the wars of the latter nineteenth century, including the Western War with the American Indian.

Although war correspondence is considered a product of the mid-nineteenth century, it had, nevertheless, a feeble beginning in more distant years. In the seventeenth century, an anonymous writer for the *Swedish Intelligencer*, published in London, wrote of Gustavus Adolphus' engagements during

[35] *Ibid., 1874,* I, *xvi–xvii.*

the Thirty Years' War, but on the basis of received information rather than on-the-spot reporting. The Napoleonic Wars also gave rise to a form of war reporting, notably by John Bell of the London *Oracle and Public Advertiser,* who wrote from Flanders. Other London papers also had men at or near the scene of action in the early nineteenth century, such as Charles Lewis Gruneison, in Spain during the Carlist-Christino War in 1837.[36]

However, the emergence of war correspondence—which involves regularity of reporting from an army in the field—dates from the Mexican and Crimean wars. By that time the daily newspaper had undergone a virtual revolution, in both technology and point of view. Advancing technology provided presses for faster and larger runs and facilities for more rapid communication—the steamship and the telegraph. A broadening of democracy, increasing urbanization, and rising literacy provided a larger reader audience for United States newspapers. Enterprising young men—James Gordon Bennett, Horace Greeley, and Benjamin Day—realized that news had a commodity value. They converted newspapers from purveyors of opinion to purveyors of news.

The one-man newspaper grew into an organization having specialized functions, including specialized reporting. "Special" correspondence appeared—dispatches—or, rather, letters —from staff men or prominent persons in other cities and countries. By the 1850's it became increasingly the practice for larger newspapers to send their own staff men on out-of-town assignments.

And so it was that when war occurred, newspapers took steps to report it. Between 1845 and 1855 the war correspondent emerged as a news-gatherer who used both old and new methods of getting the story of war and transmitting it to his paper. New Orleans newspapermen, especially George Wilkins Kendall of the *Picayune,* made the Mexican War the first to be regularly covered by daily newspapers. And then came the Crimean War, which is remembered almost as much

[36] Joseph J. Mathews, *Reporting the Wars,* 31–48.

for the appearance of William Howard Russell and the establishment of special war correspondence as for the charge of the Light Brigade.

But it was in the Civil War that American newspapers met the full task of reporting a major war. Generally, the New York newspapers excelled in coverage of the four years of fighting, although other journals had men in the field. The *New York Herald,* founded as a one-man newspaper with a capital of $500 not thirty years before, sent thirty to forty writers in the field and spent more than $500,000 covering the Civil War. The *New York Tribune* and *New York Times* were almost as energetic. And the papers in St. Louis, Chicago, Cincinnati, Baltimore, and Philadelphia all had their correspondents as well.[37]

Thus, by the time of the Western War, American newspapers had had experience in the reporting of military operations. The coverage of Indian fighting in the West can be regarded as one of the developmental stages of war correspondence, although not enough research has been done on war correspondence generally to show the relative importance of each stage. It also should be looked upon in its relation to an age of adventure. Adventure and the hero rated high in reader appeal, and war correspondents contributed their bit through accounts of their own adventures as well as adventures of others. The latter nineteenth century was an age of imperialistic wars and of smaller European wars. Just as British newspapers had specialists reporting the course of fighting on the far fringes of empire, so American newspapers sent men to report the course of Indian fighting in the West, and for much the same reason—the future of the nation was involved in the outcome. Furthermore, it made exciting reading.

[37] *Ibid.,* 79–80.

Early

2. INDIAN WAR
BEGINNING IN WEST

> *One thing in regard to my scribbling
> for a newspaper, I never discover the
> little difference between it and a run-
> ning, random conversation with some
> of "the boys," until I see the blasted
> stuff in print, and then am astonished
> to see what an amount of human cuss-
> edness and conceit a single individual
> under no restraint can produce.*
> JOE WASSON[1]

WHEN THE WESTERN WAR BEGAN in 1866, touched off by
efforts of the United States to open the Bozeman Trail to the
Montana mining region, the first newspaper reports came
from non-staff men who distorted and exaggerated the story.
Early in the summer of 1866, Colonel Henry B. Carrington
led an army column into what is now northern Wyoming with
instructions to establish two forts to guard the Bozeman Trail.
In sending him out, the government relied upon the Harney-
Sanborn treaty of 1865 in which some, but not all, of the
Sioux had agreed that the whites could have right of transit
across their hunting grounds to reach Montana. Other Sioux
had refused to concede that right, especially the militant Red
Cloud and his following, who feared that the white traffic
would destroy the richest game preserve of the Sioux. Carrington established Fort Phil Kearney, near present Sheridan,
Wyoming, on July 15, and Fort C. F. Smith, farther north,
on August 3.

Red Cloud had gone on the warpath in protest against the

[1] *Owyhee Avalanche,* Sept. 28, 1867.

government's taking of the road, and by July 31, Carrington reported a state of war existing in the area. Between July 26 and December 21, Indians appeared in front of Fort Phil Kearney fifty-one times, making hostile demonstrations. They attacked almost every person and wagon train attempting to use the new road, as well as many of the work parties bringing logs to the new fort. The climax came on December 21, when Captain William J. Fetterman galloped out of the fort to relieve a wood train then under attack. Disobeying explicit orders from Carrington, he rushed headlong into a trap set by Sioux, who used their favorite tactic of decoy and ambush. Two thousand or so Indians fell upon the command of eighty-one men, killing every one of them.[2]

No staff correspondent appeared at Fort Phil Kearney during that time, but a free-lance photographer went there to photograph Indians. He was Ridgeway Glover, who had left his Philadelphia home earlier that summer after making arrangements with the Philadelphia *Photographer* and *Frank Leslie's Illustrated Newspaper* to send them material. Even though the wagon train with which he rode from Fort Laramie to the new post had been attacked by Indians en route, Glover habitually left the fort alone and unarmed. On one such trip a group of Arapahos killed him.

Glover wrote only a few letters, but the sobriety of those indicates that a much more accurate picture of 1866 warfare might have emerged, particularly in the columns of *Leslie's*, had he lived. The accounts which came from some other free-lance correspondents often were falsified and sensationalized.

Undisciplined reporting showed up most clearly in accounts of the so-called Fetterman Massacre. Sensational, lurid, and simply faked accounts appeared in eastern periodicals, with unknown details supplied by the imaginations of

[2] Paul I. Wellman, *Death on Horseback*, 43–58; Col. Henry B. Carrington, *Ab-sa-ra-ka, Land of Massacre . . . with an Outline of Indian Operations and Conferences from 1865 to 1878, vi*, 365. Fort Kearney, as named and spelled by Carrington, was named in memory of General Phil Kearny, but accuracy in the spelling of names was not a characteristic of the period. Following Carrington, the contemporary spelling is used here.

writers and artists who "covered" the fighting from comfortable entrenchments in New York and Washington. *Harper's Weekly* and *Frank Leslie's Illustrated Newspaper* were the most culpable, along with the *Albany Argus*.[3]

A change for the better began in 1867 with the appearance of Western War correspondents. Going into the field with troops, they brought greater reliability to newspaper accounts of Indian fighting than could be obtained by correspondents in frontier towns.

Joe Wasson, one of the first staff men in the field, represented the *Owyhee Avalanche* of Silver City, a weekly in an Idaho mining community which today is a ghost town. He accompanied Crook's expedition against hostile Indians of Idaho, Oregon, and northern California.

Red-headed, muscular, and high-spirited, Joe Wasson, age twenty-six, had been in the West about seven years when he joined Crook's force. He was born in Wooster, Ohio, in 1841, where he learned the printer's trade. At the age of nineteen he left for the Far West with a company of gold-seekers, beginning an interest in mining which was to remain with him for life. En route to the West the party was attacked by Indians, an experience which prompted in Wasson a hatred of the Indians. In August, 1865, he and his brother John had established the *Avalanche* as Silver City's first newspaper.[4] Their newspaper occupied the upper floor of a rickety-looking building. Silver City, fifty miles directly southwest of Boise, had been in existence only two years when the Wasson brothers arrived.

The mining region suffered under Indian raids. In 1865, Indian raids made passage unsafe on the principal routes radiating from Boise—the road northwest to The Dalles, Oregon, the road southeast to Salt Lake City, and the road southwest to Chico, California. Defense of the roads and settlements at first was undertaken by volunteer units from Oregon

[3] Elmo Scott Watson, "The Indian Wars and the Press, 1866–1867," *Journalism Quarterly*, Vol. XVII (December, 1940), 304–308.

[4] *The Publisher's Auxiliary*, Nov. 26, 1949; *Owyhee Avalanche*, Nov. 9, 1867.

and California, then in federal service because of the Civil War, but regulars began to replace them in 1865. The army sent detachments after the Indians without success. Continuing their hit-and-run attacks, Indians on one occasion murdered fifty or sixty Chinese miners, to whom the Idaho mines recently had been opened. The Indians, exact identity unknown but usually identified as Snakes, also molested stage lines, transportation companies, and stock-raisers. At one time an express company refused to transport treasure between Boise and The Dalles because of the Indians.

When George Crook took command of the District of Boise on December 11, 1866, it seemed to him that the entire region was in a state of siege, including northern California, northern Nevada, eastern Oregon, and Idaho as far as the Montana line. Crook took command at Boise with the rank of lieutenant colonel of the Twenty-third Infantry, a new regiment, but usually he was addressed as "Major General."[5] He found morale low among the officers of his command—dissipation, a general apathy, and an indifference toward the job at hand were prevalent.[6]

Crook was a field soldier, and within a week he was at the head of troops. Reports of Indian depredations came in from the mouth of Boise River, about twenty miles downstream from Boise. He immediately started into the field, at the head of one company of cavalry. Thinking he would be gone only a week, he traveled light—one change of underclothes and a toothbrush. "But," he recalled, "I got interested after the Indians and did not return there again for over two years."[7]

All through the winter and into the summer he remained in

[5] Crook attained the rank of major general by brevet while commanding volunteer troops during the Civil War. It was customary in the Old Army for an officer to continue to be addressed by his brevet rank, even though he drew the pay and held the command of the rank in which he happened to be serving. Crook was a regular army officer, graduating from West Point in 1852, who had fought Pacific Coast Indians as a company grade officer before the Civil War.

[6] *General George Crook: His Autobiography*, 142 (hereafter cited as Crook, *Autobiography*).

[7] *Ibid.*, 144.

the field. Practically all that time he operated in eastern Oregon, never with more than two companies of cavalry—not more than one hundred soldiers or so—and a few Indian scouts. In carrying out the field operations, Crook moved from previously established military camps, each garrisoned by a small force. These included Camp Lyon, near Silver City; Camp C. F. Smith in southeastern Oregon; and Camp Warner, near Warner Lake, shown on today's maps as Warner Valley with individual lakes bearing other names.

Crook continued his operations into the summer of 1867, when Wasson joined him. Apparently, the uncertainties of frontier newspaper publication had drained the Wasson finances and the hard work required on a weekly newspaper had told on the health of Joe Wasson. As he expressed it, "To stand up to the metal-rack like a beast to stake-oats and die by inches had become my lot, or else the alternative of regaining health by taking the chances in adventure; I'm on the latter now . . . ."[8] Wasson accompanied the expedition primarily as correspondent for the *Avalanche,* but his reports appeared in the *San Francisco Evening Bulletin,* too.

His first dispatch, written while he was en route to join troops in the field, gave promise of the tone of many later stories he would write for a predominantly male audience in a western mining camp. Although he showed later that he could handle serious news creditably, he used a light touch between times. He had left Silver City on a night stagecoach on Saturday, July 13, 1867, traveling to Owyhee Ferry in what then was Baker County, Oregon—a county much larger then than now. From Owyhee Ferry he wrote the first story, describing the trip as follows:

> The moon was near its full, but no nearer "full" than the stage and its occupants. . . . The passengers were wedged in somehow and the stage got away about two A.M., and just as the moon disappeared. . . . Nothing particular occurred between Silver and old Ruby—unless besides being crowded from feet to shoulders. . . . And what with swearing and crushing of corns

[8] *Owyhee Avalanche,* Sept. 28, 1867.

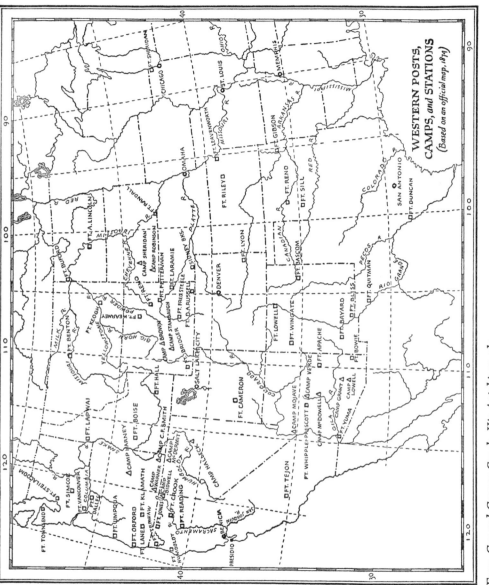

WESTERN POSTS,
CAMPS, and STATIONS
(Based on an official map, 1871)

From *General George Crook: His Autobiography*

below and the drinking of "corn" above, the mass of tangle-leg —in a double sense—managed to jog along pretty well.[9]

He started writing his first story on July 16, and added a post-script on July 18, reporting that the "Government Express" from Camp C. F. Smith had arrived that morning and would leave about 4:30 P.M. that day with him along, riding a mule. His dispatch presumably went to Silver City by stagecoach, reaching there in time for publication on Saturday.

Moving at about four miles an hour, the "Express"—presumably a courier with escort—traveled twenty-four miles through sagebrush country and camped overnight. Wasson arrived at Camp C. F. Smith the next day. This Camp C. F. Smith is not to be confused with the Fort C. F. Smith established by Carrington.

Unaccustomed as yet to the physical strain of long horse-back rides, Wasson reached Camp Smith "as nearly used up as one could be." At the time of his arrival preparations were made for a night march to begin the next evening from the camp, which contained about two hundred soldiers, approximately one hundred Indian scouts, and more than one thousand horses and mules. The officers were cordial, even to the extent of keeping him up late for a party, which they told him was customary on the evening before the start of a long campaign.[10]

The authority by which Wasson—and the later correspondents—accompanied an army command in the field would appear to be what the army knows as ground rules; that is, rules governing matters left to the discretion of local commanders. Army regulations for the period are silent about newspaper correspondents in the field. In the field, the correspondents ate with the officers. The practice was for officers to buy army rations at cost when they were in the field, and the correspondents probably contributed their share to the officers' mess fund from which the food was purchased.

[9] *Ibid.*, July 20, 1867.
[10] *Ibid.*, July 27, 1867.

Crook and the other officers told Wasson that the expedition would consist of about 150 soldiers and 100 Indian scouts.[11] Captain John Darragh, whose name Wasson often misspelled as Darrah—improper spelling was a failing not uncommon at the time in newspapers and even in official reports —had just come in with fifty Wasco and Warm Springs Indians, bringing scalps taken in a fight. Until Darragh's arrival, Crook had intended to go up the Malheur, to the north of the camp; but Darragh's opinion that the hostiles would be found to the south caused Crook to change his itinerary to the Pueblo Mountains, south of Camp Smith, and then to Camp Warner, just east of Warner Lake.[12]

Wasson wrote about both friendly and hostile Indians as he began his correspondence. The war songs of the scouts might be music to them, but as far as he was concerned they "made camp howl." Sardonically, he noted that information had been obtained which indicated that the hostile Indians, led by a chief identified as *Wee-ah-wa-wa*, were in regular communication with the Truckee country in California. The hostile Indians reportedly said they liked the California whites because they could get from them all the arms they needed, "which is a good joke on the whites—up this way," Wasson commented.

Crook wanted to get as close to the Indians as he could, Wasson reported, and was satisfied that "a good cleaning out

[11] The Indian scouts proved a decisive factor in the campaigns of 1867 and 1868, although they were organized at the insistence of civilian rather than military authorities. Legislation of 1866 authorized the enlistment of Indian scouts, apportioning them among the states and territories concerned, with Oregon receiving a complement of one hundred. Governor George L. Woods wanted Oregon's scouts divided into two companies of fifty each under commanders he would select and sent into the field to fight hostile Indians, independent of regular troops. Turned down in his request by the commanders of the Department of the Columbia and the Military Division of the Pacific, he appealed directly to Secretary of War Edwin M. Stanton, who approved the plan. Two companies of Indian scouts, drawn from the Warm Springs Reservation, were formed, under the commands of Lieutenant W. C. McKay (later promoted to captain) and John Darragh. These were the scouts operating with Crook. Hubert Howe Bancroft, *History of Oregon*, II, 530–31.

[12] *Owyhee Avalanche*, July 27, 1867.

where he is going will put a damper on their raiding out in the settlements and along the highways." Along with others being introduced to Indian campaigning, Wasson was told that a surprise would do the Indians more real harm than defeat in a pitched battle. To effect that surprise, Crook intended to march his troops at night and lay by during the day. With customary Wasson lightness the reporter concluded his story by saying that the expedition was taking rations for two months, that he would stay as long as the rations lasted, "and as close to them as I can conveniently."[13]

When Crook rode out on campaign in the early evening of July 20, Wasson rode with him, beginning his first experience as a Western War correspondent; he was to remain in the field almost four months. The first movement was a week's scout from Camp C. F. Smith, south into Nevada, back into Oregon by way of the Pueblo Mountains and then west and north to Camp Warner.

On that first scout Wasson established the routine he would follow for the rest of the campaign. He wrote chronological stories, adding to them day by day, usually indicating that he wrote from Camp No. 1, Camp No. 2, etc. When occasion offered—and it seems to have been offered frequently—Wasson sent in his stories by army courier. Regularity of communication seems to have depended upon how close they were at any given time to one of the established camps.

For a while Wasson had little to do but ride along, conditioning himself to the swing of a horse, the creak of a saddle, and the sweat-smell of a saddle blanket; to watch the countryside, to observe his companions, and bit by bit to discern the field methods of the close-mouthed Crook. Keeping up a flow of copy meant that he had to write of trivia at first, and this he did with tongue-in-cheek references to himself and humorous comments on the hostile Indians.

He usually signed his stories "Joe." As a rule they were long dispatches, each covering several days of activity. They differed from today's news stories in two major respects: Each

13 *Ibid.*

was written as a letter, ofttimes written to the *Avalanche* as though it were a person whom he could address familiarly; he seems not to have been writing to a general audience through the newspaper as a medium, which is the premise of today's reporting, but to the paper itself. Later correspondents in the Western War displayed something of the same characteristic but with the difference that their letters read as though addressed to the editor. The second major distinction was the chronological presentation of events. In the fashion of the time, he also sprinkled couplets and snatches of poetry into his prose.

Following Crook's plan of night marches to conceal the command from the enemy, they left Camp C. F. Smith at 6:00 P.M. on July 20 and rode until midnight, encamping on Trout Creek eighteen miles from their starting place. In camp the next day Wasson had a better chance to size up the command than he had had during the short stay at Camp Smith, when everyone had been busy in the hustle of getting ready for the field. He reported that it was composed of about 200 mounted men and 200 pack animals. The fighters included two companies of the First Cavalry, totaling 82 men; two companies of Warm Springs scouts, totaling 72 Indians and 22 packers; and 25 Snake Indian scouts.[14] Using Snakes to fight Snakes was part of Crook's basic technique of Indian fighting; in later years he would use Apaches to fight Apaches, Sioux to fight Sioux.

"It may be of the utmost importance to add," Wasson said whimsically, "that the undersigned is in charge of Co. I— I being the only one in the company at this time. Having one of the biggest and toughest horses in the Command, I may make an imposing appearance; but am satisfied that I am regularly imposing on the good nature of all hands and the cook—specially the latter. Such trips as this fetches one to his appetite, but frequently takes one to where there isn't anything else."[15]

[14] *Ibid.*, Aug. 3, 1867.
[15] *Ibid.*

Again breaking camp at 6:00 P.M., they made another eighteen-mile march, following Trout Creek until they reached an old stage station. "Passed through some rough canyon, high black walls on either side, resembling columns jostled over to an angle of forty-five degrees and then left to shift for themselves; at intervals, reminding one of the front of a paint-shop where green and yellow [sic] daubed regardless of expense," Wasson wrote. Pueblo Valley "looks like a billiard table stripped of its green." And in passing through the mountains Wasson the gold-seeker observed slate mixed with quartz, specimens indicating silver, and a significant amount of antimony.

He surmised that the second camp was in Nevada, but said Oregon could claim it by a mile or two until the surveyors should settle the line. As for himself, "I am not caring a cent one way or the other—nor carrying a cent, either—which is the old thing, you know."[16]

Only trouble with unbroken pack mules enlivened the march, during which Wasson observed more closely some of the men who interested him. One was a young buck captured in the fighting of the previous winter. Sometimes an older Indian would put the younger "through a dance and singing operation—a mixture of juba and coyote." Some of the "droll" characters among the troops also caught his eye. One was a bag of wind whose life Wasson said he traced through the soldier's braggadocio from the Battle of the Boyne in Ireland in 1690 to Crook's fight of the previous winter at Steen's Mountain, and "a rough estimate would require forty cords of wood and other materials to replace his sacrifices of limbs, head, etc."[17]

Up to that point, Camp No. 2, the march had been leisurely, but their Chief Scout Archie McIntosh, a half-breed with Boise blood, was ordered to the front with his detachment of Snakes. From then on, Wasson expected, there would be forced marches. "From this camp on," he said as though ad-

[16] *Ibid.*
[17] *Ibid.*

dressing the *Avalanche* as a person, "I hope to find something to interest you more than a draw on the fancy. It interests me, however, and I don't care so much for your welfare as to worry about it under such circumstances." Wasson's expectation of action was based in part upon his confidence in McIntosh. "McIntosh is no throw off, as many are in the profession he is acting. He was brought up by the Hudson Bay Co., who meant business all the time."[18]

McIntosh soon justified Wasson's confidence, for the reporter had to add a postscript to his story at 8:30 P.M. on July 22, saying McIntosh had just come in after a brush with Indians. The scout had been out all day, during which he had struck the trail of four Indians, whom he trailed, caught, and killed about twelve miles from camp.

"I get a chance to send this in to-morrow, which pleases me mightily, as I don't like any more of the memoranda business than can be got along with conveniently," Wasson wrote to his paper.[19]

McIntosh's encounter made it possible for the command to make one march in daylight, during which Wasson once more looked for mineral prospects. They camped overnight, and remained there through the twenty-fourth, on a dry creek, but obtained drinking water by digging a foot or two beneath the surface. Wasson passed the time in reading and sleeping, until the command marched late in the afternoon of July 25 for Isaac's Springs.

At least two detachments of Indian scouts stayed out all the time, scouring the country for ten miles in advance of the command. From the scout of July 25, Captain W. C. McKay, in command of one scout detachment, came in with six captured Indian children and the scalp of an adult. Several men had escaped, and McIntosh took up the pursuit. Considerable rivalry existed among the three bands of scouts.[20]

Traveling "a very rough, sagey road," the command march-

[18] *Ibid.*
[19] *Ibid.*
[20] *Ibid.*, Aug. 10, 1867.

ed through the night of July 26 until 2:00 A.M., when they decided they were lost. They halted, built fires, and "worried it out" until daylight. With dawn they moved through rocky country until they reached a dry canyon which had no water but sufficient grass for the animals. Making a dry camp, they remained there until mid-morning of the twenty-seventh.

Then they started out for Camp Warner, and ran into the first action of the campaign. About noon they came out on the road running between Camp Warner and Camp Smith, where they saw fresh Indian tracks. The scouts took up the pursuit immediately, closely followed by the command. McKay and Darragh found an Indian camp—Wasson termed it a *rancherie* —and called the soldiers for support. The cavalry started forward rapidly, but Crook called them back when he saw that the scouts could handle the fight.

Wasson, however, galloped forward to join the scouts and unlimbered his Henry rifle for two shots at the Indians. Caught by a surprise attack, the Indians fled into near-by rocks. After a skirmish of half an hour, Wasson returned to the main command. At that time he could not tell clearly what damage had been done to the Indians, a point of confusion that marked almost all Indian fighting, although it was evident that the command had struck a permanent camp, judging from the provisions, fishing nets, and other equipment found in the wickiups. Wasson observed that the Warm Springs scouts ransacked the camp for spoils with greater energy than they followed up the fleeing Indians. However, some of the scouts—joined by packers—picked up the trail of four fleeing men and then smoked them out of the rocks. Most of the hostiles were armed only with bow and arrow. Wasson said some horses with the U. S. brand were recaptured.[21]

The fight occurred at midday, and by 3:00 P.M. the command reached Camp Warner; the permanent Indian camp had been that close to the military establishment.

In Camp Warner the next day Wasson learned the results of the fight. Darragh and McKay had turned their Indians

[21] *Ibid.*

42

loose to fight in their own style, and the action had been scattered over half a mile of sagebrush and rocks. When it was over, the scouts came in with eleven scalps of warriors and eleven captured women and papooses.[22] Wasson did not make it absolutely clear that the eleven women and children were all captured, and it should be borne in mind that the Warm Springs Indians went into the field under orders from Governor George L. Woods—which they protested—to kill and destroy without regard to age or sex. Three hostile Indians had to be literally burned out of the rocks, one Indian being cooked white.

During the week since the command had left Camp Smith, it had killed and captured thirty-five Indians, about half of them warriors. For this Wasson gave credit to the scouts, among whom he thought the Snakes were the best. McKay and Darragh's scouts fought with Maynard carbines; the command would have benefited, Wasson said, had the Snakes been supplied with better weapons, although he did not say what arms they used.

By the time they reached Camp Warner, Wasson had gained through observation an estimate of Crook's ways and objectives. He inferred that Crook's idea was to keep about three bands of scouts ten to twenty miles out all the time— one ahead and one on either flank.

In saying that he "inferred" what Crook's idea was, Wasson made a statement which is interesting in the light of other comments about Crook. An officer long associated with him said that Crook was reticent and taciturn, an uncommunicative man who could talk with another person, learn all that the other knew about the matter in point, and yet never give the slightest hint of his own plans and purposes.[23]

Yet Crook seemed to welcome newspaper reporters in his command. More correspondents traveled with him than with any other general. A clue to Crook's attitude may be found in the following comment in his autobiography: "I regret to

[22] *Ibid.*, Aug. 17, 1867.
[23] John G. Bourke, *On the Border with Crook*, 109, 351.

say that I learned too late that it was not what a person did, but it was what he got the credit of doing that gave him a reputation and at the close of the war [Civil War] gave him position."[24]

In common with most of the other reporters who rode with Crook, Wasson came to respect him. "The success of the Command so far," Wasson wrote, "and upon success alone is everything judged in this practical world, implies that Gen. Crook's plan is as good as any; and I believe he has the Indian character a little nearer down to scratch than any man in the regular service. By having sufficient men to surround and whip any band liable to be met, and good scouts with change of horses, he can sweep a wide belt of country and keep it up continually."[25]

Crook took advantage of a delay in the campaign, caused by a delay in supplies, to scout for a new camp location. Camp Warner, situated on the eastern shore of Warner Lake, was exposed to heavy snows in winter and swampy conditions in warmer weather. Near it the previous winter Crook had almost lost his life in a blizzard, and for that reason had determined to relocate it. Between July 29 and August 1, he and a part of the command looked for a place to build a new Camp Warner. While traveling to the west of Warner Lake, they saw an unnamed peak to which they gave the name Crook's Mountain—shown on today's maps as Crook Peak. "It is the only thing in the country unnamed fit to receive any particular appellation," Wasson said. He observed that the mountain looked "placer-like," but did not know whether a color had been found there. "It is a section of U. S.'s domain scarcely scratched by the toenails of white men." Crook found a site west of Warner Lake for a new post, which would be known —according to plans at that time—as Camp Wood.[26]

While west of Warner Lake, they ran across fresh Indian sign, but did not have sufficient rations to follow up the trail.

[24] Crook, *Autobiography*, 141.
[25] *Owyhee Avalanche*, Aug. 17, 1867.
[26] *Ibid.*

44

However, by the time they got back to Camp Warner, Mc-
Intosh had come in with eleven more hostile Indians. He had
found a "good-sized" wickiup where his men killed two warriors and captured the eleven.

Concluding his dispatch on August 2, Wasson said he would
leave the next day with Crook for Silvies River to locate yet
another post, which would be about one hundred miles east
and north of Camp Warner. A courier to Camp Smith was to
leave Warner on August 5 and return on August 10, at which
time, he said, "I may send you some more stuff."[27]

However, nearly a month passed before Wasson appeared
in print again. In the meantime, he accompanied Crook on
a hard march to the north. En route to Harney Lake, on the
second day out, they had to march forty-five miles, from sunup until 9:00 P.M., because there was no water. Both men and
animals suffered severely, and made their condition worse
"by indulging some about noon in a puddle of warm alkali,
equally as palatable as second-hand soap-suds." Again the
next day they marched through alkali flats, greasewood, sagebrush, and rocks, a country abounding in flies which tormented the horses, causing the animals to walk stiff-legged
and swing and stumble, "rendering riding about as pleasant
as trying to run a race over a mixture of hedge and picket
fences." In the midst of the hardship Wasson frequently saw
mirages of willow-shaded streams—"the most cruelly deceptive thing one can imagine." But in the country north of Camp
Wright—which was between present Burns and Hines, Oregon, and Malheur Lake—they found a well-watered, grassy
canyon in the foothills of the Blue Mountains, where a detachment from the Twenty-third Infantry began building
Camp Steele. Then they started on their march back to
Warner, looping west to Silver Creek and the Wagontire area.
On returning to Camp Warner on August 17 (they had left
there on August 3), Wasson wrote with a note of complaint:
"Since leaving Wagontire Camp, excepting the last eight
miles, the entire route has been not nearly so much over a bed

[27] *Ibid.*

of roses as rises of bedrock—a high, bleak, barren waste. I don't wonder that there is no Indian 'sign,' as there are but few places on which they could make an impression with a cold chisel."[28] He was eager for action.

Having attended to some of the other duties of a field commander, Crook prepared to carry out his primary mission—combat. He moved his command from Camp Warner to Darragh Creek in the Warner Lake region, getting ready to move out again. As a part of the command, Wasson messed with Major David Perry, commanding Company F, First Cavalry, and shared a tent with Captain Moses Harris, commanding Company M of the same regiment.

On a lazy Sunday in camp (August 25), Wasson took time to "scribble about two columns of stuff and thus pass the Sunday," observing that it did not matter whether "it is nonsense or news set before the public, the one finds as many readers as the other." Not having received mail for a long time, he asked, "Have the exchanges stopped coming or has the *Avalanche* ceased to slide and all the proprietors vamosed the ranch?—haven't had a thing from the outside world for weeks."[29]

Crook ordered an additional month's rations packed, extending the forthcoming campaign until October 20, which brought another Wasson commentary: ". . . as I have heard of no order commanding me to leave the camp, I expect to make the round trip. I expect to get out of this adventure alive, if I can keep the officers from seeing what I have said about them till I can get away. The only orders he [presumably Crook] ever gave me were—*to help myself,* or words to that effect; and I'll bet something that in all his extensive and varied soldier life, he never saw a more willing subordinate than your humble servant."[30]

While preparations were being made for a renewed campaign, Crook's scouts met a defeat even before the command

28 *Ibid.,* Sept. 14, 1867.
29 *Ibid.,* Sept. 21, 1867.
30 *Ibid.*

could fairly get into the field. Preparatory to a general advance, McIntosh took eighteen scouts to probe the Goose Lake region south of them. On August 26, McIntosh returned, "whipped back." He had encountered a band of hostile Indians larger than his force. Unable to defeat them, he sent a peace emissary to the Indians, who indignantly replied that they would kill anyone who molested them. It was the same band which had defeated McIntosh the preceding winter and repulsed an army detachment in the spring. Wasson wrote:

> Archy says the Indian that does all this defiant talking is known as "Chee-oh"—the Warner Lake Chief. Now, I never heard of him before this affair, and am loth to believe in his corporeal existence. No sooner had I got rid of "We-ah-we-wa" than here comes "Chee-oh." Oh, d——n Chee-oh! In sounding his name abroad, you must accent the *chee* part with a good sneeze—the remaining part will naturally follow. Archy don't say that Chee-oh was killed in the last fight, and that he saw his friends *carry him off* before he had time to scalp him—as many "Indian fighters" would. I wish Chee-oh and We-ah-we-wa *were* dead and that Winnemucca would stay on the Reservation— without any mental reservation—instead of coming back with powder, lead, guns, etc.;—I'm tired of writing about something I don't see and am eternally hearing of. If Archy's scouts could exchange their weapons for some others not bearing the brand of "Harper's Ferry, 1845," and get revolvers swung to them also, their confidence would be enhanced and better accounts rendered in these skirmishes. . . . "I want a hero" worse than Byron ever did—but one that will show himself in flesh tights occasionally; not tight "in the flesh," for I see some of that now and then—and wouldn't mind being exposed to it again. However, I'm in pretty good spirits considering the delays and dullness attendant.[31]

While spending idle days in camp waiting for the command to get underway, Wasson learned to his surprise that he no longer owned part of the *Owyhee Avalanche*. The mail that arrived on August 28 included a copy of the August 17

[31] *Ibid.*

47

edition, in which he discovered that the Wasson brothers had sold the paper to W. J. Hill and H. W. Millard. The announcement of the sale appeared above the names of John and Joseph Wasson, but Brother John apparently had acted for Brother Joseph without the latter's knowledge. Reviewing their two-year experience with a mining-camp newspaper, the sale announcement said the Wassons had intended in the beginning to inform the world of the mineral wealth of Owyhee, and had succeeded in doing so through the newspapers and mining journals of New York, California, and Oregon.[32]

Even though a surprise, the sale of the *Avalanche* seems not to have bothered Wasson. He found the mail interesting —"that obituary notice in the *Avalanche,* letting me out of the institution. As a specimen of fine writing, that pleases me better than anything I've seen in that sheet for some time . . . The 'menagerie' [his term for the expedition] suits me pretty well; and better, it will leave to-morrow morning at early candle-light, to slow music. Such is life."[33]

Even though he no longer owned part of the *Avalanche,* Wasson remained with the expedition as that paper's correspondent. The command went into the field with a new military composition. It was composed of Companies F and H, First Cavalry, and Company D, Twenty-third Infantry, mounted. It included 280 soldiers, counting the Indian scouts, and a total of 360 men, counting the packers who were responsible for the mule train.

The command moved out on August 30, and on the first day experienced one of those humorous moments that relieved the tedium of a scout after Indians. They had gone up Darragh's Creek, southwest of Warner Lake, when two blacksmiths decided to go down the creek about twelve miles on business—one of them "a big blustering American" and the other an Irishman. They came back into camp after dark at break-neck speed. The Irishman said he went over his mule's head twice, and once rolled more than fifty feet, but the

[32] *Ibid.,* Aug. 17, 1867.
[33] *Ibid.,* Sept. 21, 1867.

Western Commander: William Tecumseh Sherman

83651

Courtesy National Archives.

Camp Warner, Oregon, 1873.

American wouldn't admit anything, other than to swear that they ran into fifteen mounted Indians crossing the road ahead of them. Wasson concluded that the two men had simply been frightened by a row of juniper trees. "Since Archy's late repulse, Indians are seen everywhere by packers and others."[34]

During the day's march, the command—large for that part of the country and sufficiently strong to keep several detachments of thirty to fifty men out all the time, in different directions and on fresh horses—moved along the eastern base of Crook Peak. Toward the end of the day they came to a swampy creek. It was dark by the time the pack train got in, ". . . and the animals got all mixed and filed in together—and stuck in the mud," Wasson wrote. "Such a scene I never saw. Oaths and imprecations rent the air in English, Spanish, French, Dutch, Irish, and Indian—straight; then again a mixture of all—a literal packer's pandemonium." They finally got the mess straightened out, and made camp about 10:00 P.M.

The main command remained in camp through August 31, while scouts explored for signs of hostile Indians. Crook called McKay and McIntosh to him, each with twenty Indians who formed a circle around the commander while he gave them instructions. They could dispose of hostile warriors according to their own style, Wasson reported Crook as saying, but children and captured arms, as well as horses, were to be turned over to the government. The two bands then struck out about mid-morning, moving southwesterly with three days' rations. About noon, a third band went toward the northwest.

The next day the main command moved south a short distance to the South Fork of One-Mule Creek and followed it into Camas Prairie. About noon, some of Darragh's scouts came in, reporting "hi-yu Snakes," which Wasson said could mean five or fifty. Major Perry mounted thirty men and, with the remainder of Darragh's scouts, moved in pursuit, preceded by some of McKay's scouts, who hurried out ahead of

[34] *Ibid.*

49

the main party without orders. But by night they were all back in camp, having found only tracks.

They remained at Camas Prairie through September 3, during which time Crook gave Wasson and the others a lesson in digging camas roots, a favorite vegetable of northwestern Indians. All they could do was wait for the scouts to turn up a hostile band. Darragh's scouts ran into twenty Indians, on foot but armed, who got away. McKay and McIntosh came in, drew rations for four or five days, and changed horses for another scout. Probing the country north of Crook Peak and west of Warner Lake, they continually found fresh signs of hostile Indians but failed to engage them. Wasson commented:

> I should like to take a hand in these scouts, but it is the rule that none but those properly belonging to the bands shall accompany them. Besides, some of these officers say that I couldn't be got within shooting distance of a hostile Indian anyhow. Confound them! Moreover, one of them makes it a standing bet of $4½ that I can't shoot a hole through an army tent twenty steps off-hand. Not having a cent, I have to endure this; but the worst feature of it is, no one will risk anything on it in my behalf. It looks bad. I think there is a combination to ruin my reputation, but never having had any in particular, they can't make a point off me there.[35]

His remark indicated that there was much good fellowship among the officers of the command, and that Wasson the newspaperman had fitted into the group. But the grind of campaigning was beginning to tell in other ways—Wasson's clothes were wearing out, for one thing.

From Camas Prairie on September 4 he took advantage of what might be the last chance for a long time to send in his copy. Communication toward Idaho would be accidental after that, he remarked; they were nearing the California line. And he was right. It was well over a month before his next dispatch appeared in print, and when it did, it commanded five columns.

[35] *Ibid.*

For about the first half of September Crook's scouts lanced the area bounded generally by Lake Abert, Warner Valley, and Goose Lake, going as far west as Sprague River. By that time, fresh trails were seen going southeast.[36] Crook had become convinced, through his pre-Civil War experience in California, that the hostiles would be found in California. Accordingly, he divided his force, sending Perry with two companies of the First Cavalry and Darragh and McKay's scouts northeast into the Blue Mountains. Taking a smaller party composed of Company H, First Cavalry, and Company D, Twenty-third Infantry, along with McIntosh's scouts, Crook moved southward to the west side of Goose Lake.[37] As they probed through the country, they found that the maps then in use were "nothing like correct," Wasson said.[38]

By self-enforced hardship and trail-craft the command worked its way to within a one-night march of the area in which Crook expected to find, and surprise, the enemy—and then came heartbreak through the blunder of a fraud of a frontiersman. On September 22, Crook sent out a scouting party under a man named Dad Wilson, a former stagecoach hand who had joined the command. Theretofore, Crook had not dared trust him on a responsible errand, partly because the gentleman talked too much about how many years he had fought Indians and how many scalps he had taken. Crook found it necessary to send him on that one scout, however, because Wilson had fresh horses. "About nine o'clock at night," as Wasson told it, "the old fellow discovered all his knowledge of scouting and put the natives on the lookout, by building a large fire on an exposed point in view of the camp of the soldiers—said fire being answered soon after on the Warner Range twenty-five miles east."[39]

Near noon the next day, "old Wilson came puffing and

---

[36] *Ibid.*, Nov. 2, 1867.
[37] Crook's report, dated Camp Harney, Oregon, Oct. 12, 1867, National Archives, Civil War Branch, Adjutant General's Office, Letters Received, 60057a/b.
[38] *Owyhee Avalanche*, Nov. 2, 1867.
[39] *Ibid.*

sweating into headquarters with the story that early that morning he 'fit' a camp of at least 'fifty warrior' (ten miles west), and that his Indian scouts had run, etc.," Wasson wrote. By then the enemy clearly was in a state of agitation, for seven or eight large signal fires were seen down the river.[40] When Crook, who could be brusque to the point of severity when occasion demanded, asked Wilson why he built the fire and then attacked the enemy against orders, without first reporting to headquarters, "the poor old fool stammered out something about wanting to find Archy, &c., &c., and went off with his head down like a sheep," Wasson said.[41]

The entire campaign seemed ruined. No longer did the troops have the presumed advantage of surprise. "After marching the command for two weeks over the most infernal ground, for the purpose of keeping under cover, and it had been quietly landed within one night march of its destination, and now that the whole campaign seemed to be rendered a complete failure—the disgust exhibited round headquarters was the most expressive I had ever seen," Wasson commented. Wilson's scouts returned leisurely to camp that evening, making it plain the old man had fired a few shots promiscuously "and broke like a quarter-horse for the main Command."[42] In his official report, Crook said the enemy was put on the alert "through the blunder of an old imposter [sic] of a white man who was along in the capacity of a scout."[43]

In an effort to deceive the hostile Indians, Crook marched his command in daylight down the wagon road toward Fort Crook, California, coming within twenty miles of the fort. On the way he found a place on the south side of Pit River where he could cross the river and conceal the command in timber. Marching again on the twenty-fifth, they discovered a wickiup, from which the warriors fled, but Crook did not think it worthwhile to pursue them or to capture the women who were there.

[40] *Ibid.*
[41] *Ibid.*
[42] *Ibid.*
[43] Crook's report, Oct. 12, *loc. cit.*

In camp that night, disgust, chagrin, and indignation were greater than they had ever been, Wasson reported. More, it was a dark and gloomy night with rain pelting down from black clouds. Crook went off alone under a big pine, whittling and whistling, but with "a face on longer than this report with two veto-messages added." Wasson's heart went out to him, and he wanted to go over, offer to dig some roots, and share a warm supper with the General. But he was afraid to take the liberty. Crook seemed to think the show was over. It seemed they could not go much farther or stay out much longer. McIntosh's horses were about worn out, and some of the other stock sick; the hostile Indians alert; and the command ignorant of whether the enemy had scattered or had concentrated.[44]

But the next day the command was destined to chance upon the one battle of the campaign—an engagement that came to be known as the Battle of Infernal Caverns, in an area now included within the Modoc National Forest of northeastern California. The command was moving east toward the South Fork of Pit River when McIntosh galloped in with word that he had tracked Indians into some lava bluffs within half a mile of the command. His Indians had learned that the hostile band was the same Crook had engaged at Steen's Mountain the previous winter. Crook quickly deployed his forces—cavalry under Lieutenant W. R. Parnell to the south and infantry under Lieutenant John Madigan to the north of the Indian position, with McIntosh and his scouts going into the rocks above it.[45]

Wasson went in with the scouts, holding higher ground, from which he gained a bird's-eye view of the Indian position. He found that jumbled rocks, rising gradually from the valley which lay to the east, had given the Indians a system of natural fortifications. They had improved the position to provide one fort, with portholes, on the east and two larger forts on the west. At that point, the river flowed between perpendicu-

[44] *Owyhee Avalanche,* Nov. 2, 1867.
[45] *Ibid.;* Crook's Report, Oct. 12, *loc. cit.*

53

lar walls of rock said to be at least one thousand feet high. On the western side of the river, a short ridge paralleled the main bluff, between it and the river; between the bluff and ridge were jumbled rocks, filling the intervening space up to a level with the crest of the ridge. In addition to the forts, the tops of which were on a level with the crest of the ridge, the Indian position possessed a maze of canyons, ravines, and fissures, as well as subterranean passages.

Going with the Indians, Wasson reached the more westerly bluff about 1:00 P.M. on September 26, just as Madigan's men came into position on the north, from whom the scouts received a volley by mistake. "Some blasphemous remarks (in the 'American language') in return fixed that matter," Wasson wrote. Although McIntosh's scouts immediately slithered into covered positions, Wasson stood up to survey the enemy position with glasses. However, a few bullets from the enemy, unmistakably fired in his direction, caused him to take a protected position.[46]

About an hour later, Parnell advanced on the enemy position from the south, but was repulsed by a volley which killed two and wounded two of his men. To Wasson, from a high position, it appeared that a siege was inevitable. With the enemy virtually surrounded, the attackers poured in a constant fire, "and, with the sound of the firing, mashing and glancing of balls and the yelling from both sides—the occasion was interesting to say the least." Although the scouts were above the Indians at a distance of about four hundred yards and an angle upward of forty-five degrees, they drew hostile fire with even a momentary exposure of head and shoulders. Crook continued to reconnoiter the position until late afternoon. At dark the attackers were ordered to crawl up close to the forts and cut off anyone attempting to escape.[47]

Wasson decided to remain with the scouts through the night. "But nothing ever looked so d—— ridiculous as their 'war dance' after supper—as much as to say the show couldn't

[46] *Owyhee Avalanche*, Nov. 2, 1867.
[47] *Ibid.*

go on at all without some of that sort of thing," he commented. After dark, when the scouts had inched to within one hundred yards of the forts, the hostile Indians let loose with arrows, which Wasson called "Piute toothpicks," and threw rocks at the attackers. Between the arrows and the rocks, sleep proved impossible.[48]

At daylight of September 27, Crook came up from the main camp, which had been established in the valley, and gave orders for a general attack. He had Parnell and Madigan concentrate their white troopers under the crest facing the eastern fort, and sent the scouts into the rocks on the west. Madigan and Parnell's storming parties were to crawl up the slope as far as possible without revealing themselves. Crook talked to the men "like a father," telling them that at the command, "Forward," they were to rise with a yell, move quickly, keep yelling, and never think of stopping until they had crossed a ditch separating them from the position, scaled the wall, and broken through into the breastworks.[49]

Wasson chose to go with the storming parties and attached himself to Madigan's group, which would attack from the southeastern part of the fort. The order to charge came about sunup, and Madigan's men dashed forward, but before they had gone twenty feet, they received a volley which killed Madigan and wounded six soldiers as well as another citizen, Lawrence Traynor, who went in with Wasson. But the line did not falter; the troops stormed into the ditch, found two routes of ascent, and started to climb. Scrambling up the twenty-five foot wall, they came to a natural parapet about six feet wide, which encircled the fort on the east and on the north as well. Sergeant Michael Meara of Company H jumped on to the parapet, looked into the fort, and exclaimed, "Come on, boys, we've got 'em." No sooner were the words out of his mouth than he fell dead at Wasson's feet.[50]

Wasson was one of the first men in the fort.[51] He ran around

[48] *Ibid.*
[49] *Ibid.*
[50] *Ibid.*
[51] Crook, *Autobiography,* 154.

to the north to drop any Indians who attempted to escape, but they flung their guns aside and escaped over the west side of the fort, disappearing "in an instant like so many lizards." Wasson found a soldier dead there, the man who had immediately preceded him. Down below he saw another soldier waiting for Indians to come out. Otherwise, there was not another human being in sight, except soldiers coming into the fort, whom he could see through the portholes. Then came a volley of bullets and arrows from the west fort. "The prospects for continuing in that good state of health of which I had been boasting, were not now very bright, and I went back to the southeast end of the parapet, by which time Parnell had all the soldiers up and the fort full of them," he wrote. Inside the fort they found a dead Indian, who, Wasson conjectured, might have been killed by Crook's firing over the troops' heads from the ridge where Madigan fell. "He makes few mistakes with that long 'Spencer' rifle of his."[52]

Occasional firing continued through the day and night, but the next day they learned from an Indian woman that the warriors had fled. And thus ended what Wasson at the time called the "Three Days Fight at this Indian Gibraltar." After that the command moved on north, getting back to Camp Warner on October 4. There they found mail awaiting them —including a letter addressed to Madigan, telling him he had been promoted.

Wasson's coverage of Crook's Oregon-Idaho-California campaign fitted into the same pattern in which the work of later Western War correspondents would be found. He moved into the field with troops and wrote chronological accounts, adding to them day by day until a courier could take the story in. He did not rewrite the story to bring it up to date, with the most recent incident in the lead, as a modern reporter would do. Living with troops in the field, he shared their everyday hardships, ate their field rations, and went into action beside them.

Although his copy had a playful humor about it when he

[52] *Owyhee Avalanche*, Nov. 2, 1867.

56

had little else to write, a note of familiarity which would not be found in the stories written by correspondents for larger papers on later campaigns, he also directed his attention to the same things they would—the action, the country, life on campaign, personalities, and so forth. He did not, however, provide as clear a picture of the expedition—especially regarding its members—as later writers would. It is significant, however, that Crook's report substantiates Wasson's reporting of that part of the campaign covered by both.

Wasson remained at Camp Warner with Crook until October 7, when they left for Camp Harney, the General to meet his wife there and Wasson to return to Silver City. But they would ride together on campaign again in a future year.

It was November before Wasson got back to Silver City. His brother had waited for him to return, and then they went their separate ways to San Francisco, where they were to meet. John Wasson left Silver City on November 6 for San Francisco by way of the Columbia River, with a commission as special correspondent for the *New York Tribune* and *Alta California* of San Francisco. Joe Wasson, described as "a practical printer and writer of more than average ability," left Silver City on the Humboldt Stage on November 9.[53]

In concluding his last dispatch from the field, Wasson had said: ". . . I have endeavored to give you a plain statement of how a month's operations developed from day to day.

"Had a bully time and have no excuses to make."

Henry Morton Stanley, destined within a few years to live one of the great personal adventure stories of the nineteenth century, rode out on the Kansas plains in the spring of 1867 on his first assignment as a full-fledged special correspondent. Representing the *Missouri Democrat* of St. Louis, he joined Major General Winfield Scott Hancock's force of 1,400 men, the largest that had even been sent against Southern Plains tribes up to that time.

A squat, wavy-haired, moon-faced Welshman of twenty-

53 *Ibid.,* Nov. 9, 1867.

five, Stanley made that first assignment a step upward in his rise from workhouse brat to Knight of the Bath. Indeed, his coverage of the Hancock expedition may have been the turning point in a career that took him to Livingstone four years later, for his energetic reporting in the West opened the ranks of the *New York Herald* to him, and as a *Herald* man he sought and found Livingstone.

Stanley wrote serious descriptive narratives, and if anything amusing happened during those weeks in the West, it escaped him. He was a humorless man; there had been no humor or laughter in his childhood. Born in Denbigh, Wales, in 1841, as John Rowlands, he became an unwanted waif whose family shunted him into a workhouse. Finally he shipped to sea as a cabin boy at fifteen, landing in New Orleans, where he met a merchant named Henry Morton Stanley, who adopted him. At the start of the Civil War he entered the Confederate Army, was captured at Shiloh, imprisoned near Chicago, and paroled to enlist in the Northern artillery. Ill health forced his discharge within a month afterward. Following a visit in England, he enlisted in the U. S. Navy, still during the Civil War, and wrote some newspaper articles.[54]

Until the spring of 1867 he had been only an "occasional descriptist," as he called it, but in that year was "promoted to the proud position of a Special Correspondent, with the very large commission to inform the public regarding all matters of general interest affecting the Indians and the great Western Plains."[55] The *Missouri Democrat* paid him $15.00 a week, plus travel expenses, and he stretched his income to about $90.00 a week by writing also for the *New York Herald, New York Tribune, New York Times, Chicago Republican, Cincinnati Commercial*, and other newspapers.

Stanley traveled to Solomon City, Kansas, where he took what he called a "coach" to the field headquarters of General Hancock on the banks of the Saline River, forty-seven miles

[54] Ian Anstruther, *I Presume: Stanley's Triumph and Disaster*, 8–33.
[55] *My Early Travels and Adventures in America*, I, v (hereafter cited as *Early Travels*).

away. The command then was moving from Fort Riley to Fort Larned, near present Larned, Kansas. Stepping from the coach, suitcase in hand, Stanley went to Hancock's quarters, but the commander was asleep. Rather than awaken him, Stanley strolled around camp.

The tents and blue uniforms reminded him of scenes from the Civil War. He heard soldiers talk seriously of a probable fight with the Indians, saw others preparing supper, others cleaning horses, others cleaning arms and equipment, some arranging their beds, others playing chess, cards, or other games. Later, he heard the drum and fife order retreat. Darkness descended, drums beat tattoo at eight, troops formed ranks for roll call, and were dismissed for the night, and at nine two drumbeats ordered lights out.

While Stanley was writing notes of his observations, an orderly summoned him to Hancock. Entering the General's tent, Stanley met a "hale, hearty, and tall gentleman in the prime of life" who examined the correspondent's credentials, and welcomed him to camp.

Without saying so directly, Stanley's first dispatch indicated that he learned then the general outlines of the campaign: Hancock would meet with the chiefs of hostile tribes; if peaceable, the Indians would be allowed to depart in peace; if warlike, they could fight Hancock then and there.[56]

Hancock, commanding the Department of Missouri, went into the field on the basis of rumors that the Indians intended to go on the warpath. Cheyennes, Kiowas, and Arapahos reportedly had informed frontier officers, stage drivers, and agents that they would insist on the whites' withdrawing from the Arkansas River route to New Mexico and the Smoky Hill River route to Colorado that spring.[57]

The unrest, if such it was, could be traced to the Harney-Sanborn treaty of 1865. That agreement set aside lands for all the tribes in the region south of the Arkansas, but most of the Southern Cheyennes had been hunting on the Powder River

[56] *Ibid.*, I, 1-2.
[57] Secretary War, *Report*, 1867, I, 28, 34-35.

when it was concluded. On returning south, the Dog Soldiers, a military society, refused to accept the treaty because it would take away from the Indians the hunting grounds on the Republican and Smoky Hill rivers in western Kansas, land the government wanted for the Kansas Pacific Railroad. Their refusal to give up the land caused many whites to think the Indians intended war, although the southern plains had been unusually quiet during 1866. Sherman, commanding the Military Division of the Missouri, had told Hancock that the Indians had threatened whites if they should travel either route. "This cannot be tolerated for a moment," Sherman said. "If not a state of war, it is the next thing to it."[58]

It seems appropriate here to digress briefly to explain the territorial organization of the U. S. Army in order to avoid confusion between the Military Division of the Missouri and the Department of Missouri. Although during the period of the Western War, territorial organization was changed from time to time, basically it followed a practice by which the country was divided into major commands known as military divisions, based upon the needs of continental defense rather than the requirements of Indian fighting. There were finally three such divisions—the Military Divisions of the Atlantic, of the Missouri, and of the Pacific. Each of them in turn was divided into departments. The largest, and most important from the standpoint of Indian fighting, was the Military Division of the Missouri, with headquarters in Chicago, embracing all the Great Plains and part of the mountain territories. It comprised more than one million square miles and included most of the wild, semicivilized, and civilized Indian tribes of the country. It, in turn, was divided into the Departments of Dakota, Platte, and Missouri, basically. With the construction of railroads into Texas, which altered the supply situation, Texas became a department in the division, also. Roughly, the Department of Dakota took in what is now the northern tier of states from Minnesota to eastern Montana; the Depart-

[58] *Reports of Major General W. S. Hancock upon Indian Affairs with Accompanying Exhibits*, 17–37 (hereafter cited as Hancock, *Reports*).

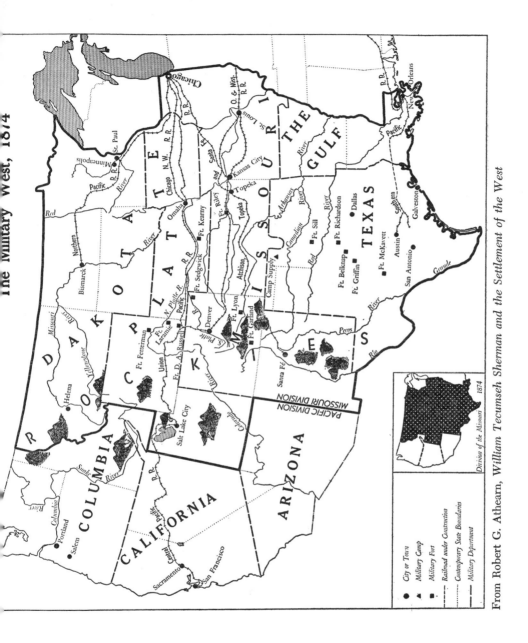

The Military West, 1874

From Robert G. Athearn, *William Tecumseh Sherman and the Settlement of the West*

City or Town
Military Camp
Military Fort
Railroad under Construction
Contemporary State Boundaries
Military Department

Division of the Missouri   1874

PACIFIC DIVISION
MISSOURI DIVISION

ment of the Platte, Nebraska, Wyoming, and ultimately a part of Idaho; the Department of Missouri, Kansas, part of Colorado, and at different times parts or all of Indian Territory. Texas was Texas.

Another journalist on the Hancock expedition was an artist, Theodore R. Davis, of *Harper's Weekly,* who had been an artist-correspondent in the Civil War. Sketches from his pad depicted many scenes on the Kansas frontier in the spring of 1867. Because his work was almost entirely graphic rather than reportorial, Davis is beyond the scope of this study.

The Hancock expedition was unimportant, despite its size, largely because the commander went into the field under equivocal orders. He was to fight or not to fight, depending upon the temper of the Indians.[59] Including elements of the Seventh Cavalry, Thirty-seventh Infantry and Fourth Artillery, plus a pontoon train, the column reached Fort Larned on April 7, where Hancock awaited a conference with Indian head men. Colonel E. W. Wynkoop—the agent for the Cheyennes, Arapahos, and Apaches of the plains—had sent runners to bring in the chiefs, but a blizzard on April 9 left eight inches of snow on the ground. Consequently, Hancock postponed the conference once, but the Indians provoked him by not appearing on schedule on April 11 on the pretext that they had found a buffalo herd near their camp and had stopped to hunt. When they came in on April 12, Hancock met them in a night council, in which he told them, among other things, that he had heard the Indians wanted to fight. If that was true, the soldiers were ready. If it was not true, the government expected the Indians to live by terms of the treaty. Tall Bull, speaking for the Cheyennes, replied that Hancock should have had representatives of the other Plains tribes there, too; only Cheyennes had come to the council. The chief insisted that his people had never done the white man any harm, and that both white and Indian should be able to go on the Smoky Hill without danger.

[59] This summary of the Hancock expedition is based upon Hancock, *Reports,* 17–37, and Stanley, *Early Travels,* I, 3–47.

Hancock marched the next day toward the Cheyenne village on Pawnee Fork, even though Tall Bull had made it clear he would have no more to say in his camp than he had said at Fort Larned. Hancock camped near the village on the fourteenth, and early that evening learned that the Indians had fled, leaving their lodges and possessions behind. Hancock sent Custer, then serving as lieutenant colonel of the Seventh Cavalry, in pursuit with four squadrons. Davis of *Harper's Weekly* went with Custer; Stanley remained with the main command.

Custer galloped through the countryside on a fruitless pursuit which helped precipitate the inglorious end of the Hancock expedition, although it was then that Custer began creating the fiction of George Armstrong Custer, Indian fighter. The failure was not all Custer's fault, however, for he had counted on finding forage stocked at Fort Hays for his horses. A slip-up in the quartermaster department had resulted in a failure to carry out Hancock's orders that grain be stored there. Without grain for his horses Custer could not continue the pursuit; he had not come anywhere near catching up with the Indians, anyhow.

Using heavier horses, the cavalry had to carry grain along with the column. The size of the horses, the fact that they were accustomed to grain, and the heavier load they carried all made it impossible for them to remain in good condition on plains grass alone. By contrast, the Indian's mustang, a smaller animal, was entirely grass-fed, adapted to the plains environment, and carried a lighter load.

Upon learning of Custer's immobilization at Fort Hays and of Indian attacks on three stage stations on the Smoky Hill route, Hancock burned the Indian village and marched for Fort Larned by way of Fort Dodge. His supplies did not enable him to remain in the field any longer. He moved on to Fort Hays, where the expedition came to an end in early May.

Hancock and his campaign were subject to much criticism. Wynkoop reported to Commissioner of Indian Affairs N. G. Taylor that the Indians had fled from their village because of "intense fear," and said that "the result of the expedition is disastrous."[60] Later writers also criticized the Hancock campaign. One, strongly pro-Indian, said Hancock and Custer "started a war without any legitimate cause whatsoever."[61] Another writer, long acquainted with the Cheyennes, said that the Dog Soldiers had traveled through deep snow to meet Hancock at Fort Larned, where the night conference aroused their suspicions because friendly councils were held in daytime. Hancock had made them still more suspicious by announcing his intention to visit their village—the village of a tribe that had been attacked in camp at Sand Creek.[62]

The expedition turned out to be unimportant, true, but in the expectation of the moment that it would be important, Stanley wrote voluminously, judging by his book of published dispatches. Writing of what he experienced, saw, and heard, especially the latter, Stanley described the countryside, each fort at which they stopped, and sometimes the individuals he met, such as Wild Bill Hickok, whom Custer also found it to his point to describe, in terms similar to those used by Stanley.[63] Stanley sometimes wrote his dispatches by tacking paper to a board that separated the halves of his suitcase.

Stanley attended Hancock's conference with the Cheyennes at Fort Larned, at which he began to learn something of dealing with primitive peoples. With that conference he began the practice of reporting the formal conversations of General and Indians in what purported to be verbatim text. In the case of the Fort Larned council, it would appear that giving the text would not have been difficult since alternate passages of English and Cheyenne probably would have allowed an attentive reporter to transcribe the English sentences in longhand without falling behind. The story of that council was the first major story written on Stanley's first assignment as a full-time newspaper reporter.

[60] Hancock, *Reports*, 98.
[61] Charles J. Brill, *Conquest of the Southern Plains*, 86.
[62] George Bird Grinnell, *The Fighting Cheyennes*, 245–62.
[63] Stanley, *Early Travels*, I, 5–6; Gen. George Armstrong Custer, *My Life on the Plains*, 68–69.

Black Kettle of the Cheyennes. Drawn by John Metcalf.

Harper's Weekly, June 8, 1867.

Fort Larned, Kansas, 1867.

Stanley's stories were sympathetic toward Hancock. He justified the burning of the Indian village in these words: "He [Hancock] was compelled to adopt this course, because, after the delivery of his speech to fifteen chiefs, they went and burned three stations on the Smoky Hill route, and scalped, disemboweled, and burnt three men employed at the Fossil Creek Station, ran off several mules and horses on that route, and gave a good scare generally to the traders." This was essentially the reason Hancock himself gave.[64]

Stanley was equally antagonistic to the two Indian agents, Wynkoop and Colonel J. H. Leavenworth, agent for the Comanches and Kiowas, both of whom had joined Hancock before he marched to the village. At the burning of the village, Stanley said, the agents raised their hands and cried, "Oh, Lord, what will become of Hancock?" He said Hancock had been kind and courteous to them, but they had been "acrimonious" in criticizing him. He emphasized that Hancock did not have to show deference to them, but wished to do so to demonstrate his willingness to be guided by their knowledge of the Indians.[65]

Upon returning to Fort Larned after burning the village, Hancock talked with Satanta, a Kiowa marauder, whose complaints gave Stanley occasion to report criticism that had been directed at Leavenworth. Satanta accused the agent of hiding annuity goods in his back room and telling the Indians he had none for them. The Indian wanted a "good and responsible man" for agent, preferably one who would bring the annuity goods to the Indians by wagon train, as an earlier agent had done. Hancock disclaimed any responsibility for the agent or his actions, but emphasized that he had burned the Cheyenne village because the Cheyennes had acted as though they wanted war. When Hancock and Satanta finished talking, Leavenworth accused Satanta of depredations in Texas and said he had orders to withhold annuity goods

[64] Stanley, *Early Travels*, I, 41–47; Hancock, *Reports*, 17–37.
[65] Stanley, *Early Travels*, I, 41–47.

until the Kiowas gave adequate assurance that they would not repeat such outrages.[66]

Leavenworth's explanation did not satisfy Stanley, who said the agent was "devoted to red tapeism," going about with pockets stuffed with official documents, the ends of which projected an inch or so from the pocket, making visible the inscription, "Leavenworth, Indian Agent." Stanley also reported that he had been told by three Indian interpreters that Leavenworth had illegally disposed of Indian goods.[67]

Sizing up the campaign on the spot, Stanley concluded that the expedition had accomplished this much: The guilty Cheyennes had been despoiled of $100,000 worth of property; their tipi poles could not be replaced without a trip to the mountains, where they would encounter old enemies, the Utes; the Santa Fe and Colorado routes would thereafter be better guarded. "Kansas is now free from all hostile Indians, and is open to the immigrant," he said.[68]

Stanley's accounts are substantiated, in the main, by Hancock's report—in the main, because the Hancock report presents a summary of events from late March to early May, devoting only paragraphs to material that Stanley expanded into full-length dispatches. Certain scenes and incidents caught his eye, which would be recorded only by a reporter presenting a running narrative from day to day. Although he reported the campaign soberly, on the whole, he did become wrought up over second-hand stories of atrocity and Indian agent cupidity.

The atrocity story, which would seem to be a standard ingredient of war reporting, appeared early in his work. As the column had moved south, he had reported, "Details that would shock even the most callous are daily poured into our ears of the scenes which have been enacted at Fort Dodge."[69] On the face of it, his statement appears exaggerated; if not,

[66] *Ibid.*, I, 62–83.
[67] *Ibid.*
[68] *Ibid.*, I, 83–91.
[69] *Ibid.*, I, 16–18.

66

then a goodly portion of the "details" probably were from the manufactory of western tall tales.

To illustrate his point, he cited the story of the James Box family of Montague, Texas. One evening in the summer of 1866, James Box, with his wife and five children, drove homeward after visiting a neighbor. Suddenly Satanta and some of his Kiowa warriors galloped up, surrounded the wagon, killed the father and one child, and then took Mrs. Box and four children into captivity. During a night march the Indians took from Mrs. Box's arms an infant whose crying annoyed them, and dashed out its brains against a tree. During the several days' journey required to reach the Kiowa village, Mrs. Box and her surviving three children occupied a common lodge at night—in which the scalp of husband and father hung before them. Once in the Kiowa camp, the eldest daughter, then eighteen, was traded from chief to chief, who spent their lust on her. Mrs. Box and the second to eldest daughter got along fairly well, but the youngest daughter—crying because separated from the others—was punished by having her feet held to a fire until the cuticle was burned away.[70]

The conclusion of the Box incident, reflecting atrocity as well as a criticism of frontier administration, appeared in Stanley's story. Obviously on the basis of second-hand information in an organization where rumor spread fast, he said that some Kiowas had brought the Box women into Fort Dodge, where the quartermaster paid $2,800 ransom for them. Without having heard the conversation himself and without any indication that a stenographic transcript existed, Stanley quoted what were purported to be Miss Box's very words at that time. Calling the commanding officer's attention to a Kiowa named Ton-a-en-ko, she said with horror: "There stands the man who slew my father. I saw him stab him in the breast, his knife reeking with his blood when he pulled it out; and he has my father's clothes on even now, and, oh, my God! you are giving him flour, sugar, and silver

[70] The details of the Box family incident were not given by Stanley but are in Custer, *My Life on the Plains,* 102–106, and Hancock, *Reports,* 43.

67

medals. Shame on you, sir! Why don't you arrest him?" Instead of "harboring the red fiends within the walls and enclosures of his fort," Stanley commented, the commander should have sent the Indians out of the fort to take care of themselves.[71]

The irony here is that Stanley wrote so indignantly about an atrocity in which Satanta figured, and then later used Satanta's charges in building a case against Leavenworth, even though Leavenworth pointed out in the conference that Satanta had been involved in the Box incident. Perhaps Stanley had forgotten.

The campaign came to an end at Fort Hays. Hancock went to Fort Leavenworth to confer with Sherman, and Stanley started on a series of journeys through the West which occupied him for the remainder of the year. In the fall he covered the Medicine Lodge peace negotiations that attempted, with no more success than other treaties, to bring peace to the Southern Plains.

Toward the end of the year, the Indian story died, and Stanley heard of a British expedition to Abyssinia which interested him. Giving up his job with the *Missouri Democrat*, he went to New York, where he mustered courage to call on James Gordon Bennett for the newspaperman's dream of that era—a job on the *New York Herald*. As a result of that conversation, Stanley went to Africa for the *Herald*.

Bennett sent Stanley overseas, but within the year the *Herald* would start sending staff correspondents to cover the various campaigns of the Western War.

[71] Stanley, *Early Travels*, I, 16–18.

First Lead

3. CUSTER ATTACKS AT WASHITA

> *. . . General Sheridan expresses his intention of making this the end of the Indian wars in this section if he is let alone. A few chicken-hearted, socalled philanthropists, may have something to say out of ignorance of the question; but economy, humanity, as well as the future security of our great thoroughfares of travel, and the settlements which will naturally spring up along them, demand a vigorous war, a rigid punishment of offenders and a durable peace.*
> DeBenneville Randolph Keim[1]

DeBenneville randolph keim had seen war before, but frontier Kansas introduced him to a new face of war. Riding a passenger train that was equipped with guns for defense against Indians impressed even a *New York Herald* man who had covered the Civil War. Likewise, he noticed that trains ran only in daytime because of the Indian threat. For his own defense Keim carried two pistols and a rifle when he went to western Kansas in late September, 1868, to report Sheridan's winter campaign against southern Plains tribes.[2]

A twenty-seven-year-old descendant of an old Pennsylvania family, Keim had spent three years covering the Civil War for the *Herald*. He was born in 1841 in Reading, Pennsylvania, which one of his ancestors had helped found, and attended Beloit College in Wisconsin, but did not graduate.

[1] *New York Herald*, Nov. 8, 1868.
[2] DeBenneville Randolph Keim, *Sheridan's Troopers on the Borders*, 14, 19–20.

While covering the Civil War, he developed a confidential relationship with Grant, but was not so fortunate with Sherman, who ordered him arrested and tried as a spy because the *Herald* had accidentally printed a confidential letter from Keim to Bennett revealing that a Union officer had broken the Confederate signal code. Instead of being court-martialed, however, he was transported north of the Ohio with orders not to return. He had reported twenty-six battles during the Civil War.[3]

Keim worked for the greatest American newspaper of its day—the *New York Herald*. Bennett had founded the *Herald* in 1835 as a penny newspaper, and, with his driving energy and recognition of news as a commodity, had built it into a strong newspaper. His son, James Gordon Bennett, Jr., succeeded his father in the management of the paper. Oswald Garrison Villard, also a New York newspaperman, considered the Bennetts "the most remarkable news men this country has ever produced." As he expressed it, Bennett, Sr., revolutionized the practice of news-getting and Bennett, Jr., created exclusive news. As an index to the paper's reliability, Villard said the *Herald* of the later nineteenth century reported local news with an accuracy which New York papers of the 1920's could not equal.[4] In sending Keim to Kansas, the *Herald* began the practice of reporting the Western War regularly.

Upon reaching Fort Leavenworth, which was headquarters for the Department of Missouri, Keim learned that Major General Phil Sheridan had established field headquarters at Fort Hays. Riding a train composed of passenger, stock, and freight cars, he reached Ellsworth, a few miles west of Fort Harker, where he first saw the roughness of the frontier and first tasted the notoriously bad food of frontier hostelries. Another daylight train trip, in the course of which he first met with the Kansas pastime of shooting buffalo from a train, and

[3] J. Cutler Andrews, *The North Reports the Civil War*, 62, 67, 374, 564; *American Biographical Directories—District of Columbia* . . . (Washington, 1908), excerpt supplied by Washingtoniana Division, District of Columbia Public Library.

[4] Oswald Garrison Villard, *Some Newspapers and Newspaper-men*, 273–75.

Keim reached Hays City about noon. He found the frontier town populated by about 200 persons—Americans, Germans, Swiss, French, Jews, Mexicans, and a few women.

In company with an infantry officer whom he met on the littered station platform, Keim went to near-by Fort Hays. Sheridan was absent on an inspection trip, but the officers and ladies of the post received Keim cordially and placed him in comfortable quarters. Sheridan returned during the day, and Keim met him that first evening.

Sheridan had taken command of the department in March, 1868—although appointed earlier to replace Hancock—and immediately had faced the threat of large-scale outbreaks, even though a peace treaty had been signed only the preceding fall. The Medicine Lodge treaty of 1867 had assigned reservations south of the Arkansas River to the Cheyennes, Arapahos, Comanches, Kiowas, and Lipan Apaches, clearing the way for railroad construction through the area bordered by the Arkansas and Platte rivers. During the winter, however, young men—especially of the Cheyennes—grumbled that the treaty concessions had been obtained by misrepresentation. When the grass greened, they unloosed fire and terror to drive the hated whites from the Indians' former hunting grounds in central Kansas.

Striking the Saline and Solomon valleys, the Indians burned homes, murdered men, ravished women. In sixty days that summer they killed 117 settlers and took 7 women into captivity. Their sudden, swift sorties, in emulation of the Sioux, who had driven back the white man, made 1868 the peak year in number of encounters between whites and Indians. The Indians achieved their desired end in part, for some settlements had been driven in and some ranches abandoned.

Against the Indians, Sheridan's troopers could do little during the summer, for in that season the Indians traveled fast and lived easily. Scattered as they were through many posts to protect settlements and guard travel routes, the troops could not be formed into enough columns to scour the country for migrant bands or gathered in sufficient force to deal with the Indians decisively. Sheridan said it was as difficult for troops to find mounted Plains Indians during the summer as it had been to find the *Alabama* on the ocean during the Civil War. The Department of Missouri embraced 150,000 square miles of frontier, including two major immigrant routes—one to Colorado and the other to New Mexico. Except for a handful of forts and a line of railroad track, it was largely unsettled. At his command on the Kansas frontier Sheridan had 1,200 cavalrymen and 1,400 infantry. Out of the 2,600 he could send only 800 into the field because of commitments at posts, along the railroads, and along the line of settlements. Against him rode, by his estimate, 6,000 Kiowa, Comanche, Cheyenne, and Arapaho warriors, each of whom had from two to ten extra horses.

Sheridan decided, therefore, on a winter campaign, because winter offered a better opportunity to thrash the Indians and impoverish them by killing their ponies and destroying their property. During the winter, the Indians confined themselves to a more restricted area, partly because their grass-fed ponies were weakened from lack of food then. Although a winter campaign had proved feasible in other departments, it was unprecedented on the plains. The task for Sheridan, then, was to find and surprise the villages of hostiles.

On matters of Indian hostilities and Indian administration the *New York Herald* held decided views, generally siding with the military. Within a few years its reporters would use the newspaper exposé to bring to light, and help to turn out, the Indian Ring. Many times through the years the *Herald* strongly recommended that Indian affairs be centered in the War Department, as it did in 1868. The *Herald* also spoke slightingly of the Commissioner of Indian Affairs, while saying that the army, if left alone, could end the eternal Indian war in one campaign. Moreover, the *Herald* traced the cause of the 1868 Indian trouble directly "to the bad management of the Interior Department and to the correlative fact that the government is the ally of the Indian and furnishes him the means to murder our soldiers."[5]

Keim's stories reflected the *Herald* editorial position. From Fort Hays he wrote on September 30 that Sheridan was determined to reduce the hostiles to "such a condition of feebleness and fear that they will be perfectly contented to remain upon their reservations" and learn to farm. He also commented: "Looking at the policy of the government with regard to the Indian question, and judging the merits of those who have its administration in their hands by their acts, without any compromise whatever, every one of them, from the Secretary of the Interior to the lowest official, might be set down as understanding about as little of the duties of their office as it is possible for any sane person to know. The management, or, rather, the mismanagement of Indian affairs is either the result of corruption or deplorable ignorance."[6]

After writing two "situationers" on September 30 and October 1, Keim turned to a news story about an incident that has since become a classic in the annals of Indian fighting in the Far West. While Keim was en route from New York, the telegraph carried the story of Colonel George A. Forsyth's fight on an island in the Arickaree River in what is now eastern Colorado. The first story was based upon the account of two scouts who had come into Fort Wallace, Kansas, for reinforcements. At that time Forsyth and the remainder of his band of civilian scouts were still besieged on the island. When word came that the survivors had reached Fort Wallace, Keim went out to interview them.

The trip to Fort Wallace, near present Wallace, Kansas, meant taking a train to end of track and then a stagecoach through hostile Indian territory. The uncertainties of frontier rail travel caused him and a handful of others to wait two impatient hours in Hays City on the morning of October 2 for the train that would take them west. Getting aboard, he found about twenty passengers, including two army wives.

[5] Issue of Oct. 1, 1868.
[6] *Ibid.*, Oct. 9, 1868.

Of the men, he said, "A fiercer, hirsute, and unwashed set I never saw." He seemed surprised to find that frontiersmen also were human, with a certain "fulness of soul." Perhaps it was that which made them pleasant companions—"under the circumstances."[7]

Within fifteen miles of Hays City, Keim began to see buffalo, several thousand of them. Within another thirty miles he saw the grassland blackened by buffalo for a distance of ten to fifteen miles, all of it new and strange to a New York newspaperman. At the sound of the locomotive, startled animals on the south of the tracks stampeded to get across the tracks to the main herd. One bull didn't quite make it, and the locomotive tossed him aside. Landing on his back in a ditch, the animal kicked furiously in the air. The train stopped to allow trainmen and passengers to cut a few humps from the animals they had shot from the moving train. With five to seven others, Keim started down the track to finish off the enraged, bellowing, pawing beast in the ditch. One man's bullet brought the bull right side up. Other shots infuriated the animal. Head down, roaring, and bleeding at the mouth, the buffalo charged Keim's party. Firing at a mad buffalo head-on would have been a waste of ammunition. "For my own part, I took occasion to make a few long and rapid strides across the track into the ditch on the other side. The rest of the party imitated this dexterous movement without many moments of reflection," Keim said. Concealed behind the embankment, the hunters got in enough shots to kill the buffalo. By then the engineer was signaling that it was time to go. They had to leave the animal where he fell, at which Keim felt "a pang of shame."[8]

Late in the afternoon the wood-burning locomotive steamed to a stop at Sheridan, Kansas, end of track on the Kansas Pacific Railroad, then one of two roads being built westward to the Pacific. Keim had come to a frontier village upon which a large war party had fired a few days earlier. Of more im-

[7] Keim, *Sheridan's Troopers*, 37.
[8] *Ibid.*, 38–40.

mediate concern to the reporter than an Indian scare, however, was the room that had been assigned him in the one hotel in town. His room was immediately above a saloon, only a thin floor separating him from the boisterous profanity and the whiskey-thin tempers of unruly men below. Having heard that six men had been shot in drunken brawls during the preceding week, Keim spent an anxious night in fear that a shooting scrape would break out below.

The next morning he boarded a Santa Fe stagecoach, which was followed by a second coach containing baggage and six Negro soldiers as a stagecoach guard. Armed and listening to his traveling companions describe Indian torture, descriptions perhaps intended for his benefit as a tenderfoot, Keim at last had fairly entered the "Wild West." Shortly he came to the end of his journey, for Fort Wallace lay only about thirteen miles beyond Sheridan.

His arrival at Fort Wallace as a stranger recently from the States was "a rare and important event in the daily routine of the garrison," and he soon was called upon to answer many questions on many subjects. Later he visited Forsyth's scouts in their camp at Fort Wallace.[9]

From the scouts and from Forsyth Keim heard the story of the defense by fifty-one men against a war party of almost one thousand warriors of several Plains tribes, mostly Sioux and Cheyenne. The Beecher Island Fight, as it came to be known, was barely two weeks in the past when he first recorded the details for publication.

During the summer of 1868, "Sandy" Forsyth served on Sheridan's departmental headquarters staff as inspector general, continuing a wartime association during which Forsyth had accompanied Sheridan on the famous ride to Winchester. As a line officer rather than a staff officer, he wanted troop duty. This Sheridan could not give him, a major in Regular rank, without injustice to senior officers. Nevertheless, an opportunity arose when Sheridan decided he wanted a company of fifty civilians—"first-class hardy frontiersmen," he

[9] *Ibid.*, 49–50.

called them—formed into a company of scouts to keep track of the Indians. Forsyth accepted the independent command, which had a freedom and mobility that would have appealed to any cavalry officer.

At Forts Harker and Hays, Forsyth organized his company during August, 1868.[10] Within five days he enrolled his company as quartermaster employees at a daily wage plus a daily allowance for their horses. The government furnished arms, equipment, and rations. Each carried a Spencer seven-shot rifle and a Colt revolver.

Forsyth regarded the company as remarkable. With one exception, he had never seen a company of enlisted men who exceeded them in general intelligence. Forty-six of the fifty were native-born Americans; several were college graduates. Practically all had seen military service during the Civil War, in one army or the other, and had drifted to the frontier afterward. They included farmers, drovers, teachers, lawyers, mechanics, and merchants.

Forsyth's second-in-command was a lame lieutenant, Frederick H. Beecher, of the clerical Beechers, who had almost missed out on preferment a few months earlier because of whiskey. The third officer was the surgeon, Dr. J. H. Moers, who had served with New York volunteers. Sharp Grover, the chief scout, was a veteran plainsman. The first sergeant was a former regimental commander brevetted brigadier general in Pennsylvania volunteers during the Civil War.

Poking into Indian country beyond Fort Wallace, they camped on the bank of the Arickaree River in Colorado on the evening of September 16. At dawn the next morning the Indians attacked, reportedly numbering almost one thousand. Forsyth hurried his men to an island in the river, where they dug rifle pits and prepared for a siege. Twice during the day yelling savages charged the island position, to be met each time by a fire from repeating weapons. The scouts claimed

[10] This account of the Beecher Island fight is based upon General George A. Forsyth's two books, *Thrilling Days in Army Life*, 3–75, and *The Story of the Soldier*, 209–32.

the Indians were armed almost as well as they. In one of the charges the famed Cheyenne warrior, Roman Nose, fell.

Forsyth was wounded, Beecher and Moers killed, two scouts killed, and at least seventeen wounded. The command lost all its horses to Indian stampede and bullets.

Without food and medical supplies, which had been left behind when the men retired abruptly to the island, the wounded suffered and all hungered. At first they ate horse meat from animals not long dead. Later they forced themselves to eat putrid horsemeat seasoned with gunpowder. During the long wait Forsyth sent out two groups of two scouts each. Each pair got through, one to Fort Wallace and the other to a military column. Relief reached the men on the island on September 25, and a larger column arrived the next day. Then came the tedious march to Fort Wallace, Forsyth traveling with his shattered leg encased in a splint made from the trunk of a tree.

Keim's interview agrees on the whole with Forsyth's accounts, although there is considerable variation in the sequence of events. However, it should be borne in mind that the excitement of battle, like any crisis, distorts the observation of participants. Thus it may be that Keim accurately reported what he had heard in the camp of the scouts and at Forsyth's bedside. Although Keim interpreted the fight as being of greater significance than it was, he reported what happened, without making it any more blood-curdling than the event itself was.[11]

Keim remembered his stay of several days at Fort Wallace as anything but pleasant. Assigned to quarters with large cracks in the wall, he developed a sympathy for soldiers whose duty forced them to live in such God-forsaken surroundings. The monotony and dull routine of a frontier post soon pressed in upon him.

The arrival of Sheridan on October 6 gave Keim a chance to escape the dreary isolation, and it also gave him another story. Sheridan—who had come to visit Forsyth and Colonel

[11] *New York Herald*, Oct. 12, 1868.

H. C. Bankhead, the post commander—brought news that the Kiowas and Comanches south of the Arkansas had gone on the warpath. With the already hostile Cheyennes and Arapahos, this would give the enemy from four to five thousand warriors. A few days before, a party of savages had charged troops at Fort Dodge, but did not fire.

Keim left Fort Wallace with Sheridan. A small party traveling in an army ambulance (a spring vehicle) and escorted by cavalry, they dashed to Sheridan, two hours away, and boarded the General's special train for Fort Hays. On the way Sheridan stopped to examine the defenses that Negro troopers had built along the railroad, giving Keim his first acquaintance with another distinctive feature of military operations on the plains—the "underground monitor." Small detachments distributed along the railroad devised their own fortifications. They dug a hole breast-deep and large enough to accommodate the number of men to use it. Around the edge they built an earthwork about eighteen inches thick and twelve inches high. Overhead they placed a plank roof, blanketed by sod. A subterranean passage connected the dugout with the entrance about thirty feet away. Once a group of Indians approached a monitor out of curiosity; thereafter, they gave all others a wide berth.

The trip gave Keim another chance to shoot buffalo, but the experience turned out unhappily. With his rifle, Keim took position on the cow-catcher and had ridden there about ten miles when the train approached a large herd which was crossing the track. He had not bargained for buffalo on the tracks. Most of the animals had already crossed, but one laggard planted himself in the middle of the track and lowered his head for combat. "As I felt no relish to be a party to any such cranial collision, and finding no other convenient place, took a conspicuous but uncomfortable position on the steam-chest, holding on by the rail. I found the temperature as far as my feet were concerned anything but desirable, but in momentary anticipation of a rare display of buffalo-meat, kept a sharp look-out for the pieces," he said. At that point the locomotive whistle startled the buffalo into moving, but not soon enough. The engine bumped the beast into a ditch.[12]

From the time of their departure from Fort Wallace, Keim attached himself to Sheridan and stayed with him during the five months he was on the frontier. He apparently had operated the same way with Grant during the Civil War. In one respect that was sensible, for the Commanding General's headquarters certainly would be the focal point for all news developments, but a sycophantic note pervaded his copy.

Writing from Fort Hays on October 11, he reported the hostile Indians much bolder. On that very day, in fact, a band had been sighted within ten miles of the fort. Others had attacked Fort Zarah; others had attacked a government provision train on the way to Fort Larned and had raided a ranch near Fort Larned; others had threatened Fort Lyon in what is now eastern Colorado; another party had, some time before, been visible all of one day from both Fort Harker and Ellsworth. Should the Indians continue their belligerence, he said, there would be no doubt of ending the Indian war soon, for the greatest difficulty in fighting Indians had been to find them. The Indians along the Arkansas and south of it had not come in for rations, which indicated they meant war. The troops along the Arkansas were willing to oblige, but needed reinforcement. Inasmuch as the Peace Commission had approved a war against the recalcitrant tribes, Keim reported optimistically that the consequent absence of interference by "deluded" philanthropists would mean the army could end the Indian trouble once and for all.

Writing frequently but not daily, Keim presented a fairly comprehensive account of military affairs in western Kansas. The *Herald* ran most of his stories at some length, usually under a standing head, "The Indian War." Their place in the paper varied considerably, seeming to depend more upon typographical convenience and a form of departmentalization than upon relative merit and emphasis. Few of his dispatches were telegraphed to New York; most were mailed.

[12] Keim, *Sheridan's Troopers,* 62–63.

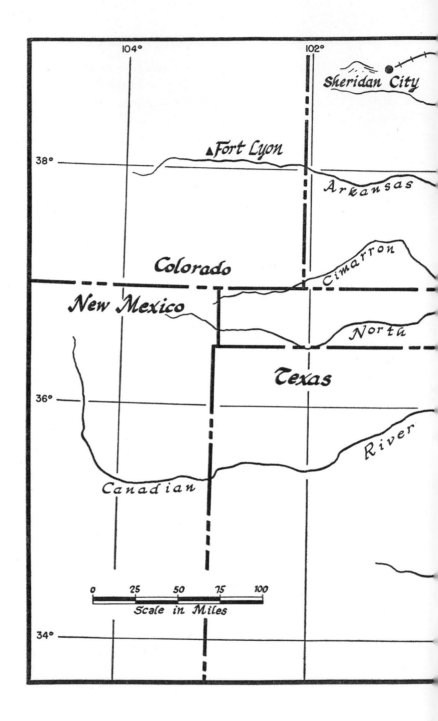

(Adapted from a map in Rister, *Border Command*, p. 68)

Area of Winter Campaign, 1868–69

Sheridan had planned carefully for the winter campaign which would end the Indian practice of summer war and winter peace, during which they had killed eight hundred whites on the plains since 1862. In proceeding with his plan, Sheridan went against the advice of many who said it could not be done. Even Jim Bridger, the old plainsman and one-time mountain man, had come out from St. Louis to dissuade him. With a winter campaign authorized, orders had been given to the Indians to report to a reservation at the Wichita Mountains, in what is now Oklahoma, if they were peaceable. Indians not in that sanctuary would be attacked.

Using almost five hundred wagons, Sheridan collected supplies at frontier posts. This was to be the first major Indian campaign in which the army had the support of the railroad so near the theater of operations. Sheridan sent 400,000 rations to Fort Dodge, 300,000 to Fort Lyon and 300,000 to Fort Arbuckle in what is now south central Oklahoma. The preliminary moves of the campaign were carried out in the early fall, with Colonel E. A. Carr and Lieutenant Colonel L. H. Carpenter flushing the Indians from the Republican River area, to drive them into the region south of the Arkansas, where Sheridan could get at them during the winter.

Sheridan planned his favorite Indian-fighting tactic—three converging columns. One column would come out of Fort Bascom, New Mexico, along the Canadian River. The second would move from Fort Lyon south toward the Antelope Hills of northwestern Oklahoma. They were to act as "beaters," driving the quarry toward the principal column, which would operate from an advance base in Indian Territory. The main column was to consist of three elements—the Seventh Cavalry, which would fight its first major battle during the campaign; a battalion of infantry; and the Nineteenth Kansas Volunteer Cavalry, commanded by Governor S. J. Crawford. The Kansas regiment, one of the few musters of volunteers during the Western War, was to be in the field by late November.

By mid-November all was ready—Sheridan thought. The main column—mostly the Seventh Cavalry—had moved toward the advance base at the junction of Wolf and Beaver creeks, where troops established Camp Supply, now marked by the town of Fort Supply, Oklahoma. The advance element was commanded by Brigadier General Alfred Sully, with Custer in command of the Seventh Cavalry.

Sheridan was to accompany the main column in the field and participate in the operation. He gave his reason: "I deemed it best to go in person, as the campaign was an experimental one—campaigns at such a season having been deemed impracticable and reckless by old and experienced frontiersmen, and I did not like to expose the troops to great hazard without being present myself to judge of their hardships and privations."[13]

With November 15 set as the date of departure from Fort Hays, Sheridan, his staff, and Keim equipped themselves. Each took two good horses, warm clothing, a buffalo robe, blankets, rifle, pistols, ammunition, tobacco, and pipe—the latter an Indian campaigner's favorite smoke, partly because he could smoke without betraying his position to the enemy. Keim was to mess throughout the campaign with the General and his staff of five officers.

Sheridan planned to move to Camp Supply with a small escort. On November 14 he sent the escort one day's journey ahead; it consisted of Company C, Tenth Cavalry; Forsyth's scouts, now under command of Lieutenant Silas Pepoon; orderlies; and a few Kaw scouts; led horses and the headquarters train. On that day Keim mailed a story to New York, detailing the preparations which had been made, giving the text of orders for the escort's advance movement, and reporting an Indian attack on an army column south of Fort Harker. An officer's wife had been with that column; during the fight she remained in a wagon with a pistol in each hand. His story also named the details to which various officers had been assigned for the campaign, either with troops in the field or in the posts in Kansas.[14]

[13] Secretary of War, *Report, 1869,* I, 45.
[14] *New York Herald,* Nov. 20, 1868.

Rain fell during the night of November 14, making the new day disagreeable. Misty morning air, chilled by a north wind, had almost a freezing temperature as DeBenneville Randolph Keim started out on his one and only Indian campaign. Before Sheridan's departure he telegraphed a story.[15]

At 7:00 A.M. on November 15, 1868, two ambulances and a light wagon were drawn up before the General's quarters, each pulled by four mules. The personal baggage of Sheridan, Keim, and the staff officers was stowed in the wagon; the men, armed, climbed into the ambulances, which often were used for plains transport because they were more comfortable than regular wagons. At 8:00 they started off on campaign.

A few miles south of Fort Hays the General's party picked up an escort from the advance party. Pelting rain, however, made a mire of the road, and the ambulances fell behind the party, with the mules showing signs of exhaustion. As nightfall neared, the driver reported mounted figures in the distance, who turned out to be watchful Indians. The tenseness was relieved by the appearance of an escort that had been sent back to find them. Using their sabers, the cavalrymen managed to goad the mules into a run, and the animals brought the ambulances into camp about an hour after dark. Keim's first night in the field was to be no better than his first day. Howling wind continued to cut at them; the rain turned to snow; the men had trouble getting the tents up; the tents, when pitched, groaned and flapped through the night; wood was scarce and wet; the ground was wet. "There was no sleep in camp that night," Keim said.[16]

On November 18 they reached Bluff Creek in south central Kansas, their line of departure for the wilderness. Through half the night Keim wrote by the light of a campfire. The next morning he entrusted his story to a courier for a trip through country roamed by hostile Indians, his last chance for some days to communicate with the outer world. The story would never reach New York.

[15] *Ibid.*, Nov. 17, 1868.
[16] Keim, *Sheridan's Troopers,* 88–90.

Crossing the undulant swells of sea-land in Kansas and Oklahoma, Keim experienced briefly something of the hardship of plains travel. The water kegs ran empty about the time the troops reached the awesomely wide flat of the Cimarron on the nineteenth. Lying athwart the land as a flat-bodied serpent ready to suck the unwary into its coils, the Cimarron offered unpalatable, alkaline water. After that they had only a chance of striking fresh water on their next day's journey— which they did.

At the camp of November 20, Keim and Sheridan strolled about a mile from camp to a knoll from which they watched hunters pursue buffalo. Walking casually back to camp, they found Indian tracks in the bed of Beaver River, near which camp had been pitched. The tracks had not been there when they had gone to the knoll. That night, three Indians tried to cut off a sentry and slip into camp, but were detected and driven away by gunfire.

On November 21, Sheridan and his escort of three hundred men—he had met two companies of the Nineteenth Kansas at Bluff Creek—arrived at Camp Supply. Keim at last was deep in Indian country—one hundred miles south of the Arkansas, two hundred from the railroad. Even there, officers maintained military etiquette, calling on the General at his tent that evening. The band of the Seventh Cavalry gave an evening concert at headquarters.

The next day Keim dashed off a bulletin and sent it by courier to Fort Hays, where a telegraph operator relayed it to the *Herald*, reporting the arrival of Sheridan at Camp Supply. After a look around, he wrote a longer story. However, his first long story from Camp Supply did not appear in print until several days after stories written later had been published. But that was one of the characteristics of the reporting from newsmen on Indian expeditions—caused, probably, by uncertainties of mail transmission from the frontier.

Keim was told that Sully had arrived four days earlier to set up the post, guided to the location by an elderly plainsman named John Simpson Smith—sometimes known as Hum-

85

ble John. As described by Keim, Smith, then past sixty years of age, had left his home in Frankfort, Kentucky, at the age of twenty-two and had gone into the West as a trapper, ultimately reaching the Pacific Coast, where he remained for seven years. Then he returned to the Eastern slope, and lived thirty years among the Cheyennes, from whom he claimed he received three sections of land in Colorado. When the Cheyennes took the warpath, Smith returned to civilization, and was living at Fort Laramie when Sully engaged him as guide. Keim said all credit for selecting the site of Camp Supply was due Smith.[17]

With Sully had come eleven companies of the Seventh Cavalry, one of the Fifth Infantry, three of the Third Infantry, and one of the Thirty-eighth Infantry, and a train of 450 wagons. Sully had started his men building a stockade for storage of supplies, an enclosure for the animals, and a fort in case of attack. The troops were to camp around the fifteen-foot-high stockade. Keim also listed the officers of Sully's staff and of the regimental units serving under him. "The officers," he reported, "were anxious for the opportunity of taking part in solving the problem of Indian administration, which it is admitted has, ever since the present policy of buying peace has been adopted, been a constant succession of failures."[18]

Keim also encountered another plainsman—a wanderer known as California Joe—who would within a week and a day bring the first report of what would in time become an important incident in western history. His full name was Moses Embree Milner, and, like Smith, he was Kentucky-born. At the time, California Joe served Custer as a scout for the Seventh Cavalry. He was a heavily bearded six-footer with a shock of long hair who usually wore a large, black slouch hat, a soldier's overcoat, and long boots into which he tucked his trousers. He was armed with a breech-loading Springfield musket, a revolver, and a hunting knife. Like many scouts, he preferred a mule to a horse because the former could live on

[17] *New York Herald*, Dec. 12, 1868.
[18] *Ibid.*

86

grass whereas the army horse had to have corn and oats. A constant smoker, California Joe almost always had a worn-looking pipe in his mouth.

Milner's talkativeness showed Custer that he had knocked around the West considerably during his forty years, including a time in Oregon which coincided with the years of Sheridan's tour there as a young officer. In response to a question, California Joe said he had known Sheridan then; he had been a wood contractor when the future general was a second lieutenant serving as post quartermaster or in some similar capacity. Joe then remarked, "I had a kind of a sneakin' notion then that he'd hurt somebody ef they'd ever turn him loose. Lord, but ain't he old lightnin'?"[19]

Originally Custer had selected California Joe as chief of scouts for the winter campaign of 1868, but after a village of Indians materialized out of Joe's bottle, Custer obtained a new chief scout. Soon after he was named chief of scouts, California Joe went out with a detachment of one hundred cavalrymen on a scout for Indians. Before leaving, he filled his canteen, but not with water. On a night march he got drunk and, without the soldiers' knowledge, rode out ahead of the column. In the darkness ahead they saw something bright, with flashing colors. With due caution they halted until a clearer view could be had of what might be a party of Indians. They looked for Joe in the column, but could not find him. Soon here he came—from in front—howling and whooping and galloping, making an imaginary charge upon an Indian village, right up the column of soldiers. Fortunately for him, they recognized him before they opened fire. Because Joe was too wildly drunk to be quieted by ordinary means, the officer in command ordered him bound hand and foot. In that condition he was returned to headquarters and demotion to ordinary scout. The bright light the troopers had seen was a tempest match with which Joe had lighted his pipe.

Sheridan experienced a disappointment upon his arrival at Camp Supply—the Nineteenth Kansas had not yet arrived.

[19] Custer, *My Life on the Plains*, 234–38.

The tardiness of the citizen soldiers could wreck the timing of the campaign and nullify all the preparations before the troops could take the field. In addition, scouts crossed a large, fresh Indian trail going north, causing Sheridan to fear that the Indians were escaping.

Snow complicated Sheridan's problem. A snowstorm struck Camp Supply shortly after his arrival in mid-afternoon on November 21, continuing into the next day. But Sheridan decided that Custer's Seventh Cavalry should take the field at once, storm or no storm, volunteers or no volunteers. Accordingly, he ordered Custer to move out on the morning of November 23. Within approximately thirty-six hours after arriving, he had a combat command on the move. He gave Custer explicit orders: Move south toward the Antelope Hills, then eastward to the Washita River, where the Indians could be expected to winter, destroy their villages and ponies, kill or hang all warriors, and bring in all women and children. A wagon train was formed to carry thirty days' rations and supplies. Few tents were allowed. Each man's baggage consisted of two blankets and the clothes on his back.

Custer had his eleven troops of cavalry in fighting trim. He had trained them during the fall in camp on the Arkansas River, and had also trained a picked corps of sharpshooters. He had had his men on the firing range daily; from his eight hundred troops he picked the forty best marksmen, whom he formed into an elite corps with the privilege of marching as a separate organization, independent of the main column. The sharpshooters also were excused from guard and picket duty. Also he had added to *esprit* by "coloring the horses"—a cavalry term for giving each troop horses of the same color, instead of having the bays and grays and whites scattered through the regiment.

Reveille brought the troops out of their blankets at 3:00 A.M. on November 23 to find snow still falling thickly. By 6:00 A.M. Custer had his eleven companies in motion. Moving out of camp, with the clop of hooves muffled by twelve inches of snow on the ground, they passed down the line of infantry tents, whose occupants turned out to cheer them. And into the swirling white snow the dark mass disappeared, the Seventh Cavalry band playing the regimental song, "Garry Owen," the words to which ran:

> *Let Bacchus' sons be not dismayed*
> *But join with me each jovial blade;*
> *Come booze and sing and lend your aid*
> *To help me with the chorus.*
>
> *Chorus*
> *Instead of spa we'll drink down ale,*
> *And pay the reck'ning on the nail;*
> *No man for debt shall go to gaol*
> *From Garry Owen in glory.*[20]

Keim remained at Camp Supply with the Commanding General, who immediately reduced the force at the camp still further by sending two hundred wagons to Fort Dodge for supplies. To meet emergencies and maintain a constant alert, guards received orders to fire on any moving object, without a challenge. Because dawn was a favorite hour for Indian attack, Sheridan ordered reveille at 4:00 A.M. daily, when every officer and man took post until the tenseness of dawn had passed. They lived well; Thanksgiving dinner included turkey, buffalo, venison, antelope, rabbit, grouse, quail, pudding, pies, tarts, champagne, whiskey, and ale. "Camp life on the Canadian, isolated entirely from the world as we were," Keim wrote later, "was found a happy episode, away from the noise and bustle of human strife, and full of interesting incidents and days of ease and amusement."[21]

And in the bright tranquility of a Sabbath morning, November 29, after the hard weather of preceding days had passed, California Joe came riding in about ten o'clock, surprising the officers, and reined up in front of the General's tent. Sheridan at first joshed him by asking, "Well, Joe, what brings you back so soon; running away?"

[20] Herr and Wallace, *Story of the U. S. Cavalry,* 160.
[21] Keim, *Sheridan's Troopers,* 103, 104, 108, 109.

Joe indignantly replied, "I've just made that ole critter of mine out thar get up and dust, for the last thirty-six hours. I tell yer it's a big thing, and we just made those red devils git."

"So you have had a fight," Sheridan said.

"Weel," Joe drawled, "we've had suthin'; you may call it fittin', but I call it wipin' out the varmints; yes, and sich a one as they won't have agin, I tell you."

California Joe then wiped his large nose with the corner of a gunny sack that he carried as a handkerchief. After that, he handed Sheridan a sheaf of dispatches. Sheridan took the papers and read their contents aloud. He, Keim, and the staff thus learned that Custer and the Seventh Cavalry had "captured" the Cheyenne village of Black Kettle on the Washita River on November 27, two days before.[22]

With the first announcement of Custer's Battle of the Washita, an engagement that helped to break the war power of Southern Plains tribes, Keim wrote three stories. The first two went by courier to Fort Hays for telegraphic transmission on December 1; the third was a more detailed story which went by mail. He seems to have predated his first story. Whereas he said specifically in his book—*Sheridan's Troopers on the Borders*—that California Joe arrived with the dispatches from Custer on November 29, his first story was dated November 28 and referred to Custer's action "yesterday morning." The second story, dated November 29, emphasized Sheridan's presence as being responsible for the action. Both stories appeared in the *Herald* on the same day, both in the same column under the telegraphic news heading, with the earlier story appearing first.[23]

The *Herald* gave the Battle of the Washita particular attention, with more emphasis than western dispatches usually received in the daily news summary on the editorial page. Theretofore, most of the other references to western events had appeared in that part of the news summary headed "Mis-

22 *Ibid.*, 110–12.
23 *New York Herald*, Dec. 2, 1868.

cellaneous." The editors gave the battle a separate heading, a bold-face line reading, "The Indians." A paragraph summarized the story, which appeared in full elsewhere in the paper.

On the next day, December 3, the *Herald* supplemented its field dispatches with information from military headquarters —something in the nature of a communiqué, as it were; the practice was to prove general throughout the coverage of Indian campaigns. A dispatch from Washington appeared in the column headed, "Telegraphic news from all parts of the world," giving the text of two telegrams, one from Sherman in St. Louis, relaying Sheridan's report to the Adjutant General, in which he said: "This gives General Sheridan a good initiation. . . . his very presence there will give assurance that the troops will act with energy and that nothing will be done but what is right." There then followed the text of Sheridan's report of Custer's attack on Black Kettle's village, dated November 29, identifying Black Kettle's band as the Indians who had committed the first depredations on the Saline and Solomon rivers earlier that year. Editorially, the *Herald* approved Sheridan's course most heartily, saying that the government had been trifling with the Indians, but Sheridan at least knew that the only effectual way to bring "these barbarians" to terms was to crush them completely.[24]

Some days elapsed before Keim's full account of the battle, the mail story dated November 29, appeared in print. Using the narrative style then common in news writing, he began his dispatch: "The stillness of this bright Sabbath morning was enlivened by the unexpected tidings of a decided victory over a powerful band of hostile savages on the banks of the Washita River, at about seventy-five miles distant from this point." He then described Sheridan's arrival on November 21 and the issuance of orders to Custer for the movement that began two days later; the camp scenes as the column rode out in a storm; and the march through snow and cold.[25]

[24] *Ibid.*, Dec. 3, 1868.
[25] *Ibid.*, Dec. 8, 1868.

Custer marched his eleven companies southwesterly until on the twenty-sixth they found an Indian trail near the intersection of the Texas border and the Canadian River—a fresh trail left by a war party estimated at not less than one hundred warriors. Since the trail pointed southeast rather than toward the Kansas settlements, the hoofprints in the snow would lead the cavalry to the Indian village for which they were looking. Custer at once cut away from his wagons, which would proceed at their regular speed while the cavalry advanced rapidly. He left with the wagons all tents and other equipment that would impede his march. He kept his troopers in the saddle until nine o'clock that night, rested for an hour, and rode again until one-thirty on the morning of November 27. At that hour Osage scouts reported a village less than a mile away. The village was near the present town of Cheyenne, Oklahoma.

Custer at once countermarched his command, taking it away from hearing distance of the village. With all the officers he reconnoitered the village personally. He saw it situated in a strip of heavy timber along the Washita River. The terrain dictated his tactics—four columns to attack from different points at the break of day. Because two columns had to march several miles before they would be in position to attack, they moved out soon after Custer formulated his plan. The others stood to horse in numbing cold through the remaining hours of night.

Dawn came, the charge sounded, the regimental band piped *Garry Owen,* and the troopers galloped into battle, cheering loudly. They caught the Indians completely off guard and unprotected. It proved to be the Cheyenne village of Black Kettle, survivors of the massacre at Sand Creek four years before. Warriors fled from their tipis to fight from ravine and underbrush. Within ten minutes the village, and all it contained, was in the Seventh Cavalry's possession—47 Cheyenne lodges, 2 Arapaho, and 2 Sioux. Custer reported 103 enemy dead; 53 women and children captured. Black Kettle was among the dead. The soldiers also captured 875 ponies, horses, and mules, besides extensive quantities of Indian supplies and food. The army attack released from captivity two white children, but resulted in the murder by Indians of two other white captives—a woman and a ten-year-old boy.[26]

But the troopers had to keep fighting. What Custer did not know when he attacked was that he had stumbled across not one village alone but one village in a chain stretching along the Washita. When he saw additional warriors coming into the fight during the morning, he learned of the other villages from captive women. Custer realized he was outnumbered and dared not undertake further offensive operations; especially did he not dare divide his command for an attack down the line of villages. Intermittently, he sent sallies against the encircling Indians, but the Indians went back only as far as driven and no farther. Sometime during the day Major Joel Elliott and eighteen enlisted men rode out to engage the Indians, and were not seen again. Ringed in by Indians, Custer began destroying the village, burning the lodges and property and killing the 875 animals. He then gathered up the captives, re-formed the regiment, and as a feint marched toward the other villages late in the afternoon. Part of his strategy was to lure the Indians back toward their villages and away from his approaching wagon train; the other part was simply to get out of there. The ruse worked, the Indians moving quickly toward their villages. Under cover of darkness, Custer marched his regiment about and joined his wagon train the next day. In the meantime, he sent California Joe and a partner on a night ride to Sheridan with a dispatch. The Seventh Cavalry suffered thirty-five casualties—two officers and nineteen men killed; three officers and eleven men wounded.

Keim's main story, appearing on December 8, was the equivalent of about eight and one-half double-spaced typed pages, plus the text of Custer's report of November 28. Story

[26] Custer's report of the Battle of the Washita, in 41 Cong., 2 sess., *House Ex. Doc. 240*, 162–65.

and report filled two columns of small type. The story itself followed that report almost paragraph by paragraph, and was an accurate account to the extent the source was accurate. However, he used certain narrative devices—common enough then, forbidden now—of describing the thoughts and feelings of the Indians at the moment of attack when he had no way of knowing what those thoughts and feelings were. He used imagination to extract inherent fact in giving some measure of realism to the scene he described; for example, an Indian woman disemboweled a white boy captive, and Keim said his entrails fell smoking on the snow. Certain geographical descriptions in the story imply that he questioned California Joe for details not included in the report.

Keim concluded his story by describing the engagement as "The Battle of the Washita." Neither Sheridan's nor Custer's report used that term. It thus may be that Keim gave to that battle the name by which it has gone into history.

Custer made a major military show of his return to Camp Supply on December 1—a General returning in victory, a master showman building a reputation. As Custer paraded in, Sheridan received the regiment in review. Down a hill rode the Seventh Cavalry, its band playing *Garry Owen*. First came the Osage scouts, one of whom carried a personal possession of which no Osage could have been prouder, the scalp of Black Kettle; then the white scouts; then Custer and his staff; then the women and captured children; next, the corps of sharpshooters; after that, the saddle-weary troopers. Following a separate line of march, a double column of wagons came over the hill, with the led horses herded in between. The Seventh went into camp about half a mile from Camp Supply. The rest of the day was a holiday.[27]

With the arrival of the men who could give him first-hand accounts, Keim recorded the sight and sounds of battle as the officers and men described them. At the charge, he was told, Black Kettle dashed out of his tipi, saw the onrushing soldiers, fired his rifle, and gave the war-whoop. Out of the other

[27] *New York Herald,* Dec. 24, 1868.

94

lodges ran the warriors, armed, for the river where some stood waist-deep to fight. Women fled toward the high hill south of the village. Into their midst moved a small figure wrapped in a blanket from beneath which came an arrow that wounded but did not dismount a bugler. The bugler killed the person, who proved to be an old warrior. At close quarters Captain Frederick Benteen fought the son of Black Kettle, losing his horse but killing the warrior—incidents and adventures of individual cavalrymen in action, too numerous to find their way, all of them, into the official dispatches. The story also gave the casualty list.[28]

Reporting the regiment's return, Keim said that the captives were camped about one hundred yards from Custer's tent, but did not mention an incident that later was handed down by the Cheyenne. As the Indians told it, Custer and his officers selected bed partners from among the women. A Cheyenne woman named Red Dress told the story, and it was corroborated, according to account, by the wife of Big Horse, a Cheyenne chief. And Monahseetah, who spoke no English but traveled with Custer as an interpreter and who knew him as Yellow Hair, bore a fair-skinned papoose whom she named Yellow Swallow.[29]

The important question in Camp Supply was, What happened to Major Joel Elliott and his eighteen men? During the fighting a scout saw them pursue a small group of warriors through the lines and heard some sharp firing, but thought nothing more of it at the time. Their absence became known later in the day. Custer said that he sent parties out to look for them, but dark was near, they could not be found, and he had to manage the rest of his command. At the moment it was a mystery, but Custer's failure to find Elliott became a festering sore within the regiment, causing part of the officers and men to distrust Custer ever after.

Keim reportedly figured in a brush between Custer and Benteen resulting from the Elliott controversy, but he did not

[28] *Ibid.*
[29] Brill, *Conquest of the Southern Plains*, 22, 45–46.

refer to it in his dispatches or his book. It came about when, later in the winter, Custer saw a letter in the *St. Louis Democrat*, unsigned but obviously written by an officer of the Seventh, which criticized Custer contemptuously for not having searched for Elliott. Custer told his officers he would horsewhip the guilty person if he learned who it was. Benteen, after loosening his revolver in the holster, identified himself as the author. Custer dropped the subject; officers' call ended. Benteen said he then went to Keim and had the reporter return with him to Custer's tent. He wanted Keim to bring along his notes of all that Benteen had told him, "as a whipping was due somebody, and I didn't want a word I'd said omitted." Keim went, Benteen said, but "Custer wilted like a whipped cur." Benteen said Keim told Sheridan about the incident, and Sheridan "gave Custer a piece of his mind about it." If the Benteen account is accurate, Keim must not have been overly impressed. Not only did he not mention the incident, but he justified Custer's conduct of the battle and belittled the criticism that resulted from Elliott's fate.[30]

Much activity at Camp Supply in late November and early December gave Keim material for several long dispatches. Camp Supply itself had become an important date line, and he described it at greater length. The rest of the Nineteenth Kansas Volunteer Cavalry finally arrived, after getting lost and running out of rations. Officer assignments for Camp Supply were announced. Officers of the Seventh Cavalry buried Captain Louis M. Hamilton, grandson of Alexander Hamilton, who had been killed at the Washita; they adopted resolutions memorializing both Hamilton and Elliott, although the latter's exact fate remained unknown. The captured women at first feared they were to be killed, and those who were wounded refused to go to the hospital, thinking they had been singled out for the first vengeance. However, a delegation of Cheyenne women inquired of Sheridan's interpreter whether they were to be killed, and upon learning the con-

[30] Graham, *The Custer Myth*, 208–209, 211–12; Keim, *Sheridan's Troopers*, 149.

trary, became livelier. They expressed their gratitude by insisting upon shaking hands with the surgeon whenever he visited their camp. Custer brought with him a handsome lodge captured at the Washita, which the women erected for him.[31]

Amid the excitement—the general atmosphere of which is discernible in Keim's dispatches—Major Henry Inman returned with the wagon train that he had taken to Fort Dodge for supplies and handed to Keim some ragged and torn paper. It was the dispatch Keim had written at Bluff Creek on the night of November 18. Upon crossing Mulberry Creek, Inman had found bloody trousers and a coat pierced by bullet holes. Investigating the area, he flushed a pack of thirty wolves in a ravine, where he found several letters strewn, including Keim's dispatch. Evidence there indicated that the two couriers—Marshall and Davis—had been ambushed at the ravine and killed by the Indians. Parts of their bodies were found near by.[32]

Custer's return, the arrival of the Kansas volunteers, and the return of the wagon train enabled Sheridan to continue the expedition into the heart of Indian country. He made Fort Cobb, at the center of the reservation area, his next objective, with a swing along the Washita River to locate any other hostile bands that might yet be out. He detached the infantry to garrison Camp Supply, assigned two companies of volunteers to escort wagon trains, and provided a company of the Tenth Cavalry for escort and scout duty. With a force of about 1,700 men—eleven companies of the Seventh Cavalry, ten of the Nineteenth Kansas, Pepoon's scouts, and fifteen Indian trailers—he left Camp Supply on December 7.

On the eleventh they camped on the Washita River, only eight miles from the scene of the battle, and Sheridan determined to visit the battlefield, anxious to know what had happened to Elliott. Keim rode with the party consisting of Sheridan, Custer, Brigadier General J. W. Forsyth, Lieutenant

31 *New York Herald,* Dec. 26, 1868.
32 *Ibid.*

Colonels J. Schuyler Crosby, A. J. McGonnigle and W. W. Cook, Dr. Morris J. Asch, Captain Charles Brewster, and Lieutenants Owen Hale, Miles Moylan, and Samuel Robbins, together with an escort. In the December cold the horses moved smartly on a trip of one and one-half hours to the immediate approach to the battlefield. Before them lay an expanse of solitude, sunlight glistening upon hoar frost. Their entrance upon the battlefield started carrion and wolf. They counted about thirty bodies of warriors and saw the debris left by Custer's torch.

The party then separated. Keim went with Sheridan, Custer, and Hale in search of Elliott on the south bank; the others went down the valley. Sheridan's party moved up a high divide, then down the other side, where they found the naked body of a white man. Negotiating rougher country, someone spied what appeared to be bodies in the grass two hundred yards away. They galloped to the spot. "A few minutes after a scene was witnessed sufficient to call forth the rebuke of every benevolent and enlightened mind against the darkened intellects of the socalled philanthropists. Within an area of not more than fifteen yards lay sixteen human bodies, all that remained of Elliott and his party," Keim said. The naked, frozen corpses told a story of savage mutilation after death. What had happened to the living, they could only guess. They surmised that Elliott and his men had pursued fleeing Cheyennes until they ran head-on into Arapahos coming into battle, and had then been surrounded. With difficulty Elliott's body was identified and prepared for transport to Fort Cobb. The others were buried on a knoll. Farther down they found the remains of Arapaho and Kiowa villages, with equipage strewn where the Indians had left it in their hasty departure. Keim estimated that one thousand lodges had filled that valley the dawn of the attack, but Custer estimated six hundred. During the day they found the bodies of a white woman, identified as Mrs. R. F. Blinn, and a white child.[33]

The column—actually a brigade since it included two regi-

[33] *Ibid.*, Jan. 4, 1869, Dec. 24, 1868.

98

ments—marched on to Fort Cobb, arriving on December 18. En route they encountered a strong war party of Kiowas. Knowing the Indians wanted to parley, Custer rode forward with about eighty men, including Keim. The result was that Satanta and Lone Wolf, notorious even among the bloody Kiowas, joined the column and later were held in custody. A threat to hang them at dawn brought the fleeing Kiowa tribe back to Fort Cobb.

Sheridan remained in the area until late February, satisfying himself that the hostile Kiowas, Cheyennes, and Arapahos would submit to the government's terms and remain on the reservation. The Comanches then were counted as friendly, although they had been considered hostile during the fall. The first to submit were the Kiowas, who seemed in awe of the show of force by the government. They interpreted the positions of Sheridan and Custer in terms of their own organization—Sheridan a big chief, Custer a fighting chief. Sheridan also gained a psychological superiority over the savage mind by holding himself aloof, refusing to talk with them directly at all, and forbidding their presence around his headquarters. After encounters with troops from the Fort Bascom and Fort Lyon columns, the Cheyennes and Arapahos also came in. Sheridan, too, eliminated, at least for the time, another sore spot—former Indian agents who were accused of having encouraged Indians to steal Texas cattle, which the white men then obtained with trade goods and in turn sold to the government. He ordered several such accused white men beyond the limits of Indian Territory.[34]

During the time they were in that area, Sheridan decided to move the troops from Fort Cobb to a new location in the Medicine Bluff area, to what later became the Fort Sill reservation. Keim accompanied the first exploring party to find a suitable location for the new post. Another time he rode into the Wichita Mountains, climbing Mount Scott. "The Wichita mountains, at the time of our visit," he wrote later, "were unexplored, and known only on the maps by location."[35]

[34] *Ibid.*, Feb. 5, Feb. 27, 1869; Dodge, *Plains of the Great West, xxix–xxx.*
[35] Keim, *Sheridan's Troopers,* 231–62.

99

Confident that the war was over and that no hostile Indians remained in his department, Sheridan started north for Fort Hays on February 23, leaving the line troops in the field. With him rode Keim, three staff officers, a cook, a servant, an interpreter, five orderlies, and thirty-eight scouts. Ahead lay a four-hundred mile trip through wilderness. On March 6 they were but twelve miles short of Fort Hays when a courier met them with a dispatch for Sheridan. It was a telegram.

There on the plains, returning from an extended and fatiguing campaign, Phil Sheridan learned that he had been promoted to the second highest rank in the United States Army —lieutenant general. Grant, formerly General of the Army, had advanced to the presidency; Sherman was to succeed him as General of the Army; Sheridan to succeed Sherman. That same day brought them into Fort Hays; the next, they were on a train headed east, Sheridan en route for Washington. Sheridan remembered, in writing his memoirs, that the group on the train included McGonnigle, Crosby, Asch, and "Mr. DeB. Randolph Keim, a representative of the press, who went through the whole campaign, and in 1870 published a graphic history of it."[36]

True, Keim had been on the entire campaign, but only in the sense that he had been wherever headquarters were. He clearly was a communiqué correspondent, sticking close to Sheridan. In a way that was wise, for accounts of important events would be communicated first to the commander. He showed good sense and perspective in keeping Sheridan—the thinker, planner, and organizer of the campaign—in the forefront and not being sidetracked by the showy, erratic Custer, who commanded the Seventh on that campaign only at the personal request of Sheridan. Between the Hancock and Washita expeditions Custer had been court-martialed for leaving his post in the field without orders, and Sheridan had entered a plea on his behalf to get him back in the field.

Generally, Keim reported the campaign creditably from the overview of headquarters, but he did a flat job of report-

[36] *Ibid.*, 298–308; P. H. Sheridan, *Personal Memoirs*, II, 346.

ing; that is, he relied almost entirely upon second-hand reports, which he handled accurately enough, but there was
neither breadth nor depth to his reporting. Aside from his
strong representation of Sheridan and his frequent contemptuous diatribes against Indian agents, he did not show
the campaign or its fighters in detail. Nowhere, for instance,
does one find any indication that he sought to describe, or
assess the role of, the Kansas volunteers. Sheridan, his staff
officers, and Custer stand out in a reading of Keim's dispatches, but the enlisted soldier remains a cipher. Since there
is no evidence one way or the other that Keim sought and
was denied permission to accompany troops when Indians
might be encountered in battle, it is perhaps unfair to criticize him on that score, even in comparison with later correspondents. Still, Keim on the Washita campaign must be
recognized as an eastern gentleman on a well-equipped camp-
ing trip.

However, there is one point on which neither Keim nor any
other Western War correspondent can be fairly criticized,
and that is not reporting the whole story. This they could not
do, because the other side—the Indian side—was not known
to them. Their competence can be assessed only on the basis
of how reliably they handled the information that was available to them at the time, and how logically they criticized
men and events coming under their observation.

The Battle of the Washita is a case in point. Custer reported
it a victory, and so it went into the records, and so it went into
Keim's dispatches. But it was not so regarded from the Indian
point of view. Long years had to elapse and much work by
amateur and professional historians had to be done before
even a part of the Indian side of the various campaigns could
be told. Reflecting the Indian point of view, one writer concluded that Custer was repulsed at the Washita, because he
retreated under cover of darkness after sacking only the small-
est village of several.[37] To be sure, Custer's own book makes
that point quite clear—if one reads between the lines.[38] Cer-

[37] Brill, *Conquest of the Southern Plains*, 13.
[38] Custer, *My Life on the Plains*, 341–75.

tainly the fuller account in his book has a tone considerably less cock-sure than his report dated the day after the battle.

For that matter, the battle became controversial almost immediately. The really sore point, within the army, was the fate of Elliott. Some of the Seventh Cavalry officers became alienated from Custer because they thought he had abandoned Elliott, and at the Little Big Horn eight years later some feared he had done the same to them. On the other hand, a sympathetic Custer biographer held that the facts did not justify the feeling that Custer abandoned Elliott, and that the tale could be traced to Benteen, who was jealous of Custer.[39] Keim concluded that, although Elliott's fate might appear as a "gross abandonment" by Custer, the latter's withdrawal was justified by the laws of war: his men had lost their overcoats, which had been left behind when they charged and later were taken by the Indians who encircled the regiment in the village; his wagon train was protected by only eighty men; the loss of the wagons would mean destruction of his entire command and perhaps the failure of the whole campaign—in short, that Custer had to think of the regiment rather than a small detachment cut off in the heat of battle.[40] As for what could be ascertained from survivors, Cheyennes said in later years that Elliott's men concealed themselves behind high grass and seemingly fired wildly over the top of the grass without taking aim; one Indian rode near them and it seemed to him that the soldiers were shooting upward, not toward the Indians.[41] Be all that as it may, Sheridan viewed the campaign as a success.

And it was from Sheridan's point of view that Keim wrote his last dispatch from Fort Hays, on March 6, 1869: "The Indian war has ended. . . . There is not a hostile Indian within the limits of the Missouri Department. The refractory tribes have been entirely subdued."[42]

[39] Col. Charles Francis Bates, *Custer's Indian Battles,* 15–16.
[40] Keim, *Sheridan's Troopers,* 149.
[41] Grinnell, *The Fighting Cheyennes,* 304–305.
[42] *New York Herald,* March 7, 1869.

The *Herald* printed Keim's exuberance in the news columns, but reserved the right to disbelieve editorially. It said the news that the Indian war had ended "is too good and too comprehensive to be true, however applicable it may be to the recent brilliant and successful Indian campaign of General Sheridan." The *Herald* felt sure that Indian hostilities had not been permanently suspended and that a long time must pass before the Indian obstruction to civilization could be removed.[43]

The *Herald's* editorial writer proved all too right, for the southern Plains tribes continued to give trouble. Irreconcilables of the various bands continued to raid and plunder—chief among them the Kiowas, who, for their size, probably killed more white men than any other tribe. By the early 1870's, open, extensive warfare raged in the Southwest, with Comanches, Kiowas, Arapahos, and Cheyennes in league. Not until the campaigns of Colonel Ranald Mackenzie and Colonel Nelson Miles in western Oklahoma and the Texas Panhandle in 1874 was the southwestern Indian menace finally dissolved.

[43] *Ibid.*, March 8, 1869.

Second Lead

4. MODOCS HOLD OFF U. S. ARMY

The news is the grand object; what it costs is but a secondary consideration.
SAN FRANCISCO CHRONICLE[1]

THE *click-click, click-click* of the telegraph brought news of Indian fighting in the north in December, 1872, but San Francisco editors disbelieved it. Neither the *Bulletin* nor the *Chronicle* would believe that the small, harmless Modoc tribe would fight either a long or serious war against the United States. After all, the Modocs wore white-man clothes and some of them spoke white-man language. Despite editorial wisdom to the contrary, local correspondents in northern California and southern Oregon continued telegraphing stories which showed that Indian hostilities had begun.

The trouble centered in a band of Modocs headed by a young leader who dreamed of being chief of all the Modocs. The Indians knew him as Kientpoos, but the white men around Yreka, California, had dubbed him "Captain Jack." The trouble went back a long way, as it usually did in Indian wars. Once the Modocs had been strong and fierce, but frontiersmen broke their power and reduced some, but not all, to living upon a reservation. An insistence that all the Modocs live on a reservation was the immediate cause of the 1872 trouble.

Captain Jack had agreed to a treaty in 1864 giving the Modocs and Klamaths a reservation in the Klamath Lake region. After trying reservation life, however, he moved his

[1] Editorial, April 19, 1873.

104

band to their favorite haunt in the Lost River country of southern Oregon, claiming ill treatment by the hostile Klamaths and near starvation by the Indian agents. Ultimately he laid claim to an area six miles square at the head of Tule Lake on the Oregon-California boundary. A. B. Meacham—Indian superintendent in Oregon, whom one historian has described as "a man with a hobby" who "believed he knew all about the savage race, and how to control it"—recognized the claim, even though white settlers already occupied some of the land.[2]

By early 1872, Captain Jack's Modocs were a nuisance. T. B. Odeneal, who succeeded Meacham as Oregon superintendent in the spring of 1872, called upon the army in November for assistance in enforcing an order from the Commissioner of Indian Affairs to place the Modocs on the Klamath reservation, "peaceably if you possibly can, but forcibly if you must."[3] That started the shooting.

Telegraph stories in early December told of the first fighting—date lines, Ashland, Oregon, and Yreka, California. Captain James Jackson of the First Cavalry—with two other officers, forty troopers, and ten civilians—surprised Captain Jack's camp on Lost River at dawn on November 29 and demanded surrender. Jack had but fourteen warriors in his camp, and Hooker Jim, encamped on the other side of the river, had even fewer. Somebody fired a shot; the Indians scattered to the brush.

After the fight the Modocs roamed the countryside, killing white men as they came upon them, but scrupulously leaving women and children unharmed, except for one boy. And then they retreated into their favorite redoubt, what is now the Lava Bed National Monument in northern California. A rock desert, the Lava Bed was cut by fissures and chasms and penetrated by caves and subterranean passages in which an Indian could elude a white man for years.

The *San Francisco Chronicle* soon had a staff man on the

[2] Bancroft, *History of Oregon*, II, 559.
[3] 43 Cong., 1 sess., *House Ex. Doc.* 122, 5–22, 38, 224 (hereafter cited as Modoc War Correspondence).

road north—Robert D. Bogart, late of the U. S. Navy and the *New York Sun*. Bogart made it sound as though the *Chronicle* had sent its own private army into the field. He reported from Yreka that the "*Chronicle*'s Indian War News Expedition" had gone into the field under the direction of the *Chronicle*'s special correspondent, who had left a special agent in Yreka to forward special telegraph dispatches to San Francisco.[4] His use of the term "expedition" appears to be an emulation of Henry Morton Stanley and the *New York Herald*'s "expedition" into Africa in search of Livingstone. What it boiled down to, however, was that one Robert D. Bogart rode from Yreka to the Lower Klamath Lake region in the company of one Ed Autenreith, a citizen of Yreka.[5] The special agent left behind perhaps was either the telegraph operator or the editor of the *Yreka Journal*, who apparently also was the *Chronicle*'s local correspondent.

Bogart arrived in Yreka on December 8, and his first dispatch indicated that hysteria had swept the region, with rumor feeding upon fear and fear upon rumor. Finding it impossible to gather information he could regard as accurate, he organized the "*Chronicle* expedition to the seat of war."[6]

Bogart penetrated as close to the "seat of war" as the Hot Creek region south of Lower Klamath lake, almost always basing his stories upon second-hand information. Some of his stories bear at least a rough approximation to verisimilitude, but others sometimes were indifferent to accuracy.

Yreka guffawed at a practical joke which exposed a spurious Bogart story, which was brought out by the *Yreka Union*, a newspaper that was *simpatico* with the *San Francisco Evening Bulletin*. Bogart arrived in Yreka on December 8, reached John Fairchild's ranch on December 11, returned to Yreka on December 14, and left for home on December 18. The *Union* said he made the Yreka telegraph office his headquarters "at the front" during his last few days in the region. Under the

[4] *San Francisco Chronicle*, Dec. 10, 1872.
[5] *Yreka Journal*, Dec. 11, 1872.
[6] *San Francisco Chronicle*, Dec. 12, 1872.

heading, "A Brace of Munchausens," the *Union* reported a story which it said was too good to keep: On the evening of December 16, when Bogart was "headquartered" at the telegraph office, in came E. H. (Lige) Heard of Yreka, asking to be introduced to him. Heard claimed to have come directly from Captain Jack's camp and offered to take Bogart into the Lava Bed for an interview. Heard had been out of town the week before, but not to the Lava Bed. Through the practical joke Bogart had—in the slang of the time—been "sold" by Heard. When Heard was reproached for it in Yreka, he merely shrugged his shoulders and asked who was the bigger liar —Heard or Bogart. For Bogart had antedated his story to December 14 and date-lined it Van Bremer's Hill, which was about ten miles from Captain Jack's camp. Moreover, Bogart had said in the story that he had been entreated on all sides not to accept the risk of going into the Lava Bed for an interview. The *Union* considered that remark "something exquisite," and it also relished the irony that Heard would thereafter be known to fame by the wrong name, for an error somewhere along the line made his name appear in the *Chronicle* as "T. H." instead of E. H. Heard. The *Yreka Journal*, however, defended Bogart, saying the telegraph operator likewise had been "sold" and through him the Associated Press as well.[7]

The Modoc war story broke about a month after Bogart's departure. On January 17 the army sent four hundred regulars and volunteers against Captain Jack's stronghold. This group attempted a pincers movement, but dense fog cut off communications and made artillery useless, and the men moved through a nightmare of weird rock formations from which an unseen enemy poured a raking rifle fire into their ranks all day. The first news of the defeat appeared in the newspapers of January 21, the *Chronicle*'s story coming from Yreka, where the local correspondent had obtained his information from H. C. Ticknor, who had arrived with dispatches from Lieutenant Colonel Frank Wheaton, commanding, to

[7] *Yreka Union*, Feb. 1, 1873, Dec. 21, 1872; *Yreka Journal*, Dec. 25, 1872.

107

Brigadier General E. R. S. Canby, who commanded the Department of the Columbia with headquarters in Portland. The troops lost about forty in dead and wounded; the Indian losses were unknown then, but subsequent Indian statements claimed not a man was lost. The story based on Ticknor's information paralleled Wheaton's report of January 19.

Approximately fifty entrenched Indians had defeated and turned back a double-pronged army attack. Ticknor and Wheaton both predicted it would take one thousand men to dislodge the Modocs. Calling for reinforcements, Wheaton moved his camp northward from Van Bremer's ranch to a more central location on Lost River.

The Modoc War was on, and a group of war correspondents made for the remote battle area of northern California. Before the end of January, Bogart returned for the *Chronicle*. A few days later, strapping, long-haired Edward Fox came by stage into Yreka to cover the Modoc War for the *New York Herald,* and would within a month be compared with Henry Morton Stanley because of his daring. With Fox came burly H. Wallace (Bill Dadd the Scribe) Atwell, representing the *Sacramento Record.* Two days after Fox and Atwell came mustachioed Alex McKay, a Yreka surveyor on special assignment from the *San Francisco Evening Bulletin,* the only nonprofessional newsman in the group. By February 8 all had written under date lines from the isolated lake country of northern California and southern Oregon. They composed the largest group of correspondents who had appeared up to that time in any campaign of the Western War, and they would engage in the only fierce news competition of that war.

Bogart, then about thirty years old, had been in California less than a year. He had been born and reared in Princeton, New Jersey, had edited a Hoboken newspaper, had served as a navy paymaster, and had written for the *New York Sun* before coming west.

Bogart waited in Yreka five days, going north on January 30 with Colonel Alvin C. Gillem of the First Cavalry, who was to relieve Wheaton. Their trip to the Hot Creek region, where

Fairchild and P. A. Dorris had neighboring ranches, was a hard one. On the second day out they traveled fifteen miles through snow six inches deep, Bogart riding with Gillem in the light, springed headquarters wagon. On the way, Bogart remarked upon the eagerness of speculators to have the war continue, but in the ranch country he noted that the ranchmen said the war could and should have been avoided. Because of the snow, Bogart worried about getting his story back to Yreka for transmission to San Francisco, inasmuch as regular communications had not yet been established. However, Gillem had by February 7 established a courier service to Yreka. After they reached Hot Creek, they continued to suffer from snow; the troops had only shelter tents; Bogart stayed in a log cabin through the chinks of which the wind forced the snow; he awakened one morning to find his blankets covered by a half-inch layer of snow.

As the tension of the Modoc War had begun to build, James Gordon Bennett, Jr., of the *New York Herald* learned through army sources that a good interviewer might be able to reach Captain Jack. At the suggestion of City Editor Ned Flynn, Bennett gave the assignment to Fox, the yachting editor. Fox was an Englishman who had served in the British Army, his later career in England and Australia indicating that he came from a substantial background.

Traveling across the continent, Fox reached San Francisco, and, in spite of messages saying snow had made the roads nearly impassable, he took another train to Redding. A thirty-six-hour stagecoach ride brought him into Yreka late on Monday, February 3. There he said he intended to interview Captain Jack by hiring a guide and an interpreter. In Yreka, a mining town of about 1,500 population, where merchants were "rather jubilant" over the good trade brought by hostilities, he met the same difficulty Bogart had encountered in December—"it was hard to find two people with the same stories." He made arrangements at a livery stable for transportation to army headquarters, about seventy miles away. Upon learning that the army had no accommodations for visitors there, he bought a rubber sheet "and plenty of blankets." He left early Tuesday morning with Atwell.[8]

Atwell, then forty years old, had been a California newspaperman for twenty-two years. Born in Windsor, Vermont, he had migrated to California, where, in the course of his life, he edited newspapers in Stockton, Visalia, and Marysville. Only a few months before taking on the Modoc War assignment for the *Sacramento Record,* he had edited the *Marysville Defender,* which ceased publication soon after he sold it in late 1872.

By February 5, Fox and Atwell were at Fairchild's ranch and had met Gillem, to whom most of the correspondents referred as General Gillem, using his brevet rank.

Alex McKay, a thirty-five-year-old Rhode Islander who had stated his occupation as surveyor when he registered as a voter the previous fall, arrived in Yreka on February 5 and later went to the front as correspondent for the *San Francisco Evening Bulletin* and *Yreka Union.* He made his way to the Dorris ranch, where he slept "on the soft side of the kitchen floor," apparently meaning the dirt part of the floor.[9]

Once in the field, the correspondents found that, paradoxically, they were not to cover a war but a peace parley, because a wedding of Oregon politics and the Grant peace policy had substituted talk for ammunition in the Modoc difficulty. A group of Oregon politicians, who happened to be in Washington at the time of the Lava Bed battle, endorsed a suggestion by one of their number that a peace commissioner treat with the Indians. To reach Secretary of the Interior Columbus Delano, who had supervision over Indian affairs generally, they worked through an Oregonian in the cabinet, Attorney General George H. Williams. He arranged an interview between them and Delano. Delano accepted their suggestion and appointed a peace commission. Following the recommen-

---

[8] *New York Recorder,* March 22, 1895; William Simpson, *Meeting the Sun: A Journey All Round the World,* 371; *The Western Mail* of Perth, West Australia, March 9, 1895; *Yreka Journal,* Feb. 5, 1873; *New York Herald,* Feb. 21, 1873.
[9] *San Francisco Evening Bulletin,* Feb. 18, 19, 1873.

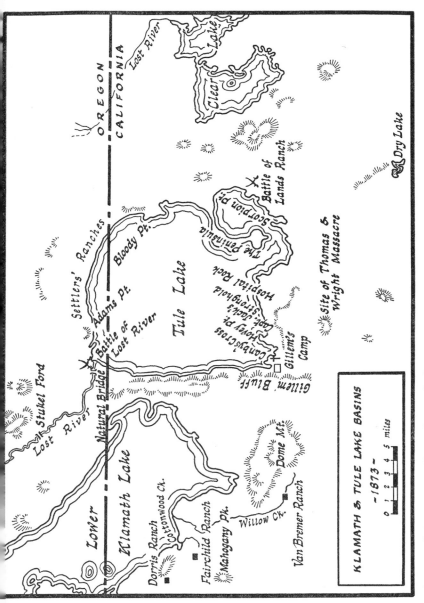

KLAMATH & TULE LAKE BASINS
– 1873 –

0 1 2 3 4 5 miles

From Keith A. Murray, *The Modocs and Their War*

dations of the Oregonians, he named a small-time Oregon politician as chairman, A. B. Meacham, the erstwhile superintendent of Indian affairs in Oregon. Meacham was in Washington then as Presidential Elector for Oregon. Delano also named Odeneal and J. H. Wilber, agent of the Simcoe Reservation, to the commission. Meacham, however, refused to serve with the other two. After notifying Odeneal and Wilber of their appointments, Delano then removed them from the commission and upon Meacham's recommendation substituted Samuel Case, agent of the Alsea Reservation in Oregon and Jesse Applegate of Yoncalla, Oregon. The commission was to determine the causes of the Modoc difficulty and to devise means of restoring peace. In the meantime, Sherman ordered Canby to place his troops on the defensive and let the commission try to settle the Modoc problem.

Because of slow transportation, a month intervened between the battle of the Lava Bed and the commencement of peace talks. In the meantime, the correspondents gathered material to inform their readers of the general situation in the Lava Bed region.

The outstanding story of the waiting period came from Fox. In a long mail story he gave a full account of the Lava Bed battle of January 17. Even though he wrote the story three weeks after the battle and the story appeared in print more than a month after the fight, his account was the most comprehensive that appeared. He interviewed participating officers and used the text of reports to provide a story that by modern equivalents would have filled about twenty-five double-spaced pages. He gave the full text of the field order directing the engagement; the combat report in full of Major John Green, who commanded the line; and excerpts from two other combat reports. In matters of substance, he was accurate, but his copies of the texts vary in several instances from the reports as printed, in details of phraseology, initials, and punctuation. A four-column map of the area accompanied the story, which took up practically all of a six-column page in the *Herald*. The *Yreka Journal* said Fox's map was considered accurate, but the man who drew a similar map for the *San Francisco Chronicle* "must have been a little boozy."[10]

The Peace Commission had first been named at the end of January and reconstituted on February 5, but as late as February 7 the reporters and officers in the field had no idea who the commissioners were. By the light of an inch of tallow candle, Bogart wrote a "think" piece in which he expressed the optimistic belief that there could not be the slightest doubt of the Peace Commission's final success. He was due to change his mind radically.

With surprise the men at the Hot Creek headquarters learned on February 12 the names of the peace commissioners. The news came from Frank Riddle, a white man married to a Modoc woman, who had just come from Yreka. Riddle told McKay that the Peace Commission was composed of Meacham, Applegate, and Odeneal.

McKay, the local man, reacted strongly: "If this is the case, I am inclined to the opinion that the Commission will be a failure, as Mr. Meacham was Indian Agent at Yaniox [*sic*] Reservation at the time the Modocs allege they were starved. The Applegate family were at the same time in some way connected with contracts for supplying the reservation with beef, and if it was not Jesse Applegate, it was some of this numerous family; and that is sufficient to render him objectionable in the eyes of Jack and his followers. Such a Commission as this can hardly be expected to gain the confidence of the Modoc warriors or the people, who are familiar with the history of these men. What a Commission to ventilate the abuses of the Yaniox Reservation!"[11]

McKay had reached a conclusion without all the facts. It had been Jesse Applegate's nephews—Ivan and Oliver—who had been connected with the reservation. However, much of the opposition to Applegate as a member of the commission came from his family name rather than his personal involve-

[10] *New York Herald*, Feb. 24, 1873; Modoc War Correspondence, 53–63; *Yreka Journal*, Feb. 12, March 5, 1873.
[11] *San Francisco Evening Bulletin*, Feb. 19, 1873.

ment. He had been one of the first Oregon immigrants in the 1840's.

With Gillem, Fox rode to Linkville, Oregon, arriving on February 15, the date set for the first meeting of the Peace Commission. In the story, Fox referred to himself as the "*Herald* Commissioner," a stylish term among *Herald* men. He found, however, that only Applegate and Case had arrived, and that O. C. Applegate had been appointed clerk of the commission. The only order of business was a letter from Governor L. F. Grover, of Oregon, who insisted that Oregon was the only jurisdiction competent to try the Modocs for murdering sixteen Oregon settlers after the battle of November 29, protesting in advance any effort the commission might make to locate the Modocs on Lost River, which already was settled by whites, and urging that the Modocs either be placed on their own reservation or be assigned a new one beyond the limits of settlement. "Both gentlemen appeared rather 'flabbergasted' at the letter," Fox reported, "and some remarks were made concerning the sanity of the aforesaid Governor." Applegate and Case tabled the letter.[12]

Grover was a Democrat, addressing a commission of Republicans. Applegate replied to him in an open letter, as a private citizen, in which he said the commission was a federal body and could not receive instructions from any state executive. In a written report to Meacham, Applegate said that when he saw the Governor's secretary at Linkville, he suspected "some cunning advantage was being sought by the inveterate enemies of the Federal Government." Telling Meacham about his reply to Grover, Applegate said, "You will perceive I have been mild and courteous toward the governor. You know, as well as I, Mr. Grover is not entitled to such treatment at your hands or mine."[13]

In Linkville they met Canby, who was to be on the ground continuously thereafter. The entire group—military, Peace Commission, and correspondents—headed back toward the

[12] *New York Herald*, Feb. 17, March 6, 1873.
[13] Modoc War Correspondence, 251–52.

114

Hot Creek region. Fox rode in an army ambulance to begin with, but the road was so rutted and precarious that he had to hang on the outside at times to act as ballast. On the night of the sixteenth they slept on the floor of a storeroom, and on the seventeenth they moved on to Fairchild's.

Settling down at Fairchild's ranch, the correspondents shared limited accommodations with officers, peace commissioners, and civilians. Fourteen men slept on the floor of a room about fifteen feet square, seven slept in an adjoining room about nine by fifteen, and Canby and his staff occupied a shed about eight feet square. The ranch served two meals a day, one at 8:00 A.M., the other at 4:00 P.M., with beef as a staple at both meals. Flour made up to resemble hot biscuits, as Fox put it, also were served; there were no vegetables. "The sugar bowl is an article of antediluvian extraction, coated with a brown crust of dirt, which has accumulated by its constant service during the past few years without being introduced to water. . . . The fluid in use is called coffee, and has a brown appearance resembling a liquid we have seen before bearing the same name; but perhaps, on the whole, a man might make a campaign under worse auspices."[14]

Just as Fox did, most correspondents in the Western War gave details of their personal experiences and the conditions under which they lived, sometimes in a tone of criticism as above, and sometimes in terms suggesting self-pity or self-glorification through hardship.

Meacham arrived on February 18, a Tuesday, and the Peace Commission held its first regular meeting, in an outbuilding furnished with two short benches and a three-legged stool. They met in private session for about two hours, while the reporters waited to learn what the public body was considering. After the meeting, Meacham told them that the commission had sent for two Modoc women, whom they would send into the Lava Bed to feel out the entrenched Modocs.

From that very first meeting, the Peace Commission and

[14] *New York Herald*, March 8, 1873.

115

the press collided over the issues of freedom of information and secrecy in government. By holding private meetings and attempting to keep the press from getting any information except what they chose to give them, the peace commissioners let the reporters understand that they were to get only what information it might please the representatives of a democratic government to make public. Another correspondent reported the press had been "religiously" excluded from commission meetings.[15]

One might ask the premise upon which the newspaper comments were based, to which the reply would be that United States newspapers, functioning under the Constitutional guarantee of freedom of the press, maintain that freedom of inquiry is their right. American newspapermen also maintain that agencies of a democratic government are beholden to report their activities to the public and to function in full public view. The press is the only agency through which the citizen can have direct daily contact with government and its workings.

At first the correspondents trusted Meacham to tell them the truth about commission sessions, but before the week was out, they decided they had made a mistake. Matilda Whittle—the wife of a white man, Robert Whittle—arrived on Wednesday night, and on Thursday morning she and Artinie Choakus, another Modoc woman, went into the Lava Bed. When the women returned on Friday afternoon, Jesse Applegate met them at the corner of the fence and instructed them to talk with no one before they reported to the commissioners. After the meeting Meacham told the reporters that the Modocs had evinced a strong desire for a peaceful settlement. That was well and good; but he also said that the Indians had been willing to talk with the men who came from a long way off, meaning the commissioners. Later, the correspondents were told by Matilda Whittle and her white husband that the Indians had said nothing of the kind; they did *not* want to talk

[15] *San Francisco Evening Bulletin*, Feb. 25, 1873; *San Francisco Chronicle*, Feb. 23, 1873.

with the men who came from a long way off; they preferred to deal with men they knew and trusted, specifically Elijah Steele of Yreka and his former law partner, Judge A. M. Rosborough.[16]

The newspaper stories indicated that the reporters thought Meacham had lied to them, and from then on the swords were drawn. On Saturday, Whittle and his wife rode into the Lava Bed to arrange a conference with the Indians, who still wanted Rosborough and Steele present for a meeting the next Tuesday. Since Rosborough and Steele could not get there that soon, another delegation was to go to the Lava Bed on Monday—composed of Fairchild, Whittle, and Matilda—to so advise the Indians.

Having come west to interview Captain Jack as well as to cover the main story, Ed Fox of the *New York Herald* sought permission from the commissioners on Sunday, February 23, to accompany Fairchild and Whittle to the Lava Bed the next day. His request was peremptorily denied, and Meacham gave Whittle specific orders not to allow any member of the press to go along.

Fox was not to be denied. It would not have been in keeping for a *Herald* man to allow a political appointee like Meacham to stand in the way of news reporting. Concluding that "Mr. Meacham had no authority to govern my going and coming in this section of the country," Fox determined to reach the Modoc stronghold on his own responsibility. He knew, however, that his movements would be watched if he remained at Fairchild's. Moving with circumspection, he left the ranch Sunday afternoon on the pretext of spending the night with officers of the Fourth Artillery at Van Bremer's ranch to the southeast on Cottonwood Creek. In an offhand manner he asked Fairchild what time they planned to leave the next morning, and was told at seven. He then rode away. "I felt considerably relieved," he wrote, "when I got clear of the headquarters of the Peace Commissioners, as Mr. Mea-

[16] *New York Herald,* March 8, 1873; *San Francisco Chronicle,* March 2, 1873.

117

cham might have asked General Canby to give orders that I was not to leave the neighborhood, which would naturally have left me in rather an awkward position."[17]

From the sutler at Van Bremer's he bought two pounds of tobacco and filled up his flask "in case I should require a little stimulant to help me out." Arising at reveille on Monday, he found the ground covered by three inches of fresh snow. After eating breakfast and saddling his horse, Fox was on the road by 7:30 A.M., moving back toward Fairchild's ranch, planning to intercept the Fairchild-Whittle party at a bridge over Willow Creek which they would cross.[18]

When he arrived at the bridge, he saw from the undisturbed snow cover that the Fairchild party had not yet come along. He continued on toward Fairchild's to meet them on the way. In time they rode into view, Fairchild and Artinie riding abreast in front, followed by Whittle and Matilda on their horses fifty yards behind.

Fox rode up to Fairchild—whom he had described in an earlier dispatch as "a very good fellow"—and told him he wanted to go along. Fairchild raised no objection but said Fox must get permission from Whittle, who was in charge. Whittle refused, saying he would have been glad to take Fox in before the Peace Commission employed him, "but now I am in the government employ, and you know yourself what my instructions were." Fox tried to persuade Whittle to let him go, but Whittle ended the conversation by saying, "I am very sorry; but either you or I must go back." Fox said he considered going in alone, but realized he probably would fail, since all he knew of the Indian camp was that it lay about twenty miles to the east.

Accepting defeat, Fox trotted back toward Fairchild's ranch, but within half a mile he noticed that the tracks of the horses were clearly imprinted on the fresh snow. "It suddenly flashed across my mind that those tracks would lead me to

[17] *New York Herald*, Feb. 28, 1873.
[18] This account of Fox's trip is based upon his two stories in the *New York Herald*, Feb. 28 and March 17, 1873.

the lava bed, and the Commissioners could throw no blame on Whittle," he wrote. He immediately wheeled around, confident the tracks would lead him to Captain Jack.

Fox's lone ride into the land of the murdering Modocs called for more than ordinary courage or naïveté. The other four were going as emissaries to Indians who knew them, who would recognize and let them pass. But there was Fox, an unknown white man riding into the lines of an enemy who for three months had been killing all white men who were caught in the open.

As Fox told the story, he moved slowly at first, so as not to overtake the party. On reaching hills, he would stop, dismount, and peer over the crest to make sure the others were out of sight. He followed that procedure until he felt certain he was in Indian country, and, catching sight of the others, he hurried to close the gap.

Fairchild and Whittle saw Fox and reined up to wait for him. Whittle seemed annoyed but concluded, "Well, well, now you have come, and you had better keep up close, as we have been seen by the Modocs before now." Less than an hour later they reached the bluffs that line the western edge of the Lava Bed. Gathering sagebrush, the two women lighted a fire to let the Modocs know the group had arrived.

Within twenty minutes they saw three Indians approaching the base of the bluff. The Indians came up to them. Fox was introduced as the Paper Man to Modoc Dave, Hawker Jim, and Steamboat Frank. "These three gentlemen were all armed to the teeth," he said. Two carried muzzle-loading rifles; the third, a cavalry carbine; each had a revolver and sheath knife. Dave did not wear paint, but Hawker Jim [the name also appears as "Hooker Jim" and "Hooka Jim" in various accounts] had a black, greasy paste on the lower part of his face. Dave wore buckskin pants and a soldier's overcoat. Jim, dressed in a flannel shirt and worn gray pants, shook hands sullenly. "There was certainly no friendship evinced in that shake," Fox noted, "and a look at the gentleman's countenance did not tend to reassure me of his pacific intentions."

119

Frank said Captain Jack wanted to see Fairchild in camp, and Whittle asked whether he and the Paper Man should come along. Frank said yes.

On foot they descended the bluff, leading their horses, and at the base Fox learned personally what the soldiers had learned on January 17 about the Lava Bed. "I discovered that what I had taken to be a flat plain was a rolling surface, covered with sharp edged rocks, and interspersed with large and deep holes, half filled with broken scoria."

They now were within hostile territory, a remote fastness from which the Modocs fought a war that led the *Herald* to headline one of Fox's stories "Rob Roy Mac-Modoc." At any moment they might meet death from an impetuous savage.

A ride of about half an hour into the rocky, creviced Lava Bed brought them to a group of six Modoc scouts who were talking and laughing beside a sagebrush fire. "They were a wild looking group, nearly all clad in woollen shirts and second hand soldiers' clothes," Fox said. "They were all armed to the teeth and painted." The greasy paint gave the Indians a "hideous" appearance, "and coming upon this group standing around the blazing fire, each with a musket in his hand and a revolver and knife at the belt" made Fox realize once more that he was not visiting peaceful, innocent gentlemen of nature. Fox and his group dismounted, and joined the Indians at the fire.

Fairchild introduced Fox as "the Paper Man from afar off, from the big town by the sea, in Boston Illihee." He explained to Fox that Indians in that part of the country called all white men Bostons; "Illihee" meant a far country. After a round of handshaking, Fox sent his pipe the rounds a second time. "My smoking qualities were evidently much admired by the Modocs," he said, "and they also expressed themselves favorably on the quality of my tobacco."

They remained at the scouts' fire only a few minutes before resuming their march, reinforced now by nine Indians. Another mile and they came to a camp of about fifty men, women, and children. Fox noticed that the Indian costumes were heterogeneous. Most of the men wore army overcoats; the women seemed partial to red petticoats, the latter putting him in mind of a gypsy camp. There Fox met John Schonchin, brother of the Modoc chief Schonchin who lived on the Yainax Reservation.

Once more they were on their way after a halt of only a few minutes, with all the Indians in train. The road became steadily worse, and even the horses had trouble with footing. In common with many other white men who attempted to describe the country, Fox said simply, "It defies description." Another common description of the Lava Bed was to liken it to a sponge in appearance. Fox then understood how fifty or so Indians had demoralized four hundred white soldiers on January 17.

Soon afterward, things became lively. First they met a friendly, nice-looking Indian of about twenty years of age, Bogus Charley, who spoke good English. One of the Hot Creek band, he greeted Fairchild in a friendly manner. But shortly thereafter they met an unfriendly Indian. "Our march was presently interrupted by the arrival of Charley Miller, a repulsive-looking Indian, who waved us back with his hand as he came." Fox learned later that Charley Miller—or Miller's Charley, as he is identified in some accounts—was one of the worst of the Modocs. Charley Miller's violent talk and gesticulation brought him into a heated argument in Modoc with Bogus Charley and Steamboat Frank.

Although the Indians spoke in their own tongue, Fox detected that the visitors were the center of the argument. "I must say that I did not like the look of things, as the Modocs were evidently getting very hot over their talk, and it did not appear improbable that they would wind up with a fight. Such a conclusion I did not desire, as an Indian with his blood up might not have much respect for a newspaper correspondent, especially for one who had hair about ten inches long," Fox recorded.

Matilda told Fox that Charley Miller said that Captain Jack had sent orders for them to camp where they were. Bogus

Charley, Steamboat Frank, and Modoc Dave objected, Bogus Charley insisting Fairchild should sleep at his "house" and Dave that Whittle and Fox should stay with him. "I cannot say that at this moment I was very grateful to Mr. Dave for this exercise of hospitality, as I concluded that, should these gentlemen come to blows over the little question of etiquette, the guest would probably fare the worst of all." Scarface Charley rode up and settled the argument by saying the entire party was to come into camp.

At that juncture the party of five visitors separated—Fairchild and Artinie taking the left-hand trail toward Captain Jack's and the others going to the right with Dave, who led them toward the home of his cousin, Wild Gal. "I now dismounted, as the trail became nearly impassable, and after passing through a wild-looking gorge, with walls of craggy rock, about twenty-five feet in height, we climbed up some rocks, and then, suddenly descending a nearly perpendicular wall of broken scoria landed in a chasm, surrounded by walls about thirty feet in height, formed of broken rock, apparently piled indiscriminately one on top of the other," Fox said. There he saw three or four Indian *"rancherias"*—he insisted upon using southwestern terms to describe habitations of northwestern Indians. They unsaddled, tied their horses to rocks, and entered the *"rancheria."* Fox, like the others, squatted Indian-fashion beside the fire which had been kindled in a cavity formed by two rocks forming the apex of an equilateral triangle. He saw that the dwelling was built only up to the rocks, so that the fire actually was in the open. During a half hour or so at the fire, Fox distributed tobacco and met other painted Indians. Matilda told him there was a debate about whether he would be admitted to the council with Captain Jack.

Presently a messenger arrived with instructions to bring Fox, Whittle, and Matilda to the council cave. "I followed our guide, and after clambering up the rough walls of one chasm we walked, or rather crawled, about one hundred yards over some broken rocks, when the guide suddenly disappeared down a dark hole. The *Herald* correspondent followed, but, not being acquainted with the nature of the country, went down faster than necessary, and found himself in a large cave, lit up by the blaze of a fire, which was burning in the centre and gave sufficient light to enable me to see fifty or sixty Modocs seated round in circles four or five deep."

Fox made his way to the front circle. There he shook hands with the hostile chief himself—Captain Jack. He also shook hands with an Indian known as Scarface Charley, "on whose left, with considerable courtesy, I was placed." Looking about him, Fox decided that no troop of Italian bandits could have made a wilder or more picturesque group. He felt himself the center of attention, favorable attention. With Bogus Charley as interpreter, Fairchild once more explained that Fox was the Paper Man from the big city by the sea, that he had followed their tracks in the snow to get there, and that he was anxious to hear the Indian story of their troubles. The speech met general approval, "expressed by a chorus of grunts, sounding like a gutteral pronunciation of the letter 'a'." Fox also noticed that most of the Indians had washed off their paint and had come to the council unarmed.

Even though Captain Jack was ill—he sat wrapped in a blanket and supported himself on a root digger stuck in the ground in front of him—the council proceeded. Fairchild read his instructions from the Peace Commission, sentence by sentence in English with Bogus Charley interpreting sentence by sentence. The message simply informed the Modocs that the President's peace commissioners were willing to delay a grand council until the Indians' friends, Rosborough and Steele, arrived from Yreka.

Schonchin then talked for about two hours, with Bogus Charley and Steamboat Frank interpreting. In essence, he said he knew Meacham; was treated badly at Klamath Reservation; the whites started the fight at Lost River; he had given away all his country, but wanted to keep a little piece of country on Lost River. Bogus Charley described the Lost River fight in terms of a people surprised in their early morn-

FOLLOWING THE INDIAN WARS

ing sleep and still puzzled at why the soldiers started shooting.

The council adjourned, Fox went to Wild Gal's for supper, and then Schonchin, Scarface Charley, Bogus Charley, and other Indians came to see him. The Indians told him their story of mistreatment on the reservation—that they had been moved three times, that the men received only half a blanket apiece and the women none in winter, that they had to dig in the cold ground for camus roots for food and kill their horses for meat.

Before retiring, Fox went back to talk some more with Captain Jack. He quoted Jack as saying that he had known Meacham a long time ago, but was afraid he did not know him now; perhaps Meacham "don't feel good"; Jack had one heart, but perhaps Meacham had two; he did not want Meacham to be afraid, they should all come to the council; he talked with one tongue, but perhaps Meacham had two; Meacham had too many friends; perhaps half the white men were good and the other half bad; he would tell Meacham the truth; "I want tell him gas before fight, same as white man after fight"; he wanted to see people travel anywhere they pleased, and he was sorry the white man was afraid to travel; "Tell Meacham I want him to come to no gassing. Tell him not be scared this man from paper afar off."

Fox returned to Wild Gal's for the night. She arranged the bed by shaking out the matting and placing the blankets on top. He removed his boots and crawled into bed with four men and three women, on a matting eight feet wide. Even with that much animal warmth, Fox was so cold he could not sleep, and remained awake all night. They were up a little before daylight, Matilda building a fire which Fox welcomed. After a light breakfast and a pipe, he joined the others in going to Jack's cave, where the council was in session.

They found Jack looking a little better than he had the night before, although his wife supported him around the waist. Fairchild sought to find out how many men the Indians would bring to the council with the commissioners and whether they objected to soldiers coming with the white ne-

124

gotiators. Jack and Schonchin objected to soldiers, but Jack said twelve or fifteen white men should come, and the paper man should come, too.

When Schonchin finished talking, the emissaries saddled their horses and made their way back to headquarters, arriving about 7:00 P.M. on Tuesday, February 25, and Fox summed up his impressions. From what he had seen of the Modocs in the Lava Bed and from what he had learned of their history, he believed they had been badly treated and that the origin of the war could be traced to a few Oregonians. He remarked that the California settlers had never had any trouble with the Modocs. Having seen the Modoc stronghold, he repeated the remarks of military men that one thousand troops would be necessary to carry it, and then only with fearful loss of life. Because the white men attacked first on Lost River, the Modocs did not consider themselves guilty of any wrong in killing white men. The peace commissioners "need not for one moment flatter themselves" that they could bring the Modocs to give up the Indians who had killed the settlers; the Indians would rather fight to the last man, convinced they had done no wrong. However, he said, the Modocs were willing to go on a reservation, but the whites must keep faith and Indian agents must not be allowed to rob them of supplies. Still Fox doubted that the present Peace Commission could make peace with the Indians.

Fox wrote two stories about his adventure. The first story went by wire. In it he apparently gilded the lily with just a touch of the melodramatic, for his lead sentence read: "I write this despatch in Captain Jack's cave, in the lava beds . . . ." Nowhere in either account does he allow for time to write a story there. He date-lined the first story, "Headquarters Captain Jack's Camp, Lava Beds, Feb. 25, via Yreka, Feb. 26, 1873." The *Herald* gave over all of page three to it on February 28, page three being the first news page in a paper that devoted the first two pages to advertising. Once again the *Herald* used his four-column map to illustrate the story, which ran over for almost a full column on the next page. The multi-deck headline was almost one-half column in depth. The *Yreka Union* said the telegraph toll for that one story was $500 or $600; the *Herald* reprinted the *Union*'s comment in full, sanctioning the accuracy of it.[19] Fox's second story was mailed to New York, in the usual pattern of Western War correspondents, giving fuller descriptions of some incidents.

Inasmuch as Fox's story represents perhaps the outstanding individual feat of the entire Modoc War, it is surprising that it has been ignored in most secondary accounts which have mentioned later activities of other correspondents. Even if confirmation of the story were lacking, the authenticity of phrasing and exactness of description would show that it was not made of whole cloth. There is, however, sufficient contemporary verification of the story. The *Yreka Union* was most enthusiastic about it, saying that while the *Bulletin*, *Record* and *Chronicle* men were fussing about the Peace Commission, Fox quietly saddled his horse and rode into the Lava Bed. "This feat of Fox," said the *Union*, "has placed the *Herald* in the van, and distanced all competitors in the race for news! It is, no doubt, intended by the *Herald* office, which planned, and Fox, who executed this move, that it shall rank only second to Stanley's search for Livingstone in Central Africa." Stories in the two Yreka papers from both McKay and Atwell confirmed that Fox had followed the Fairchild-Whittle party into the Lava Bed. Meacham, who as things turned out could hardly have had any love for Fox or any other correspondent, said that Fox, by going into the Lava Bed, "performed an act of undisputed courage, which entitles him to a place among the dauntless heroes of any age." Meacham also said that only Scarface Charley's abiding basic friendship for the whites kept Hooker Jim (whom Fox named as Hawker Jim) and Schonchin from killing Fox while he was there.[20]

Proud of Fox, the *Herald* said editorially, "The feat which

[19] *Yreka Union,* Mar. 1, 1873; *New York Herald,* March 19, 1873.
[20] *Yreka Union,* March 1, 1873; *Yreka Journal,* March 5, 1873; A. B. Meacham, *Wi-ne-ma and Her People,* 83.

he has accomplished is no inconsiderable one, and will remain as a record of that daring which is peculiarly the attribute of the *Herald* correspondent in the pursuit of his duty." *Herald* men closer to home were many times called on to exercise similar dash and tact, the editorial said, but the surroundings of Fox's feat "make the *Herald* correspondent's work among the Modocs verge towards a genuine heroism."[21]

The reaction in the theater of war was no less vigorous. Fox reported in his mail story that Steele told him his visit "had done more to establish confidence between the Indians and whites than anything that the Peace Commission had yet accomplished." He reported of the peace commissioners: "They are very indignant at the *Herald* correspondent for having dared to furnish news and truth to the public without its coming through their hands."[22] Returning on Tuesday, he wrote on Wednesday from Van Bremer's that three Modocs had come in, and when they returned to the Lava Bed, they went with instructions not to permit anyone to talk with them without a written order from the peace commissioners.

Fox had come through with the sort of exclusive story upon which the *Herald* had built its reputation, but within the week the other three correspondents also saw Captain Jack in his stronghold. The visit of Bogart, Atwell, and McKay resulted from a new turn that peace negotiations took later in the week.

At Canby's suggestion, Judge Rosborough of Yreka had been added to the commission on February 19. He arrived at Fairchild's on Thursday, February 27, with Steele. Both men knew the Indians well, and the Modocs had asked specifically that they be among the negotiators for peace. Rosborough and Steele had been law partners in Yreka before the former began his career on the California bench in 1856.

"It was astonishing to note what a soothing effect the presence of the member [Rosborough] had upon Meacham & co.," Bogart reported.[23]

[21] *New York Herald*, Feb. 28, 1873.
[22] *New York Herald*, March 1, 17, 1873.
[23] *San Francisco Chronicle*, March 3, 4, 1873.

The arrival of the two lawyers meant that for the first time the doors were opened to the reporters, who attended the commission meeting on February 27. Meacham, who was a great talker anyhow, opened with a long speech about what had been done up to then. When Meacham finished, Rosborough suggested it might be a good idea to start out by deciding what terms would be offered Captain Jack.

The commission agreed that the Indians first should surrender to United States forces, because the Oregon indictments complicated matters to such an extent that the Indians could not be left subject to civil authority anywhere; that it would be impossible for the Indians to remain in that part of the country because of the high feeling in the area; that the tribe should be moved to a reservation in Arizona, Indian Territory, or southern California; and that Steele should present the terms to Captain Jack in the Lava Bed the next day, Friday. Steele also had power to offer amnesty for all, on condition of removal to a distant reservation by way of Angel Island.

Steele left about 9:00 A.M. Friday, undeterred by a snowstorm. With him went Bogart, Atwell, and McKay. No reason was assigned in any of the dispatches for Fox's not going. Fairchild, Frank Riddle, and Riddle's Modoc wife, Tobey or Wi-ne-ma, accompanied them.

Supplied with blankets, warm clothing, and forage, they reached Jack's camp, "imbedded in the wildest rocks I ever beheld," as Bogart put it, about 5:00 P.M. Delighted to see Steele, the Indians gathered around him like children.[24]

After a supper of hardtack, bacon, and coffee at Wild Gal's fire, they went to Jack's cave for a council; descriptions of the cave tallied with Fox's. Steele explained the terms to the Modocs, and they seemed to assent. After a talk of several hours, Jack—still sick—ended the council for the evening. The correspondents and Steele slept in Jack's cave that night. Another council was held in the morning, lasting until almost noon. Again, the tone and tenor of the council were friendly,

[24] *Ibid.*

128

leading Steele to report upon his return that peace was assured. However, the Indians insisted upon making peace with Rosborough and Steele; they wanted nothing to do with the Peace Commission, especially Applegate and Meacham, as the correspondents reported the Indian attitude. Jack was glad the newspapermen had come. He said he could not write but could think, and was glad their talk was being written down, for that way it would not be forgotten. They left the stronghold at noon and arrived at Fairchild's at dark.

"It was a horrible ride, and the party are thoroughly tired out," Bogart reported.[25]

Taking advantage of Bogart's fatigue, Atwell and McKay tried to steal a march on him by getting into print first. They told him they did not intend to send their stories to Yreka until the next day, and he took it easy. Meantime, his two competitors slipped off and wrote their stories. At 11:00 P.M. they announced to Canby that they were sending dispatches into Yreka by special courier, who could take anything he might have. The courier left, and Bogart started writing immediately. Using a crackerbox for a desk and a candle for light, he wrote until 4:00 A.M. Sunday, and then hired an Indian boy to take his dispatch to the Yreka telegraph office. If the boy delivered the dispatch to the telegraph operator before sundown, he was to receive $40. The boy made it, and Bogart's story appeared in Monday morning's paper. Because of Sunday, Bogart at least broke even, and got into print ahead of McKay, whose story appeared in the *Evening Bulletin* of Monday afternoon.[26]

Steele returned to Peace Commission headquarters at Fairchild's confident that the Modocs had accepted terms of peace. He was jubilant, and his message brought a sense of relief to the camp. The correspondents sent in stories indicating, on the strength of Steele's interpretation and their own observations, that the Modoc trouble was about over. The

25 *Ibid.*
26 *Ibid.*, March 31, 1873; Anon., *The San Francisco Chronicle and Its History*, 7–9.

Peace Commission telegraphed Washington, "Everything looks favorable for peace." The telegram said the Modocs would surrender as prisoners of war and be moved to a warmer climate, with amnesty for all. However, Bogart was not sure the Indians had fully understood what Steele had meant.[27]

Fairchild also voiced serious doubt that the Indians had understood, but Steele remained steadfast. The problem called for a secret session of the Peace Commission, at which they discussed whether the Indians had understood. The eight Modocs who had returned with Steele were sent for, and the terms were explained to them much more specifically than Steele had presented them. Meacham explained that they would be removed to Angel Island at San Francisco until a reservation could be made ready for them in southern California or Arizona. Canby promised food, clothing, and transportation for the whole tribe, amnesty to all, and protection against their enemies, provided they surrendered to him. However, the Indians had come to listen, not to talk.

Unshaken by doubts, Steele started back to the Modoc camp on Monday morning, March 3, just one week after Fox had followed Fairchild and Whittle, empowered to make peace on terms enumerated by the commissioners on Sunday. Steele invited Fairchild to go along, but he declined. Atwell, however, had courage enough to go. The party included Steele, Atwell, Riddle, Tobey, and the eight Modocs.

Shortly after starting out, Atwell detected in the Indians' demeanor that something had gone wrong, but at first he could not learn what. As they jogged toward the Lava Bed, an Indian woman who rode beside Atwell asked him why white men told so many different stories. She said a white man had informed the Indians at Fairchild's that the peace talk was a trick to get the Indians out of the Lava Bed and hang them. That was Atwell's first intimation that "cursed

[27] *San Francisco Evening Bulletin,* March 3, 1873; *San Francisco Chronicle,* March 4, 1873; *New York Herald,* March 3, 1873; A. B. Meacham, *Wigwam and War-Path,* 428.

knaves had been tampering with the Modocs" at Fairchild's. He could not dissuade Lucy from the conviction there would be more fighting.[28]

Once at the Lava Bed, Steele and Atwell saw that something was badly wrong, but pretended not to notice. En route, Bogus Charley and some others had ridden ahead, reaching the stronghold before the white men. As Steele and Atwell rode in, they saw only two or three Indians, who looked sullen; none came out to greet them as before. They cooked and ate supper at Wild Gal's again, and then waited for a messenger to lead them to the cave for council, but none came. When they tired of waiting, they went to the cave on their own. Approaching the cave in the company of Indian women, they heard loud arguing from within. Once inside the cave they saw sixty-nine warriors, more than Fox had counted, which led to later surmises that the Snakes had reinforced the Modocs.

Worse, they received only scowls and cold handshakes from Jack and Schonchin. Scarface Charley sat down beside Atwell; it turned out that he and two confederates were the only Modocs in the cave friendly to the white men. Steele outlined each of the points named by the commissioners, and suggested they think them over until morning. "This was a little piece of strategy on the part of Mr. Steele to avoid a discussion of the matter at that time, for it was easy to see that the Modocs were in an evil humor, ripe for treachery and bloodshed," Atwell reported.

Instead of breaking up the council, however, the Indians started talking, with Jack making "a surly, inflammable speech, accusing Steele of duplicity and double-dealing." He refused to go out to see the commissioners, but insisted they come to him instead. Schonchin delivered "a violent tirade" against Steele, Canby, the commissioners, "and almost everybody else." Darkness in the cave prevented Atwell from taking notes, "but they were not needed to enable me to remem-

[28] This account of Atwell's experience is based upon *San Francisco Chronicle*, March 11, 1873.

ber it, and one used to the Indians needed no interpreter to learn its import." He said of Schonchin, "The old heathen chafed and fumed like a caged tiger." As Schonchin spoke, Indian faces lighted with passion, and hands played nervously with revolvers and knives. Steele and Atwell put a good face on it, behaving as though unconcerned, "but it was all put on, for I knew a single spark would set things going in that cave, and our little unarmed party of three men and one woman would not probably whip sixty-nine well-armed desperate Indians."

The first direct intimation that the Indians threatened treachery to Steele and the others came when Schonchin asked Steele if he was not afraid to sleep in the Modoc camp that night, after having talked to them with two hearts. Steele replied that he feared no man, and if he died, he would die with a good heart. Steele threw back at Schonchin the charges of speaking falsely. He also explained about the commission, the Oregon indictments, and the safety the Indians would gain by surrendering to Canby. When Steele finished, Scarface Charley and his two friends responded affirmatively, "but the rest preserved an ominous silence." Jack and Schonchin spoke violently once more.

Jack had remarked, however, that those who came to his home should be protected, "and I trusted to that and my natural stupidity to get me through in time to write an account of it," Atwell said. When the council finally broke up, Scarface Charley whispered to Atwell that he should sleep there in Jack's cave with Scarface beside him. Atwell and Steele bedded down in Jack's cave, next to the rock, after Scarface had whispered a warning to Atwell against going outside for a look around. Scarface, Jack, and Mary formed a protective ring around them in the night, and Scarface's two friends stood guard at the cave entrance. "To the protection of these three Indians I am satisfied we owed our safety," Atwell said.

Morning brought only a slight lessening of their peril. When they had breakfasted at Wild Gal's and returned to

Jack's for council, they met not a single word of welcome. Jack and Schonchin spoke at length, the burden of their talk being that they had been deceived. They refused to give a second thought to moving to a distant reservation; they would accept no terms of peace other than amnesty and the privilege of living on their lands in northern California as they had done before. They remained steadfast in their insistence that the commissioners come to the Modocs, not *vice versa*. Steele worked his way out by agreeing, as a ruse, that the commissioners would come to the Modocs. This the Indians liked, and they agreed to meet the four commissioners, Steele, Fairchild, and the newspaper reporters. No other whites must come. The Indians, however, must have the privilege of bringing all their warriors; they wanted to shake hands with the commissioners. One by one they eliminated the whites, saying Rosborough, Steele, Canby, and Case need not come, "but they insisted that Applegate and Meacham should come, for they were their *particular friends.*" Atwell remarked, ironically, how strange it was that the Indians had changed their minds about Applegate and Meacham, "for at our last interview they positively refused to have anything to say to them, saying they were bad men and their enemies." Intended Modoc treachery again was evident. However, Steele made arrangements for the meeting the next day. Thus, with the "anticipation of bigger game having cooled their animosity toward us in a great measure," as the reporter interpreted it, Steele and Atwell saddled and left, with only Scarface Charley to bid them good-bye. Boston Charley, Mary, and some women accompanied them to Fairchild's. "I did not draw a free breath until I reached the top of the bluff, three miles from the Modoc camp," Atwell said.

Canby and the Peace Commission gave the Indian point of view short attention. The next day, March 5, they sent by Mary and Boston a peremptory refusal of the Modoc terms and an ultimatum: Jack and his head men must come to Fairchild's by March 6, when the Peace Commission again would offer the proposed terms. If the two parties should fail to agree, the Indians would be allowed safe passage back. Should the Indians not come, the Peace Commission would go home and turn the matter over to the army.

The sudden change from friendliness to belligerence on the part of the Indians was blamed on a white man named Charles Blair. Atwell identified him as a Linkville citizen, "a worthless fellow, who, report says, has at one or more times graced the inside of the Penitentiary." Similar blame and characterization appeared in the *New York Herald* and in a report to Washington from Meacham, who said he was "a man of disreputable character, and violently opposed to peace commission."[29] The similarity of the accusations implies a common source.

At any rate, war seemed in prospect as of March 5. It had been a busy ten days since Fox rode off for the Lava Bed, during which time the whites had probed for an answer to the question of war or peace. First, there had been uncertainty, then jubilation at the prospect of peace, and again uncertainty, but now the odds were in favor of war. Fox spoke for the others when he reported: "I believe this will end my peaceful correspondence."[30] He wrote as a reporter stating the situation, without any indication that he particularly looked forward to reporting a war. And in summing up, Atwell said, "So ends the first chapter of the Peace Commission, which has been fraught with dangers, blunders and serious mistakes."[31]

The best that can be said of the first stage of peace negotiations is that it ended in failure—fiasco might be a more accurate word—under circumstances that would appear to have vindicated the press in its denunciation of the Peace Commission. More significant than the newspaper statements themselves as criticism is the extent to which officials in

[29] *New York Herald,* March 26, 1873; Modoc War Correspondence, 264.
[30] *New York Herald,* March 18, 1873.
[31] *San Francisco Chronicle,* March 11, 1873.

Washington assessed the members of the commission much as the correspondents did.

Bogart wrote with a meat-ax, splitting somebody's skull— or trying to—in almost every story, usually Meacham's or an Applegate's, and he was much more contemptuous of the commission than were any of his colleagues. He dubbed it the "High Old Joint Commission"; when he wanted to be especially disrespectful, he called its members the "High Old Joints." Atwell wrote as bluntly but more responsibly. McKay, as the knowledgable local man, often became indignant. Fox, the outlander, pursued his own inquiries, but often appeared to follow the lead of his California colleagues in characterizing some of the commissioners and their personal interests.

Fox said that the commission was careful about what news it gave the reporters and then gave it "as a special favor." He declared that one of the commissioners had offered him all the current news, provided Fox would submit his stories to the commission for approval before sending them to New York. Both Applegate and Meacham were at odds with the reporters; Applegate was quoted as saying they should have no information except what he chose to give them; after the secret sessions of the commission, Meacham would come out and tell "a cock-and-bull story to the correspondents."

The correspondents rebuked the commission regularly. One story summed up the commission in the folksy expression that the Peace Commission could not get elected because it had the wrong men on the ticket. As the correspondents saw more of the commission, they described it in terms of "political trickery," consultation of private interests ahead of public welfare, "a stupendous humbug," and a "farce." Within three days after the first full meeting of the commission, the *Chronicle* reporter thought Applegate and Case would have little to say, with Meacham there to "rule the roost," and he asked, "Can there be any doubt that the tribunal of arbitration has been packed?"

Meacham was caricatured and condemned, particularly by the *Chronicle* and *Herald* men. Both described him as a smooth-talking operator. Bogart said, "The words roll from his silvery tongue like green peas from a hot platter," and Fox used the same expression, quoting "a contemporary." Bogart also said Meacham could "talk the legs off a cast-iron pot in just ten minutes." Fox described him as a "Micawber politician" who had engineered the Peace Commission as a means of settling with Odeneal, who had displaced him as Oregon Indian superintendent. The reporters seem to have deduced from Meacham's free conversation that his primary interest had been to place the onus of bad management upon Odeneal and upon Captain O. C. Knapp, who had been a subagent under Meacham. Moreover, Fox quoted one of the other two commissioners—the context suggests Applegate—as saying the commission was a humbug being used to cloak Meacham's attack on Odeneal. Meacham was described as having arrived on the scene "like a conqueror come to deliver an oppressed people," confident he could manage both Applegate and Case, but soon found they had minds of their own. However, Bogart did not think Meacham himself had stolen anything while Indian agent, although he was sure there had been stealing under Meacham, and he also felt that Meacham would deal fairly with the Indians in the showdown.

Applegate received harsh treatment because of his family connections. Bogart, who dealt most severely with him, said: "This Indian business up here is a good deal like a decayed egg. Puncture the shell anywhere and you will find an Applegate flavor at the same time." In time, the correspondents showed greater respect for Applegate when they learned he was not to be manipulated.[32]

Official Washington assessed the commission much as the correspondents did. As a result of frequent communication between Delano and Secretary of War W. W. Belknap, Sher-

[32] The foregoing summary of press comment is based upon *Yreka Union*, March 1, 1873; *New York Herald*, Feb. 27, March 8, 17, March 26, 1873; *San Francisco Chronicle*, Feb. 21, Feb. 23, Feb. 26, March 1, 2, 13, 1873; *San Francisco Evening Bulletin*, Feb. 18, 19, 26, 1873.

man telegraphed Canby, "All parties here have absolute faith in you but mistrust the commissioners." Delano, in a day when Indian administrators and military officers were as compatible as horses and mountain lions, finally gave Canby full authority to discharge and appoint members of the commission on the spot and to work out a peaceful solution on his own if he could. On February 26, Applegate wrote a letter of resignation, effective upon termination of the peace negotiations, but Delano did not wait for the outcome; he accepted it forthwith.[33]

The collapse of peace negotiations signified by Steele's return from his second trip to the Lava Bed, on March 4, marked the end of the first peace commission. Meacham sent Delano a frenzied telegram, reporting that the Modocs had rejected all offers and threatened treachery to himself and Applegate. "The mission is a failure," he said. Delano replied the next day that the mission should not be a failure, that negotiations should continue, and added, "Think I understand now their unwillingness to confide in you."[34]

The commission disintegrated. Case felt official duties required his presence elsewhere, and Applegate's resignation had already been accepted. Before Applegate left, the commission met for the last time, but could not agree on a report, leaving each member free to file a minority report. That Applegate did. And he used keen-edged words which made Meacham appear to be an imbecile. Applegate was not a man to be led by the nose. He concluded with the statement that the commission was an "expensive blunder"[35]—which was what the correspondents had said all along.

About the same time, a change occurred in the press corps when Bogart left the field on March 5. There was no explanation why he had been recalled, but the *Yreka Union* said that, if reports from the front were true, Bogart was a "signal instance" of a "martyr in the cause of 'live journalism'."[36] Per-

[33] Modoc War Correspondence, 69, 71–72, 73–74, 258, 267.
[34] *Ibid.*, 261.
[35] *Ibid.*, 265–66.
[36] *Yreka Union*, March 8, 1873.

haps his unrestrained personal attacks upon the Applegates had been more than the *Chronicle* could stand the risk of continuing. Certainly much of his work had been irresponsible and inaccurate. His exaggerated style, especially in the personal references to the Applegates, make it appear that he was ineptly trying to whip up a sensation.

Bogart himself soon made news. The U. S. Navy arrested and tried him by court-martial on an old charge of embezzling $30,000 while he was a navy paymaster in 1869. The story remained alive during his trial and imprisonment, but languished in the long interval between the decision of the court-martial and approval by Secretary of the Navy George M. Robeson. By the time Robeson approved the finding of the court-martial on December 23, 1873, and ordered Bogart imprisoned for twenty-three months at Mare Island, where he had been held and tried, the Mare Island commandant could only report: "The person . . . having escaped and I am ignorant of his address." Navy court-martial records do not indicate that Bogart ever again was apprehended.[37]

Atwell replaced Bogart as the *Chronicle* correspondent and continued to represent his other newspapers. The *Chronicle* editors wired him on March 7: "We want the first, the best, and all the news, and will rely on you for it. We will increase your pay one-third. Don't allow yourself to be beaten. If a battle occurs telegraph full details without regard to expense. Answer."[38]

"Been doing so the last week. Will continue . . . ," Atwell replied two days later.[39]

Several times in later telegrams the *Chronicle* impressed upon Atwell that he was to spare no expense in getting news to the *Chronicle*, and that he should employ special couriers

[37] *Yreka Union*, March 29, 1873; *Yreka Journal*, March 26, 1873; San Francisco *Alta California*, March-May, 1873; *Record of the Proceedings of the Naval General Court Martial of Robert D. Bogart*, quoted in letter to the author from Elbert Hubert, War Records Division, National Archives.

[38] *San Francisco Chronicle*, April 19, 1873.

[39] *Ibid.*

freely. Before the war was over, the editors had raised his pay twice.

The three remaining correspondents—Atwell, Fox, and McKay—watched the Modoc War move to a new anti-climax and settle into a war of attrition. The anti-climax came when Captain Jack accepted the ultimatum which had been sent to him on March 5, after Steele's second trip to the Lava Bed; and after several exchanges promised to come in on March 10. But the Modocs failed to come. When Canby reported this, Sherman telegraphed him to be patient but implied that extermination of the Modocs would be justified if they again attempted deceit and treachery. Canby, however, was willing to be even more patient. Nevertheless, he began a tactic of compression, ringing the Lava Bed with troops to prevent the Modocs from escaping, hoping by a show of force to awe the Indians into surrender, although he ordered his men not to fire on the Indians.

A second peace commission was appointed, and the correspondents treated it with more respect than they had shown its predecessor. It included Meacham; Rosborough, who ultimately gave his proxy to Canby because of his duties on the bench; Rev. E. Thomas of Petaluma, California; and L. S. Dyar, Indian agent of the Yainax agency. McKay said that Thomas seemed to understand his duties better than any other member of the commission, but Atwell attacked Dyar as the "howling kind" of Christian, accusing him of keeping Mrs. Dyar on the payroll as a schoolteacher at the agency even though a school had not been established. Control of the entire situation—military and Peace Commission—remained with Canby. The new commission, however, did not arrive on the scene as a group until late March.[40]

The reporters had little to write about until later in the month. In the meantime, troops in the area were increased to

[40] Modoc War Correspondence, 70–73, 261, 266–68; *San Francisco Chronicle*, March 9, 12, 16, 1873; *San Francisco Evening Bulletin*, March 10, 12, 14, April 5, 1873; *Yreka Journal*, March 19, 1873.

approximately six hundred. As the month wore on, the reporters found Canby silent on his military plans, certain that the Modocs would learn of his plans through the Indian women and men passing back and forth. This was the only time during the Western War that intelligence security limited the information available to newsmen.

During the interim, Fox acted as a hostage when Canby and Gillem talked personally with Captain Jack during a chance encounter at the edge of the Lava Bed. The incident occurred during a reconnaissance of the Lava Bed region by Canby and Gillem with two troops of the First Cavalry. Fox and McKay rode along with them when they left Van Bremer's to scout the edge of the bluff overlooking the Lava Bed and get the bearing of different points in the Lava Bed and along the south end of Tule Lake.

When the scouting party reached the bluffs about noon, Canby and Gillem surveyed the Lava Bed through their glasses, picking out a group of Indians on a ledge about a mile away who shouted for someone to come down and talk. Dr. T. T. Cabaniss of Yreka, serving as an army surgeon, was about halfway down the bluff at that time, and he obtained Canby's permission to find out what the Indians wanted.

Cabaniss presently returned, saying Captain Jack wanted to talk with the two officers, and asked that someone else go with him. Another officer offered to go, but Canby thought his companion should not be a soldier. Fox, having met the Indians, joined Cabaniss, and the two went to the Modocs. Arrangements were made for Captain Jack to meet Canby and Gillem at a juniper tree halfway between the foot of the bluff and the Modoc outpost.

Jack refused to go unless Fox and Cabaniss agreed to remain as hostages. While Jack talked with the two officers, Fox talked with the other Indians, whom he described as painted for war and stripped to the waist. The Indians, he reported, appeared nettled by the recent capture of some of their horses by the cavalry. "I told them," Fox said, "they were taken by a hundred new soldiers, hoping that the knowledge of such an addition to our forces might have a wholesome effect, but I am grieved to say they did not look very scared." Fox said he noted that one Indian carefully stroked a scalp of curly brown hair, which decorated his shot pouch, at the news of more whites in the area. That proved enough to convince Fox that he should have his ten-inch hair cut off when he got back to Van Bremer's, which he reported he did.[41]

The talk between Canby and Jack amounted to nothing, and on the way back to Van Bremer's, Canby told Fox he thought the Indians did not want peace unless they could remain on Lost River. Fox also quoted the General as saying he thought nothing actually could be done with the Modocs until the troops demonstrated who held the upper hand. Fox's role in the meeting was not mentioned in the official reports, but was confirmed by McKay.

On April 2, Canby moved the troops from Van Bremer's to a camp in the Lava Bed itself, only a short distance from Captain Jack's stronghold. Thomas, Dyar, and Meacham moved to the camp with the army, and on the first night there Indian women and civilians played on Meacham's fears to such an extent that he informed Canby that the Indians would attack the camp that night. To allay the peace commissioner's fears, Canby strengthened the pickets. Meacham even suggested they should all dig pits to sleep in. For himself, he slept with his boots on. And a good time was had by all, at his expense. Fox observed that Thomas was the only one of the commissioners who dealt with the Indians as though he was not afraid of them.

Rosborough arrived on April 3, and several talks were thereafter held with the Modocs. The reporters were excluded from the meetings, although they gained from Indian sources a version of what had taken place. The situation was that the Indians refused to leave that part of the country, while the commissioners insisted they had to leave. A council tent was pitched between the army camp and the Modoc stronghold for negotiating sessions. During this time identical and nearly

[41] *New York Herald*, March 25, April 7, 1873.

141

identical stories appeared in the *New York Herald* and the *San Francisco Evening Bulletin*, but nothing indicated what arrangements had been made that resulted in the dual use. The army had two camps in the Tule Lake region, one on the east and the other on the west—with the Modoc stronghold between—communicating through signal stations.

Came Good Friday, 1873, and the patient commissioners once more went out to negotiate with the Indians, and once more refused the press the privilege of attending. Canby, Meacham, Thomas, Dyar, Riddle, and Tobey rode out of camp at about 11:00 A.M. for the council tent a mile away. The reporters watched them go and then returned to their tents, Atwell to write, Fox to read; McKay's story did not say what he did. From the signal station atop the bluff, Lieutenant John Q. Adams, First Cavalry, kept his glasses on the commissioners as they wound through the rocks to the council tent. The camp remained quiet through midday.

A yelling soldier, running down the bluff, broke the quiet about 1:30 P.M.: "They're firing on the Commissioners!"[42]

Fox and Atwell rushed from their tents, the former buckling on his revolver, and the long roll of the drums brought infantry and artillery into line. Fox encountered Gillem, who said Mason's camp on the other side of the lake had been attacked, and showed the *Herald* reporter a note he had just started to write to warn Canby of danger. Fanning out in skirmish formation, the troops moved as rapidly across the broken rocks as they could.

At the picket line of the camp they met Dyar, a tall, powerful man, who came bounding toward them over the rocks. Behind him came Riddle and Tobey, the latter crying like a child.

"Where are the others?" they were asked.

"All dead; killed by the damned Indians," Riddle replied. "Oh, the devils! It has turned out just as I thought it would, and now I guess they will believe me and her when we tell them there is danger."[43]

[42] *Ibid.*, April 13, 1873; *San Francisco Chronicle*, April 14, 1873.

Reaching the council tent area, they first came upon Meacham, whom Atwell described as a "terrible-looking object" from gunshot wounds and attempted scalping, seriously injured but alive. On the council ground lay Canby and Thomas, dead. Canby had been shot in the head and stripped naked; Thomas, shot and stripped to his pants. Atwell first covered Canby's naked body with his coat and then cut a piece of canvas from the tent to cover him. Fox apparently went on a little distance farther with the troops, for he saw some of the Indians running in the distance. However, Gillem soon ordered recall, for his troops could not go into action without preparation, and he could not attack without orders from Washington that would change the previous standing order forbidding hostile action against the Modocs. Atwell went back to Meacham, who was conscious and attended by Dr. Cabaniss. Atwell got some of his details from Meacham before the latter was borne back to camp on a stretcher.[44]

By 3:00 P.M. Fox was back in his tent, hurriedly writing a story which reflected the fury of the moment against the Modocs, with a courier waiting to make the eighty-mile ride to Yreka and the telegraph. His lead ran: "Peace policy and the Indian Bureau have accomplished the bitter end, and offered as martyrs to the cause the lives of General E. R. S. Canby, commanding the District of the Columbia, and the Rev. Mr. Thomas." Atwell wrote a much longer story, which began with equal fury: "The peace negotiations with the Modoc Indians, which have occupied the attention of the country for the past two months, resulted today in the consummation of the most damnable plot that ever disgraced even the Indian character."[45]

Their stories went on the wire at Yreka on Saturday, and made the Sunday editions of their respective papers. The *Evening Bulletin* had the story on Saturday afternoon, a sub-

[43] *San Francisco Chronicle*, April 14, 1873.
[44] *Ibid.*, April 13, 1873; *New York Herald*, April 13, 1873; Meacham, *Wigwam and War-Path*, 504–505.
[45] *New York Herald*, April 13, 1873; *San Francisco Chronicle*, April 13, 1873.

dued narrative account based on information from Dyar and Riddle, indicating that McKay had remained in camp when the others went to the council tent area.

The *Chronicle*'s story came in Saturday afternoon when the streets were thronged with people leaving matinees or shopping. The *Chronicle* chalked the first news on its bulletin board. Additional details were chalked up as they came in, read by a growing crowd. "People seemed to discredit their own eyes," said the *Chronicle*, "and acted as though dumbfounded." The newspaper issued an extra, which sold out as fast as it could be printed. Working the local angle of the story, a reporter went to headquarters of the Military Division of the Pacific and learned from a janitor that General Schofield was at the Pacific Club, where the reporter found him. Schofield had already heard the news from Thomas' son-in-law, John R. Jarboe, an attorney. With the reporter Schofield went to the *Chronicle* office, where he read proof sheets of the extra, and later stopped at the Western Union office, receiving a telegram from Gillem that confirmed the tragedy. The *Chronicle* gave over all of page one to the story, placing on it a headline which extended almost a full column in depth, the first line reading, "THE RED JUDAS."

The *New York Herald* started the story in the far right-hand column of the editorial page, an unusual procedure, under the headline, "Massacre." In all, the *Herald* gave the story about six columns, including the story from Fox and supplementary stories from Washington and San Francisco, background of the war, and stories about Canby.

The short *Bulletin* story appeared on page three, the markets page, also under the headline, "Massacre."

The first stories coming from the Lava Bed were incomplete and contained errors, because of the confusion and lack of knowledge at that moment. On the basis of information from the military, they reported there had been an attack on Mason's camp east of Tule Lake, which they corrected when more accurate information was received. Fox said the troops reached the scene of the murder in about five minutes; Atwell,

Gillem's Camp and Tule Lake.

U. S. Troops Prepare for the Attack on the Modoc
Stronghold, 1873.

an hour. The confusion of crisis also distorted even the official reports. In three separate reports of the sequence of events, Gillem gave as many different versions. Some variations also appear in the Fox and Atwell stories. Fox obtained his information from Dyar; Atwell apparently got some facts from Dyar and some from Meacham.

Back in camp, officers and correspondents more coolly assessed the situation, deducing that the Indians had intended to capture or kill all the commanding officers, for they had lured two lieutenants from Mason's camp with a white flag, asking for the commanding officer, and then fired on them, mortally wounding one. Sketchy signal communication perhaps had been responsible for the original distorted information about the affair at Mason's camp.

Knowing that Atwell would have written a longer mail story, supplementing his first telegraphic story, the *Chronicle* editors on Sunday wired the Yreka postmaster to take Atwell's story from the mails and send it by telegraph, which thus gave them another story on Monday morning. The story remained alive and fresh from the Lava Bed for San Francisco editors, but not for eastern editors, for a storm on the Great Plains snapped telegraph wires in Nebraska, although not before Fox had made the Monday edition with a follow-up story and not before Sherman had issued orders to exterminate the Modocs.

The war correspondents then had a war to cover, for military operations began promptly, consisting of an assault phase and a guerrilla phase. Under orders issued immediately by Sherman and Schofield, Gillem began advancing on the following Monday.

Troops from the two camps on either side of the stronghold fought the Modocs for three days, April 15, 16, and 17, driving them from their stronghold in what the correspondents called the "Three Days Fight."

In covering the Three Days Fight, the reporters worked out a pooling arrangement, a news-reporting method that reached much greater refinement in World War II. McKay

145

and Atwell took turns—one remaining in camp while the other went out with troops. Fox went with troops each of the three days. The two with troops got eye-witness views of the fighting; the man in camp had access to headquarters information and from the signal station watched movements across the entire battlefield, keeping an hourly log of movements. Atwell patronizingly referred to McKay, saying he had left an "assistant" in camp or had sent "another reporter" with troops. McKay retaliated by saying he had left an "agent" in camp.[46] The reporters had tried to arrange a pool even earlier. When the Peace Commission had first sent out the women to talk with the Modocs in February, the reporters, having been refused permission to witness the commission session when the women returned, unsuccessfully sought to have one reporter attend, representing all newspapers.

On the first day of fighting, Fox picked up a Springfield and went forward with an artillery command under Colonel Marcus Miller. Atwell's story of the first day's fight, based upon his observation from the signal station, reached Yreka in the "unusually" fast time of fourteen hours. A courier left camp with the story at 8:30 P.M. and delivered it to the Yreka telegraph operator at 10:30 the next morning, riding one horse seventy miles. The most graphic accounts of the first two days of fighting came from Atwell.

Early on the third day of battle Atwell and Fox were caught in an ambush. They left camp about 7:00 A.M., riding leisurely along the lake edge toward the advanced lines. Atwell, a civilian, and Gillem's orderly rode in advance. Fox and Dr. Henry McElderry, an army surgeon, rode about 150 yards behind. Another 200 yards in the rear rode two Yreka citizens, Eugene Hovey and Sam Watson.

Atwell's group had just come abreast of Captain Jack's original stronghold, from which the Modocs had been driven, when concealed Indians opened fire at about 300 yards. Armed only with a six-shooter, Atwell made a run for it, hav-

46 *Yreka Journal*, April 23, 1873; *San Francisco Chronicle*, April 18, 19, 1873; *San Francisco Evening Bulletin*, April 22, 1873.

ing to cross an exposed sagebrush flat before he could reach Hospital Point, half a mile away. One shot tore the sole from his boot, the impact stinging his foot so badly that he had to return to camp by boat on Tule Lake later in the day.

When Fox saw the shooting, he thought it was funny, remarking that Atwell was doing well as a sprinter even though he had a game leg. McElderry interrupted the *Herald*'s laughter by saying, "They must be firing this way." Four or five bullets cutting past them caused them to dismount. McElderry led his horse behind a ridge. More bullets cured Fox of hesitation; he let go his horse and sprinted for a cluster of rocks about one hundred yards away, "and I don't think I could have been more than thirteen seconds making the distance, hampered as I was with cartridge box and Springfield." Taking cover, Fox tried to get a shot at the Modocs, but they had the drop on him, putting two rounds so close that one made his ear tingle. He told the story in facetious terms. The shots, he said, "changed my tactics, so that I made a flank movement, left my rear open to the fire of the enemy, and rejoined the Doctor after a brilliant dash of some two hundred yards." Officers who had watched through field glasses, he said, "acknowledged that I had made the most brilliant retreat of the day."[47] Hovey, still in his teens, was killed in that ambush.

The reporters continued to use their pool system in the extensive field operations that followed the Three Days Fight. During the fighting the troops took the Lava Bed stronghold, but in the night the Modocs escaped through a gap in the army lines. Immediately afterward the cavalry went out on a scout in an effort to re-establish contact with the enemy. McKay rode with the cavalry, reporting that Fox and Atwell would cover for him from camp, "and I will telegraph for all from the front."[48]

The press corps was augmented at the same time by William Simpson, a special artist of the *London Illustrated News*,

[47] *New York Herald*, May 7, 1873; *Yreka Journal*, April 23, 1873.
[48] *San Francisco Evening Bulletin*, April 19, 1873.

who remained but a week. In the course of a journey around the world, Simpson had been in San Francisco when the story of the Canby murder came in, which caused him to make an excursion to the Lava Bed.

Reduction of the Lava Bed stronghold, which was accomplished largely through mortar fire, caused the Modocs to flee and break into small parties, which meant the start of the guerrilla phase of military operations. A marauding band ambushed a wagon train between the two army camps, and another crept up to within eight hundred yards of the camp on the south side of Tule Lake. Their harassing fire, which was stopped only by a well-placed mortar shell, caused the commanding officer to issue carbines to the few men stationed there. Atwell remarked that he wrote with a carbine by his side, and would keep it handy. The start of guerrilla fighting aroused fears of a general border war.

News coverage thereupon suffered two disruptions. With the Indians fanning out, couriers refused to ride between the Lava Bed and Yreka. Both Fox and Atwell reported that a courier carrying news dispatches had been fired upon. The second disruption came from a horse disease, ungrammatically called the "epizootic," which made almost every horse in the command ill. The horse disease had started in the East during the previous fall, causing suspension of streetcar operation in Philadelphia, and gradually spread westward, striking cavalry mounts and other horses in northern California in the spring.

By the end of the week following the Three Days Fight, operations had dwindled to such inconsequence that Fox decided to return to New York, but the Modocs furnished him with one last story. On the morning of April 26, Fox reported that there was a difference of opinion concerning what had happened to the Modocs. Scouting parties had reported that the Indians had fled, but Donald McKay, who had arrived with Warm Springs auxiliaries in time for the Three Days Fight, was convinced that the Modocs still hid in the caves and crevices of the Lava Bed. Personally, Fox felt sure they would not stand together as a body again, but would have "to be exterminated by ones and twos." On the same day McKay wrote a story saying Fox intended to leave the next day for New York. By evening, however, another story had developed in the Lava Bed which would sting a nation with indignation.[49]

On that Saturday morning when Atwell climbed the signal station to survey the Lava Bed through field glasses as the correspondents had been doing regularly, he watched a reconnoitering party advance southeastward. Composed of two artillery batteries and one infantry company, the force of about seventy men was to seek a route for pack animals and mortars to a spot about four miles away. Atwell watched them go and kept them under surveillance during the morning. He saw them stop for a noon break and then saw a great commotion in the rocks, but could not tell what was happening, except that they had found Indians or *vice versa*.

About one-thirty stragglers started coming in. Demoralized and scared out of their wits, as they were described, they told stories which did not quite make sense but pointed to a fearful disaster. Other soldiers, who had run in the face of the enemy, also came straggling in, but the full story of what happened was not revealed during that day. Night came, and the men in camp had to wait for what they were sure would be bad news. On Sunday morning a reinforcing party, bringing in dead and wounded, filled out the account. Commanded by Major Evan Thomas of the Fourth Artillery, the patrol had been surprised by a smaller force of Modocs who had the advantage of both the element of surprise and superiority of fire. About one-third of the men stayed with the officers; all line officers were killed. The other two-thirds fled. It proved to be one of the most disastrous engagements the army had had to record up to that time. Casualty figures varied; Gillem reported eighteen dead and sixteen wounded; Atwell reported twenty dead, seventeen wounded, and six missing,

[49] *New York Herald*, April 29, 1873; *San Francisco Evening Bulletin*, April 28, 1873.

which was a closer count than Gillem's, for a casualty report in June showed twenty-three dead and nineteen wounded. The correspondents, especially Atwell, referred to the retreat of the men who deserted their officers as panic-stricken; the same term was used by Gillem and with biting contempt by Major General Jeff. C. Davis, who arrived six days later to replace Canby. The stories of Atwell, Fox, and McKay naturally contain considerably more detail than Gillem's official report of the twenty-eighth, but even so, there are several variations among the three newspaper accounts and between them and Gillem's report. The reporters did not write their stories until Sunday and Monday.[50]

The fight did not keep Fox from leaving, however. Traveling with Simpson, he arrived in Yreka on April 28, and may have received there the information upon which he based his account of the fight. There he received a telegram from New York, asking him to stay a while longer. He complied, remaining in Yreka for two weeks, during which time he was lionized by the belles of Yreka at a church social. But at length New York agreed he might as well come home. Taking the stage on May 11, he reached Redding the next day, where the local correspondent of the *San Francisco Chronicle* described him "as fat and rugged as a California grizzly."[51] Ever thereafter he was known to New York newspapermen as "Modoc" Fox.

Atwell took over as Modoc War correspondent for the *New York Herald.* Through the rest of the campaign he represented the *Herald, San Francisco Chronicle, Sacramento Record,* and *Chicago Inter-Ocean,* although the *Inter-Ocean* gave the Modoc War less attention than the other papers did.

In leaving the field, Fox crossed the path of a new reporter coming into the Modoc story—William Mitchell Bunker, a top man of the *San Francisco Evening Bulletin.* Nantucket-born, Bunker then was twenty-three years old and had been in

[50] Modoc War Correspondence, 82–84, 108; *San Francisco Chronicle,* April 30, 1873; *San Francisco Evening Bulletin,* April 29, 1873; *New York Herald,* April 30, 1873.

[51] *Yreka Union,* May 3, May 17, 1873; *San Francisco Chronicle,* May 13, 1873.

California for ten years. The son and grandson of newspaper-men, he had begun his newspaper career in the back shop of the *Bulletin,* on the side writing a series of letters on California politics for an eastern paper. When the *Bulletin* editors, who had clipped and reprinted the stories, found the author in their own composing room, they moved him into the editorial room, where he developed a reputation as one of San Francisco's better reporters, later becoming city editor and news editor of the *Bulletin.* Bunker arrived in Yreka on May 9 and reached Davis's headquarters at the front two days later. Atwell's detailed reporting had placed the *Chronicle* ahead of the *Bulletin,* and Bunker apparently came to take charge of *Bulletin* coverage, rather than to displace McKay, who remained in the field. However, McKay seems also to have been writing quite a bit for the opposition *Chronicle* under the pool arrangement with Atwell.

Thus, three reporters again were on duty for the final stage of the Modoc War—Bunker, Atwell, and McKay—but some days elapsed before definitive operations were undertaken. Finding morale low, General Davis moved slowly until he felt his command ready to fight. In the meantime, the army learned definitely through two Indian women, who had been sent to spy out the land, that the Modocs had fled the Lava Bed. The scene of operations then shifted to the east of the Lava Bed, toward the Clear Lake country. Cavalry encountered the Modocs at Sorass Lake and drove them back into the Lava Bed. Whereupon Davis used the fighting plan he had favored from the beginning. He sent all his troops into the Lava Bed, where they formed a series of bivouacs from which they could fight when opportunity offered and rest between fights, as the Indians did.

In the meantime, Atwell went into Yreka for a short visit, returning to the front on May 18 with S. A. Clarke, a Salem, Oregon, editor on assignment for the *New York Times.* Clarke was one of the Oregon politicians in Washington whose petition through Williams had helped to create the first peace commission. On the road they learned that the Modocs had fled the Lava Bed and were then to the west of it, in the vicinity of Fairchild's ranch, and that a mail rider had been shot at near Dorris's ranch the day before. Considering discretion the better part of valor, they turned back to Ball's ranch, nearer Yreka, to wait for an escort to Fairchild's.

The Indians in the Fairchild vicinity were the Modocs who had lived there originally. They broke with Captain Jack in the Lava Bed, and the two groups went their separate ways. About seventy-five men, women, and children surrendered to Davis at Fairchild's on May 22.

Through them Davis learned that Jack and the other Modocs were toward the east, in the Clear Lake–Goose Lake country. Dividing his cavalry into three detachments—the cavalry was all west of the Lava Bed at that time—he moved them back toward the east, basing them at Boyle's Camp on the east of Tule Lake. In the meantime, a group of surrendered Modoc warriors offered to help find Captain Jack. Accepting their offer, Davis went with them to Jesse Applegate's ranch in the Clear Creek country; he had a home there even though Yoncalla had been listed as his residence. The turncoat Modocs found Jack on Willow Creek (not the same Willow Creek which Fox crossed), whereupon Davis ordered two cavalry detachments, under Captains H. C. Hasbrouck and James Jackson, forward from Boyle's camp. Thereafter, he reported, the pursuit was "more of a chase after wild beasts than war."[52]

On May 29, the two cavalry detachments left Applegate's, accompanied by Atwell and Bunker. That day and the next they found Jack's band, capturing Jack's sister and most of his remaining warriors, but Jack and a few others remained out.

On June 1, Bunker returned to Applegate's house with a detachment of soldiers and the captives, Atwell apparently remaining with the troops. During the day the troops captured Captain Jack with the aid of Warm Springs scouts in Langell Valley in southern Oregon. That incident ended the Modoc War.

[52] Modoc War Correspondence, 110–11.

On a $300 mule, Atwell tried to take a short-cut to Ashland, Oregon, and the telegraph office with the story. But his mount stumbled and broke its neck, injuring Atwell, who made his way to Boyle's camp and later received medical treatment in Yreka.

During the day, the troops returned to Applegate's, and the story of Captain Jack's capture was written not by Atwell but by Bunker. In fact, most of the stories of the last three days of the campaign came from Bunker. They appeared in the *Bulletin* above his initials; identical stories appeared in the *Alta California* above his name; identical stories appeared in the *Chronicle*, without initials but leaving the impression that they came from a staff man. Crying "foul," the *Bulletin* charged that the *Chronicle* had stolen news "as any sneak thief might have stolen a hat or an overcoat" and "lied" by pretending the stories came from its own correspondent. The same stories also appeared in the *New York Herald*. The *Bulletin* said it published an extra when the news came in on Sunday and the *Chronicle* took the capture story from that.[53]

Even though dogged by bad luck, Atwell had at least one stroke of good fortune. The *Herald* not only paid one-third of the cost of his dead mule, but gave him a $100 bonus.

Although Atwell had favored extermination of the Modocs when they were under arms and insisting upon continuing the war, especially after the Canby murder, he sought justice for them as prisoners after their capture. The Modocs who were involved in the murder of Canby and Thomas were tried in July by a military commission at Fort Klamath, composed in part of army officers who had fought them. Before the military commission findings and sentences were approved by the President, Atwell wrote Delano to urge that action be deferred until a full and fair investigation could be made of the circumstances leading to the war. He said the Indians had been tried without counsel. Moreover, he said that Riddle

[53] *Yreka Journal*, June 4, 11, 1873; *San Francisco Evening Bulletin*, June 2, 3, 1873; *Alta California*, June 2, 3, 1873; *San Francisco Chronicle*, June 2, 3, 1873; *New York Herald*, June 3, 16, 23, 1873.

and Tobey, who also acted as interpreters at the trial, were not trustworthy. "We know he is illiterate," he said, "can neither read or write; cannot translate the idioms of our tongue; cannot even understand good English. We know the squaw with whom he cohabits has shielded her relatives in his interpreting at the expense of others. We know that gross wrongs have been committed by whites on these Indians, and will show them, if permitted to do so." He also charged that the war had been brought about by designing white men for selfish purposes. His plea went unheeded, however, and Grant approved the findings, sending two Indians to prison for life and four to the gallows—Captain Jack, Schonchin, Black Jim, and Boston Charley.[54]

With the hanging scheduled for October 3, newsmen gathered once more and made elaborate plans to best one another in the race for a telegraph key. Fox returned, making an eleven-day trip from New York to Fort Klamath, and sent many columns of copy, including lengthy advance stories which incorporated his jail-cell interviews with the condemned. Atwell was there to cover the execution for the *Sacramento Record* and *Yreka Journal*. Colonel H. S. Shaw, city editor of the *San Francisco Chronicle*, came with correspondents of Washington and Cincinnati papers, exciting suspicion in Yreka that his wagon contained carrier pigeons. Fox, Atwell, and the Shaw group were on the same side. Although each would do his utmost to get the story in ahead of the others, they represented newspapers which opposed the Western Union telegraph monopoly and the Associated Press connection therewith. Their opposition was William Turner of Jacksonville, Oregon, representing the *San Francisco Bulletin* and the Associated Press.

Because Fort Klamath was isolated, a ninety-mile race to the one telegraph wire at Jacksonville was necessary. Acting in conjunction, Fox and Shaw had a line of courier stations between Fort Klamath and Jacksonville—three couriers and nine horses for a trip estimated at seven hours. Keeping his

[54] Modoc War Correspondence, 202–203, 323–24.

own counsel, Turner had an old Indian trail cleared, shortening the distance to seventy-five miles. Atwell sought to beat them all by sending his couriers to Ashland. On the day of the execution, Fox sent an early courier to place a story on the wire, marked "more to come." When the trap-door was sprung at 10:25 A.M., the couriers grabbed the copy and were off at a gallop. Even by taking the regular road, the *Herald* couriers were in position to beat the *Bulletin,* but at Rogue River the *Herald* rider encountered trouble, which led to suspicion of trickery. Instead of a saddled horse waiting for him on the ferry-boat, he found the horse in a stable, unsaddled, and the boat on the opposite shore—result, a twenty-minute delay. In addition, a bucking mule delayed him another ten minutes. The *Bulletin* courier made it in first, completing the trip in six hours and thirty minutes, or about 5:00 P.M., too late for most afternoon papers. The *Herald* rider came in only twenty minutes later, but the *Herald* and *Chronicle* had the jump on the opposition because of the story filed earlier in the day. Because of the time difference, it already was night in New York, and the *Herald,* even as a morning paper, could have missed out on a staff story if the *Bulletin* and AP had held the wire for several hours. The *Chronicle's* carrier pigeons, which were supposed to wing their way to Yreka, disappeared. As for Atwell, it would seem that Ashland was a jinx to him, because one of his riders got drunk on the road, fell off his horse, and lost six hours.

Schofield commented that the Modoc War was "more remarkable in some respects than any before known in American history."[55] The same might be said of the news coverage, in relation to coverage of the other Indian campaigns. The Modoc War was the first campaign of the Western War to be covered extensively, it was the first in which newspapers competed energetically to be first in print with the news, and it was one of the earliest of all wars in which the pool was used in war reporting. Moreover, the correspondents reported a

[55] Secretary of War, *Report, 1873,* I, 52.

war and concurrent diplomacy, as it were. Four reporters had the unusual experience of crossing enemy lines and interviewing the enemy commander during a truce period.

Seven accredited correspondents reported from the Lava Bed region; five were there long enough to do a measurable job of war reporting; the other two were on the ground only briefly. A generalization to summarize their work can be drawn only with caution. Bogart is the one reporter whose work can be dismissed in large degree as sometimes inaccurate. Fox, Atwell, McKay, and Bunker did workmanlike jobs, on the whole. Viewed from the consideration of how well they informed the public of what was happening, their reports presented all points of view—not always objectively or balanced and sometimes through indirection—including the Indians' side on the three occasions when a reporter had the opportunity to hear the Modocs in the Lava Bed, although many of the stories that were published were antagonistic toward the first peace commission.

There are discrepancies between the newspaper accounts and the official army reports, but almost always these involve minor matters, except for the casualty figures for the Thomas defeat, and there Atwell's report came closer to the final casualty report than the army's report at the time. However, news reporting rests so often upon the intermediate source rather than first-hand information that allowance must be made, in battle accounts written on the spot, for inaccuracy on the part of officers who provided information during the stress of continuing combat.

The violence of the reporters' reaction to the first peace commission presents the Modoc War in a light different from most secondary accounts, except Bancroft's. The reporters' reactions probably were made more violent than they would have been had not the Peace Commission appeared to them as deliberately obstructing the press in its access to information. Personality conflicts, especially with Meacham, also appear to have colored the news reports. Since the reports of commission activities were toned down considerably after the appointment of the second peace commission, which coincided roughly with Bogart's departure, the question arises whether Bogart might not have been a trouble-maker, transferring to the other reporters some of his animus, but the available evidence does not supply an answer to the question.

Very often, one asks, "Where did the reporters get that information?" Unfortunately, the accounts—written in a news style quite different from modern style—do not indicate sources clearly. Nevertheless, the construction of the stories, when they are read as a group, leads to the guess that Fairchild supplied the reporters with much of their information, especially on the background of the Indians and the personality of Oregon Indian agents. In this respect, the reporters sometimes appear to be vulnerable, especially in instances like Atwell's contemptuous dismissal of Dyar, since he gives no indication whatever that he had ever known him, but on the contrary, leaves the impression that his information was second-hand. The influence of the military upon the reporters is obvious, and—parenthetically—the Modoc War correspondents were as one with their colleagues of other campaigns in the respect and admiration they showed for the American soldier, especially the officers of the Old Army. Frequently, the reporters used terms which showed their stories were based upon information obtained from officers, even when the accounts were not so attributed. Two cases in point can be taken from the assault phase of military operations in April. Gillem had wired Schofield that no Modoc would be left alive to boast that he had killed Canby or Thomas, and those words showed up in the news stories. Similarly, Gillem said the attack on Boyle's camp on April 11 indicated a preconcerted plan to capture the commanding officers, and the reporters also used the word "preconcerted." It would be naïve, however, to suppose that the newsmen's phraseology always followed the lead of the officer. There appears to have been considerable freedom of communication within the camp, and the exchanges of information between officers and reporters may well have given the reporting officer an apt expression as phrased by a reporter. Officers also may have given the reporters some of the information about the Indians and Indian agents.

Irony touched Atwell, who, alone among the correspondents, covered the entire story from February through October. In fact, hard luck dogged him. On the final major story of the war, an accident threw him behind the opposition in reporting Captain Jack's capture. Later, a drunken courier placed him behind in reporting the hanging. And then came the final ironic touch. Traveling south from Yreka after the hanging, he rode a stagecoach that was held up. The highwaymen got approximately $4,000 from the other passengers and the strongbox, but Atwell had only "two bits." When he told the robbers he was broke and a long way from home, they let him keep the change.[56]

[56] *Yreka Journal*, Oct. 15, 1873.

5. CROOK FIGHTS SIOUX AT ROSEBUD

> *I insisted that I was going in to fight.*
> *. . . It was my business as a correspon-*
> *dent to get the news, and I couldnt*
> *think of getting it from the rear.*
> ROBERT E. STRAHORN[1]

CITY EDITOR Clinton Snowden singled out lanky, red-faced John F. Finerty as the man to cover the Sioux campaign of 1876 for the *Chicago Times*. White-bearded Wilbur Storey had made the *Chicago Times* one of the great newspapers of its day. Holding himself aloof from his staff other than departmental heads, he treated subordinates with asperity, once firing a man who wore creaking boots because the noise disturbed the other men at work in the editorial room. As an editor he was ahead of his time in developing the newspaper as an organ for printing the news and in publishing a newspaper more nearly akin to today's papers than most of its contemporaries. Continuing the forthright individualism that got him into trouble with the authorities during the Civil War, he sent a correspondent to cover the Franco-Prussian War in 1870 and established a London bureau to cable general news, other than just war news. At home he developed a city staff of educated, traveled, and qualified writers. Among that group Finerty stood out, a younger colleague recalling, "It seemed to me, he possessed the widest sweep of classical and

---

[1] Robert E. Strahorn, "Ninety Years of Boyhood," unpublished autobiography, Strahorn Memorial Library, College of Idaho, 124, hereafter cited as Strahorn, Autobiography.

medieval lore and history of all the men of that remarkable news force."[2]

Early in May, Snowden told Finerty that Storey wanted a man to accompany an expedition that soon would take the field against the Sioux. "There is apt to be warm work out there with the Indians," Snowden said, "so if you don't care to go, you needn't see Mr. Storey."

"I care to go, and I'll see Mr. Storey," Finerty replied.[3]

Finerty went in to see Storey, who informed him that he would go with Crook. Finerty objected, saying he had understood he would accompany Custer, whom he knew. Brusquely, Storey told him Crook; Crook was expected to do the hard work of the campaign; Custer was not even in command.

In the nine years since he had undertaken the Oregon campaign, George Crook had built a reputation among both Indians and whites and had been promoted to brigadier general. After quelling the hostile Indians of Oregon and northern California, he had whipped the Apaches in Arizona, earning from them the nickname "Nan-tan Lupan," meaning Chief Gray Wolf. General Sherman came to call him the best Indian fighter in the United States Army. After his service in Arizona, Crook had been transferred in April, 1875, to command of the Department of the Platte, with headquarters in Omaha, which stretched from the Missouri River to Great Salt Lake. It was that command which placed him in the 1876 campaign against the Sioux and Northern Cheyennes.

Various strands complicated the cause of the Sioux war, but in essence it was a war of aggression, by which the United States took what it could not buy. The treaty of 1868 had barred whites from the Black Hills, the sacred Pa-Sapa of the Sioux, and from the entire area north of the North Platte between the Black Hills and the Big Horn Mountains. Most of the Sioux had moved to reservations, but irreconcilables con-

[2] Charles Sanford Diehl, *The Staff Correspondent,* 54–55, 58, 71–72; Franc B. Wilkie, *Personal Reminiscences of Thirty-five Years of Journalism.*
[3] Finerty, *War-Path and Bivouac,* 25.

General George Crook's Infantry in the Black Hills, 1876.
From a Photograph by S. J. Morrow, Deadwood.

Horse Travois Carrying Casualty after the Battle of Slim Buttes, September 9, 1876. From a Photograph by S. J. Morrow, Deadwood.

tinued to roam the Sioux homeland, insisting upon expulsion of whites under the treaty. That became exceedingly difficult after Custer's expedition of 1874 found gold in the Black Hills.

White adventurers streamed into the Hills in spite of Indian reprisals and despite army efforts to intercept and expel them. In the fall of 1875 the government tried to buy the Black Hills, but the Sioux spurned the offer. With the 1876 presidential election near and with the effects of the Panic of 1873 still pinching the nation, President Grant opened the Black Hills to white miners by subterfuge. At a small conference on November 3, he had confidential orders issued to the army not to hinder whites in reaching the Black Hills. Six days later an Indian inspector, a political appointee, recommended that the army conduct a winter campaign to drive in the Sioux who were still out. Some Northern Cheyennes also were with the wild Sioux. This recommendation, however, was modified to the extent that the Indians were given until January 31, 1876, to move to a reservation or be turned over to the army. Because of difficult traveling in the winter, the Sioux could not have complied with that ultimatum even had they been of a mind to do so, as most were not, although at least one small band did try to come in. The dead line came and passed.

Crook was the first to go into action, sending a column northward in March, 1876, which struck an Indian village— assumed at the time to be that of the Sioux leader, Crazy Horse, but actually that of a Cheyenne band. Although much of the Indian possessions were destroyed, most of the Indians fled to Crazy Horse farther north.

Sheridan, commanding the Military Division of the Missouri from Chicago, decided to use his favorite tactic—three converging columns. Brigadier General Alfred Terry, commanding the Department of Dakota, headquarters in St. Paul, would lead about 1,000 men westward from Fort Abraham Lincoln, near Bismarck, North Dakota. Colonel John Gibbon, with about 450 men, would move eastward from the Montana posts and join Terry. Crook would move northward from

Fort Fetterman with another 1,000 men. They were to converge in the region of the Big Horn and Yellowstone rivers, although Sheridan did not expect Crook and Terry to operate in conjunction. Up to that time the army knew only from Indian agents that the strength of the hostile Indians would be about 500 warriors. That was one of the great understatements of American history, for the Sioux and Northern Cheyennes gathered in one of the greatest encampments they had ever known, possibly the largest, and could place several thousand mounted warriors in the field at one time and one place. They were capable of consolidating against each of the smaller army columns and crushing them in detail. Once in the field, even though they were less than 100 miles apart, Crook and Terry could communicate only by a 2,000-mile line around the rear.

Throughout all the correspondence between the War and Interior departments and their subagencies during the period of preliminaries, the name of Sitting Bull appeared regularly as the one hostile leader who had to be whipped. The government letter writers, whose decisions were made public, created the image of Sitting Bull as the enemy Sioux general.[4]

After receiving instructions from Storey, Finerty drew expense money from the business office, bought weapons and riding clothes, and called on Sheridan for a letter of introduction to Crook. Sheridan warned him Crook would be a hard campaigner. Telling his friends good-bye, Finerty boarded a train and rode out of Chicago in a driving rainstorm on May 6. The next day he stopped in Omaha to meet Crook, an athletic man of forty-eight with close-cropped hair and a blonde beard, dressed in mufti. In a good-humored conversation, Crook inquired about Finerty's marksmanship, which was good enough to hit a haystack at close distance, and advised him, "We'll have some tough times, I think." Finerty went on to Cheyenne by rail. At near-by Fort D. A. Russell he made arrangements to mess with Captain Alexander Sutorius of the

[4] 44 Cong., 1 sess., *House Ex. Doc. 184.*

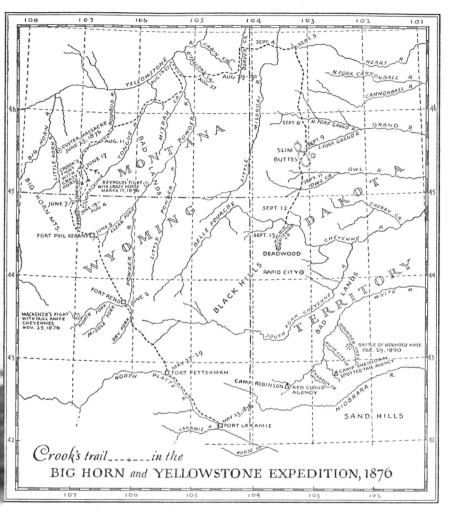

Crook's trail _ _ _ _ _ _ _ _ _ _ in the
BIG HORN and YELLOWSTONE EXPEDITION, 1876

From *General George Crook: His Autobiography*

Third Cavalry during the campaign, and met Colonel J. J. Reynolds, commanding the post, who advised the greenhorn war correspondent, "Never stray far from the main column, and never trust a horse or an Indian."[5]

The troops from Fort Russell formed one wing of the expedition. The other wing would move north from Medicine Bow, farther west on the Union Pacific. Both would unite at Fort Fetterman on the North Platte, under Crook. The Fort Russell contingent, including several companies of cavalry, a few of infantry, and a great part of the wagon and mule train equipment, ultimately went north by way of Fort Laramie, where they could cross the North Platte on an iron bridge and avoid the risk of a ferry crossing of the flooded river at Fort Fetterman.

With several days to wait before the column moved out, Finerty visited old friends in Cheyenne, buying a horse in the meantime. Cheyenne he found to be "a quiet kind of hell," with gamblers and harlots flourishing. Applying an Old Country description to western lawmen, he wrote, "Half a dozen Peelers suffice to keep peoples' throats from being cut." On the crowded streets he was jostled by scouts, miners, Mexicans, and troopers. Listening to them, he decided public attention was focused on Crook's forthcoming expedition, with every day bringing word of another Sioux attack on miners. Although personally unwilling to believe all the claims made for the Black Hills, he observed that "it is rank treason in Cheyenne to say aught against the Black Hills country," for the mining fever fattened the merchants.[6] Finerty received word that the main body from Fort Russell would leave on May 17, but "his" company, Company E, Third Cavalry, would ride two days later as escort for Colonel W. B. Royall, commanding.

During his final stay in Cheyenne he met T. C. MacMillan, who had just arrived to cover the campaign for the *Chicago Inter-Ocean*. MacMillan, too, arranged to mess with Sutorius.

[5] Finerty, *War-Path and Bivouac*, 26–35.
[6] *Ibid.; Chicago Times*, May 15, 16, 1876.

Since the newcomer had to buy a horse and some equipment, he and Finerty decided not to leave with the troops at day-break on May 19, but to mount and equip MacMillan and then follow the troops. After the *Inter-Ocean* man completed his purchases, they set out for Lodge Pole Creek, eighteen miles distant, accompanied part way by Sheriff George O'Brien. They went the rest of the way alone to Lodge Pole Creek, an area struck only a few days later by a flying party of Sioux raiders. There they rode, a Scot and an Irishman, commissioned to inform the American public of a military campaign against aborigines.

Reaching the army camp shortly before sundown, they took some kidding as they began their western campaigning; Captain Elijah Wells of the Second Cavalry said that by having their hair cut, they were cheating the Sioux out of their scalps. Sleeping in Sutorius' tent, Finerty heard occasionally through the night MacMillan's "eternal cough."[7]

The next day, Finerty, MacMillan, and a third correspondent with Royall—R. B. Davenport, *New York Herald*—learned what it was like to ride with a combat command in the Old West. His throat dried out by the alkaline dust scuffed up by the horses, Finerty drained his canteen and suffered from thirst afterward. Sutorius taught him to place a small pebble in his mouth as a relief from thirst. At the end of another day's marching, a tired and hungry Finerty could not wait for supper. He ate some raw bacon and hardtack and fell asleep on a horse blanket beneath a tree. A poke in the ribs awakened him to share a cooked meal then being served in the Captain's tent.

For men accustomed to city cushions, forking a horse proved a strain. On the second day out, a stiff Finerty was "devoutly grateful" for every halt. He seems to have bought an "American horse," as they were called in the West, but MacMillan had been bilked into buying a broncho. The bron-

[7] Finerty, *War-Path and Bivouac*, 45–47. Much of Finerty's book is composed of his newspaper dispatches, edited to provide a more continuous narrative.

cho, or mustang, was fine for a western man, especially since it could live on grass, whereas the American horse had to have grain, but not for a newcomer. As Finerty expressed it, bronchos, which had to be broken afresh every morning, "are simply virile mules, and life is too short to undertake their education."[8]

MacMillan at least found humor in his daily contest with a bucking broncho. In his words:

Ah! the tractable disposition of such a steed! Every morning we take an hour's exercise before starting on our journey. It seems a matter of fun to the pony, this hour of exercise. He usually rises with the sun, and, if you want to go West that day, he is kind to take you the other way. We shuffle off blankets at 4 o'clock every morning. This is one of the luxuries of the march. From 5 to 6 o'clock the pony and myself have gymnastics together, that is, he is the performer, and I am—sometimes another. We are ready to mount. There is a plunge. You think it is fun. The reins are tightened and your feet dive into the stirrups as if you were looking in your boots for the latest coinage of the "three silver pieces in a dollar." As your feet touch the fiery untamed, the pony remembers what you have forgotten. The spurs you wear are sharp and wonderfully ticklish. He dashes away at top speed to come to a sudden standstill. This is to try your powers of playing leapfrog over his ears. When he finds that putting on brakes doesn't make you bite the dust, he changes his cavalry tactics. He stands on his head. Then it grows exciting. Tooth, mane and narrative are subsidized to retain position. What makes it worse is that everybody is looking at you and enjoying the joke. Some campfollower (the miserable fellow) cries out, "This way to the hippodrome, ladies and gentlemen, and see the marvelous feats of the champion bareback rider of the wor-r-rld!" This decides you. If it moves heaven and earth you will break in that broncho—or yourself. The pony rights himself again, and you think that he is tamed. Alas! he will only be quiet in the form of Spaulding's glue. Never, while he has a leg at each corner and a head at the end. You are just well seated when he rears and is pawing the air. His neck is wide

[8] *Ibid.; Chicago Times,* May 31, 1876.

enough for your arms, and the plan succeeds. Once more he assumes his natural attitude, and now, surely, you can believe that you have neither lived nor labored in vain and for nothing. . . . he enters into a foul horse-conspiracy with a vicious, kicking mule of the wagon train. One takes you near enough, and the other tries to keel you off. A twist of the bridle gives your broncho the blow intended for yourself, and now, indeed, you feel that broncho-brain has exhausted itself in its efforts to shuffle off its mortal coil. . . . By sheer cussedness the pony brushes you off. You are forced to get your feet out of the stirrups or be crushed by the diminutive bit of horseflesh which you bought because they had "bottom" to them, and would wear out any American mule (or man) in the outfit. You want to find the man you hate most, and give him the broncho . . . you purchase a brace of pistols and carry them day and night to shoot the man who sold you the gentle, easy-riding, strong, perfect, grass-fed broncho that has scarcely ever been ridden much, but is just the animal for such a trip among the mountains.[9]

Davenport did not dramatize his discomforts as much as Finerty and MacMillan, but welcomed just as much as they a day's enforced stay in camp on the Chugwater because of rain. With rain pattering on canvas, he snuggled in his blankets with a single-minded determination to get comfortable. Finerty and MacMillan more than welcomed the day in camp, because both were "exceedingly fatigued" after three days in the saddle. The day itself was pleasant enough; the officers relaxed their military reserve, visited back and forth, exchanged cigars, and drank. Nevertheless, the "shivering correspondents damn the weather, the mud, and themselves, and begin to look upon 'glory' with jaundiced eyes."[10]

During the march they met parties of had-been miners returning from the Black Hills, chased out by the threat of the scalping knife (and no luck). A sharp-tongued soldier taunted one group by asking, "So you've turned tender-feet, 'ave ye?"

[9] *Chicago Inter-Ocean*, June 7, 1876.

[10] *New York Herald*, June 9, 1876; Finerty, *War-Path and Bivouac*, 50–51; *Chicago Times*, May 31, 1876.

167

His comrades thought that marvellously funny, and the next day that same taunt, all down the line, greeted other returning wealth-seekers.[11]

When the column went into camp across the river from Fort Fetterman on May 27, the correspondents—as Finerty embellished it—had to take their lives in their hands in getting their dispatches to a telegrapher. They were told the ferry to Fort Fetterman, which lay on the south side of the swollen Platte, had broken down; but they found it had been patched up and decided to try it. Unless they reached the fort, they could neither mail nor telegraph their stories, nor receive any mail that might have been addressed to them there. They boarded the ferry, went out into the stream, and had almost reached the south bank when the rope broke. The rapid current swept the craft downstream. They were saved from possible drowning, Finerty said, by Lieutenant J. W. Bubb, Crook's commissary officer, who spurred his horse into the stream, caught a cable which was thrown to him from the ferry, and towed them to safety.

When the two wings of the expedition came together at Fort Fetterman, the full press corps of five correspondents was present for the first time. They were well fed, well clothed and well equipped on that May day as they started on campaign, but would be worn and hungry before it was all through. Their number included men of varying ages and personality, all with some experience in the West and some who had participated in other campaigns. Here they are:

Joe Wasson: Riding with Crook for the second time, he reported for the *New York Tribune, San Francisco Alta California,* and the *Philadelphia Press.* He reached Fort Fetterman either with the Medicine Bow column or with Crook, who had come by way of the Red Cloud Agency in Nebraska.

Since the end of the 1867 campaign in Oregon and California, he had continued to move around the West. He spent some time in California; founded the *Winnemucca Argent* as a Grant paper in Aurora, Nevada; with his brother John es-

[11] *New York Herald,* June 9, 1876.

tablished the *Arizona Citizen* in Tucson; returned to Nevada, where he published another Grant paper; and worked for a time in San Francisco. His time in Arizona overlapped Crook's tour there, bringing acquaintance with Crook's aide, Lieutenant John G. Bourke, who remembered him as a capable newsman who "approached every duty with the alertness and earnestness of a Scotch terrier."[12]

One observer on the campaign unabashedly called him "a genius" and "a clear able writer [who] gives you facts boiled down and in language that can be easily understood." A good-natured, affable man, he stood about five feet, nine, had a sandy complexion, light red hair and matching moustache, and gray eyes.[13]

Wasson's dispatches showed that he had changed considerably in the nine years since the battle of Infernal Caverns. For maturity he paid the price of spontaneity. Gone from his copy was the eclectic irreverence of Oregon; absent was the Rabelaisian quality suitable for Silver City but not for San Francisco, Philadelphia, or New York. Gone was the detailed reporting of long treks across sage flats. In their place appeared abbreviated, irregular dispatches which, as a whole, would not have told the whole story of the campaign. But still it was Wasson the gold-seeker. Even before the troops had all assembled at Fetterman, he wrote about the hopes and prospects of gold in the Big Horn Mountains, more tightly guarded by the Sioux than even the Black Hills.

Robert E. Strahorn: Writing under the pen name of "Alter Ego" for the *Rocky Mountain News*, Strahorn picked up other accounts for the Sioux war, including the *Chicago Tribune, Omaha Republican, Cheyenne Sun,* and *New York Times.* Then twenty-four, he was a solidly built man, also about five feet, nine inches in height, with black eyes, dark hair and whiskers, and regular features.

Finerty described Strahorn as "a distinguished Western

[12] Strahorn, Autobiography, 140; *The Publisher's Auxiliary,* Nov. 26, 1949; Bourke, *On the Border with Crook,* 94–95.
[13] *Rocky Mountain News,* Aug. 8, 1876.

newspaper correspondent," although he probably was hardly that at the time. Born in Center County, Pennsylvania, in 1852, he had been educated in the public schools and printing shops of Stephenson County, Illinois. As printer and writer he had been in the newspaper business since the age of fourteen. He went to Colorado in 1870, working as a printer at Central City and Black Hawk in 1871, later joining the staff of the *Rocky Mountain News.*

Strahorn was the one correspondent who remained with Crook winter and summer until Crazy Horse, a leader of the wild Sioux, surrendered. A personal friendship with Paymaster T. H. Stanton brought Strahorn an invitation to accompany Crook's campaign of the previous March against Crazy Horse. When the column commanded by Colonel J. J. Reynolds came in sight of the village and prepared for a surprise attack at dawn of St. Patrick's Day, Strahorn insisted upon riding to the charge with forty-seven men of the Egan Grays—Captain Teddy Egan's company of the Second Cavalry—who were almost cut off through faulty management of the battle when they dismounted to fight the Indians in the village.

Strahorn ruined his voice for life in that battle. The wild, full-throated yelling of the charge in weather 39 degrees below zero silenced him for several days after, and the voice strain of the moment interfered with his speech for the rest of his life; he usually lost his voice entirely during hard colds; never again could he give a lusty yell. Slight compensation though it might be, Reynolds mentioned him in his official report, the Secretary of War thanked him for his part, and he was commended for gallantry.

He remained with Crook, and in mid-May went with him to Red Cloud Agency in an unsuccessful effort to get Sioux scouts. On the way back, he gave an alarm which may have prevented Crook and his escort from being murdered by Agency Indians. He then rode to Fort Fetterman with the General, waiting for the rest of the troops to arrive.

During later life, when Strahorn retained close relations

with Crook, the reporter's wife remembered having heard the General say, "It mattered not what the coat was; Bob was every inch a soldier . . . and he never failed to work his rifle as well as his pen."[14]

Strahorn was not the only correspondent for the *Chicago Tribune* on the campaign. An infantry officer, Captain A. S. Burt, also wrote for the *Tribune* as well as for the *Cincinnati Commercial*. This sometimes results in difficulty in determining authorship, since only some of the stories were signed.

Thomas C. MacMillan: A twenty-five-year-old Scotsman, the *Chicago Inter-Ocean* correspondent was a slender, pale man of medium height, in poor health at the time. At that period his strong religious convictions, which in later life made him a lay leader of the Congregational church, also influenced his journalistic attitude, causing an observer to remark, "It is not believed that any inducement of possible gain to himself or the paper he represents could be strong enough to persuade him to write anything he does not believe to be true."[15]

Born in Scotland, MacMillan came to America at the age of seven with his parents. Attending Chicago schools, he suffered from poor health as a youngster. For a short time he studied at the University of Chicago, and then entered the newspaper business, becoming a reporter for the *Inter-Ocean* in 1873. A colleague once said that MacMillan was the best police reporter the *Inter-Ocean* ever had.[16]

The assignment to cover the Crook expedition marked his second trip into the West. During the previous summer he had accompanied the Jenney-Newton expedition to the Black

[14] *Ibid.;* Finerty, *War-Path and Bivouac,* 61–62; Carrie Adell Strahorn, *Fifteen Thousand Miles by Stage,* 2, 27, 30, 179, 540; Strahorn Folder, Elmo Scott Watson Papers, Newberry Library, Chicago (hereafter cited as Watson Papers); Strahorn, Autobiography, 116, 124, 128–29; Vestal, *New Sources of Indian History,* 179–80; Bourke, *On the Border with Crook,* 254, 259–64, 270–82; Report of Col. J. J. Reynolds, April 15, 1876, Letters Received, Adjutant General's Office, Civil War Branch, National Archives, 2732/12–AGO–1876.

[15] *Rocky Mountain News,* Aug. 8, 1876.

[16] MacMillan Folder, Watson Papers.

Hills, which confirmed the discovery of gold by miners with Custer's expedition of 1874.

Reuben Briggs Davenport: Davenport represented—indeed, he *represented*—the *New York Herald.* He had "New York Herald" on his bridle, blankets, haversack, and canteen, as a sarcastic observer wrote, adding, "He has not branded his horse '*Herald*,' but he has got him so he looks like a *Herald* horse." Also a man of middling height, perhaps a bit shorter than the others, he was light complexioned with black hair and whiskers and gray eyes.[17]

Davenport apparently suffered from personality difficulties. He came to criticize the command with carping severity, and in turn some of the officers remembered him in unflattering terms. As an avid questioner he made a nuisance of himself, becoming the butt of jokes by Plainsmen who told him exaggerated western stories and thought he swallowed them. His dispatches show, however, that he was a knowledgeable young writer. As the commentator on the correspondents remarked, Davenport was always "hungry" for news. "Whenever he talks with you, you are impressed with the fact that he is suffering for news, and if you fail to tell him anything out of which he can frame an item the look of disappointment that comes over his face is painful to behold. The temptation, therefore, to give Davenport news, though it is manufactured out of whole cloth, is very great, and the young men of the command have occasionally perpetrated 'whoppers' on him."[18]

Then twenty-four years old, he was a native New Yorker. He had been graduated from the College of the City of New York in 1871 and in the following year had become a member of the *Herald* staff.

He, too, had covered the Jenney-Newton expedition of 1875. His persistent questioning then had also caused officers and civilians to tell him some tall tales, but those yarns would seem to have been the dross extracted, for his stories show a sardonic, even supercilious, regard for many of the men he

[17] *Rocky Mountain News,* Aug. 8, 1876.
[18] *Ibid.*

met in the West. After the expedition, he rode alone through part of the Black Hills, a dangerous thing for anyone to do, in obeying a *Herald* order to cover the negotiations for purchase of the Black Hills. While reporting the negotiations, he interviewed the friendly Sioux chief Spotted Tail with the help of an interpreter, Louis Bordeaux, and then reported the interview in both Sioux (or what purported to be Sioux) and English. He explained in later years that the Oglala vernacular was slowly taken down by "a very intelligent half-breed interpreter," and was worked into the story, the first time any such thing had been done in a newspaper. "Of course," he wrote, "it had no special utility, and was only excusable as an effort to furnish the pale-face readers of the journal with a unique linguistic curiosity."[19]

John F. Finerty: ". . . the gem of the lot," as one officer of the command said of Finerty. Another observer wrote: "If Davenport is always hungry—for news—Finerty may be said to be always thirsty—for liquids and news, and he can hold any quantity of either. . . . when he writes about the troops being willing to storm the gates of hell he means it, and if they ever do so rash an act Finnerty [*sic*] will be there, and he won't be in the rear of the command either." The same observer said, however, "The *Times* must have news, and if there happens to be a dearth of incidents he invents them." His colleagues on the *Times* held him in high esteem. One recalled him as "one of the most valuable men on the *Times* . . . a reporter in city matters, a social writer, and a species of factotum."[20]

Then twenty-nine years old, Finerty had been in America only twelve years. The son of an Irish editor from whom he received a classical education, Finerty became an Irish rebel and fled his homeland. In America he remained a radical advocate of Irish independence. He had come to America in

[19] *New York Herald*, Aug. 26, 1875; *Hot Springs* (S. D.) *Times-Herald*, June 17, 1927.

[20] Charles A. King, *Campaigning with Crook*, 153; *Rocky Mountain News*, Aug. 8, 1876; Wilkie, *Personal Reminiscences*, 177–78.

1864, and served in the Ninety-fourth New York Regiment during the Civil War.

After the war, Finerty went to Chicago, where he worked first as a reporter and then as city editor of the *Chicago Republican* from 1868 to 1872. Until 1875 he wrote for the *Chicago Tribune*. The date of his affiliation with the *Times* is not known.[21]

Fort Fetterman was the jumping-off place for the Big Horn and Yellowstone Expedition, and its telegraph office was to be the point of contact for the correspondents. Situated near present Douglas, Wyoming, it was one of the larger western forts. There Crook concentrated his command of 47 officers and 1,002 soldiers. He had fifteen troops of cavalry from the Second and Third regiments and five companies of infantry from the Fourth and Ninth regiments. Colonel William B. Royall commanded the Third Cavalry and all the horse troops, and Colonel Alexander Chambers of the Fourth Infantry, the foot.

Crook had 100 wagons, but he made a pack train of 295 mules the heart of his transportation. His aide said that Crook had "made the study of pack trains the great study of his life." Whereas other large columns would flounder along with wagons, Crook could take his mules wherever he had to go and could diamond-hitch with the best packer. The mule trains of that era, incidentally, gave to army slang an enduring term—shave-tail. Green mules had their tails cut off so that the packers could recognize them instantly and were called shave-tails. Pack-train terms then came to be used to describe officers—shave-tail for young officers, bell-sharp for the experienced.[22]

The swinging route-step of the foot soldier paced the col-

[21] Diehl, *Staff Correspondent*, 71–72; Milo Milton Quaife's "Historical Introduction" to the Lakeside Classics edition of John F. Finerty's *War-Path and Bivouac* (Chicago, 1955), xl, xliv. This is not to be confused with the 1890 edition of *War-Path and Bivouac* cited in other footnotes.

[22] Bourke, *On the Border with Crook*, 150–54; *Chicago Tribune*, July 5, 1876.

umn into motion on May 29, and the long line of men, wagons, and mules stretched out for four miles. Behind the infantry lumbered the one hundred wagons, each pulled by six mules, with their white canvas covers bobbing over the rough ground. Behind the wagons rode the fifteen cavalry companies, in column of twos, with just enough interval between companies to mark the commands. Striding afoot into Sioux country that summer, the infantry—known by the Indians as "walk-a-heaps"—wore a new type of shoe, and soon let the Inspector General know they didn't like it. The soles were fastened to the uppers with oval brass screws which worked through the soles and gouged into the soldiers' feet on the march. Most of the soldiers were young men—Irish and Germans mostly, but Anglo-Saxons were noticeable especially among the noncommissioned officers.

Their first destination was old Fort Reno, where Crook expected to meet a contingent of Crow scouts. With him, the principle of using Indians to hunt Indians was fundamental; he had followed it in both the Northwest and Arizona. But when they reached the site of the former fort at the end of a four-day march, they found no Crows. At the site of the fort, which the Sioux had burned after the army withdrew in accordance with the terms of the 1868 treaty, Wasson, Davenport, and Bourke looked over the cemetery, where lay buried men who had died in the service of their country. They found not a headboard standing.

Moving northward along the old Bozeman Trail toward old Fort Phil Kearney, the correspondents by then had settled into the routine of march life. In camp they shared wall tents with officers. Finerty and MacMillan messed with Captain Sutorius of the Third Cavalry. Strahorn, crowded out of Crook's mess when two new aides were appointed, ate with Chambers of the infantry. Wasson's mess perhaps was with Crook, and Davenport ate with Royall or other officers in the cavalry command.

Around the campfire at night, men asked the question that was on the mind of most—where were the Sioux? Never mind, a seasoned troop commander of the Second Cavalry would tell them, the Sioux would come when the troops least expected them.

On the march one day Strahorn rode out on the right flank, just out of sight of the troops. When he came upon a covey of grouse, the temptation was too great for him to abide by the strict orders that had been issued against firing. After shooting two grouse, he hid them in his raincoat on the saddle. His shots had been heard, and skirmishers, quickly thrown out in that direction, found him and hustled him to Chambers.

"Mr. Strahorn," the Colonel asked sternly, "did you do that firing?"

When Strahorn admitted it, Chambers asked, "At Indians, or what?"

Strahorn said he had shot at grouse, explaining, "I was so hungry for grouse that I just couldn't help it; so I am ready to pay the penalty. What is it?"

Since they were in the same mess, the Colonel commented quietly, "Well, it will make a damn sight of difference whether you got a grouse."[23]

Arrival at the site of former Fort Phil Kearney gave the correspondents occasion to review its history and the Fetterman massacre. Finerty reported what he had heard in idle hour conversation—the story that the first Mrs. Carrington had forced Colonel Carrington to establish the fort there by refusing to go any farther, and that the lady who became the second Mrs. Carrington, at that time the widow of an officer killed in the Fetterman incident, had berated Carrington for the disaster. "Thus, you see," Finerty commented, "military heroes, the chivalry of the land, as it were, can gossip about as much as the members of a Massachusetts sewing-circle."[24]

When Crook went into camp on the Tongue River on June 7, his troops began the army guessing game. "We all put this up as the permanent camp; but nobody knows but Gen.

[23] Strahorn, Autobiography, 141. The text does not make clear the exact period of the campaign when this occurred.
[24] *Chicago Times*, July 1, 1876; San Francisco *Alta California*, July 6, 1876.

Sitting Bull.

Sitting Bull's Camp in the Big Horn Mountains, 1873. From a Painting by Henry A. Cross.

Crook, and he won't tell," one writer remarked. "The General doesn't make any confidants."[25]

Crook encamped at the Tongue to wait for the Crows—for whom two scouts, Frank Grouard and Louis Richaud, had been sent—and on the first night in camp an incident occurred that gave cause for apprehension for their safety. About midnight some figures appeared on the bluffs opposite the camp and yelled at the soldiers. A half-blood answered in Sioux. The visitors asked whether the Crows had yet arrived, and the soldiers interpreted the question as mockery by Sioux visitors who knew what had happened to the Crow allies.

During the next two days of waiting, the troops started rumor going. The night visit by Indians "swelled into gigantic proportions." And the story went the rounds that the Sioux had spies among the packers, many of whom were half-bloods. However, neither Crook nor Royall placed any stock in the rumors.[26]

Sioux attacked the camp late on the afternoon of June 9. Cavalry troopers had just brought in their mounts from grazing and were grooming them on the line when a band of Sioux—estimated at from fifty to two hundred—made a surprise attack. They were detected by infantry pickets. Crook ordered a squadron of the Third Cavalry, under Colonel Anson Mills, the man who later patented the web equipment used by U. S. troops, to dislodge the Indians from the bluff from which they were firing into the camp.

Finerty rode into action with the troopers. He took his place at the head of the column, carbine on pommel, pipe stuck in his mouth, and in shirt sleeves. "Hell appeared to have broken loose in the bluffs and all around the north side of the camp," Finerty reported. He splashed through the Tongue, dismounted, and climbed the steep and slippery bluff with the cavalrymen. Once atop the bluff, they saw the Indians hightailing it, although the savages paused to fire at them. The soldiers returned the fire. By that time the Indians had re-

[25] *Chicago Tribune,* July 5, 1876.
[26] *Chicago Times,* July 1, 1876.

tired to a ridge farther back, where they could have been reached only by cannon. The cavalrymen could not carry the attack farther with any good effect, because of broken and rocky ground between them and the Indians. Finerty borrowed a field glass to look at the Indians who were prancing around to display their horsemanship. "Not more than a dozen were in view," Finerty reported, "although at least 50 must have fired upon us in the first place. Those that I saw were dressed in a variety of costume. One fellow wore what seemed to be a tin helmet, with a horsehair plume. Another chap wore a 'war bonnet,' but most of them had the usual eagle feathers. To say the truth, they did not seem very badly scared, although they got out of the way with much celerity when they saw us coming in force."[27]

The next day Crook decided to move his camp eleven miles back to Goose Creek, which was done on June 11, and from that point the correspondents sent in their stories of the attack at the Tongue. The courier was to be one Ben Arnold, a frontiersman who had been engaged by Major George M. Randall, chief of scouts, for messenger service. Before Arnold left, Davenport called him over and told him to deliver the press dispatches first and the government dispatches later.

Leaving camp at night, so that he could travel in the dark and hide by day, he rode until dawn, when he smelled the odor of a campfire. From a concealed point on a ridge, he saw a small party of Indians half a mile away. His horse and an Indian pony chose that moment to nicker to each other, and then there was the devil to pay. Arnold ran to his horse and had just remounted when he saw three Indians coming on him at a gallop. He outdistanced them up a ridge, dismounted, and opened fire with a repeating rifle. He killed two Indian ponies, setting their riders afoot, and the third Indian scampered out of sight. Arnold put as much distance between himself and the Indians as he could, and then hid for the day in

[27] *Ibid.; Rocky Mountain News*, Aug. 8, 1876; Bourke, *On the Border with Crook*, 296.

a brush thicket on one of the branches of Powder River. Continuing his journey of almost two hundred miles, he reached Fort Fetterman the third night out and awakened the telegrapher, to whom he handed the press dispatches. "Two and a half hours later I turned in the government dispatches. I did not question why I was so instructed; I did as I was told to do, and there my duty ended. New York City, Chicago, Omaha, and other cities had sent out newspaper correspondents to cover this campaign, and each of them sent dispatches and news letters back by me. I received $250 for the trip," he said later.[28]

Crook's new bivouac was on Goose Creek, a clear mountain stream, two branches of which flowed around the camp. Finerty thought the "absolutely delightful" place equal to the finest sections along the Hudson River. Strahorn's stay there led to establishment of a large ranch in the vicinity: some years later he was asked if he could recommend one place above all others for a ranch, and he directed the inquirer to the Goose Creek section.

It also was described as a "royal place" for the correspondents, who could have a courier to Fort Fetterman about once every ten days. Ordinarily, the correspondents used the regular government courier, but when they had a story—such as the battle story yet to be written—they could employ their own couriers, from the group collected by Randall, to take the story to the Fort Fetterman telegraph operator. In that case, each courier was expected to leave as soon as the reporter could write his story and make the 190 miles in forty to fifty hours, riding one horse and leading a remount; couriers for the government could take an extra twenty-four hours. Approximately $200 was the usual price for a trip by a government courier, but the correspondents, it was said, had to pay $300 to $500 if they wanted the rider to make the addi-

[28] Lewis F. Crawford, *Rekindling Camp Fires: The Exploits of Ben Arnold (Connor)*, 236. Arnold said that he was given these instructions by "Captain Davenport." There was no officer by that name, but the instructions are in keeping with reporter Davenport's methods.

tional haste through a country in which he might face ambush and death.[29]

While the soldiers were waiting for the Crows, the great object of life became to kill time pleasantly; and to while away the hours, Wasson and Bourke agreed to read a Shakespeare play or a Macaulay essay each day and discuss it. Much time was spent on the stream by "trout maniacs"; others read and wrote; packers ran foot races with "jawbone" and "wind" bets of five and ten thousand dollars, although only small coin actually changed hands. Lieutenant A. H. Von Luettwitz, a German officer, made his comrades laugh with a ballad of lamentation, rendered in broken English, the chorus of which ran, "Crows, dear Crows, vere the devil you are?"[30]

In the meantime, Crook received intelligence via Fort Fetterman that approximately three thousand Sioux warriors had left the agencies to join Crazy Horse in the field. He learned also that the Fifth Cavalry would come forward to reinforce him. But concerning Crook's plans, his officers and the correspondents remained in the dark. As one writer expressed it, "Everybody again supposes that we are to leave the infantry and wagon-train here, and start out with pack-mules; but nobody knows anything about it but Gen. Crook, and he has a faculty for silence that is absolutely astonishing. There is one thing very certain; none of the General's plans will ever be discussed until after they are executed,—a priceless quality in a commanding officer. Grant is loquacious when compared with him."[31] All the correspondents could do was just what the troops did: sit, fish, talk, wonder, and wait.

Ennui evaporated in a trice and excitement rippled through camp when the Crows arrived on June 14. Grouard and Richaud (whose name appears variously as Reshaw, Richard, and Richards) came in with the Crows late in the afternoon, and a group of Snakes arrived about two hours later. While

[29] Strahorn, Autobiography, 144; Rocky Mountain News, July 11, 1876.
[30] Bourke, On the Border with Crook, 297–99; Finerty, War-Path and Bivouac, 75.
[31] Chicago Tribune, July 5, 1876.

the number of Indian auxiliaries varies among the different accounts, both Finerty and Davenport reported 180 in the first group to arrive and 86 in the second, although Finerty called both groups Crows. In honor of the occasion, Crook formed his troops in regimental front to receive the allies on a flat now covered by the northern end of Sheridan. With the fifteen cavalry companies in close order, stirrup touching stirrup, and the five infantry companies in double column, the regimental front extended almost one mile in length. Crook feasted the Indians and held a pow-wow with them, learning that the Sioux held Gibbon at bay on the Yellowstone, that the main body of the Sioux were on Tongue River, and that Crazy Horse was thought to be on the Tongue. "All during the night they kept up a fearful racket, beating their tom-toms, and howling in a manner calculated to aggravate the most even-tempered individual, provided he wanted to sleep," one writer observed. Finerty was more succinct: "Their music is fitter for hell than for earth."[32]

Finerty interviewed Grouard, repeating the story that Grouard consistently told of his parentage, that he was half French and half Polynesian. In fact, the Sandwich Islander version of Grouard's life, in which he came to live with the Indians after being captured by them as a boy, seems to have prevailed among contemporaries, although there is evidence that Grouard may have been born half Indian and half Negro in the Missouri River country. At any rate, Finerty got from Grouard a story of his adventures in reaching the Crows; Grouard said that the Crows had attacked his small party in the belief they were Sioux. When Grouard arrived, the troops learned that the Indians who spoke to the camp from the bluffs on June 7 had been Crows who feared they had stumbled on a Sioux encampment.

Crook was "bristling for a fight," and made immediate preparations to take the field. The following day was spent in getting ready. The wagons were to be left where they were, and the column was to be entirely mounted. Each man was

[32] *Ibid.; Chicago Times,* July 1, 1876.

to carry four days' rations, one hundred rounds of ammunition and one blanket. The big show of the day came when two hundred infantrymen were detailed to be mounted on mules for the trip. Strahorn enjoyed the performance, as did the others, when the doughboys who didn't know how to ride climbed aboard mules that had never been ridden. "No circus ever furnished a better show," Strahorn recalled.[33] But by end of day the infantrymen and mules had reached an understanding, and on the morrow they would be cavalry.

"We expect," said a diarist in the *Chicago Tribune*, "to have the biggest Indian fight, about the 18th, that has ever taken place west of the Mississippi, and finally settle the business for the Sioux nation, or else—"[34]

Reveille at 3:30 A.M. on June 16 awakened the strongest Regular Army force ever sent against the Sioux—approximately 1,300 men, including Indian auxiliaries and 20 packers who were going along to fight. Before leaving, the correspondents followed the example of many soldiers by placing dried elk meat in their saddle pouches to augment the limited four-day ration of hard bread, coffee, and bacon. The Snakes impressed Davenport with their particolored blankets, white or pinto ponies whose tails and manes were daubed with red or orange paint, and coup sticks which he called long white wands.

An accident befell Strahorn during the advance. At the beginning of a shower, the men put on light rubber raincoats strapped to their saddles, but without dismounting or reining up. "While my arms were helplessly entangled in the garment," he said, "the flapping of its ample folds scared my horse and he bucked me off ingloriously into the midst of the headquarters staff, with one foot, however, still clinging to the stirrup. Then, with increasing fright, he started to run, bucking and kicking, dragging me face downward through a patch of thickly growing prickly pear and cactus. General Crook and the others, with about a company of cavalry, finally

---

[33] Strahorn, Autobiography, 148.
[34] *Chicago Tribune*, July 5, 1876.

surrounded and rescued us. When I was picked up it was found that my face and arms, which were dragged over the prickly pear, were as full of the sharp barbed thorns as the quills on the fretful porcupine. It took me weeks, with all the help of the surgeons, very painfully to extract those barbs whose sharp spearlike forms drew them persistently inward. Needless to say, with such utter discomfort, I was in good mood for an Indian fight or any other distracting adventure."[35]

Finerty also had a narrow escape. While he was remounting after a halt, the muzzle of his carbine struck the hammer of his revolver, which had been left down on a cartridge. "An explosion followed. I felt as if somebody had hit me a vigorous blow with a stick on the right rear of my pantaloons, and my horse . . . reeled under the shock." A cavalry officer, Captain Guy V. Henry, came galloping back to inquire if Finerty were hurt. "Is the bullet in your person?" Henry asked.

"I don't know," Finerty replied.

Vastly amused by the Irishman's indecision, Henry replied, "Then, by Jove, it is about time you found out," and rode away laughing. The joke speedily went through the ranks.[36]

During the day, scouts reported the column was on the trail of a large force of Indians. While a picked force of Snakes and Crows went forward to reconnoiter, other Indians hurriedly put on war-paint, went into a war dance, and galloped back and forth until they were frenzied and their ponies lathered. Strahorn asked Grouard what the galloping was all about, and the scout, who had once lived with Sitting Bull, replied, "Oh, they are only making brave; that all stops when we get into a fight."[37]

They camped for the night in an amphitheater in the valley of the Rosebud, in southern Montana. Having left their tents behind, they slept on the ground, forming a circle around their animals to guard against stampede by the Sioux. The last words Finerty heard that night were spoken by Captain

[35] Strahorn, Autobiography, 149.
[36] Finerty, War-Path and Bivouac, 115–16.
[37] Strahorn, Autobiography, 149–50.

Sutorius, who slept next to him: "We will have a fight to-morrow, mark my words—I feel it in the air."[38]

Everyone was awake and up shortly before dawn the next morning, June 17. The brave Indian allies of the day before had become strangely reluctant, and had to be prodded into activity by the scouts. Crook permitted the men to build small cooking fires for coffee. Soldiers joked in low voices, borrowed and lent chews of tobacco. Some caught a few extra winks while holding to the pommel after their horses were saddled. Then the troops moved out, the infantry advancing first on their mules, and marched until 8:00 A.M., when they halted in another part of the Rosebud valley, where wild roses grew in profusion, in a country green with pine and sweet grass.

During this halt the troops unsaddled, and Finerty lay down on the ground, resting his head on his saddle. Sutorius and Von Luettwitz sat near him, talking. In such circumstances John F. Finerty, who came to be known as the "Fighting Irish Pencil Pusher" and later as dean of Indian war correspondents, found himself in his first Indian battle, for gunfire broke Finerty's repose. About twenty Indian scouts galloped into view on a crest to the north, and Mills, without waiting for further orders, told his squadron to saddle up. Shortly after, "panic stricken" Crows and Snakes dashed into camp, shouting, "Heap Sioux! Heap Sioux!" Behind them were seen Sioux in large force.

"How do you feel about it, eh?" Sutorius asked Finerty.

"It is the anniversary of Bunker Hill," Finerty said he replied. "The day is of good omen."[39]

Too well disciplined to cheer, the troops waved their carbines to acknowledge Finerty's observation.

Thus began, from the point of view of one newspaper correspondent, the greatest Indian battle in United States history in terms of the number of fighting men engaged, although more Indians fought at the Little Big Horn. Crook had taken the field with Indian Bureau assurance that there were only

[38] Finerty, *War-Path and Bivouac*, 118–19.
[39] *Ibid.*, 123–24.

five hundred hostile Indians in the North, although other information available to him showed otherwise. He had started out to find and take by surprise what he assumed would be the main village of the wild Sioux. What he did not know was that the enemy had sought him and would fight on its own choice of ground. He also did not know that Crazy Horse was at the head of an attacking force at least as large as his and possibly larger. Army accounts, based on information obtained some months later from Crazy Horse, reported that Crazy Horse placed 1,500 warriors in the field and had 5,000 in reserve, which sounds ridiculous because no one Indian chief could have controlled that many individual fighters in battle. Even though the Sioux had turned to Crazy Horse as a new kind of leader in their hour of desperation, it would seem that the Indians, who usually fought as individuals rather than in military units, would have committed themselves against Crook's smaller force if there had been 6,500 of them. Another version, based upon Indian sources in part, does show, however, that Crazy Horse led about 1,000 warriors to battle and that others came up later.[40] Crook's total force numbered about 1,300, although the use of every fourth soldier as a horse-holder reduced the number of white and Indian effectives to about 1,000.

The battle lasted five or six hours.[41] The attack came from north of the Rosebud, and Crook moved his troops across the stream to meet it, leaving two dismounted companies to hold a high point south of the river. Sioux and Cheyenne warriors bore down upon the troops from all directions, including flank and rear, like a swirling, flooded river that has burst the levee. Crook attempted to fight in Civil War style, trying to form his troops in one line and expecting the Indians to do likewise. But he had at last encountered the disconcerting mobility of the Plains Indian.

The fight was not many minutes old before the army com-

[40] Bourke, *On the Border with Crook*, 311–18; Mari Sandoz, *Crazy Horse, the Strange Man of the Oglalas*, 315–19.

[41] This summary of the Battle of the Rosebud is based upon J. W. Vaughn, *With Crook at the Rosebud*, 47–67.

mand was split and divided, fighting three separate battles. Crook was in the center. Royall, with cavalry dismounted, fought on the left, out of sight of the commanding general. The two companies on the south bank fought separately.

Hour after hour of intermittent charge and counter-charge locked Sioux and soldier in brief deadly combats in ravines, on ridges, along crests, in timber, and across rocky ground. There seems to have been more galloping than shooting. During the fighting Crook decided to concentrate his command and move down the Rosebud to the hostile village which he thought was only about eight miles away. Mills with his cavalry complied with the order to join Crook at the center, but Royall could not. Royall had to fight every step of the way, and the way was blocked by yelling savages who made repeated efforts to capture his horses, held by horse-holders while the rest of the men fought dismounted. After a long period of fighting, Royall was able to join Crook, but only by running a gantlet of fire in a hollow where his men were virtually surrounded by warriors.

In the meantime, Crook had detached Mills and sent him down the valley of the Rosebud with orders to attack and hold the village until Crook could arrive with the entire command. At the head of eight companies of cavalry, Mills advanced down the narrow defile of the valley, a natural for ambuscade and massacre. Ultimately Crook realized the trap into which he had sent the cavalry. To call Mills back, Crook sent his aide, Captain Azor Nickerson, who galloped with a single orderly to carry the message down canyon. After he received the counterorder from the dust-grayed officer in buckskin, Mills defiled out of the canyon, rode westward, and took some of the Sioux in the rear, although most had begun to withdraw by then.

Early in the afternoon the Sioux and Cheyennes withdrew from the field, leaving it in possession of the soldiers. Why? An Indian historian explained, "They were tired and hungry, so they went home."[42]

[42] *Ibid.*, 147.

186

Crook, too, withdrew. Surprising the village was out of the question. His wounded needed attention, and he decided he needed reinforcements before he could deal with the mass of warriors confronting him, some of whom were armed with the most recent weapons. Army men often claimed that the Indians also had more reliable ammunition than they; a frequent complaint against carbine ammunition was that it jammed in the breech after five or six shots had been fired.

The correspondents were in the thick of the fighting. Davenport rode through the battle with Royall, Finerty and Mac-Millan with Mills. Strahorn stayed with Crook, as, presumably, did Wasson. Crook did not mention either of them in his cryptic summary report, but Royall and Mills mentioned the correspondents with them, in their more detailed individual reports. Finerty said the cough-racked MacMillan displayed marked gallantry through the day, and that the officers that night commended the courage of Wasson, Strahorn, and Davenport.[43]

Davenport did his share of the fighting during Royall's retreat under orders from the left to join Crook in the center. Moving back slowly with a skirmish line warding off the Sioux on their north, Royall's men bunched on a slope near an open hollow which they had to cross. But they were virtually surrounded by Sioux. Davenport had taken his place in the skirmish line in fighting to that position. An enfilading fire made the slope untenable, and the Sioux were swarming in to cut off the cavalrymen. Davenport saw "a swarm of Sioux" one thousand yards in his front, and heard their shots in the rear as they cut down the rear guard. With the one soldier attending him as an orderly, Davenport had with the others been pressed back on the slope. At that moment he had to decide whether to remain and cross the hollow with the battalion, which would make a larger target for the converging

[43] Reports of the Battle of the Rosebud, National Archives, Civil War Branch, Adjutant General's Office, Letters Received, 3994–AGO–1876; Vaughn, *With Crook at the Rosebud*, 237; Finerty, *War-Path and Bivouac*, 135.

Sioux, or ride pell-mell the half-mile to the hill occupied by Crook.

He chose the latter course, and galloped through ravines to reach the slope opposite the one he had left, although he did not make clear whether the orderly rode with him or had been left behind. As he went up the second slope, he heard "the yells of the savages close behind, and the reports of their rifles, as I emerged from the safer ground, sounded remarkably near and loud." Looking behind him, he saw a dozen Sioux surround a group of soldiers who had straggled behind in the retreat. He said six soldiers were killed in that one spot, including a recruit who surrendered his carbine to a painted warrior, only to have the savage crush his skull with a tomahawk.[44]

Moving into the center of the line on a high point with Crook, Strahorn saw Sioux in every direction. Every mountain in the area, each a fortress in itself with rocky ledges and ravines, was peopled by savages in the splendor of the warpath. "Right, left, front and rear alike were faced by the incoming braves, and it seemed as though the whole surface of the country for miles around was one vast skirmish line," he reported.[45]

During the fight, Strahorn said, he heard Crook summarize the feelings of a man who is exposed to fire for hours at a time. With Crook and several officers, Strahorn stood on an exposed mound of dry, hard earth against which the striking bullets sounded as though they were hitting pavement. Captain Burt had ridden up with some intelligence, but before leaving, he asked Crook, "General, many say that they get so hardened to this sort of thing that they don't mind it, and I often wonder whether you feel like I do in a position of this kind?"

"Well," Crook replied, "how do *you* feel?"

"Why," Burt said, "just as though, if you were not in sight, I'd be running like hell!"

[44] *New York Herald,* July 6, 1876.
[45] *Rocky Mountain News,* July 4, 1876.

"Well, I feel exactly that way myself," the General said.[46]

Finerty and MacMillan rode into action with Companies E and A of the Third Cavalry, but their dispatches do not detail their personal experiences.[47] Immediately after the attack began, Mills charged the bluffs in the center. Galloping to the charge, Finerty saw the Indians wait until the troops were within fifty paces. They rode at such speed that carbines could not be used. Instead they fired their revolvers, and broke into "a mad cheer" as the Sioux went back as though reeling under the impact of that charge. The Sioux retreated to the next ridge—the ground ahead seemed to be one ridge after another—there riding in circles, "slapping an indelicate portion of their persons at us, and beckoning us to come on." After several hours had passed, Crook ordered Mills down the canyon to find, strike, and hold the village, the mission from which he subsequently recalled him. Several weeks later, they saw that the Indians had built an abatis from which they could have slaughtered the troops in the narrow canyon.

Wasson's place and part in the fight are not clear. His detailed story of the Battle of the Rosebud for the *Alta California* apparently miscarried in the mails, and his mail story of the battle in the *New York Tribune* was sketchy.[48] Since all the other correspondents are accounted for, it should be noted that Strahorn in his autobiography referred obliquely to a correspondent who habitually remained in the rear with the pack train, although that does not sound like Wasson. Crook suspected that Wasson's telegraph story to the *Tribune* had been suppressed in the Fort Fetterman telegraph office, implying skullduggery in the competition of *Herald* vs. *Tribune*.[49]

After the battle, the quiet of a pleasant summer evening enwrapped the battlefield and its masses of fragrant wild plum and crabapple blossoms. Crook encamped his command there

[46] Strahorn, Autobiography, 153–54.
[47] *Chicago Times*, June 24, 1876; *Chicago Inter-Ocean*, June 24, 1876.
[48] *Alta California*, July 28, 1876; *New York Tribune*, July 6, 1876.
[49] Vaughn, *With Crook at the Rosebud*, 124.

for the night, buried the dead, rigged up travois to transport the wounded, and marched the next morning. The soldiers reached their camp at the Tongue on the day following, June 19.

There the reporters wrote their stories of the battle and sent them to the telegraph operator at Fort Fetterman. Theirs was a difficult task. The battlefield was four miles long and two miles wide, in which three battles within a battle were fought simultaneously, without any one individual's having a commanding view of the whole, although Strahorn claimed many years later that he had held such a position. The fact that each reporter had been borne into the excitement and frenzy of battle, restricted his point of view. The plight of the reporters can perhaps be best explained by the observation of the Duke of Wellington that no one person could get an adequate personal observation of the detailed movements of numerous bodies of men extended over several miles. Speaking to Edward Everett at a dance, the Duke suggested that the American reflect upon how difficult it would be to recall the next morning the position and movements of all the groups of dancers then on the floor.[50]

Necessarily, the correspondents wrote first of what they had seen and experienced, and then obtained from officers details of other actions. Combining personal observation and second-hand information, their stories provided faithful accounts of the battle, as it came within the view of themselves and the troops. Probably with more truth than anyone else who has ever written about it, Wasson said it "can hardly be called a battle." The newspaper stories and official reports are in general agreement, but, as in earlier engagements, there are some points on which the two cannot be compared, since each contains some information that is lacking in the other. For example, Crook carefully refrained from estimating the enemy loss other than to say thirteen dead Sioux were seen. The correspondents mention that figure, too, but they also gave estimates ranging from 100 to 150 enemy dead and

[50] Andrews, *The North Reports the Civil War,* 76.

wounded; Strahorn implied that the estimate came from army officers.

One of the most remarkable features of their stories is that they one and all identified the attacking Sioux as Sitting Bull's force, although Wasson also mentioned Crazy Horse. Undoubtedly their assumption stemmed from the Indian Bureau's repeated references to Sitting Bull before the campaign. Sheridan tried to set the record straight later in the year, saying he had always interpreted "Sitting Bull" in the Indian Bureau correspondence as synonymous with "hostile," although he understood how newspaper accounts would compound the confusion created by the Interior Department. He said Sitting Bull had never been more than an "insignificant" warrior with a "few thieving followers," and concluded that Crazy Horse's Oglala Sioux and the Northern Cheyennes had done practically all the fighting. Time bore him out.

The reporters wrote with some restraint. Not one called the fight either a victory or a defeat, then. And for good cause. No one knew. Crook considered it a victory since he had fought on the enemy's choice of ground and had been left in possession of the field, but the candid Sheridan said that if it was a victory, it had been barren of results since Crook did not follow it up. At least one troop commander concluded they had been humiliated.

Another noticeable quality in the stories is the extent to which interpretation was colored by the point of view of the officer with whom the correspondent rode. Strahorn—who had been with Crook—wrote a glowing and sanguine summary of the entire action. Davenport, on the other hand, reflected Royall's hostility toward Crook, saying Royall had been circumscribed by contradictory orders from Crook, a charge that is implied in Royall's report. Royall continued his disagreement with Crook when he told Omaha reporters ten years later that the Rosebud defeat was due to Crook's faulty generalship. In a meeting in Crook's Omaha home, the General told Royall to his face that Royall's conduct had caused the failure of Crook's plan.

If anyone knew for certain how many men were killed and wounded in the Battle of the Rosebud, his figures certainly did not bind any others who gave casualty figures. The official casualty report shows nine soldiers dead and twenty-one wounded, remarkably low for the numbers engaged and the hours in contact. In addition, one Indian ally was killed and several wounded. From there on, it is a free-for-all. The newspaper casualty reports are not uniform in that some separate white and Indian casualties, while others do not. However, they all revolve around the figure of ten dead, which would include both white and Indian. Considerable variation appears in the number of wounded reported. That this was not due alone to faulty reporting is indicated by recent research showing one estimate of twenty-eight killed and fifty-six wounded and the fact that the National Archives do not contain battle reports from the three commanders whose companies were said to have lost the most men. The names of dead and wounded in the newspaper accounts do not agree in every instance with the names on the official casualty report.[51]

Davenport, MacMillan, Finerty, and Wasson sent telegraphic dispatches to Fort Fetterman by courier, presumably on the night of June 19 after their arrival at the Goose Creek camp. Both Chicago reporters date-lined their lead battle story from Rosebud Creek, June 17.

In addition, Davenport and Finerty sent duplicate dispatches by a courier or couriers who left on June 20 or 21. Something happened to Davenport's courier along the way, for by June 25 he had not been heard from, and it was feared he had fallen to the Indians. However, he apparently reached his destination, for Davenport's mail story appeared in print. By that time, Finerty had developed a strong distrust of the

[51] *New York Tribune,* July 6, 1876; *Chicago Times,* June 24, 1876; *Chicago Inter-Ocean,* June 24, 1876; *Rocky Mountain News,* July 4, 1876; *New York Herald,* June 24, 1876; Reports of the Battle of the Rosebud, National Archives, *loc. cit.;* Secretary of War, *Report, 1876,* I, 442–43, 447, 500; 44 Cong., 1 sess., *House Ex. Doc. 184,* 58; Anson Mills, *My Story,* 409; Vaughn, *With Crook at the Rosebud,* 65, 66, 124, 134–37, 146–47, 165–66, 213–38.

General George Armstrong Custer in Montana Territory in the 1870's.

Chief Joseph of the Nez Percés. From a Photograph by DeLancey Gill.

couriers, questioning their honesty and saying they were "very unreliable" and "the chief annoyance" of the correspondents, although he acknowledged they took a great risk in traveling through Indian country.[52]

Once Crook had returned to Camp Cloud Peak on Goose Creek, he sent his wagon train back to Fort Fetterman for supplies, and waited for reinforcements. The wounded went back with the wagon train.

Medical officers recommended that MacMillan return, too, because his health had grown worse daily. Acquiescing, in part because he thought there would be no more fighting, MacMillan left with the wagon train on June 21. Bourke, Crook's aide, recalled that MacMillan "had shown as much pluck as any officer or soldier in the column, but his strength was not equal to the hard marching and climbing, coupled with the violent alternation of heat and cold, rain and shine, to which we were subjected." Another observer remarked, "How he came to stay with the command as long as he did can only be accounted for by a nervous energy that will hold out long after his slender physique gives way."[53]

MacMillan's departure left four correspondents—Finerty, Davenport, Wasson, and Strahorn—to wait out the long delay with Crook and his men as they reconnoitered the Sioux country and wondered where Terry was.

[52] *New York Herald*, June 26, 1876; *Chicago Times*, July 5, 1876.
[53] Finerty, *War-Path and Bivouac*, 141; Bourke, *On the Border with Crook*, 319; *Rocky Mountain News*, Aug. 8, 1876.

Flash

6. CUSTER COMMAND WIPED OUT

> *I go with Custer and will be at the death.*
> MARK KELLOGG[1]

THE UNITED STATES celebrated its centennial in July, 1876, while its soldiers were in the field fighting a war that was not recognized as such. For the civilians living in a land at peace, Philadelphia became something of a hundredth-year mecca, with a Centennial Exposition that became the place to visit. The *New York Herald* said there appeared to be "a Centennial fever" across the country as every city, town, and village planned its appropriate celebrations. And all across the land, crowds by the thousands, speakers by the scores, proudly marked the success story of man's freedom in a republic that could endure, on the Fourth of July.

On the fifth of July, the telegraph operator in Salt Lake City placed a story on the wire for the Associated Press: Custer and five companies of his regiment had been annihilated.

The story was based upon a message brought to Fort Ellis, Montana, by a scout named Muggins Taylor. Generals in the East discredited the report immediately. Sherman and Sheridan, both attending the Centennial Exposition, refused to believe it. After all, they had received no official word. Besides, said Sheridan, frontier scouts had a way of spreading stories. As for Taylor, said an unidentified officer in Sheridan's company, his reputation would not justify anyone's accepting the story without reservations.

And then on the morning of July 6 the telegraph operator

[1] *Bismarck Tribune*, July 12, 1876.

194

in Fargo, which was the end of the twenty-hour wire in the Northwest, recognized the "fist" of J. M. Carnahan opening the day wire from Bismarck—telegraph operators tapped the key with mannerisms as individualistic as fingerprints. Fargo heard Carnahan demand a connection with St. Paul.

"What's up?" asked Fargo.

"Cut us through and listen," Carnahan replied. "All the Custers are killed."[2]

For the next forty-eight hours, with only three hours' rest, Carnahan controlled the wire, tapping out the words that told of one of the most stunning military reverses in American history, at almost the moment of the centennial. Approximately 40,000 words of press dispatches came from Bismarck during those two days, taking second place to official dispatches which confirmed that George Armstrong Custer and five companies of the gallant Seventh Cavalry—the one regiment that had been formed for the special purpose of whipping Indians —had been wiped out on the Little Big Horn. With the aid of an unemployed telegrapher, S. B. Rogers, Carnahan "jerked lightning" from the morning of July 6 until the morning of July 8.[3]

Custer's defeat—to go down in romance as "Custer's Last Stand" and the "Custer Massacre"—was one of the great news stories of the nineteenth century. But the only newspaperman who had accompanied Terry had died with Custer.

C. A. Lounsberry, owner of the *Bismarck Tribune*, had intended to accompany Terry's Yellowstone Expedition as correspondent, but illness in his family caused him to change his plans at the last moment and delegate the assignment to Mark Kellogg, sometime telegrapher, erstwhile train dispatcher, and small-town hack writer.

Then forty-three years old, Kellogg had been a telegrapher during the Civil War, had been assistant editor of the *Council*

[2] Carnahan, quoted in newspaper clippings in Kellogg Folder, Watson Papers.
[3] *Ibid.; Bismarck Tribune*, July 19, 1876.

Bluffs Daily Democrat in 1868, and, when that proved financially unrewarding, had become a train dispatcher on the Northern Pacific. He went to work on the *Bismarck Tribune* when Lounsberry established the paper in 1873. Sometime during the next year, he lost his job on the paper, and after that he supervised work in a haymakers' camp north of Bismarck. He had rejoined the *Tribune* by 1876.[4] A widower, he had two daughters in La Crosse, Wisconsin, where he had preceded Carnahan as telegrapher.

Kellogg accompanied the Terry expedition as the only accredited newspaper correspondent with the column. Primarily representing the weekly *Bismarck Tribune,* he also would send letters to the *New York Herald, Chicago Times,* and *Chicago Tribune,* although none of the metropolitan papers shared the expenses of outfitting him.

The plans for Lounsberry to accompany the expedition appear to have been made during the winter when it was expected that Custer, who commanded Fort Abraham Lincoln across the river from Bismarck, would command the entire expedition. Having friendly relations with New York editors, Custer encouraged the presence of newspaper correspondents with his command.

On February 26, Custer wrote a confidential letter to Whitelaw Reid, editor of the *New York Tribune,* asking that the *Tribune* send a staff man along. Custer used persuasive lure, saying: ". . . the most extensive preparations are being made for a combined military movement against the hostile Sioux that have been attempted since the war.... There is scarcely a chance of avoiding a general Indian war this coming season."[5] But the *Tribune* did not see fit to send a staff man.

Nor did the *New York Herald* send a staff man, even though Custer had helped the *Herald* expose Indian Ring corruption the previous year. The *Herald* had sent out Ralph Meeker,

[4] John C. Hixon, "Custer's 'Mysterious' Mr. Kellogg," *North Dakota History,* Vol. XVII (July, 1950), 145–63, 152–53; Col. Clement A. Lounsberry, *Early History of North Dakota,* 315; *New York Herald,* July 19, 1876; *Bismarck Tribune,* July 19, 1876.

[5] Royal Cortissoz, *The Life of Whitelaw Reid,* I, 312.

who, with Custer's help, got a job at the Berthold Indian Agency, an undercover position from which he gained the information for an exposé of corruption in Indian management. This exposure—in which Edward Fox, the correspondent of the Modoc War, participated—along with one in the *New York Tribune*, led to the resignation of Columbus Delano as secretary of the interior. Custer personally fed the flames by writing a story, entitled "Belknap's Anaconda," which helped bare the sale of post traderships, which involved Secretary of War W. W. Belknap.[6]

Possibly at Custer's urging, Lounsberry, who was also Bismarck correspondent for the Western Associated Press, may have taken on the *New York Herald* as a temporary assignment. At any rate, Custer-Lounsberry made a compatible team. Both Michigan men, they had been friends since the Civil War, and their friendship was renewed when Custer and the Seventh arrived at Fort Abraham Lincoln in 1873. Through that association, the *Bismarck Tribune* had published the first story on the discovery of gold in the Black Hills in 1874, because the stories of the *Tribune* correspondent reached Bismarck through Custer's official dispatch rider. The *Chicago Inter-Ocean*, which is usually credited with having the first stories of the gold discovery, did not get into print with the story until two weeks after the *Tribune* carried it.[7]

However, the exposures turned out to be Custer's downfall as well as Belknap's. When Custer's connection with the newspaper stories came to light, he was summoned to Washington, where his testimony before a Congressional committee placed him at odds with President Grant, because it involved the President's brother, Orvil. Taking matters into his own hands, as he usually did, Custer left Washington without permission, and was detained by orders in Chicago. The net result was that he was not even to command his regiment, let alone the expedition, during the Sioux cam-

[6] Lounsberry, *Early History of North Dakota*, 313–15; *New York Herald*, July 23, 1875; Marshall Sprague, *Massacre: The Tragedy at White River*, 32–38.

[7] Hixon, "Custer's 'Mysterious' Mr. Kellogg," *loc. cit.*, 152–53.

paign of 1876. However, he won the intercession of his departmental commander, Terry, who was to command the expedition in person as a result of Custer's disgrace, and of Sheridan, who had interceded for him under similar circumstances in 1868. According to Terry's brother-in-law, Custer got down on his knees to ask Terry's intercession.[8]

When Lounsberry had to change his plans, he obtained permission from Terry for Kellogg to report the campaign.[9] Apparently, Terry paid little heed to Sherman's telegram: "Advise Custer to be prudent, not to take along any newspapermen, who always make mischief, and to abstain from personalities in the future . . . ."[10]

The absence of newspaper comment on Sherman's telegram to Terry indicates that no newspaper encountered difficulty in getting a correspondent assigned, probably because no others asked, anyhow. The two most energetic news-gatherers already were represented by Kellogg—the *New York Herald* and the *Chicago Times*. Others, such as the *New York Tribune* and the *St. Paul Pioneer-Press,* would receive stories from officers, to whom free-lance writing provided an addition to army pay. In short, the newspapers of the country—at least those interested enough to pay the expenses of staff coverage—seem to have concluded as Storey did that Crook would do the fighting, that the Terry-Custer expedition was not likely to produce much news.

Astride the horse originally provided for Lounsberry and wearing Lounsberry's Civil War belt, Kellogg rode out to Terry's camp on Sunday, May 14, expecting the column to march the next morning. That evening, however, a storm blew up, forcing Terry to hold his men in camp south of Fort Lincoln another two days, with the march scheduled for Wednesday, May 17.

[8] See Edgar I. Stewart, *Custer's Luck,* 120–39.
[9] *Bismarck Tribune,* July 19, 1876.
[10] Col. Robert P. Hughes, "The Campaign Against the Sioux in 1876," *Journal of the Military Service Institute of the United States,* Vol. XVIII (January, 1896), 14, text of article reprinted in Col. W. A. Graham's *The Story of the Little Big Horn.*

Excited by the bustle of an army camp in which 1,200 men prepared to take the field for the summer, Kellogg worked his way through the camp, talking with Terry and other officers. From Terry he learned that the column would move almost due westward, along the route of survey of the Northern Pacific Railroad, to the Yellowstone River, where Missouri River steamboats would meet them with supplies. Also on the Yellowstone, near Glendive Creek, Terry would meet Gibbon, who had been in the field since April. In the interview, Terry said that during the summer the Indians, as Kellogg phrased it, "must be taught that the Government was not to be trifled with, and such measures would be taken as would learn the Indians to feel and recognize that there existed in the land an arm and power which they must obey." Writing more of his story on Monday for the weekly *Tribune*, Kellogg said, "I have visited every department and every position of the camp, and find everywhere perfect preparation, order and system. Everything is moving along like clockwork."[11]

Following an almost standard practice of Western War correspondents, Kellogg in his first story detailed the composition of the column, with names of the officers. Comprised of 1,207 men, it included all twelve companies of the Seventh Cavalry, the first time since the Civil War that an entire regiment had been together on campaign; three companies of infantry; an infantry detachment manning a battery of three Gatling guns; 45 Indian Scouts; and 190 civilians—a chief wagonmaster, chief packer, chief herder, clerk, guides, interpreters, master mechanic, blacksmiths, wheelwrights, assistant packers, assistant wagonmasters, teamsters. He was not overly careful in giving figures for the various components; his figures do not add up.

Although it looked good on paper, the command was deficient in experienced Indian fighters. Terry had no experience whatever. A lawyer trained at Yale, he had won his star during the Civil War and had remained in the army for a career. Beloved of his officers and men, he bore the air of a scholar

[11] *Bismarck Tribune*, May 17, 1876.

rather than a soldier. Custer's reputation was spun of gos-
samer, for it took considerable first-hand experience to teach
even a professional officer how to fight Indians, and Custer's
battle experience had been limited. Several Seventh Cavalry
officers were absent, including the regimental commander,
Colonel Samuel D. Sturgis, and the two senior majors, one
of whom was an experienced Indian fighter. Under Custer,
the lieutenant colonel of the regiment, was the junior major,
Marcus Reno, who had never fought Indians. Some of the
company commanders had fought Indians, and so had some
of the men, but many troopers were green—just as green as
the regiment's horses, which had not yet been trained to the
noise of battle and the smell of Indians.

Jealousy and resentment still rankled in the Seventh Cavalry, stemming from the fate of Major Elliott at the Battle
of the Washita. That it could not have been otherwise within
the regiment is not surprising, considering Custer's cut.
George Bird Grinnell, the naturalist who accompanied Custer
on the 1874 trip to the Black Hills, illustrated his view of
Custer's egocentricity with a story about the latter's hunting.
Custer often bragged of his own shots, he related, but did
not show much interest in the marksmanship of others. One
day Grinnell took a saddle of venison to Custer, telling him
that Luther North had killed three running deer in three shots.
Custer responded, "Hah, I found two more horned toads
today."[12]

Cold fog enwrapped the camp in the valley when reveille
brought the troops out of their tents at 3:00 A.M. on May 17.
At 5:00 they marched westward and then north, but Kellogg's
story did not mention the dramatic moment, recalled by
Custer's widow, that came when Terry led the column across
the parade ground of Fort Abraham Lincoln to reassure the
apprehensive women and give the men a last look at their
loved ones.[13] With the Seventh Cavalry band playing "Garry

[12] Mills, *My Story*, 409; Bates, *Custer's Indian Battles*, 26; Bourke, *On
the Border with Crook*, 351; Brill, *Conquest of the Southern Plains*, 14n.;
George Bird Grinnell, *Two Great Scouts and Their Pawnee Battalion*, 239–43.

Owen" and the cavalry's sentimental "The Girl I Left Behind Me," the long line of troops marched toward a point two miles west of the fort, where Terry formed the column in order of march.

Taking post on a high point of ground, Kellogg watched the command, creaking, clopping, treading into motion to the strains of martial music. Custer rode ahead to pick a campsite for the first night, accompanied by Mrs. Custer, who was to go back the next day, two companies of cavalry, and forty scouts. At the head of the column rode Terry, accompanied by Chief Scout Charley Reynolds, Interpreter F. F. Girard, Terry's staff, and the band. Behind him, in order, came the Seventh Cavalry, artillery, ambulances, and forage wagons, with infantry scattered here and there to defend the wagons and with cavalry flankers on left, right, and in the rear.

For three weeks they marched westward. Terry originally planned to strike the Yellowstone River at the mouth of Glendive Creek in eastern Montana, near which an infantry force occupied Stanley's Stockade, built during the expedition of 1873. En route, however, he received word from the stockade that Gibbon was near the mouth of the Rosebud River. Terry accordingly changed his route to the Powder River, which he reached on June 7.

During the march, Kellogg regularly sent dispatches and kept a diary, which contradict the secondary accounts that say he came upriver on Captain Grant Marsh's steamboat, the *Far West*. The *Bismarck Tribune* published four of his stories, three of which were signed "Frontier," and appears to have synopsized a fifth.[14] The signature "Frontier" also appeared on one story in the *Chicago Times*.[15] At least two of Kellogg's letters appeared in the *New York Herald*;[16] two other stories in the *Herald*, reporting departure and progress of the column, suggest they were written and dispatched by

[13] *Bismarck Tribune*, May 24, 1876; Stewart, *Custer's Luck*, 210–11; Elizabeth B. Custer, *"Boots and Saddles,"* 262–63.
[14] *Bismarck Tribune*, May 17, 24, June 14, 21, 1876.
[15] *Chicago Times*, May 25, 1876.
[16] *New York Herald*, June 27, July 11, 1876.

Lounsberry, through whose hands all of Kellogg's work passed.[17]

Two other stories appeared in the *Herald*, of unverified authorship, although Custer is the suspected author.[18] One, printed after the battle of the Little Big Horn and appearing under the headline, "A Voice from the Tomb," was identified as coming from a "prominent officer" killed in the battle; Custer was the only "prominent" officer killed there. Each of the two contains references to subjects to which Custer alluded in letters to his wife.[19] A man of seemingly unlimited energy, Custer did spend time writing during the campaign. He wrote an article for the magazine *Galaxy*, and a letter to his wife implies that he also had written at least one newspaper letter, as this type of communication was called.[20]

Kellogg wrote long, chatty letters in a disjointed style. In getting information, he had full run of the column, including headquarters, where, he said, Terry's letter book was open to him. However, he had little to write about before the column reached the Powder River, other than the countryside and the long tedium of day upon day—creaking saddles, swishing tails, braying mules, groaning axles, and bellowing teamsters—of an Indian expedition, differing from others only in locale.

In referring to the officers, he always put Terry first, describing him as a "gentleman soldier," a popular, kind, and considerate commander. And then, as if he had been bowing to propriety and holding himself in leash, he went into paeans of praise for Custer—using such terms as "brave," "dashing," "always out in front," "unbounded energy," "fearless," "electric mental capacity," "iron frame and constitution." In truth, Kellogg wrote as a sycophant. But he also gave a realistic picture of Custer in other terms—"hell-whooping" over the prairie and "on the scoot," as the troops called it.[21]

17 *New York Herald*, May 18, 24, 1876.
18 *Ibid.*, June 19, July 11, 1876.
19 *Ibid.*; Elizabeth Custer, *"Boots and Saddles,"* 304–12.
20 Elizabeth Custer, *"Boots and Saddles,"* 304–12.

He sent most of his stories by courier, but he almost lost one story in an accident at the mouth of Powder River on June 12. His story, Custer's *Galaxy* article, and mail were given to a detachment of three men who were to go down-river in a rowboat to another steamboat. Just as they were starting, the boat overturned, a sergeant was drowned, and the mail sack sank to the bottom. The accident occurred near the *Far West*, whose crew fished the mail sack from the river with boat hooks. Kellogg and Marsh spent the night drying out the letters, which finally were sent on their way about four o'clock the next morning.

Traveling as a guest of the Seventh Cavalry, Kellogg seems to have become part of Custer's campaign family, which included the General's youngest brother, Boston, and his nephew, Autie Reed. Young Custer traveled as forage master and Reed as herder. Another brother, Tom Custer, commanded a company in the regiment.

Because his horse played out and there was no remount for him, Kellogg shifted his saddle to a mule and rode out the rest of his adventure in that fashion.[22] Terry could grant him no favors other than transportation for his personal effects.

Kellogg's activities seem to have been limited to keeping his place in the line of march, except for a hunting trip with Charley Reynolds, a brief scout with the same Reynolds, a steamboat trip on the Yellowstone, and possibly a scout with Custer. On June 12, after the column had reached the mouth of Powder River, Kellogg made a one-day trip to Stanley's Stockade and back with Marsh on the *Far West*, which he described as an "unexpected experience."[23] It may have been that one-day trip with Marsh which led to the erroneous account that Kellogg traveled by boat rather than riding with the troops.[24]

Kellogg's stories had a trained-seal quality. Through all of

[21] *Chicago Times*, May 25, 1876; *Bismarck Tribune*, May 24, June 14, 1876; *New York Herald*, July 11, 1876.
[22] *New York Herald*, July 10, 1876.
[23] *Bismarck Tribune*, June 21, 1876.
[24] See Joseph Mills Hanson, *The Conquest of the Missouri*, 249.

them only Custer can be seen, after a quick bow to Terry, who is shoved from the stage immediately each time. If a later report is to be believed, Custer actually had no command during the march, in the course of which the Seventh Cavalry was said to have been divided into two wings under Reno and Benteen. If that is true, Kellogg's stories must be criticized as not presenting a fully accurate picture.

The trained-seal quality came out most strongly when Kellogg accused Reno of disobedience after that officer had completed a reconnaissance, which Terry ordered. Upon reaching the Yellowstone on June 8, Terry established contact with Gibbon, farther up the Yellowstone, who reported the Sioux in force south of the river. With most of the officers believing the Sioux would be found on the Rosebud or Big Horn rivers, Terry thought it necessary to make sure they were not in the Powder or Tongue valleys and sent Reno to find out.

Reno began his eight-day scout, with six companies of the Seventh Cavalry, on June 10, with orders to proceed up the Powder River, cross over to the Tongue, and follow the Tongue to its junction with the Yellowstone, at which point the rest of the command would meet him. Reno, however, went farther west and came down the valley of the Rosebud, which was the one move Terry did not want him to make for fear of alerting the enemy. When Reno reported on June 18, the day after Crook fought the Battle of the Rosebud, he told of crossing a large Indian trail on the Rosebud, pointing toward the Big Horn. That perhaps was the trail left by the Indians who had moved their large camp from the Rosebud to a tributary of the Little Big Horn shortly before the fight with Crook.

Kellogg said that "Major Reno was unfortunate enough not only to exceed but to disobey the orders and instructions of General Terry."[25] Another *Herald* story of the same date, the one presumably written by Custer, accused Reno of having

[25] *New York Herald*, July 11, 1876.

acted "in positive disobedience to the strict injunctions of the department commander."[26]

With his plans for systematic scouting disrupted, Terry devised an alternate plan. In conference with Gibbon and Custer on June 21, he decided to send Custer with the full twelve companies of the Seventh Cavalry up the Rosebud on June 22, have them cross over to the Little Big Horn, and work down the Little Big Horn at the same time that Terry, Gibbon, the infantry, and Gibbon's few companies of the Second Cavalry moved up the valley of the Big Horn toward the mouth of the Little Big Horn. Some accounts of the controversial battle, which need not be detailed here, have been based on the premise that Terry intended the two columns to meet on June 26, but others hold that such a premise is insupportable because of the freedom Terry gave Custer and because Custer took fifteen days' rations, enough to keep him on the move until July 6.[27]

As Custer made preparations June 21 for a move the next day against an Indian force which the officers estimated at 1,000 to 1,500 and the scouts at no less than 5,000, there was, indeed, as an Irish cavalryman put it, "a mighty foin chance for a fight or a foot race."[28]

Establishing himself on the *Far West*—it is possible that Kellogg may have taken up quarters on the boat some days before when Terry transferred his headquarters to the steamboat—Kellogg worked far into the night on his dispatches. He wrote a story of approximately two thousand words for the *Herald*, his last, and enclosed with it a note which shows him to be a humble, even a deferential, man. Referring to the accident to the mail sack at the mouth of the Powder on June 12, he wrote the *Herald* editor: "Please find manuscript, which I have been forced to write very hurriedly, owing to the want of time given me for the purpose. My last was badly demoralized from wetting, as then briefly explained, and I have feared

---

[26] *Ibid.*
[27] See Stewart, *Custer's Luck*, 240–50.
[28] *Ibid.*, 242–43; *New York Herald*, June 27, 1876.

it would not prove acceptable on that account. The officers of the expedition have written generally to their friends to watch for the *Herald*, as they know I am to record their deeds. I will endeavor to give you interesting letters as we go along. I have the liberty of the entire column, headquarters and all, and will get down to bottom facts in all matters connected with the expedition."[29]

He also wrote at least a note to Lounsberry, saying, "We leave the Rosebud to-morrow, and by the time this reaches you we will have met and fought the red devils, with what results remains to be seen. I go with Custer and will be at [*sic*] the death."[30]

Kellogg worked until after midnight in the stillness that pervades a river at night, broken only by the gentle sound of insects and lapping water. A little after midnight he came out on deck, where he met an officer, believed to have been Major James Brisbin of the Second Cavalry, who had come out to smoke a cigar before retiring. Kellogg told Brisbin that he was through writing and his letters were ready for the mail the next day. He talked a long time about the campaign, hopeful that the Seventh would have an opportunity to fight in the next few days.[31]

At noon the next day Custer announced that his regiment was ready to march and ordered a regimental parade for the leave-taking. Terry, Gibbon, and Brisbin lined up as the reviewing officers—the latter two held brevet rank as general officers. Astride his mule, with canvas saddlebags containing writing material, Kellogg took post on the right of Gibbon for the review.

Mounted on a blooded sorrell, "Vic," which had white feet and a blaze, Custer rode at the head of his regiment. Wearing a broad-brimmed whitish-gray hat with a low crown and a fringed buckskin suit, the blouse of which was double-breasted with military buttons, Custer carried as personal

29 *New York Herald,* July 11, 1876.
30 *Bismarck Tribune,* July 12, 1876.
31 *New York Herald,* July 8, 1876.

arms a Remington sporting rifle with octagonal barrel, two self-cocking English white-handled pistols with a ring in the butt for the lanyard, a hunting knife in a beaded sheath, and a canvas cartridge belt.[32]

With cavalry cantering ahead, Custer turned back for final instructions and a last good-bye from Terry, who shook his hand and said, "God bless you." Custer reined Vic toward the column. Terry turned back toward the boat.

Kicking his mule, Kellogg started off after Custer, but Terry called him back for a personal good-bye.[33]

Three days later, Sunday, June 25, 1876, Custer's regiment charged into a force of Sioux and Cheyennes perhaps five to ten times their number. Custer's battle occurred only eight days after Crook had met the same force of Indians at the Rosebud and only a short distance from Crook's battlefield.

After a night march with tired horses and tired men, Custer in the early morning of June 25 came within striking distance of the largest Indian village ever collected in the Northwest, where, a scout told him, there were more hostiles than the soldiers had bullets.[34] Reports from front and rear indicated that the Indians had discovered the regiment. Convinced that concealment until the next day would be impossible and certain the village would scatter, leaving the long, tedious job of rounding up the Indians to be done all over again, Custer decided to attack. Halting about noon on the divide between the Rosebud and the Little Big Horn, he divided his command into four parts. He gave Benteen command of three companies and sent him off on a scout to the left; Reno took three other companies as another battalion; Custer himself, five companies. The remaining company guarded the pack train. About 2:15 P.M. Custer sent Reno's battalion across the Little Big Horn to pursue and attack a group of fleeing In-

[32] Letter from Gen. Edward S. Godfrey, Jan. 16, 1896, to the artist Edgar S. Paxon, quoted in Albert J. Partoll, "After the Custer Battle," *Frontier and Midland,* Vol. XIX (Summer, 1939), 277.

[33] *New York Herald,* July 8, 1876.

[34] This summary of the Battle of the Little Big Horn is based upon Stewart, *Custer's Luck,* 271 ff.

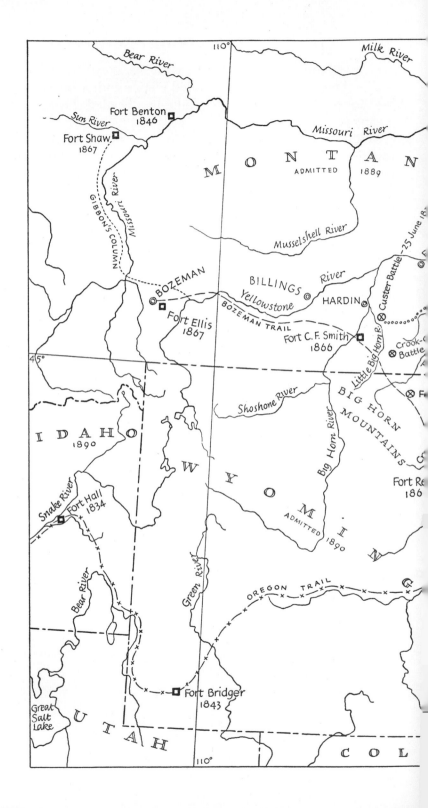

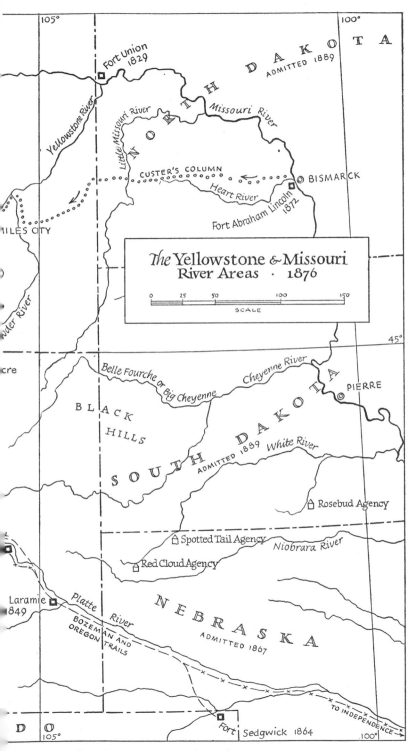

105°

Fort Union
1829

N O R T H   D A K O T A
ADMITTED 1889

Yellowstone River

Little Missouri River

Missouri River

CUSTER'S COLUMN

Heart River

BISMARCK

MILES CITY

Fort Abraham Lincoln
1872

Powder River

The Yellowstone & Missouri
River Areas · 1876

0   25   50   100   150
SCALE

100°

45°

cre

Belle Fourche or Big Cheyenne

Cheyenne River

PIERRE

B L A C K

H I L L S

S O U T H   D A K O T A
ADMITTED 1889

White River

Rosebud Agency

Spotted Tail Agency

Niobrara River

Red Cloud Agency

Laramie
849

Platte River

BOZEMAN AND
OREGON TRAILS

N E B R A S K A
ADMITTED 1867

TO INDEPENDENCE

D O
105°

Fort Sedgwick 1864

100°

From Edgar I. Stewart, *Custer's Luck*

dians, with the promise that he would support him with the rest of the forces. Kellogg rode with Custer when the commander diverged to the right with five companies.

Reno met a fierce counterattack from Indians who forced him to retreat into trees along the river; later, after and with heavy loss, he retreated rapidly across the river to take up a position on a bluff. Meantime, Custer, riding off to the right at first, came back to the Little Big Horn and ran into a horde of warriors. He sent a trumpeter with orders to Benteen to hurry forward with the ammunition packs. That was the last ever heard from Custer. The trumpeter encountered Benteen, who had returned to Custer's march route after finding nothing on the left, and Benteen moved forward, ultimately meeting the badly whipped Reno. He and Reno placed their six companies in a defensive position on the bluff in mid-afternoon.

About six o'clock, after the pack train had come up, Reno and Benteen moved downstream; some of the men had heard heavy firing, which had started and then stopped, in late afternoon, and which told them Custer had been in action. Reno's and Benteen's advance was slowed by the fact that many of their men were on foot, having lost their horses in the fighting, and by the transportation of the wounded—each wounded man was carried in a horse blanket supported by six soldiers. From a high point Reno's and Benteen's men saw what later became known as the Custer battlefield, but accounts of what they saw vary, although one officer reported seeing thousands of Indians moving downstream. And then the troops, whose command Benteen gradually assumed, saw the Sioux coming at them in full force.

The soldiers retreated to the position on the bluff which they had left shortly before. By 7:00 P.M. they were surrounded, and in the remaining hours of daylight the troops lost eighteen killed and forty-six wounded. And there they remained for the night, and the next day, and the next night, some suspecting that Custer had ridden off and left them to their fate, as in the case of Major Elliott on the Washita.

There they were found and relieved on June 27 by Terry and Gibbon, who advanced up the Little Big Horn with five companies of the Seventh Infantry and four of the Second Cavalry. Not until then was the annihilation of Custer's forces even suspected. Five companies of the proudest cavalry regiment in the service smashed. Every man with him killed—more than two hundred of them.

What happened to Kellogg? As with everything else connected with the Battle of the Little Big Horn, the accounts are contradictory. The officer who supplied material for the *New York Herald* story of the battle, and who knew Kellogg, said his body was found near that of Lieutenant James Calhoun, who commanded Company L on the east of the battlefield.[35] The core of the other account is the story related by Gibbon that he found Kellogg's body on June 29, identifying it by the peculiar construction of a boot, since decomposition made identification by other means impossible.[36]

Another point of contradiction is the location of Kellogg's personal papers. According to one version, Kellogg's portfolio lay beside the body and was recovered by Terry.[37]

Subsidiary evidence seems to favor the Gibbon version. In his report of June 27 from the field, Terry mentioned Reed and Boston Custer among the slain but did not refer to Kellogg. A story written on July 1 by an officer for the *St. Paul Pioneer-Press* and relayed to other newspapers said that Kellogg's was the last body found.[38] On the other hand, Reno said that his men buried Kellogg on June 28.[39]

If the body found by Gibbon was Kellogg's, the remains of the mule-mounted correspondent were found by accident. Gibbon, who had been ill and busy, had not had an opportunity to visit the battlefield until a delay in camp gave him

[35] *New York Herald*, July 8, 1876.

[36] Gen. John Gibbon, "Hunting Sitting Bull," *American Catholic Quarterly Review*, Vol. II (October, 1877), 669.

[37] Hanson, *Conquest of the Missouri*, 282; Usher L. Burdick, *The Last Battle of the Sioux Nation*, 125–26.

[38] *Chicago Tribune*, July 8, 1876.

[39] Charles E. DeLand, "The Sioux Wars," *South Dakota Historical Collections*, Vol. XV (1930), 556–57.

that opportunity on June 29, after the burial details had completed their work. Reaching the field, he found a valley which would appear to have been a good escape route. There on a grassy slope his party came upon the body of a white man, badly decomposed. It had not been stripped, as had many other bodies on that field, but it had been mutilated; scalped and one ear cut off. Since the clothing showed it to be the body of a civilian, Gibbon had the underwear and stockings removed in search of a name, but none was found. However, the boots had a strange construction. A strip of leather reinforced the heel and terminated in two straps in front, one with a buckle, When the boot was taken to camp, it was recognized as belonging to Kellogg.[40]

It also seems more likely that Kellogg left his diary and notes, written on a pad of coarse gray paper of about the texture of a child's school tablet, aboard the *Far West*. They were forwarded to Bismarck, the diary and Kellogg's satchel of personal belongings going to the reporter's friend, J. P. Dunn, a Bismarck druggist. A dispatch, or at least a note, went to Lounsberry.

In passing, it should be mentioned for the record that fanciful stories were told, based upon the version that the body was found on the twenty-seventh. According to this yarn, the Indians had neither stripped nor mutilated Kellogg because they knew him as their friend and because of the supernatural powers he was supposed to possess as the man who made the paper talk.[41] A much more reasonable explanation was that he, as well as several others who were not stripped, had fallen some distance from the immediate field of battle and the Indians either overlooked him or did not bother.[42]

In reporting that a full regiment of the United States Army had lost 51 per cent of its men in the greatest victory Indians

[40] Gibbon, "Hunting Sitting Bull," *loc. cit.*, 669.
[41] Lounsberry, *Early History of North Dakota*, 315; Burdick, *Last Battle of the Sioux Nation*, 125–26.
[42] Lt. James H. Bradley, letter to the *Helena Herald*, July 25, 1876, quoted in full in Graham, *Story of the Little Big Horn*, 166.

ever obtained over trained troops, Terry sent messages both east and west—Fort Ellis to the west and Bismarck to the east. His dispatch to be telegraphed from Fort Ellis went by Muggins Taylor, Gibbon's scout. His other dispatch went to Bismarck aboard the *Far West,* which took the wounded to Fort Lincoln.

During his night ride Taylor ran into the Indians. They chased him, but he reached the sanctuary of the *Far West,* then tied up on the Big Horn waiting for instructions. He remained with the boat until it reached the Yellowstone on June 30. Then he struck across country toward Fort Ellis.

En route to the commanding officer at Fort Ellis, who would telegraph Terry's report from Bozeman, Taylor reached Stillwater on the night of July 1. There he told the story to W. H. Norton, correspondent of the *Helena Herald.* Taylor reached Fort Ellis on July 3, delivering Terry's report to Captain D. W. Benham, who took it to the telegraph office personally. Two days later Benham learned it had not been telegraphed, but had been placed in the mail only that morning. The telegrapher claimed that the wires were down, but Benham said they were not. It is significant, however, that as late as July 1, the *Chicago Times* had reported that Sheridan's headquarters had declared that telegraphic communication with Fort Ellis had been closed for several weeks because of obstructions.

The first news stories of the Custer defeat came from Bozeman and Helena. From Stillwater, on July 2, Norton sent a story to Helena by a courier who had to make a 180-mile ride, a circumstance which may substantiate the claim that the telegraph was down at Bozeman. The courier was Horace Countryman, who had a ranch near Stillwater. Worn out by his long ride, Countryman reached the office of Andrew Fisk, editor of the *Helena Herald,* about noon on July 4. Because of the holiday, Fisk had to round up his assistants to put a paper together, an extra which came out late on the night of July 4, the one hundredth anniversary of the United States. He later relayed the story by telegraph to Salt Lake

City, and that was the story which appeared in morning newspapers of July 6, giving the first news of the Custer disaster.[43]

In the meantime, Taylor had reached Fort Ellis on July 3 where the *Bozeman Times* put out an extra at 7:00 P.M. on that date, the first newspaper publication of the defeat. That Bozeman did not in turn forward the news immediately seems to substantiate again the story of a break in the telegraph wire. However, the *Bozeman Times* story also went out from Salt Lake City on July 5, dated Bozeman, 7:00 P.M., July 3. Along with the Helena story via Salt Lake, it appeared in the morning papers of July 6. The *New York Herald* received the story at 3:00 A.M., July 6.[44]

The *Helena Independent* also received its own story of the Custer battle from a correspondent with the Diamond R. Transportation Company, which supplied Gibbon's command with wagons and teamsters. The identity of the Diamond R. man is not known, but his story reached Bozeman by courier, and was telegraphed to Helena on the night of July 5, appearing in the *Independent* the next day.[45] Although the identity of the Diamond R. correspondent is not known, Matthew Carroll, who had charge of the wagons, kept a diary which shows him to have been not only articulate but a careful recorder of detail.[46]

Before the *Far West* shoved off from the mouth of the Little Big Horn, a point to which no other steamboat captain had ever dared navigate, willing hands had taken up the task for the dead Kellogg. He had started a story, or had written a note, before the Seventh Cavalry marched from the Rosebud, and that fragment was directed to Lounsberry in Bismarck. In addition, Brisbin filled a passbook with details as

[43] Graham, *The Custer Myth*, 349–51; E. A. Brininstool, *Troopers with Custer*, 251–54.

[44] Graham, *The Custer Myth*, 349–51; *Chicago Times*, July 6, 1876; *New York Herald*, July 6, July 7, 1876.

[45] "Hugh McQuaid Told World of the Custer Massacre," *Contributions to the Historical Society of Montana*, Vol. IV (1903), 287.

[46] See *Contributions to Historical Society of Montana*, Vol. II (1896), 229–40.

he saw them on the battlefield, sending it to Lounsberry with the request that it be given to the *New York Herald*.[47]

Terry had written two reports, one an official report which would be made public and the other a confidential report that found its way to the press immediately though inadvertently. In addition, at least two officers had written newspaper accounts, for the *St. Paul Pioneer-Press* and the *New York Tribune*. Besides that, hundreds of private messages, reportedly, were to go on the telegraph at Bismarck, as well as the long official casualty lists.

After being delayed at the Yellowstone two days to ferry Gibbon's command to the north bank, Marsh ordered full steam up and pointed the *Far West* downstream with its load of wounded soldiers. Also on board were Terry's adjutant, Captain E. W. Smith; an infantry officer, Lieutenant John Carland; and a medical officer who had been with Reno, Dr. H. R. Porter.

Marsh kept up as high a head of steam as he could in safety, and the *Far West* scooted down the Yellowstone and Missouri on a record run. Leaving the mouth of the Big Horn about 5:00 P. M. on July 3, the *Far West* moved swiftly on the fast-flowing currents of a summer rise, arriving in Bismarck about 11:00 P. M. on July 5, having made a run of 710 miles in fifty-four hours.[48]

Excitement, consternation, and frustration are said to have rippled through Bismarck when the boat docked, for at that hour there was no way of telling the world what had happened. Not until morning could telegrapher Carnahan get the wire, and then he held it for forty-three of the next forty-eight hours, assisted by Rogers. First they moved Terry's confidential report—the official report having gone by Bozeman—and then private messages and then press dispatches. Through the long hours they sent the messages to operators

---

[47] Lounsberry, *Early History of North Dakota*, 315; Diehl, *Staff Correspondent*, 127.

[48] Frank Fiske, *Taming of the Sioux*, 125; Hanson, *Conquest of the Missouri*, 306.

William H. Gridley and Charles E. Hughes in St. Paul, who worked twenty-one hours at a stretch without even rising for food. Probably one received from Bismarck and the other relayed. Toward the end, Hughes commented, "My God— ain't we having lots of fun?"[49]

The first news stories from Bismarck were brief. On the basis of a short statement by Captain Smith, outlining the main facts but misleading in the casualty figure, Lounsberry forwarded a story to the *New York Herald*. Another brief story, fattened by the inclusion of Terry's order to Custer at the start of the march, went to the *New York Tribune*. Another story went to the *St. Paul Pioneer-Press* and was relayed to the *Chicago Inter-Ocean*, becoming a general press dispatch on the wires the next day.

And then Lounsberry developed the major story of the disaster, forwarding 18,000 words to the *New York Herald* at an estimated cost of $3,000. Starting with material that Kellogg had prepared, he wrote the lead story, running about 7,500 words as it appeared in the *Herald*, in the first person, presumably basing it upon the material sent in by Brisbin, an elderly officer whose interest in Montana's agricultural possibilities caused his troops to nickname him "Grasshopper Jim." Filling out the details with information from Dr. Porter, Captain Smith, and the others who came down on the *Far West*, he gave to the *Herald* a good example of the rewrite. The lead story, which would have required more than two hours for Morse transmission, filled all of page three, the first news page, except for a four-column map, and ran over to page four. In all, the *Herald* of the eighth used three pages for the story, with sidebars.

The unknown scribbler who rode a mule in a cavalry fight became a posthumous hero. The *New York Evening Post* of July 11, then edited by William Cullen Bryant, wrote his elegy in prose, saying: "If it is heroic to face danger and meet death calmly in the discharge of duty, then Mark Kellogg, the correspondent of the *New York Herald*, who died

[49] *Bismarck Tribune*, July 19, 1876; Kellogg Folder, Watson Papers.

with Custer, was a hero . . . his duty as a correspondent was to go with Custer, and he went in pursuit of duty, not of honors. The danger was as great to him as to any soldier in the column that he marched with, and he encountered it as coolly as they."[50]

Both the *New York Herald* and the *Chicago Tribune* claimed Kellogg as its own, and James Gordon Bennett, Jr., sent $500 to the two Kellogg girls in La Crosse. The claims of the metropolitan papers were just too much for Lounsberry to bear.

Petulantly, defiantly, Lounsberry wrote a story claiming for all time that Kellogg represented the *Bismarck Tribune*, that he was the only accredited correspondent with the Terry expedition, that other papers received stories from officers, that the *Herald* and other papers accepted Kellogg's dispatches through Lounsberry's hands, but the full cost of outfitting him had been borne by the *Bismarck Tribune*. "In view of these facts the *Tribune* asks for the credit for enterprise to which it is duly entitled, and expects that Mark Kellogg will be known in history as its special."[51]

In developing the Custer story with a speed and efficiency that would have been impossible before American newspapers learned the lessons of extensive and rapid news coverage in the Civil War, some of the major dailies immediately placed Custer and his fatal blunder in proper perspective. But the image of Custer was too strong to keep it in perspective. Romantic, sentimental, and sensational writers were tempted and yielded.

Terry's lengthy official report, which went by way of Bozeman, was written late in the day of June 27. It told with the drama of simplicity what had happened, but when he read it to his assembled staff officers by candlelight, they protested against his "excluding the fact that disobedience had occurred and had caused the miscarriage of a well-consid-

[50] Quoted by *New York Herald*, July 12, 1876, and *Bismarck Tribune*, July 19, 1876.

[51] *Bismarck Tribune*, July 19, 1876, Jan. 24, 1877; *New York Herald*, July 10, 1876; *Chicago Tribune*, July 8, 1876.

ered plan that promised a great success." Nevertheless, Terry intended to bear personally any hurtful imputations that might arise.[52]

But on July 2 he wrote the confidential report to Sheridan and forwarded it by the *Far West* for telegraphic transmission from Bismarck. In Philadelphia, Sheridan showed it to Sherman, who handed it to a man he supposed to, be a government messenger, intending to have it sent to Washington.[53] The messenger, however, was a reporter for the *Philadelphia Inquirer,* in which paper it appeared the next morning, July 7.[54] The confidential report also appeared in the *New York Herald* of July 7.

As printed in the *Herald,* identified as a confidential report, Terry's report implied that Custer had disobeyed, without using the word, by saying that the plan had been for Custer to take long enough on his scout to the southward to arrive on the Little Big Horn in time to co-operate with Gibbon's slower-moving column coming up from the south. Terry had instructed Custer not to follow the main Indian trail to the Little Big Horn, but that is what Custer did do without wasting time. Somehow, the last three paragraphs of Terry's report were omitted when it was relayed by telegraph from Sheridan's headquarters in Chicago to the General in Philadelphia. The last paragraph is said to have read: "I send in another dispatch a copy of my written orders to Custer, but these were supplemented by the distinct understanding that Gibbon could not get to the Little Big Horn before the evening of the 26th."[55]

Sheridan was attending a meeting of the Army of the Cumberland in Philadelphia in addition to attending the Exposition, and a *Herald* correspondent talked with other officers to get their views. One, identified as an "officer of distinction, who did not care to have his name mentioned," gave a penetrating insight into Custer. As reported by the *Herald,* he said:

[52] Hughes, "The Campaign Against the Sioux in 1876," *loc. cit,* 19.
[53] *Ibid.;* Graham, *Story of the Little Big Horn,* 110.
[54] Graham, *Story of the Little Big Horn,* 110.
[55] *New York Herald,* July 7, 1876; Graham, *The Custer Myth,* 216.

The truth about Custer is that he was a pet soldier who had risen not above his merit but higher than men of equal merit. He fought with Phil Sheridan and through the patronage of Sheridan he rose, but while Sheridan liked his valor and his dash he never trusted his judgment. . . . While Sheridan is always cool, Custer was always aflame. He was like a thermometer. He had a touch of romance about him, and when the war broke out he used to go about dressed like one of Byron's pirates in the Archipelago, with waving, shining locks and broad, flapping sombrero. Rising to high command early in life he lost the repose necessary to success in high command . . . but you see we all liked Custer and did not mind his little freaks in that way any more than we would have minded temper in a woman. . . . Custer's glorious death and the valor of his men will become a legend in our history. . . . We all think, much as we lament Custer . . . that he sacrificed the Seventh cavalry to ambition and wounded vanity.[56]

The *Chicago Tribune*, which said editorially that Custer's "own madcap haste, rashness, and love of fame" caused the defeat, received a report from a St. Louis correspondent quoting the Seventh Cavalry's commander, Colonel Sturgis, who had lost a son with Custer. Sturgis characterized Custer as "a very selfish man . . . insanely ambitious of glory, and the phrase 'Custer's luck' affords a good clew to his ruling passion." Public opinion of Custer had been formed largely by Custer's writings and from newspaper reports, when the truth was that Custer did not know enough about Indian fighting to come off victoriously in a contest with the Sioux, Sturgis said.[57]

But somehow the hero factor, the martyr factor, went to work. The truth wasn't good enough. George Armstrong Custer became something of a demigod.

[56] *New York Herald,* July 7, 1876.
[57] *Chicago Tribune,* July 7, 19, 1876.

Add Custer

7. TERRY TAKES FIELD AGAIN

> *There is no use trying to conceal the*
> *fact that the victory of the Sioux, so*
> *terrible in its completeness, has low-*
> *ered the morale of our troops; not*
> *much, perhaps; but if one listens to*
> *the soldiers as they discuss among*
> *themselves the campaign the convic-*
> *tion is forced that they no longer look*
> *upon victory as certain.*
> JAMES J. O'KELLY[1]

TWO CORRESPONDENTS hurried forward to Terry's command within the week that the Custer story broke, and a third went later in the month. For first-hand coverage, the *New York Herald* sent one of its better reporters, James J. O'Kelly, who had once made an international incident of himself. The *Chicago Tribune* selected "Phocion" Howard, a tall, portly eccentric. The *Chicago Times* assigned to the story a stripling of twenty-one, Charles Sanford Diehl, who in maturity would direct the Associated Press.

They went to the Indian country by way of Bismarck and river steamers up the Missouri and Yellowstone, traveling with the reinforcements sent to Terry. The earlier route of the romantic Audubon and the fur traders had been converted into a highway for war.

Howard reached Bismarck by July 12, O'Kelly by July 17, and they both arrived at Terry's camp on the Yellowstone by the end of the month. Diehl did not start until late in the month, and it was the middle of August before he reached the theater of operations.

The Custer disaster, what happened and why, still called

---

[1] *New York Herald*, Aug. 18, 1876.

for investigative reporting, but O'Kelly was the only one of the three who consistently dug at the facts. However, Terry later showed Diehl a copy of the orders given Custer, and told him Custer would have been court-martialed, had he lived, for arriving at the Little Big Horn ahead of time.[2]

A soldier of fortune with a striking personality, O'Kelly collected adventures as some men collect stamps. A stout Irishman of thirty-one, he had fought as a soldier on three continents before becoming a reporter for the *New York Herald*. In 1863, at the age of eighteen, he had left his home in Ireland to join the French Foreign Legion, and had fought in North Africa and for Maximilian in Mexico. Mexican troops captured him in northern Mexico, but he escaped one night, found a dugout canoe, and crossed the Río Grande into Texas, eventually making his way back to Ireland.

He returned to the French Army to fight in the Franco-Prussian War of 1870. When the tide turned against the French, he was sent secretly to Ireland to raise an Irish brigade, but was left high and dry there by the defeat of France. At that time, he turned toward New York where he went to work for the *Herald*. A knowledge and appreciation of art made him the paper's art critic, a position in which he remained until the *Herald* needed a man who could get through the Spanish lines in Cuba and interview leaders of a revolution there in 1873. Despite threats that he would be shot as a spy if he left the Spanish lines and tried to return, O'Kelly made his way to the insurgents, got his interview, and returned, about the same time Fox penetrated the Lava Bed. Spanish authorities arrested him, but the intervention of British consular authorities saved him from immediate execution. With the *Herald* beating the drums, his case became an international matter, and the Spanish government transported him to Spain for trial but released him. After that he went to Brazil for the *Herald*, and had just finished escorting Emperor Dom Pedro on a tour of the United States when

[2] Diehl, *Staff Correspondent*, 107.

he was assigned to cover the Sioux campaign. He arrived in Bismarck on July 15.

The men who covered the Civil War called themselves Bohemians and did their best to live up to the name, but James William "Phocion" Howard seems to have been the only Bohemian who covered any of the Indian campaigns. He lived up to the name.

Forty-three years old in 1876, Howard had a long and checkered career. He was born in Rising Sun, Indiana, on July 4, 1833, the son of a steamboat captain. He once attended a theological seminary, but he also worked as an apprentice in a newspaper's backshop, which turned him toward journalism. During his earlier years he published newspapers in Kentucky; he ended his management of an Illinois paper with perhaps the shortest leave-taking on record: "Ta-ta."

"Commanding in height and contour," Howard habitually dressed in a long, blue frock coat set off by brass buttons, blue dress military trousers (he had served in the Civil War, although accounts vary as to how and when and where), a black military field hat, and a frilled shirt front. He also carried a cane with a concealed stiletto. Once he drew the stiletto in an argument and was arrested for assault, but won acquittal with the claim that the law was unconstitutional.

Howard, who went into newspaper work in Chicago in 1865 or 1866, once outmaneuvered the opposition in interviewing Jay Gould by jumping on Gould's train just as it left the station, waving good-bye to his colleagues and interviewing Gould on the trip to St. Louis. During his career he reputedly worked on newspapers in New York, Michigan, Iowa, Ohio, Pennsylvania, and Canada, and had been on at least one expedition into the Sioux country for the *Chicago Tribune* before 1876. He arrived in Bismarck by July 12.[3]

The Sioux war assignment lifted young Diehl from the anonymity of city railroad news. He had been on the *Chicago Times* three years, but on newspapers since the age of fourteen. Born in Maryland, he grew up in Ottawa and Wenona,

3 Howard Folder, Watson Papers.

Illinois, where his classicist father was school principal and Diehl's only educator. Detailed to replace Kellogg, he rose for the first time to the position of staff correspondent, which, on the *Chicago Times,* meant that his stories would be signed more often than not, even if only by his initials. In the last week of July he joined a party of officers at St. Paul for the trip to Bismarck and thence to Fort Buford, hoping to push on from there to join Terry.

The story they went to cover had become unlike any other Indian campaign, because for once a spirit of war supported Indian fighting. A military disaster of the magnitude of Custer's defeat would have shocked the nation at any time, but its coincidence with the United States centenary had an inevitable emotional impact. Perhaps it was that which caused some contemporary accounts to say that not even the assassination of Lincoln had produced such shock as the news of what had happened to the Seventh Cavalry.[4]

Troops sent to the front as reinforcements saw demonstrations of that sentiment. En route from Fort Leavenworth to support Terry, Colonel Nelson A. Miles and his Fifth Infantry were cheered every time they passed a gathering of citizens. Through towns and villages it seemed to Miles much as during the Civil War. He saw many public buildings and private houses draped in mourning.

Phocion Howard found the same thing as he traveled westward by rail from St. Paul. All along the route, he reported, the Indian war and Custer's defeat absorbed the conversation, on the train and in the stations. At every station a large crowd greeted the train, expecting to see troops moving toward the front. Since there were no troops on the train, the trainmen satisfied the townsmen by pointing out Howard as "Standing Bull, the great chief of the Indian Peace Commission."[5] At least that's what he wrote. What he wrote and the truth don't always appear to have been on speaking terms.

Sheridan drew reinforcements not only from throughout

[4] Stewart, *Custer's Luck,* 5.
[5] *Chicago Tribune,* July 15, 1876.

his Military Division of the Missouri but from the Atlantic and Pacific as well. In addition to the Fifth Infantry and other infantry units which had been stationed in the Department of Dakota and which went to Terry, Sheridan pulled out all ten companies of the Fifth Cavalry, that were then stationed in new posts along the Kansas-Pacific Railroad, for Crook. He had to use every available soldier in his department, but not entirely for the front. For the army also had been given control of all Indian agencies within the theater of war, necessitating many troop transfers to reinforce garrisons already at those agencies.

Transporting, equipping, and supplying the necessary reinforcements took most of July, and the Crook and Terry commands waited in the field until the new men arrived before renewing operations.

After a wait in Bismarck, O'Kelly and Howard were assigned space on the steamboat *Carroll,* leaving on July 20 with reinforcements from the Twenty-second Infantry—mere skeleton companies, Howard called them. Three hundred and eighty persons had been thrust suddenly upon the decks of a steamboat, which had not been built to carry that many, leaving little more than standing room for the 1,000-mile trip. The upper deck was propped to keep it from collapsing under the added weight of many men. Young recruits—eager and confident on their first trip to battle—hurried aboard, each man grabbing the best place he could find, the first ones aboard taking sheltered positions. Good fortune blessed a few officers with staterooms, but half had to sleep on cots on the cabin floor or on blankets or buffalo robes, with no protection from mosquitoes.

Arriving at Terry's camp at the mouth of the Rosebud, the infantry reinforcements caused "considerable stir." Only the arrival of Miles's Fifth Infantry was awaited before Terry moved southward in search of the hostiles.[6]

O'Kelly was after the Custer story. He began digging for it in Bismarck, where, he reported, he saw a book that Custer

[6] *New York Herald,* Aug. 7, 1876.

had been reading before he left on his last march. It was Mrs. Alexander's *Her Dearest Foe,* a new three-volume English novel that had just come out in 1876. "I have just been shown the book, and find many passages showing the strongest affection and the most kindly and forgiving spirit marked, but this: —'I have faith in my own fortunes, and believe I shall conquer in the end,' struck me most forcibly," O'Kelly wrote.[7]

Also from Bismarck, O'Kelly reported that Custer had been without a command until he started up the Rosebud. Previously, his regiment had been divided into the two wings under Reno and Benteen. "Much of the time," O'Kelly reported on the basis of what he learned in the frontier river town and, presumably, Fort Lincoln, "was spent with his brothers, and a few trusty men, hunting and scouting on his own account. Generally he was with the advance, but not in command of it. Two or three times he was called upon to find passes through the Bad Lands or mountains, and once Terry said no other officer but Custer could have conducted the command through difficulties which seemed insurmountable so successfully."[8]

O'Kelly or his informants may have exaggerated, but certainly that which he made explicit is implicit in both the Kellogg dispatches and Custer's letters to his wife.[9] During the march to the Powder River the Seventh Cavalry had been divided into two wings, and the main facts of the O'Kelly report—Custer in the advance, Custer with scouts, Custer with his brothers, Custer hunting—are supported by Kellogg's descriptions, the "hell-whooping" over the prairie and "on the scoot."

Such activity does seem an odd occupation for an acting regimental commander on campaign. The explanation might

[7] *Ibid.,* July 18, 1876. "Mrs. Alexander" was the pen name of Mrs. Annie French Hector, whose novel, *Her Dearest Foe,* appeared in a three-volume edition in London in 1876. In the seventh edition, a one-volume edition, published in 1895, a quotation substantially the same as that given by O'Kelly, but not exactly the same, can be found on p. 75. Unfortunately, Custer's published letters to his wife do not refer to his reading on campaign.
[8] *Ibid.*
[9] Elizabeth Custer, *"Boots and Saddles,"* 304 ff.

lie in Terry's sagacity and Custer's record. After Custer had won reinstatement for the expedition, he had bragged that he would swing clear of Terry as he had of Stanley in 1873. Division of the regiment, with the commander reduced virtually to independent status, would have been an astute means of neutralizing Custer.

O'Kelly kept after the Custer story when he arrived on the Yellowstone. Within five days of his arrival, he wrote a long story based upon interviews with Reno and Benteen.[10] In beginning the story, he noted that officers of the Seventh Cavalry were annoyed by the "incorrect and garbled accounts published in some papers" and written by officers who knew nothing of the fight at the Little Big Horn. He did not say whether the condemnation included the *Herald*'s story based in part upon Brisbin's material.

The middling tall, swarthy Reno impressed O'Kelly as a soldier whose appearance and temperament indicated he would be the last person in the world to leave a comrade in trouble without trying to save him. He said the gray-haired Benteen, called the "Saviour of the Seventh," had a kindly, gentle expression which belied "the decision of character" he showed in battle.

Reno had just been stung by a letter written to the *Minneapolis Evening Tribune* by General T. L. Rosser, a former Confederate officer who had been chief engineer of the Northern Pacific and who had accompanied the survey expedition of 1873 which Custer helped escort. Reno let O'Kelly have his reply in full, in which he emphatically denied Rosser's assumption that Custer had specified a rendezvous in case either his or Reno's battalions should be repulsed, as well as Rosser's further assumption that Custer's attack would have succeeded had Reno with the other seven companies fought through to Custer immediately. Reno wrote that "both the premises are false, and consequently all the conclusions of your letter fall to the ground." He said Custer had sent orders to him to attack the village with the promise of support "by

[10] *New York Herald*, Aug. 8, 1876.

the whole outfit." Reno charged the village, found that the Indians outnumbered him ten to one, and discovered that Custer was not riding to his support. It was then, Reno explained, that he retired to the timber along the river and then to the bluffs across the river. Maintaining that—since he was the first in action—his battalion should have been supported instead of being expected to support another, Reno made this point: "Custer's disaster was not the defeat of the Seventh Cavalry, who held their ground for thirty-six hours after with a force outnumbered ten to one."

After that, O'Kelly interviewed Benteen, who took out his notebook and sketched the battlefield for the reporter. In the interview, Benteen said his scout to the left, looking for valleys where Indians might be camped, had been fruitless, and he returned to the main trail. Several miles later, while hurrying on the main trail without having sighted the enemy, he saw fighting in the valley and part of the regiment retreating across the river. He did not know which part of the regiment it was, but he was certain they had been whipped. Benteen said he then marched to their support and discovered it to be Reno's command. While the command waited for the strung-out pack train to come up with the ammunition packs for which Custer had asked, they sent a company forward in the direction supposed to have been taken by Custer, but the company proceeded only a mile before being attacked and driven back. By that time, he said, Custer's command had been annihilated, although he claimed he had not heard any heavy firing from any quarter.

When Benteen said additional details should come from Reno, O'Kelly interviewed Reno, who told of being forced back to the bluffs when he attempted to move forward to Custer's possible position, the fighting of the evening and early hours of the next morning, and the withdrawal of the Indians the next day through huge clouds of dust and smoke, the latter from the prairie which they had set afire.

But O'Kelly could get no further with direct questioning, and had to wait for the rest of the information to come forth

227

gradually. As he described it, he almost literally soaked up the story in the weeks that followed as he traveled, lived, and slept with the men of the Seventh Cavalry. Listening to camp-fire talk in the evening, noticing especially what questions they asked of one another, observing the unguarded words dropped in the heat of argument, O'Kelly continued trying to piece the whole story together for the nearly two months that he was in the field.

Upon leaving the field, he wrote a long story from Fort Abraham Lincoln,[11] in which he demanded a governmental investigation of the Little Big Horn disaster and placed full blame on Reno and Benteen. Men there were who could speak, he said, but who dared not speak against their superior officers who were just as much the enemies of Custer dead as of Custer alive. Only if compelled to, would the officers of the Seventh Cavalry tell what they knew. The story showed that Reno's favorable impression upon O'Kelly had vanished.

Linking together all that he had heard, O'Kelly said he was convinced that the Custer disaster resulted from a "blundering want of soldierly sympathy—a failure on the part of men to do their duty or lukewarmness in supporting General Custer—that might be called by an ugly name." No experienced Indian fighter, he wrote, would question Custer's wisdom in attacking the village when he did, and the officers with Terry felt sure that had the full regiment fought together, the Little Big Horn would have been a victory rather than a defeat.

No confidence could be placed in the official report of the battle, which had been read with "astonishment" by officers who had fought there, O'Kelly declared. As a case in point, he said Reno retreated to the timber in the face of not an overwhelming force of Indians but, rather, no more than fifty Indians. He charged bluntly that Reno retreated pell-mell to the bluffs, instead of charging to the bluffs, because there were no Indians in the way to be charged. "There is a strong impression," he reported, "that had a tougher fight been made

11 *Ibid.*, Sept. 21, 1876.

in the bottom the Indians could not have overwhelmed Custer with their whole force." O'Kelly denied that Company D had been sent forward from the bluff to try to reach Custer; rather, he said, the company went voluntarily, without orders. Nothing prevented the seven companies on the bluff from charging to Custer's assistance, he continued. Further, he said, Benteen was no more than seven or eight miles away from where Custer fell after he came back on the main trail. Only a searching investigation, the reporter claimed, could bring light to the Little Big Horn disaster.

An investigation was conducted, but at Reno's demand. An Army Court of Inquiry convened in Chicago in 1879 and heard testimony which developed that Reno and Benteen could not have acted other than they did. The court concluded that Reno was not guilty of any action requiring "animadversion."[12]

In reaching his conclusions, O'Kelly moved into one of the two main schools of opinion that developed about the Little Big Horn controversy; he joined with those who damn Reno; the others damn Custer. Who influenced O'Kelly is not named in the story, but the opinions he reflected appeared in subsequent writings. While the command was in camp in August, Captain Thomas B. Weir, who had led the one company toward Custer, said something about Custer and Reno which caused Custer's enemy, Benteen, to call him a "damned liar" and offer to shoot it out right then. There were still in the regiment several, if not many, officers who were devotedly loyal to Custer and critical of Reno, such as Weir and his lieutenant, Edward S. Godfrey. Both Weir and Godfrey firmly held unfavorable opinions of Reno. F. F. Girard, the interpreter, said that Reno's movement to the bluff was a rout, not a charge. George Herendeen, a scout, claimed that not more than two hundred Indians attacked Reno. Captain Myles Moylan, a troop commander, also held Reno in con-

[12] Graham, *The Story of the Little Big Horn*, 102–104; Col. W. A. Graham, *Abstract of the Official Record of Proceedings of the Reno Court of Inquiry*, 266.

tempt, although he thought him justified in getting his three troops out of the bottom. Captain T. H. French said that Reno ran away, and he hinted darkly that he had thought of murdering Reno because, he thought, the troops could have won. One enlisted man, William D. Taylor, said, in 1910, that Reno "proved incompetent."[13]

If one assumes that those men held those same opinions in 1876 and that they and others muttered them in soldier talk, one can see where O'Kelly obtained his information and who influenced him. Having reported both sides of the story, although not in the same article, he likewise was justified in saying an investigation was called for; the differing opinions certainly were of such volatility as to make a searching investigation the only means of getting at the truth.

O'Kelly found other things at which to become indignant during the few days he had to wait between his arrival on the Yellowstone and the time Terry resumed field operations. The first was the absence of ambulances to transport the wounded. Kellogg had reported ambulances with Terry originally. "Let the humanitarians who howl over the sorrows of a stricken mule," O'Kelly wrote, "do something for the poor fellows who are daily risking their lives that their fellow citizens may dwell in peace and security." The second was the callousness which he reportedly found in regard to the wounded. He said that when he asked several cavalry officers what would happen to their wounded without ambulances, they replied that the wounded soldier was out of luck not to have been killed.[14] O'Kelly, however, emphasized Terry's solicitude for the wounded.

Howard was much less systematic in his reporting, and seemed to write more for the entertainment of the *Chicago Tribune's* readers than O'Kelly did for the understanding of his readers. His first story from Fort Lincoln included a section based upon an "almost complete history" of Sitting Bull, heard from the lips of no less reliable an authority than a

---

[13] Graham, *The Custer Myth*, 196, 217, 251, 264, 333, 335, 342, 344.
[14] *New York Herald*, Aug. 13, 1876.

steamboat captain. With a perfectly straight presentation, he wrote that Sitting Bull had learned French from the Jesuit missionary, Father DeSmet, and that he had read the French history of Napoleon's wars, modeling his generalship upon Napoleon's.[15] That was the sort of bunkum which contributed to the myth of Sitting Bull.

In mid-July, however, O'Kelly had reported from Bismarck —before going upriver to Terry's camp—that Crazy Horse rather than Sitting Bull had commanded the Indians who had fought Crook at the Rosebud. And by the end of July the press had part of the truth about Indian leadership at the Little Big Horn. Lieutenant Colonel J. S. Poland, commanding at Standing Rock Agency in Dakota, reported seven Sioux from the hostile camp had identified Crazy Horse and Black Moon as the Indian leaders at the Little Big Horn and said that Sitting Bull remained in the council tent during the battle.

Meantime, Diehl had started upriver after a wait at Fort Lincoln, where the mosquitoes were so troublesome the men wore balloon-like wire helmets covered with netting for protection. He found transportation aboard the *Key West*, which carried materials for construction of a new army post near the mouth of Powder River, approved by a begrudging Congress after the Custer calamity. However, the *Key West* drew too much water to go beyond Fort Buford at that season of lowered water stage, and at Buford he had to wait for the lighter draught *Josephine* before he could proceed to Terry's camp. Going up the rivers, they maintained a watch for hostile Indians, who fired on the boat on at least one occasion, killing a soldier. The boat tied up on the opposite bank to return the fire. When a barricade was formed of grain sacks and boxes of hardtack, Diehl took his place there with a carbine, but Captain John F. Weston of the Seventh Cavalry spotted him, and commanded, "Come out of that. You are not paid to be killed. We are."[16] Diehl did not arrive on

[15] *Chicago Tribune*, July 15, 1876.
[16] Diehl, *Staff Correspondent*, 34, 97–99; *Chicago Times*, Aug. 10, 1876.

the Yellowstone in time, however, for the start of Terry's field operation.

Reinforced until he had a strength of almost 1,600 men, Terry took the field once more, beginning a southward march in search of hostile Indians on August 8. But in his column, with its lumbering wagons, there were more infantry than cavalry, going after a completely mounted enemy. The soldiers looked more like irregular than regular troops, dressed in any manner their fancy and purse might permit, some in regulation blue, some in white corduroy breeches and tall riding boots with shirts to suit, and some in the elaborately fringed buckskin jackets of the frontier.

Some there were who predicted battle, but some "bell sharp" campaigners said there would be no fight. The veterans predicted the Sioux would divide into small parties, making battle impossible.

Terry led his command up the Rosebud Valley—cavalry, infantry, Gatling gun batteries, and 203 wagons, each pulled by a six-mule team. At the end of the first day's march, Terry sent five Crow scouts out in an effort to make contact with Crook, known to be south of them. Two scouts returned the next afternoon, reporting "Heap Sioux" in front. Terry camped for the night, prepared to repel attack.

On the tenth the ponderous column moved forward again.

A dust cloud appeared on the near horizon, moving down a pass between spurs of the Wolf Mountains. Crow scouts dashed in, crying, "Sioux! Sioux! Heap Sioux!"

Terry prepared for battle.

Add Crook

8♦ SIOUX PUSH "FIGHTING IRISH PENCIL PUSHER"

*The soldiers, on the eve of seeking an-
other battle, with the terrible fate of
Custer and his men so fresh in their
memories, are by no means as gay as
they were when they last started
toward the Yellowstone. But there is
a grim resolve evinced in their manner and their faces to seek vengeance
for the slain of the Little Big Horn.*
REUBEN DAVENPORT[1]

To CROOK, as Wasson quoted him, the Battle of the Rosebud
had been "a mere scratching of the boil," and he ached to
draw its core, provided he had plenty of help. He dared not
move forward again until reinforced and resupplied, knowing now that thousands rather than hundreds of Sioux and
Cheyennes were in hostility, many of them well armed. He
began a long wait on Goose Creek, after reaching camp on
June 19.[2]

Before two weeks were up, Finerty complained that the
waiting had become "physically and mentally nauseating."
And he had come to the discomfiting conclusion that Crook
intended an all-summer campaign, which no one had expected.[3] In isolation two hundred miles from the telegraph
and three hundred from the railroad, the men felt the lone-
liness and inactivity acutely.

And so they remained in Camp Cloud Peak, on the broad
level benches flanking either side of Goose Creek, with the

[1] *New York Herald*, Aug. 18, 1876.
[2] *Alta California*, Aug. 1, 1876; Bourke, *On the Border with Crook*, 320.
[3] *Chicago Times*, July 12, 1876.

Big Horns towering to south and west. On the north bank, imposing wall tents marked the headquarters of the Big Horn and Yellowstone Expedition. For several hundred yards on either side of headquarters were regular rows of snow-white infantry and cavalry "A" tents. Across the stream, cavalry-men lived in one long line of identical "A" tents. Beyond in any direction stretched wilderness.

Fretting and anxious because the infrequent couriers brought no word of Terry or Gibbon, Crook took a detach-ment of about twenty men to the summit of the Big Horn Mountains, where with powerful glasses he could sweep the country to the northeast for signs of smoke, dust, camps, or other evidences of the unheard-from columns.

Leaving on July 1, Crook took along all four correspondents —Finerty, Wasson, Strahorn, and Davenport. Mounted on mules and carrying food for four days, they climbed to the 12,000-foot area where Crook could see vast stretches of Indian country but no sign of the other army columns.

Crook returned to camp on the centennial Fourth, and decided on another expedition. If he could not locate Terry, he wanted at least to know where the Sioux were. To that end, he formed a scouting party of Frank Grouard; Lieutenant Frederick W. Sibley and twenty-five picked men from the Second Cavalry; another scout, Baptiste Pourier, who was known as "Big Bat" to distinguish him from Baptiste Garnier, known as "Little Bat"; and a packer known as "Trailer Jack."

When Finerty learned from an officer that the patrol was going out toward the Little Big Horn, he sought permission to accompany it. Crook was reluctant to let him go, but finally consented, warning him there might be more trouble than he had reckoned on. When the word spread that Finerty was to go, some of the officers kidded him about it, Bourke asking what kind of an epitaph he wanted.

About noon of July 6 the party, provisioned for several days, rode from camp to Big Goose Creek, thirteen miles away, and camped until sundown. On the way, they thought they saw a horseman watching them from a ravine, but decided it was a stray elk. After dark they moved forward again, everyone silent. Under the light of a full moon, they marched with the appearance of a "phantom company." At 2:00 A. M. they halted, forty miles from camp.[4]

On the morning of July 7 they rode until they reached a point near the Little Big Horn, where Grouard ascended a rocky mound, alone, for a look at the country. Excitedly, he summoned Big Bat to his side, and both scanned the country through their glasses. They galloped back to the others.

"Be quick, and follow me for your lives," Grouard cried.[5]

Wheeling their horses, the men followed Grouard on what was described as a hair-raising ride through rough country until they reached a place where the horses could be concealed while the leaders watched the countryside. The four men with field glasses—Finerty, Sibley, Grouard, and Pourier —crawled up into the rocks to see what was coming. As they watched, Grouard told them he had seen Sitting Bull's war party. Soon Finerty and Sibley saw for themselves—Indians in war costume on the bluffs to the north and east. Tensely, they waited to see whether the Indians would cut their trail. Their glasses were trained on an Indian in a red blanket, who suddenly started riding around in circles—the Plains Indian's sign for enemies sighted. The Sioux had found their trail.

Sibley had sense enough to trust the whole matter to the plains wisdom of Grouard, who said the only hope of escape was to lead their horses into the Big Horns and try to cross them. Rejoining the troopers, Sibley told them they had been discovered, might have to fight, and that no man should surrender because of the merciless treatment they could expect from the Sioux. Moving westward at a brisk trot, they traveled about five miles before Grouard thought it would be safe to rest.[6]

[4] Finerty, *War-Path and Bivouac*, 161–79. Accounts of the Sibley scout vary. Since Finerty's account was based largely upon newspaper dispatches written immediately after the event and Grouard's account was based upon memory, after a lapse of several years, and then written by another person, the Finerty version is followed here in tracing the course of the adventure.

[5] *Ibid.*

[6] Sandoz, *Crazy Horse*, 338, based upon Pourier's recollection.

During the hour's halt, in which the men brewed coffee, Big Bat poked fun at Finerty. Now, he said, Finerty really would have something to send his paper. Yes, Finerty replied, and it would be the last scout he would accompany for the sake of news. Big Bat told him he could expect some stirring times ahead.[7]

That hour's halt came near to proving fatal. Resuming their march—it was early afternoon by then—they came within sight of the Big Horn's snowy range, riding single file through parklike country on the mountainsides.

"The Indians! The Indians!" came a shout from two men in the rear. Finerty turned to see Indians behind and uncomfortably near.[8]

At that time, they were on a narrow plain in the mountain range—the exact locale of the action is not made clear in any of the accounts—with woods on their left and front, high rocks and timber on the right. Grouard told them to keep well to the left, close to the woods. His instructions were punctuated by rifle fire directed at them from the rocks and timber on the right. Having seen what route the whites were taking, the Indians had maneuvered to cut them off and ambush them.

After the first fire from the Indians, Grouard saw Finerty lying flat on his back. Thinking the reporter had been shot, he asked where he was hit. Finerty replied that he was not wounded, but had been thrown by his horse, which had been hit.[9]

Under orders from the mixed-blood Grouard, the soldiers retreated hastily to the woods, where they tethered their horses, formed a semicircular skirmish line, and opened fire. Using trees and fallen timber for breastworks, they fought an enemy whose number gradually increased, including Cheyenne as well as Sioux warriors. The Indians recognized Grouard, whose Indian name was Grabber, and called out

---

[7] Baptiste Pourier Interview, Interview No. 15, Eli S. Ricker Collection, Nebraska State Historical Society, excerpt supplied by Archivist Donald F. Danker (hereafter cited as Ricker Interviews).

[8] Finerty, *War-Path and Bivouac*, 161–79.

[9] Joe DeBarthe, *Life and Adventures of Frank Grouard*, 140.

to him: "Do you think there are no men but yours in this country?"

The "no surrender" order passed along the short line of white men, and Grouard told the men to save the last shot for themselves. Three or four began to cry when he said that, others receiving the words with differing emotions, but Finerty—as Grouard recalled—had the happiest attitude of all.[10]

No man there expected to leave with his life, knowing that the sound of battle would attract every Sioux and Cheyenne within hearing distance, while the whites were a good fifty miles from any hope of relief whatever. During the fighting, the Indians aimed for the horses to make escape impossible. "We were truly looking death in the face," Finerty wrote, even though he was able, during lulls in the firing, to pick mountain crocus and forget-me-nots which he pressed between leaves of his notebook. "Life seemed particularly sweet throughout that eventful day. Close acquaintance with death is not a pleasing situation."[11]

Even at that moment Big Bat could make a joke of it. There on the skirmish line he nudged Finerty and said, "You will have lots to send to your paper when you get back to camp."[12]

"Damn you, Bat, you are always making fun of me!" Finerty responded, and repeated that he would not go out on another scout for news.[13]

Presently the order to slip back quietly came down the skirmish line to Finerty. Sibley ordered the men to take all their ammunition from the saddlebags and retreat on foot, up through the thick timber and rocks, abandoning their horses. Grouard had recommended the stratagem, and had the men fire some random volleys to deceive the Indians. Although the Indians had been prodigal of ammunition, the soldiers had frequently reserved their fire, and another silence would help cover their retreat since the Indians would not notice it immediately. Single file, they slipped through the

[10] *Ibid.*, 141.
[11] Finerty, *War-Path and Bivouac*, 161–79.
[12] Ricker Interviews.
[13] *Ibid.*

trees, waded a stream waist deep, and scaled the slippery rocks of a mountain ridge where mounted Indians could not, and dismounted Indians probably would not, follow them. Finerty kept falling down, tripping over brush and grass which snagged his boots, the toes of which turned upward like the front end of a prairie schooner. They had gone about a mile when they heard five or six volleys, probably the final fire before the savages charged their former position. "That means we are safe for the present," Grouard said.[14]

But they were far from safe for good, with fifty miles between them and camp. They would have to travel afoot and hungry, because they had also left their food in the saddle-bags. In the heat of the day they threw away superfluous clothing as they marched, climbed, and scrambled over obstacles which at any other time would have been insurmountable. When utter fatigue finally made them stop at midnight, they bivouacked under a pile of rocks on an unknown summit. During the night, a wind and hail storm lashed the mountain, uprooting trees and tormenting the men with cold.

At dawn they stumbled their way onward again, reaching a southern branch of the Tongue, which placed them about twenty-five miles from camp. But they had to turn their backs on the invitingly easy travel of the valley, which was good game country where they might meet Indians. With a rapid march through an exposed part of the valley, they crossed the stream, and then Grouard hurried them up a precipice on the right bank. They went up diagonally, along what Finerty called a "squirrel path" not more than one foot wide, with a sheer drop of five hundred feet below them. Even though the men were dog-tired and suffering from hunger, Grouard dared not stop. Twenty miles distant they saw the point of mountain which marked camp, food, and comrades. Scant comfort it was, though, as they continued their flight, making only one descent into a deep valley for water—their sole refreshment.

After a quick drink, Grouard hurried them into the moun-

[14] *Ibid.;* Finerty, *War-Path and Bivouac,* 161–79.

238

tains again, and they had scarcely gained the timber when he sounded the warning, "Hush." Grouard threw himself on the ground, signaling the others to do the same. Around the base of the mountain they had just crossed came a party of Indians. "Some were anxious to fight this small body of Indians in front of us, especially Mr. Finerty," Grouard recalled.[15]

But the Indians did not see their trail, and passed from view. That short wait robbed them of vitality. Exhausted, they fell asleep and did not awaken until dark. They were hungry to the point of pain when they woke up, and were certain they could not endure any more of the mountain route.

Caution thrown aside, they struck out across the plain in a night march. At 3:00 A.M. they waded Big Goose Creek, up to their armpits in water cold from melted snow. At the creek two men balked, refusing to cross since neither could swim. Sibley left them there, to hide until horses could be sent out for them. Dawn brought the others to a point about a dozen miles from camp. By that time every step was hurtful in feet skinned by rocks which had broken their boots. So great was their desperation that they made no effort to hide when, in the gray dawn, they saw Indians in the east, but the Indians did not pursue. About six-thirty they came upon two cavalrymen who had obtained permission to go hunting. Sibley sent them to camp for horses, food, and an escort for the two men left on Big Goose. A detail from the Second Cavalry came out to them an hour and a half later with cooked food and led horses.

Finerty, as well as the others, was described as almost hysterical upon reaching camp about mid-morning on Sunday, July 9. They were in a state of collapse—ragged, bleeding, exhausted, and famished. Strahorn remembered Finerty's outburst thus: " 'I lost my saddle and bridle. I lost my pipe and blankets, and I lost my horse.' Then, bursting out with a loud cry, he reached the climax by raising his voice to its utmost pitch with:

" 'But the worst of it all is I LOST MY TOOTHBRUSH.' "[16]

[15] DeBarthe, *Grouard*, 143.   [16] Strahorn, Autobiography, 192.

Crook mentioned Finerty by name in his official report to Sheridan, made public at Sheridan's headquarters in Chicago.[17]

Upon their return, they found that Crook had gone into the mountains to get fresh meat for the command. Although he liked to hunt, Crook also was distressed more than he cared to admit over the lack of word from Terry and Gibbon. Trips into the mountains gave him more chances to search the countryside through field glasses.

That is where Crook was the next day, July 10, when couriers Ben Arnold and Louis Richaud brought a dispatch from Sheridan reporting the Custer disaster—the first news that had reached Crook's men of the defeat that had occurred to the north of them. Arnold had been sick in bed at Fort Fetterman when the telegrapher brought him the dispatch. Even so, he saddled his horse and, with Richaud, brought the news to the men on Goose Creek. At first, the news shocked the officers and men into silence, and then wild excitement followed.

Annihilation of the Custer command and the near disaster of the Sibley scout caused immediate apprehension about Crook's safety. Crook had called for mules to bring in his kill of twenty elk, and the officers feared Sibley's attackers might find the trail of the mule train. Anxiety led Royall to send Mills with a battalion in search of Crook; the cavalrymen met him and the returning mule train about two-thirty that afternoon.

Back in camp, where the twenty elk were a delicacy to men who had been living mostly on bacon and trout for a month, Crook read the dispatches. "Crook said very little when he heard of our adventure and Custer's disaster," Finerty reported, "but he kept up a big thinking."[18]

Crook received another telegram from Sheridan, saying, "Hit them again and hit them harder!" Crook commented:

[17] *Chicago Tribune,* July 26, 1876; Bourke, *On the Border with Crook,* 331–33.
[18] *Chicago Times,* July 26, 1876.

"I wish Sheridan would come out here himself and show us how to do it. It is rather difficult to surround three Indians with one soldier!"[19]

For a time, each successive day brought new excitement. First, Sibley's men returned in what was regarded as a miraculous escape. The next day, news of the Custer disaster. The third day, Washakie arrived with 213 Shoshone allies, who would give their alliance with the pony soldiers another trial.

And then on the fourth day, July 12, three dirty, ragged men rode into camp. To the astonishment of Crook's men, they identified themselves as Privates James Bell, William Evans, and Benjamin F. Stewart of the Seventh Infantry. They were all the more welcomed when they produced a message from Terry, addressed to Crook. They were all the more honored for having made the ride from the mouth of the Rosebud which no frontier scout had been willing to make. A few days later some Crow scouts arrived from Terry's camp, and still later Crook found a man—a scout named Kelly —who was willing to take a message to Terry.

And on the next day, infantry reinforcements reached camp, along with a wagon train of supplies, but at the same time Crook received orders from Sheridan not to take the field immediately. Sheridan thought it better if Crook waited for the arrival of Colonel Wesley Merritt, who had taken command of ten companies of the Fifth Cavalry. Merritt had started out, but on the sixteenth had had to make a detour to cut off Cheyennes moving from the Nebraska agencies to the camp of the hostiles.

By that time, it was obvious that the army was engaged in a major war against the Sioux Nation. Criticizing Crook for preferring separate operations to the co-operation suggested by Terry, Davenport said, "All other Indian wars sink into insignificance compared with this." Even when the Fifth Cavalry should arrive, he wrote, the combined forces of Crook and Terry "would not be too strong to cope with the formid-

---

[19] Finerty, *War-Path and Bivouac*, 181. This story may be apochryphal, in the light of later orders sent to Crook.

able enemy now aroused."[20] Strahorn wrote that the war had become "an affair of amazing proportions," with the Sioux estimated at more than 3,000 warriors—his being just one of the many estimates of enemy strength, all of which were mere guesses. When the expedition should take the field again, Strahorn continued, "the fight this column will be expected to make will be merely one with the odds all against it,—all except the known courage of our troops, and the judgment and unexcelled ability of our commander for such work."[21]

Having twice felt the impact of the enemy's war power, once disastrously, the army seems to have heeded the military axiom that a commander should not underestimate the enemy. Knowing from personal experience that the Indians were armed, the whites seem to have assumed that the Indians were uniformly well armed. The exact extent to which the Indians were armed is not absolutely clear, but Indian testimony indicates that the white assumption may have been well based. For example, Kill Eagle, a Blackfoot Sioux who told an Indian agent that he had come into the big Sioux encampment while hunting and was there at the time of the Rosebud battle, was quoted as saying that the Indians seemed to have plenty of guns and ammunition, including Henry, Winchester, Sharps, and Spencer rifles, plus muzzle-loaders, and that many warriors had two or three revolvers each. Kill Eagle, indicating the number of warriors, said they were "like maggots on a carcass" in a village six miles long and one mile wide, in which the tipis were as close together as they could be. An officer at Standing Rock Agency also reported that three representatives had come in from the hostile bands and reported to the other Indians that they "had any quantity of ammunition and more guns than they needed."[22]

The Sioux let the soldiers know they were still around, attacking near midnight of July 9, renewing the attack at the same hour the next night when they set the grass afire, and

[20] *New York Herald*, July 16, 1876.
[21] *Chicago Tribune*, Aug. 2, 1876.
[22] Graham, *The Custer Myth*, 52, 54, 55, 99.

thereafter making regular nightly attacks. In succeeding weeks, the Indians burned off the grass for what was said to be 100 miles in every direction.

Otherwise, the camp settled into the monotony of the enforced wait for Merritt's Fifth Cavalry, under which the correspondents chafed and at which they complained. At first, hunting and fishing had offered some diversion, with a minimum of 15,000 trout caught during the first three weeks after the Battle of the Rosebud, by Bourke's calculation. After the Sibley scout and news of the Custer disaster, and with the night attacks by war parties, even hunting and fishing became too dangerous to be diversions. The officers kept the troops occupied in drilling and in frequent changes of camp as the command moved from creek to creek in the Tongue valley to find fresh pasturage for the horses. Finding fresh pasturage steadily became more a problem as the Indians burned off the grass in an effort to starve out the troops' horses. Wasson complained at the lack of reading matter, books being almost nonexistent except for a small library of paper-backs owned by two officers. Newspapers, twenty days to a month old. Cards, tiresome. The days in camp were hot, especially from eleven to four, but the nights were cool. However, Davenport found even the evenings unpleasant because of the noise made by the friendly Indians and by the wolves. Each day, for about an hour before sunset, he reported, the young Shoshones raced their ponies, a favorite Indian amusement. And then in the evening they sat in their shelters made of boughs, singing a monotonous chorus until ready for sleep. After that, prowling wolves set up a chorus, "and thus," he reported, "the civilized campaigners suffer martyrdom."[23]

One topic of conversation recurred around the campfires— the late battle on the Rosebud. From those conversations the correspondents gained a better perspective and evaluation of what had happened.

Finerty directed ridicule at Davenport when he read the

[23] Bourke, *On the Border with Crook*, 328, 329; Finerty, *War-Path and Bivouac*, 143; *Alta California*, Aug. 1, 1876; *New York Herald*, Aug. 3, 1876.

Herald story. "A flashy New York sheet calls for his [Crook's] removal, because he did not please that paper's reporter on the day of Rosebud," Finerty said. "The *Herald's* warrior must have been awfully excited if he calls Rosebud fight a defeat." Another newspaper report that the battle had been a victory he also discounted. "With all due respect for these great ink-bottle generals," he continued, *"The Times* correspondent would mildly venture to opine that neither is correct. Crook set out from Goose Creek to thrash Sitting Bull and allowed himself four days in which to do the job. Sitting Bull swooped down on Rosebud to meet Crook and, to all appearance, gave himself only an hour or so to finish the whole command, *a la* Custer. There was a fight—that much I am sure of—the Indians were repulsed at every point.[24]

The increasingly critical tone of Davenport's stories might betoken his rising gorge in personal arguments that would have been bound to arise after Crook and his staff had read his stories. Writing in late June, he said the battle had been fought over "a thousand times by the light of the camp fires." Out of the conversations had come Grouard's opinion that Crazy Horse had been among the attacking Indians—not only among them, as later information was to reveal, but at their head.[25]

Wasson, close to Crook, also took a swing at Davenport, who had spoken bitingly in his first story of the conflicting orders that had reached Royall during the fight. "The talk about 'conflicting orders' is the veriest nonsense," he wrote for the opposition *Tribune*. "There is more or less dissension —or has been—prevailing, the origin of which dates back to and beyond the battle with Crazy Horse last Winter [Wasson meant the Reynolds attack in March]; but the fate of Gen. Custer has served to teach officers and soldiers the seriousness of the situation." Not only had the Custer disaster taught them how serious the situation was, he said, it had strangled any further criticism of Crook's generalship on the Rosebud, the

[24] *Chicago Times,* Aug. 1, 1876.
[25] *New York Herald,* July 13, 1876.

244

officers admitting "his superior foresight and promptness" in recalling the troops to the center.[26]

Humor also enlivened the camp from time to time, although none of the correspondents reported one of the incidents—the arrival of Calamity Jane. Dressed as a teamster, she arrived with a whiskey peddler. Bourke and Mills mentioned her by name in their books, but Finerty merely said in his book that "two abandoned females, disguised as mule drivers" came into camp with the whiskey peddler. The troops thought it was funny, especially when she claimed to know Mills. The women and the peddler were ejected.[27]

For more of army humor, Strahorn related the following anecdote about an occurrence one night after Indians had attacked the camp: "After a scattering fusillade had been indulged in for an hour or more one night, and the camp believed to be thoroughly aroused, a brawny Irishman, yet asleep, was suddenly awakened by a stray shot. Jumping as though himself hit by the bullet, he broke the momentary stillness by yelling terrifically, 'Hip, thur, byes! *Wake up!* WAKE UP! *The Enjuns is here!*' The soldiers who had been formed in a hollow square around the outer edge of camp and were lying on their arms quietly awaiting a more determined onslaught, understood the situation instantly, and more than one bursting laugh had to be repressed."[28]

In short, it was "a village of 1,500 healthy, jolly men"[29] from which the correspondents reported during that most familiar part of all wars—the waiting. And the stories written during that long wait presented a picture of life in an advance army camp—the trials, the laughter, the brief diversions, the danger, the confidence, the situation, the plans, and the gossip.

Finerty revealed himself as an Indian-hater in his few stories, appearing from one to three weeks apart in the *Chicago Times,* signed sometimes by his full name and some-

[26] *New York Tribune,* July 27, 1876.
[27] Finerty, *War-Path and Bivouac,* 200; Bourke, *On the Border with Crook,* 299–300; Mills, *My Story,* 401.
[28] *Chicago Tribune,* Aug. 2, 1876.
[29] *Ibid.*

times by his initials. The frequency of appearance indicates that he sent in copy by the regular couriers. In turn, this demonstrates that the news of the Indian campaign, even news from a command which was doing a great deal of nothing, completed successfully for column inches against the Centennial and the presidential campaign as the summer went on. Indian war news likewise competed successfully in papers represented by Wasson, Strahorn, and Davenport, although Strahorn got crowded out of the *Rocky Mountain News* later in the summer by political news, and the *New York Tribune* used shorter pieces than the other papers. The *Chicago Times* leaned toward alliterative headlines, such as "Braving the Braves," which appeared above one of Finerty's stories.

In describing the country, Finerty became enthusiastic about the grazing possibilities of "magnificent Montana, a land that would maintain millions of people in living if there were enough emigrants to settle it and if the whole tribe of Indians, friendly and otherwise, were exterminated." At another point in the same story, he said, "I detest the race . . . ."[30]

In a "situationer" in late June, he recognized that it would be impossible to surprise the Indians, who by then controlled the place and timing of battle if there was to be one. "How strange," he commented, "that our civilized administration should permit its post traders and agents to arm the Indians, provide them with the ammunition, feed their women and children, place them, in a word, on a war footing, and then enlist unsuspecting white men in the regular army, arm them, train them, feed and clothe them for the purpose of shooting down the very warriors whom the government itself has rendered formidable. Thus we have the interior and war departments fighting each other in the field. The men killed on both sides fall by government bullets."[31] Finerty here echoed the bitterness that is found in the writings of Old Army officers.

Finerty grew caustic in reporting the size of military units. "By the way," he wrote, "all our so-called companies are short

30 *Chicago Times*, July 5, 1876.
31 *Ibid.*, July 12, 1876.

of their legal complement by 25 men on an average. This shows how deceptive a muster-roll can be. When we hear of a regiment, we receive a weak battalion. Is this war, or humbug?" In a later story he said cavalry companies [the designation "troop" did not come into official use until several years later, although it was used interchangeably, but unofficially] averaged forty-five men and infantry, thirty-five. "Will not any unprejudiced person remark that this state of things is simply damnable?" he asked.[32]

Perhaps because of the practice of writing chronological stories, Finerty subordinated his account of the Sibley scout to his recital of the July 1–4 trip to the Big Horns. He told first of the mountain exploration and then of the Sibley scout. The irony is that Finerty, one of the heroes of that reconnaissance and the only newspaperman along, was beaten on that story. Possibly because the Finerty story went by mail and the *New York Herald* more regularly used telegraph, the *Herald* reported the Sibley scout and Finerty's part in it ten days before Finerty's own story appeared.

Davenport made enemies with the same ease that Finerty made friends. Davenport's Rosebud story especially grated on the men who had fought there, and one writer—presumably Captain Azor H. Nickerson, Crook's aide, who went back to Omaha after the battle to arrange for Ute scouts to join the command—went to some pains to contradict him. Davenport had written that Crook had sent the Mills battalion up the canyon, toward the supposed village, and then discovered it was in the opposite direction. The truth of the matter, said the commentator on the correspondents, was that Crook never did receive any information indicating the village was in any direction other than down the canyon. "Probably Davenport did not mean to misrepresent, but he took this as he does other cock-and-bull stories, for news, and the world will read the lie before the truth gets started."[33]

Another officer also became indignant about Davenport's

[32] *Ibid.*, July 26, Aug. 1, 1876.
[33] *Rocky Mountain News*, Aug. 8, 1876.

battle story. Referring to Davenport as "this Field-Marshal of the *Herald's*," he complained in a letter to the *Chicago Tribune* that Davenport's stories indirectly charging Crook with incompetency had led to "absurd" editorial demands that the General be replaced. Using the ludicrous descriptions of its own reporter as a starting point, he said, *Herald* editorial writers spoke in "crisp phrases of authoritative blat!"[34]

To give the devil his due, Davenport at least had the courage to keep writing what he thought about the Crook command, even though he lived with the men in an isolation "nearly as complete here as within the walls of a prison." He also took Bourke to task for exposing himself in fighting beside friendly Indians when, thought Davenport, "the commonest of manly qualities" in that case would keep an aide-de-camp beside his general.[35] Since Bourke was in position to give information to the correspondents, Davenport's apparent tactlessness may have resulted from blunt honesty, if one disregards the possibility of spite.

The *Herald* generally gave good play to Davenport's stories, which were never signed, in accordance with *Herald* practice. An entire page was used when a story justified it, as in the case of a long mail story rehashing the Battle of the Rosebud, the third story from Davenport about the fight. It also gave more than three columns to his story of the Big Horn trip.

Davenport continued criticizing the management of the expedition. The Sibley scout, he noted, left camp in broad daylight, "with a strange absence of precaution, for which somebody superior to Sibley in rank is responsible, it being usual to disguise such movements under the shelter of darkness." Writing after the return of the Shoshones and the opening of communications with Terry, the young New Yorker said the Shoshone displeasure with "the management of our

[34] *Chicago Tribune*, Aug. 2, 1876.
[35] *New York Herald*, July 13, 1876. Davenport's criticism of the management of the campaign is one with his criticism of the management of the Jenney-Newton expedition of the previous summer. Not enough is known about Davenport to judge whether the pattern of criticism was due to personal maladjustment or whether it was a reader-appeal device.

fight of June 17 is not yet appeased," and added that unless Crook acceded to Terry's request for joint operations, "Other disasters may be anticipated."[36]

Late in July, Davenport commented that the troops had been inactive for more than a month, that only a little "desultory" scouting had been done, that all of Crook's plans seemed to hinge upon the obtaining of reinforcements, that opportunities had not been improved for definitely learning something about the enemy's position and movements, and that "the guides and scouts seem to have been permitted to exercise their presumable function of observation just so little as has suited them."[37]

Wasson, who was friendly toward Crook personally and in his dispatches, did not get into print as often as the others, possibly because he was not a staff man. He corroborated Davenport's version of Terry's first message to Crook, suggesting a union of the two commands but allowing Crook, the junior officer of the two, to make and carry out the plans. Parenthetically, Wasson said Terry "plainly implies that Gen. Custer was a victim of his own rashness." But Crook thought, Wasson reported, that it would be better to keep the two commands separate, with Terry's as a reserve which would join Crook only after he had engaged the enemy. Since Crook traveled with a packtrain and Terry with wagons, the Platte commander thought the Indians would see Terry's column long before they could be brought to battle. In considering the over-all situation and their past experience, Crook considered one mounted Sioux equal to two cavalrymen, since one in four troopers had to hold horses. But Crook the infantryman calculated the foot soldier with Springfield rifle worth six mounted Sioux.[38]

Crook faced a difficult problem, Wasson said. If he and Terry joined together, the Indians would see them and scatter. Then the troops would have to disperse for the pursuit, with

36 *Ibid.,* July 16, 1876.
37 *Ibid.,* Aug. 3, 1876.
38 *New York Tribune,* July 27, 1876.

the possibility that the Indians could reunite to slaughter the soldiers in small units. Crook wanted additional infantry, anticipating that the Indians would flee to the mountains, where foot soldiers could wear them out. Crook's force was also handicapped with recruits "raw as swamp grass" as well as jealousy and incapacity among some subordinate officers. Some of them, he added, had "lost no Indians" while others were too ambitious, as Custer had been. "Terry was ordered to the field for the reason that Custer was unfit to command, and yet the latter managed to give him the slip—and slipped up." His stories were signed "José" in the *Alta California*.[39]

Strahorn, who signed his stories "Alter Ego," was a Crook partisan. He wrote that "careful investigation" revealed it was cheaper to support troops in the field than in garrison, but the figures he gave in support of his thesis are not convincing. Aside from the probable loss of life, he said, field service in the summer was "beneficial to all connected with it, just as a summer's travel and relaxation are beneficial to those who are compelled to make a treadmill of life anywhere."[40]

Considering the prejudices of the other three, Finerty appears the most impartial of the correspondents with Crook. He criticized when he felt occasion demanded, but he criticized objectively; that is, without the sting of personal criticism which Davenport left. This is not to say he was completely impartial, for he reflected the army point of view almost exclusively.

Irregular courier service carried the news dispatches through country where war parties could be expected at any time. As a rule, a courier rode to and from Fort Fetterman once every three weeks. Couriers were cautious about making the trip. Once, late in July, a courier took six days for the normal seventy-two-hour trip because he ran into a party of two hundred Indians at the Powder River, and hid in the timber for twenty-four hours. Upon reaching Fetterman, he raised fears that couriers sent to Crook six days earlier had

[39] *Alta California*, Aug. 1, 1876.
[40] *Chicago Tribune*, Aug. 2, 1876.

not made it through, for he had seen their trail south of the Powder but not above.

With July nearing its end and Merritt long overdue, Crook became impatient to attack. Crow scouts reported strong Sioux parties near the Little Big Horn. To Finerty it seemed that Crook was exasperated, swinging like a pendulum between a desire to fight at any cost and the caution that warned him he might be as rash as Custer in trying to tackle an enemy who outnumbered him. Finally, he gave orders to march directly to the Little Big Horn and engage the Sioux. His men learned with dismay that they would leave their tents and bivouac for the rest of the season. And then, on the afternoon of August 2, a courier arrived from Merritt, reporting the near approach of the ten troops of the Fifth Cavalry.

Merritt also brought along more correspondents. Of the new group, however, only Barbour Lathrop, of the *San Francisco Evening Bulletin,* and a man named Mills, said to represent the *New York Times,* were remembered by other men on the expedition as bona fide accredited correspondents. Neither Finerty's book nor Strahorn's memoirs mentioned the new men, but Bourke described the group:

[Lathrop and Mills], I believe, were the only real correspondents in the party, although there were others who vaunted their pretensions; one of these last, name now forgotten, claimed to have been sent out by the New York *Graphic,* a statement very few were inclined to admit. He was the greenest thing I ever saw without feathers; he had never been outside of New York before, and the way the scouts, packers, and soldiers "laid for" that man was a caution. Let the other newspaper men growl as they might about the lack of news, Mr. "Graphic," as I must call him, never had any right to complain on that score. Never was packer or scout or soldier—shall I add officer?—so weary, wet, hungry, or miserable at the end of a day's march that he couldn't devote a half-hour to the congenial task of "stuffin' the tenderfoot." The stories told of Indian atrocities to captives, especially those found with paper and lead pencils, were enough to make the stoutest veteran's teeth chatter, and at times our newly-discovered acquisition manifested a disinclination to swallow, unstrained, the stories told him; but his murmurs of mild dissent were drowned in an inundation of "Oh, that hain't nawthin to what I've seed 'em do." Who the poor fellow was I do not know; no one seemed to know him by any other designation than "The Tenderfoot." He had no money, he could not draw, and was dependent upon the packers and others for every meal; I must say that he never lacked food, provided he swallowed it with tales of border horrors which would cause the pages of Boys Own Five-Cent Novelettes to creak with terror. I never saw him smile but once. . . . He left us when we reached the Yellowstone, and I have never blamed him.[41]

Whether or no Mr. Graphic was staffer or camp-follower, the *New York Graphic* printed three sketches of scenes of Crook's camp, drawn by Charles Holtes. That was the only time the *Graphic* used anything about the campaign that was not clearly second-hand. Likewise, the *New York World* —to whose reporter there is a later reference—had only one story, appearing in mid-September and signed with the initials "J. J. T." There was a later reference to a Mr. Talbot, who was identified as a New York newspaperman.

Lathrop was an experienced newspaperman of thirty. Virginia-bred and Harvard-educated, he was the only Western war correspondent to come from a background of wealth, which in his later years allowed him to become a philanthropist who improved America's breakfast table and American horticulture through the plant importations of David G. Fairchild. He had been in San Francisco for several years, where he had helped found the Bohemian Club, when he went out to cover the Sioux war.[42]

Lathrop had hurried from San Francisco within the week after the publication of the Custer story, but he had been detained at Fort Fetterman for want of transportation. Writ-

[41] Bourke, *On the Border with Crook*, 346.

[42] *San Francisco Chronicle*, May 18, 1927, Feb. 12, 1928, clippings in Lathrop Folder, Watson Papers; Nelson Klose, *America's Crop Heritage*, 113–14.

ing from Fort Fetterman on July 14, he reported there was difficulty in getting couriers to carry messages to Crook; not even an offer of $250 for the trip would tempt a rider just then. Once he thought he would be able to leave with a courier, having made arrangements to ride with one through the Sioux country, but at the last moment the "valiant scout" failed to appear. He then had to wait until Merritt arrived.[43]

With Merritt also came the Fifth Cavalry's chief of scouts, Buffalo Bill Cody, taking time out from his Wild West show, for which he also got some new material; that was the summer of his "duel" with Yellow Hand. Cody's assistant was Captain Jack Crawford, the "poet scout," in all truth more a rhymester than a poet.

Merritt joined Crook on August 3, and 2,100 men of the Big Horn and Yellowstone Expedition were organized for a march to begin on August 5. Crook believed the hostile Indians would be found two days northward in the bluffs and uplands of the Rosebud. The command included 25 companies of cavalry from the Second, Third, and Fifth regiments; ten companies of infantry from the Fourth, Ninth, and Fourteenth regiments; 225 Shoshone scouts; 25 Ute scouts; and 30 white and half-blood scouts and civilians.

Crook was cutting loose from his wagon train entirely, leaving it under command of an officer and about two hundred civilians, parked and fortified until the field command returned. With three hundred pack mules, the command was equipped and rationed for twelve to fourteen days, but they were skimpy rations of bacon, hardtack, and coffee. Each man was allowed only the clothing on his back, plus one blanket and an overcoat. Each man also was to carry 100 rounds of ammunition on his person, while the mules carried another 150,000 rounds. Determined not to be hamstrung by wounded as he was at the Rosebud, Crook had had two dozen Indian travois built to transport any wounded, and he assertedly intended to keep after the Indians, halting for nothing short of a general engagement. In the event of a fight, the cavalry

[43] *San Francisco Evening Bulletin*, July 15, July 17, Aug. 9, 1876.

253

and the allies were to follow through with a hard pursuit that would either overcome or thoroughly disperse the Indians.

Having learned at the Rosebud what confusion the Indian allies could cause, Crook had his men tear up flour sacks so each friendly Indian could wear a white flag above the scalp-lock or on the war bonnet.

Major J. V. Furey, the quartermaster, with two hundred teamsters, would lock his wagons in place in a circle, with the short intervals between them laced with ropes and chains to form a barricade as well as a corral for the one thousand horses and mules to be left there. Rifle-pits around the outer edge of the circle provided the civilians with fortifications.

With Saturday, August 5, 1876, dawning clear and bright, cavalry trumpet and infantry bugle brought the men out with reveille. Roll call was over quickly, and troopers groomed their horses. Officers and correspondents gathered around their mess chests for a large breakfast; it would be ten weeks before they would know the "luxuries" of the wagon train again. The "general" ordered troops to strike tents, hurriedly load wagons, and place them in the quartermaster corral. Then the infantry, described as a tough, wiry bunch, moved out with the scouts.[44]

A short time later, the cavalry trumpeters sounded "boots and saddles," and the troopers brought in their horses. "Lead into line!" the sergeants ordered. Carefully, the officers of the yellow ribbon inspected men and animals—blanket, poncho, overcoat, side-line, lariat, picket pin, canteen, haversack, one hundred rounds. "Mount," sounded the trumpet.[45]

Twenty-five companies of cavalry walked their horses out on campaign, with the correspondents scattered through the commands. The troopers rode at ease, talking, laughing, and singing if they wished. The only thing required of them was that they not lounge in the saddle and that they keep their distances, riding at a steady walk. From 7:00 A.M. until 2:00 P.M. they marched, and then went into camp.

[44] King, *Campaigning with Crook*, 57–59.
[45] *Ibid.*, 62.

On the second day's march they encountered a twisting small stream. For the eleventh time in one morning the infantrymen had stripped off their lower garments to wade the stream, when a tall, red-headed Irishman sent his comrades into laughter with a quizzical comment: "Fellers, did e'er a one of yez iver cross on a bridge?"[46]

When they reached the valley of the Rosebud on August 7, a frontier scout reported that the whole Sioux Nation had been encamped there within less than two weeks. He claimed to have ridden ten miles downstream without reaching the end of the village.

In the Rosebud valley, which they entered about six miles north of the battleground and one and one-half miles from the point where Mills's battalion had defiled out of the narrow canyon, they saw where the Indians had felled trees in their path and on the sides of the ravine. Had they gone another half-mile during the battle, Finerty said, not a man of that battalion would have come out alive, and the five companies of the Second Cavalry behind them would have met the same fate, for the narrowness of the canyon allowed no room to deploy or rally. Continuing through the valley of the Rosebud toward the Yellowstone, Finerty thought "that part of the world looked utterly unfinished," and hazarded the opinion that Darwin might have been able to find the missing link there somewhere.[47]

On the eighth, Crook ordered a night march, probably repeating his stratagem of Oregon and California, hoping to come that much closer to the Indians without their knowing the exact whereabouts of the approaching column. Riding in pitch darkness, the men sang Negro melodies and Irish songs. Looking back and forward, the correspondents could have traced the outline of the column by the embers of pipes smoked by troopers.

During the march, Wasson, Strahorn, and Bourke rode with

[46] *Ibid.*, 71.
[47] Finerty, *War-Path and Bivouac*, 215, 221–22; *Alta California*, Sept. 26, 1876.

a rough bunch of white scouts who called themselves the "Montana Volunteers," commanded by Strahorn's old friend, Paymaster Stanton. Their general reputation was reflected by Bourke in his sardonic comment that there was a rumor in camp to the effect that one or two of the volunteers had never been indicted for murder, but he thought the story had been started by Stanton to give his men a better name. At any rate, Bourke claimed that he, Wasson, and Strahorn sat on their saddles many a night to make sure they would still have them at sunrise. One of the men with the volunteers was not a white but a Ute, known as Ute John. Ute John was proud that he was a "Klishchun," having been "heap wash" by the "Mo'mon."[48]

On August 10, when scouts reported the Sioux trail diverged eastward toward the Tongue, the correspondents and officers saw a large dust cloud boiling up on the near horizon.

"They are Sioux!" some of the officers exclaimed.[49]

Crook threw skirmishers forward.

[48] Bourke, *On the Border with Crook*, 348–49.
[49] Finerty, *War-Path and Bivouac*, 223.

Add Crook

9. WHERE ARE THE INDIANS?

It will require good generalship to save this campaign from being a miserable fiasco.

CHARLES S. DIEHL[1]

WHEN CROOK'S FORCES sighted the dust cloud, a young Shoshone rode up beside Finerty and said, "Heap pony soldier." Cody said marching troops raised the dust, and he galloped off to reconnoiter. Satisfying himself, Cody galloped back to report to Crook that it was Terry, with enough wagons for an army corps, and asked whether they were to catch Indians with such lumber as that.[2]

Coming together entirely by accident in an area where each had expected to encounter Sioux in force, Crook's men were surprised, Terry's astonished, "and one of the most comical sights I ever witnessed was this meeting, and one of the most unanswerable questions ever asked was, 'Why, where on earth are the Indians?' "[3]

Four thousand United States soldiers bumped into each other in the middle of nowhere. A medical officer punned that it would have been "Siouxicidal" for them to have fought. But the joy at meeting comrades was tinged with resentment on the part of Crook's men. Forced to live like Spartans, without even shelter tents, they saw that Terry's men not only had tents but some officers had Brussels carpets in their tents, and lights, too.

Finerty expressed what seems to have been in the minds of

[1] *Chicago Times*, Sept. 5, 1876.
[2] Secretary of War, *Report, 1876*, I, 506; Finerty, *War-Path and Bivouac*, 222–24; *Chicago Times*, Aug. 19, 1876.
[3] King, *Campaigning with Crook*, 54–55, 78–79.

many: "Great doubts as to the success of the enterprise are entertained." Davenport reported: "There is great uncertainty regarding the enemy. It is impossible to shape any conjecture as to the occurrence of a fight."[4]

The two forces camped together that night. Since Crook had stripped his column "to the buff," as Howard described it, Terry decided to do the same. Although a mule pack train had never been organized in his department before, Terry had brought along packsaddles, and he cut out enough mules from the wagon train to form a mule train. Before Terry's wagons left, Crook drew a fresh supply of rations.

Two *New York Herald* correspondents divided the reporting chores. Davenport reported the union of the two forces. O'Kelly returned to the Yellowstone to cover Miles's patrol of the river. Immediately after the two forces met, Terry had sent Miles and his Fifth Infantry back to patrol the river on steamboats, trying to keep the hostile Indians from fording the Yellowstone and fleeing into the vastness of the north.

Crook and Terry began their joint expedition in joint discomfort. On the night of August 11, a wind and rainstorm drenched the tentless troops. Rains continued for several days. One rainy night, Lathrop, having found the bond of mutual friends in Lieutenant Charles King of the Fifth Cavalry, joined him in making a double wickiup of twigs and saplings. King remembered the reporter as one "whose vivacity was unquenchable, even by such weather as this."[5]

Beginning their march on August 12, the combined expedition had anything but the shine and polish of a well-equipped army column representing a powerful nation. Every mile of the way, Finerty said, they lost horses; Crook's mounts had been without grain since May, and looked like bone heaps when the march had begun on August 5. Day after day of continuing rain made marching difficult. Although Crook's seasoned troops swung along like Sherman's infantrymen

[4] *Chicago Times*, Aug. 19, 1876; *New York Herald*, Aug. 21, 1876.
[5] Finerty, *War-Path and Bivouac*, 226–31; King, *Campaigning with Crook*, 85.

marching through Georgia—Howard's expression—many of Terry's young, green infantry simply lay down in the dirt, exhausted. They were picked up by cavalry or carried on pack mules or travois. Almost every company in Crook's cavalry had to shoot or abandon used-up horses as the march continued through the sterile badlands of Pumpkin Creek, which Finerty said were so repulsive that it made "one's heart sick to look at the place."

Continuing along, some of the infantry suffering from bleeding feet and swollen legs, they suddenly missed an officer's cook. Terry sent some Crows back to look for him, and found he had lain down under a tree to die; they brought him in a raving maniac. Finerty's own horse, he said, was a "fair specimen" of the horseflesh in Crook's command—his shoulders covered with scabs and blood, stumbling at every step, he had to be led more than half the time. Terrible waste occurred during the march. Terry's green mule train dropped, lost, and damaged more supplies on the first day's march than Crook's had from the start of the summer, a condition which Howard described: "The improvised pack-train of wagon-mules played sad havoc with the limited stores, as the line of march for miles was strewn with broken packs and inverted mules."[6]

The broad Indian trail led them eastward toward the Tongue and Powder rivers, but five or six days of continuing rain helped to blot it out. By the time they reached and scouted the Powder Valley, it seemed that the trail led toward the Little Missouri River, a favorite wintering ground of the Sitting Bull band.

In need of supplies, the column turned northward to the Yellowstone, which they reached on August 17. Crook went into camp on the east bank and Terry on the west bank of the Powder at its mouth, where they remained six and seven days, respectively, before taking up the trail again. In the meantime, Terry's supplies were brought down from the

[6] Finerty, *War-Path and Bivouac*, 226–31; Bourke, *On the Border with Crook*, 352–56; *Chicago Tribune*, Sept. 9, 1876.

Rosebud. Once in camp, Terry's men went back into their tents and ate well from their stores. Crook's men still slept in the open and had only the clothing on their backs. Their diet was limited to bacon, hardtack, and coffee.

Davenport's resentment of Crook's management came out in a description of what happened when a trading boat came down from the Gallatin valley of Montana:

> An illustration of the eagerness with which they sought a change of diet was a ludicrous scene which occurred on the arrival of the first sutler's stores at the camp. A Mackinaw boat dropped down the Yellowstone from Fort Ellis, Montana, and was moored near the shore. No sooner had it come into sight than there was a grand rush of officers and soldiers to the water's edge, and confused shoutings assailed the ears of the boatmen. Before touching the bank they were surrounded by horsemen, who rode into the water. I urged the trader to open his boxes. He soon was in the midst of a lively commerce.
>
> Rank and degree were forgotten in the expression and attainment of a multiplicity of desires, which were burlesqued in the earnestness of the pleading. One individual wanted a "frying pan," another a "coffee pot" and every one asked for canned fruits, with an avidity which met only with disappointment. This scene, which I have not attempted to describe, but merely to hint at, was repeated on the arrival of other boats. The privation of the troops was depicted in the contrast between their browned and wrinkled faces, overgrown with beard, and the smooth, well content lineaments of the river traders who sold them a few of the most meagre necessities at enormous prices. Two-thirds of them were so ragged that their nakedness was exposed. The government had not had foresight sufficient to provide a supply of clothing at the Yellowstone for the poor wretches, and they spent a great part of the pittance which they received for soldiering in remedying the deficiency.[7]

Crook's severe camp separated the men from the boys among the correspondents, so to speak. Only the four original correspondents remained with him thereafter—Finerty, Wasson,

[7] *New York Herald*, Oct. 2, 1876.

Strahorn, and Davenport. Lathrop shifted to Terry, with whom he remained until the campaign came to an end. The other unnamed correspondents—including the one known as Mr. Graphic and the one known as Calamity Jim, otherwise unidentified—were said to have taken one of the steamers downriver.

The coverage during the period of joint operation had been divided into two areas. O'Kelly was on the river with Miles, along with Diehl, who had arrived by that time. With the troops in the field were Finerty, Strahorn, Davenport, Wasson, Howard, Lathrop, and those who were thought to be mere camp-followers rather than correspondents. Contact with Terry had given Crook's correspondents a line of communication, steamboats to take copy to Bismarck for telegraphing and mailing. Otherwise, the Crook correspondents would have been an indefinite time away from any sort of courier communication. On at least one occasion, Howard used Gibbon's courier route to the Bozeman telegraph office. Once a *Herald* man sent a courier by boat to Glendive Creek, whence he was to go overland to Bismarck.

By the time the two commands reached the Yellowstone, the correspondents reported, disgust existed throughout the ranks. Interestingly, they displayed strong biases against the other commanders—those with Crook flayed Terry (except for Davenport who made Crook his favorite monster), and those with Terry bemeaned Crook. Otherwise, the reporters had little to write about beyond the juncture of the two commands and their fruitless march through eastern Montana.

Finerty showed boredom and disgust by the phrasing of a date line: "Big Horn and Yellowstone Expedition, Commanded Not by the Great Jehovah, but by Crook and Terry, In the Field on Pumpkin Creek, Montana, Aug. 12." Concluding a story written August 18, he wrote:

Incertitude is the order of the day at present. Many camp followers, including some of the correspondents, are leaving the expedition. I have not yet made up my mind what is best for me to do. I hate to leave at this stage of the futile campaign, and yet by remaining I shall see very little else than mud, misery, and rough country. One good battle and a decent wind-up to this wretched business would just suit me now. But I fear very much that the last shot of this section of the campaign has been fired. This comes of the official imbecility which, at the outset, sent an insufficient force to fight a powerful enemy, and, in the end, sent green infantry to impede our movements, and left us cavalry horses fit only for the purposes of a glue factory.[8]

O'Kelly wrote that the troops had suffered in health since the start of a "theatrical" campaign which he attributed to Crook. Allowing troops no eating utensils other than a tin cup was "patent humbug campaigning," he wrote. "Only that Crook happened to meet General Terry he would long since have been compelled to turn back to Goose Creek, where he left his wagon train in accordance with the clever system of campaigning adopted on the Plains, which resembles nothing so much as a Chinese stage battle, where the combatants are constantly rushing in an excited manner after invisible enemies they never seem to catch, but who now and then manage to catch the pursuers." Soldiers are not made better Indian fighters by getting dysentery and rheumatism, O'Kelly declared.[9]

While O'Kelly was on the river, he wrote a story from the *Far West* on August 15, describing the campaign generally and the meeting with Crook particularly. Under a subhead which read, "What is the matter with Crook?" there appeared the statement that Crook did not come out of his tent to meet Terry, the senior officer, and that the circumstance had occasioned comment. Elaborating, O'Kelly said: "The conduct of this officer throughout the campaign has been, to say the least, peculiar." He suggested, with a sneer, that perhaps Terry's volunteer background and Crook's West Point background "may, perhaps, have something to do with it."[10]

[8] *Chicago Times*, Sept. 22, 1876.
[9] *New York Herald*, Sept. 12, 1876.
[10] *New York Herald*, Aug. 24, 1876. Bourke confirms that Terry did come

On the other side of the river, Wasson criticized Terry. Had Terry not run into Crook, he said, "He would doubtless have been going yet up toward the Big Horn Mountains, directly opposite to the enemy's course." While the two commands traveled together, there was no comparison—"it was all contrast"—between them, he wrote. "Crook's ship was trimmed down to fast-sailing condition—every man's outfit complete in itself, and the pack-train on the Pacific Coast plan, better organized still," he added. "When Terry cut loose from his elegant wagon camp, he was in a miserable plight, and his shoulder-strapped equipage became a severe impediment to all concerned." The junction, according to Wasson, had delayed the pursuit for five days, while a rainstorm had almost obliterated the trail. Terry, the senior officer and operating in his own department, had insisted the whole force move down to the Yellowstone, and Crook was "hugely disgusted" at the delay. "Terry's scouting force," Wasson continued, "is of no account whatever, while Crook's scouts have worn out their animals in keeping track of the trails, and so the case stands. . . . All this big outfit needs to perfect it is half a dozen brass bands and *Herald* correspondents. Perhaps James Gordon Bennett's fleet of yachts would be necessary." Wasson noted that the enemy had done something unprecedented—kept his entire force in a compact mass from beginning to end, judging by the trail the soldiers had followed.[11]

In a later story Wasson said Terry was loth to leave the Yellowstone once he was there, "that interesting base of supply, consisting largely of officers' stores, including untold barrels of ale and all the delicacies of the season." Still Terry was anxious "to cling to Crook's coat-tails and thus divide up the responsibility of a successful or unsuccessful campaign, as much as possible." At the same time, Wasson disclaimed any ill thoughts of Terry, whom he described as "a big, good-natured school-boy—totally ignorant of the distracting con-

to Crook first, but not to a tent: They met under a tree where Crook waited for his senior, and the meeting was "most cordial." *On the Border with Crook*, 351.

[11] *Alta California*, Sept. 26, 1876.

ditions of Indian warfare; wanting to do something for his country, but not knowing, of himself, how to go about it." In the river camp Terry's men even had washstands with marble tops, he reported with some disdain, or secret envy.[12]

Howard, whose stories in the *Chicago Tribune* were signed simply "Phocion," wrote with a pomposity barely equaled by the Washington columnists of the present century. Terry's troop organization, he said, "could not have been better," but Crook would have to answer before some committee on the conduct of the war how he let the Indians get away from him. During the joint march, it was a question of whether they were following the Indians or whether part of the army had left Goose Creek "to go on a wild-goose chase." Terry's troops, he said, were "disgusted" and "a hundred times a day" asked, Where were Crook's Indians? Terry, he added, was at the mercy of scouts and guides. Crook had Cody and Grouard. Terry had Girard, whom he identified as a former job printer on the *Missouri Republican*, George Herndon (more properly, Herendeen), and Muggins Taylor of Montana. "Individually, I have no doubt, these are severally good men and experts; but, collectively, they don't amount to a cuss," Howard wrote, explaining that jealousy and rivalry had riven the group. In self-importance, Howard said the river patrol meant that Terry "seems to have heeded the suggestion I made in a former letter." As for the Indian trail they had followed, he declared it had been made by Indians stealing the corn that Terry had stored at the supply depot at the mouth of Powder earlier in the summer. "This trail," he wrote, "to quote an old doggerel—

> *Twisted in and twisted out,*
> *Leaving Terry still in doubt,*
> *Whether the injun who made the track*
> *Was going north or coming back."*[13]

[12] *Ibid.,* Sept. 17, 1876. Although Terry's officers may have had a wine mess, as officers did on some other campaigns, a trader had opened a bar after Terry first reached the river, which might account for the ale. Stewart, *Custer's Luck,* 228.

264

Fortunately, Howard pictured some of the other correspondents. With his not infrequent exaggeration, he referred
to the twenty-five or thirty reporters with Crook, including
Finerty and Davenport. He said Finerty had won the hearts
of the cavalry, but should he suddenly appear on Clark Street
none of his friends would countenance him. "He is 'bearded
like a pard,' ragged as Billy Barlow, and bronzed deeper than
Daniels' injun tobacco image," he wrote. "Yesterday his nose
began to peel for the fifth time, and the new epidermis, contrasting with the old, gave his face the appearance of a lump
of smoked topaz set in moss-agate."

For Davenport he showed contempt—"a little, weazened-
faced fellow, sharp, quick-witted, and full of resources." Referring to the story that Davenport had delayed the government dispatches after the Battle of the Rosebud—and thereby
seemingly confirming the Ben Arnold account—he reported
that Davenport had offered the courier $100 to delay Crook's
dispatches twelve hours. "I have been a reporter over a quarter of a century; but it was left for Davenport to learn me how
to get news through on sight," he said. He concluded his description by saying: "News is news; and the general impression among military men is, that, the less the *New York Herald*
prints, the more the public will know as to the actual situation
of affairs on the Yellowstone."

By being on the river with Miles, Diehl gave the *Chicago
Times* double-front protection, just like that which the *Herald*
had; however, his reports during the middle part of August
were routine accounts.

Lathrop also reflected army grumbling. "Everybody has
grown dissatisfied with what they claim to be the continued
mismanagement of the officers, and criticise the conduct of
the officers severely, and frankly express their disgust at having anything to do with a campaign, which is evidently based
upon false theories."[14]

Crook and Terry were in a predicament at that time. With

[13] *Chicago Tribune*, Sept. 9, 1876.
[14] *San Francisco Evening Bulletin*, Sept. 4, 1876.

the strongest force ever sent against Plains Indians, they had
lost the Indians. Crazy Horse, Gall, and the other Sioux leaders had kept their people together; always with scouts to
watch and report the progress of the two army columns, they
knew when Crook and Terry moved and they knew when
they had been reinforced; they knew when they joined. Getting their women and children out of the way, the Indians
moved eastward across Terry's front. Because the Indians
were well supplied with horses, they made it difficult for
troops to overtake them. However, the continued threat to
their safety, from the army's nearness through the summer,
restricted their hunting. Camp remains found by Crook
showed that the Indians were eating ponies and dogs instead
of game; Indian accounts show that was not true earlier in
the summer. While retreating, the Indians kept lookouts to
advise the main body of approaching pursuers. When pursuit drew too close, the Indians branched off from the main
trail group by group, choosing hard places where their tracks
would not be seen. Eventually the trail faded to nothing, and
the soldiers—dependent upon civilian scouts—were in a quan-
dary. Perhaps Phocion Howard was right—the scouts didn't
amount to a cuss.

On August 24 and 25 the two commands took the field
again, going up the Powder River, but they pulled away from
each other for good on August 26 when Terry received a
report that hostiles had fired on his infantry detachment at
the mouth of Glendive Creek. Swinging eastward, Terry followed the Yellowstone and Crook operated farther south, hoping to snap a trap on the Sioux and their Cheyenne allies.

The old Wasson irreverence cropped out finally, when he
spoke of "Terry & Crook's co-operative society or combination
troupe, for the suppression of Sitting Bull" which had again
started on "the old dried-up and drowned-out warpath."[15]

Marching eastward to the area of Beaver Creek, with a
recent and an older Indian trail pointing to the east and south,

15 *Alta California*, Sept. 17, 1876.

Crook's scouts skirmished a time or two with small groups of Indians, but the column never did get close enough for a major engagement. The march continued until they reached Heart River on September 5, thirteen days away from their starting place on the Powder.

Then came the day of crisis—September 5, 1876, on Heart River—when Crook made the decision that sent his two thousand cavalry and infantry on one of the most severe and trying marches the United States Army ever made. Crook's situation was critical. His men had been in the field thirty-one days, with no change of clothing, sleeping in the open, often in the rain. It looked as though Crook had been whipped without a fight. He had only two and one-half days' rations left. He would have to march from four to eight days to reach supply, depending upon which route he chose. He was in what is now western North Dakota. He could follow the Heart to Fort Lincoln or go westward to Terry's supply dump at the mouth of Glendive Creek, either route involving a four- or five-day march. And he was at least eight days from the settlement in the Black Hills.

The tactical situation complicated matters. Although the Indians had scattered, their trail pointed south—toward the Black Hills. White men had continued to populate the Hills, and the Indians had continued trying to depopulate them. By going to Fort Lincoln, in another department, Crook might be tied up indefinitely, leaving the white settlers in the Black Hills, in his department, unprotected. What would Crook do?

Correspondents went over to talk with him, to find out what lay ahead. Whether they went as a group or singly or whether they talked with him on the same or on succeeding days, is not indicated in the dispatches. Wasson, who said he had known him "quite intimately" for nearly ten years, found Crook "much more silent and determined in his manner than I ever saw him." The General was about ready for bed when Wasson talked with him—bed being a saddle-blanket and overcoat under a cottonwood in a cold, drizzling rain. Surprisingly, Wasson said, the interview was the most pleasant, in terms of results, he had had with Crook for over a month.[16]

Crook told Wasson what he told the others. They would march for Deadwood, 150 to 200 miles south, not only through wilderness but through badlands. A march of six to eight days on two and one-half days' rations. Finerty remonstrated, amazed that Crook would attempt a 200-mile march in wilderness with worn-out horses and tired infantry and so little food. Crook conceded that it looked hard, but the march had to be made. Half-rations would be issued. No one knew much about that part of the country, but it looked as though it might furnish some game. "If necessary," Crook added, "we can eat our horses."[17]

Finerty said that suggestion fell upon him "like a splash of ice water." When he relayed the information to Lieutenant Joseph Lawson, a white-haired veteran with whom he messed, the old soldier exclaimed that he would as soon think of eating his brother as his horse.[18]

Crook was sending a courier to Fort Lincoln with a telegram asking Sheridan to forward supplies to Crook City or Deadwood. Since this would mean a chance to get their stories in, all the reporters wrote.

"I wrote my dispatches that evening under a half blanket, precariously supported by poles cut in the neighboring marsh, while the rain came down as if it had not rained before in several years," Finerty recalled.[19] Under the date of September 5 on Heart River, he wrote a story which was telegraphed from Bismarck on the eighth. In it he said that Crook was convinced the Indians had broken up, some going to the British possessions, others to the Black Hills, others to the agencies. Cold rain drenched them continually, and no one in the command was prepared for bad weather. "As a matter of fact," he observed, "this column is in an unserviceable condition, utterly unfit to do more than act as infantry. The

[16] *Alta California*, Sept. 17, 1876.
[17] Finerty, *War-Path and Bivouac*, 245–46.
[18] *Ibid.*
[19] *Ibid.*, 247

horses are too poor and broken down for active pursuit of the enemy. Gen. Terry's column is living in comparative luxury, while we have marched almost continuously for a month on the poorest kind of rations and without so much as a shelter-tent to keep the men dry during this rainy season. . . . Dysentery, rheumatism, and fever are spreading fast among the soldiers, and the sick have to be borne all the way from here to the railroad posts, a distance of about 500 miles, in mule litters."[20] In another story on that march, Finerty noted that Crook was unpopular with the troops and was disliked by most of his officers, except those who had served with him longest. "Crook is a singular man," he said, "and one impossible to estimate at a glance or even on long acquaintance."[21]

Davenport's story, too, was short, giving just the essential facts of the contemplated march, which he predicted would mean near starvation. A sort of dull resignation seems to pervade Davenport's account from Heart River. His story is also interesting in another respect: Whereas the stories of the other three correspondents left Bismarck September 8 and appeared in the editions of September 9, Davenport's cleared the wire a day later and appeared a day later. The circumstance suggests that Crook's courier may have had orders to hold up Davenport's story in retaliation for that reporter's past schemes to get his account in first.

On September 7, Crook detailed Mills to take 150 picked men and ride ahead to the Black Hills settlements to buy food and send it back to meet the troops. Strahorn and Davenport went with Mills's column, which also included sixteen packers and sixty-one pack mules.

Already ragged and ravenous after a prolonged diet of bacon, hardtack, and coffee, and reduced rations at that, Crook's main command started out, and by September 8 was reduced almost to starvation and to misery. Due south by compass they marched, their horses dropping day by day. The exhausted animals carried "half-starved men who could

[20] *Chicago Times*, Sept. 9, 1876.
[21] *Ibid.*, Sept. 30, 1876.

not sit up in the saddle, and couldn't so frequently dismount on coming to steep, slippery descents" where they ordinarily would dismount to favor the horses.

Day after day it rained, making it impossible for the men to build fires, even had the country afforded firewood, which itself was scant enough. That meant the men could not even have coffee, which was the only thing left by September 8. The rain had washed their little sugar and salt out of the saddlebags. A few on occasion were lucky enough to get a fire going, and Davenport—riding with the scouts—sometimes shared deer or antelope which they bagged.

Even then a bit of humor leavened the situation. Showing that not everyone had literally heeded the restrictions on food, Strahorn and Major Gerhard Luhn of the infantry clowned when they divided their last spoonful of beans. Strahorn held the spoon in one hand, his revolver in the other. Likewise holding his revolver, Luhn drew his knife and carefully divided the beans down the middle. Each flourishing his pistol, they ate their last beans, in a pouring rain, to the merriment of those around them.

As they marched through gumbo, an occasional pistol shot told that another cavalryman had shot his mount. Soon two to three hundred cavalrymen marched in the rear of the infantry. Finerty said that he, too, would have shot his horse, which was becoming a burden, except that he needed him to carry the writing material in the saddlebags. Many of the horses fell dead, others simply lay down and quit.

And then on September 8—when the hardtack had either been ruined by the rain or consumed, when the dab of coffee could no longer be cooked, when the bacon was gone, when the salt and sugar had been washed out of the saddlebags— then there remained but one choice of alternatives, as Finerty put, "to eat one another or our animals." That day he and Lawson saw a group of soldiers taking meat from a dead horse. That was the beginning of horsemeat and ultimately mulemeat rations. Crook then ordered that officers select as many horses each day as would be necessary to feed the men. Finerty gave his opinion of equine flesh:

> As I sampled all kinds of equine meat on the trip, I will give my opinion of that style of diet in brief: Cavalry horse meat, played out, sore-backed subject, fried without salt, stringy, leathery, blankety and nauseating. Cavalry horse, younger than preceding and not too emaciated, produces meat which resembles very bad beef; Indian pony, adult, has the flavor, and appearance, of the flesh of elk; Indian pony, colt, tastes like antelope or young mountain sheep; mule meat, fat and rank, is a combination of all the foregoing, with pork thrown in.[22]

A cavalry officer complained that to eat his horse seemed like cannibalism.

Straggling, famished, worn-out, ragged, wet, discipline almost gone, they went into battle.

Mills and his men had stumbled upon an Indian village while riding to the Black Hills to get food, whereupon Mills sent a courier to Crook, asking for support.

When Mills was detailed on September 7 for the trip to the Black Hills, Strahorn and Davenport chose to go with him, although, as Strahorn said, "all knew it was a case of taking our lives in our hands." The sense of danger was heightened because troops that day found a fresh trail of six hundred lodges on the right flank, heading toward the Black Hills. Davenport wrote, "I determined to incur the perils of the ride with the hope of escaping the sooner from the privation of the field." Finerty would have gone, too, "but my horse was useless, and I was compelled to remain with the main command."[23]

In early evening of September 7, Strahorn and Davenport took their places in Mills's column, whose 150 men were picked

[22] Finerty, *War-Path and Bivouac,* 248
[23] Strahorn, Autobiography, 201; *New York Herald,* Oct. 2, 1876; Finerty, *War-Path and Bivouac,* 247–48.

271

as having the best horses left in the regiment.[24] "The mist circumscribed us so that our world seemed very small and beyond it dwelt the terror of the unknown," Davenport recorded. For two hours they moved in silence, with the pack mules closely guarded to keep them from fleeing, and in a darkness that obscured landmarks. Occasionally Grouard, as guide, flicked a match to see the compass. In time the air cleared of rain and mist, the Big Dipper and North Star shining through, but only long enough for them to verify their course. Of a sudden clouds again curtailed the stars and dumped more rain upon them. About midnight they halted, picketed their horses, and tried to get some sleep in the mud and rain.

At 4:00 A. M., with the sky just beginning to lighten behind the still-falling rain, Mills put his troops in motion again. After an eleven-hour ride in which they made only twenty-five miles because of broken country and muddy footing, Grouard reported an Indian village ahead.

Mills scouted the village with Grouard, consulted his officers, and remembered his instructions from Crook—to strike any village he might encounter. While waiting for Mills to complete a reconnaissance, the men shivered in a shallow hollow, clammy mist wrapped about them. Wiping the barrels of their guns as best they could and brightening cartridges with numbed fingers, Davenport reported, the men did not seem to care whether they advanced or retreated. "A dull apprehension of disaster reigned," he reported, "but none knew what to do to dispel the dread." Deciding against an attack during the afternoon, Mills moved his men back two miles and concealed them in a gorge, planning to attack the village at dawn.

That was another miserable night—dark, cold, rainy, muddy—withal, "one of the ugliest" Mills had ever spent. For

[24] This account of the march and the attack on the village is based upon Davenport's two stories, *New York Herald*, Sept. 17 and Oct. 2, 1876; a story in the *Chicago Tribune*, Sept. 17, 1876, presumably by Strahorn; Strahorn, Autobiography, 202–206; and Mills's official report in Secretary of War, *Report*, 1876, I, 509–11.

supper the soldiers had hard bread and a few scraps of bacon. The packers, however, feasted on a soup made of flour and grease, which Davenport shared, eating it "with an eagerness I never before would have conceived of." They tried to get a little sleep, in wet blankets on greasy canvas taken from the mule packs. Before going to sleep, Davenport watched the grotesque images created by the glare of campfires against the mist. Dropping off to sleep, he soon was awakened by "a fierce trampling and snorting over my head." Some mules had attempted to stampede, but were checked by the picket lariats, only just soon enough to keep Davenport and his bedfellows from being trampled. Later, other animals broke for freedom, including Davenport's horse, Nigger. "I searched for him in a rather desperate mood," Davenport wrote, "and was delighted at last to find him standing passively near the camp. He rubbed his nose against me familiarly when I touched him, as if to declare that he knew it would be very ill conduct to desert me in such an emergency as then beset me."

Strahorn did not even attempt sleep. Through the night he and others alternately sat and stood, holding their horses in the cold rain and mist. "Never before or since," he wrote in later years, "were hours so laggard or anxiety so great for the coming of dawn when we could at least do something that would heat the blood and cheer the soul to forgetfulness of that everlasting soaking patter, patter of the freezing rain."

About one or two o'clock Mills roused his men for an advance to the position from which they would make the dawn attack, in which both correspondents were to participate. Strahorn was to ride in the charge that was to be made by twenty-five mounted men to scatter the Indian pony herd. One hundred cavalrymen were dismounted for the attack. Another twenty-five were to remain hidden in a ravine a mile or so back, holding the horses and mules. Davenport was detailed to remain with the horses and pack train.

Before the full plan could be carried out, the Indian pony herd stampeded, neighing the alarm to Indians, who cut their way out of tipis for an escape to the hills. Mills revised his

273

plan and sent both the mounted and dismounted men into the attack. Very shortly they had the village in their possession, but the braves—having placed their women and children in protected places—fought from rock and brush near by.

Meantime, Davenport and the others waited in a ravine about a mile from the village, to advance when they heard firing. If the enemy should prove too powerful, they were to take a strong point and hold it until relieved. "There was in these arrangements," Davenport wrote, "an anticipation like that which befell Custer and his gallant Seventh. The waiting in the chill, wet darkness, straining the ear in rain for the sound of the fray, was full of dread, anxious suspense." Soon Captain Jack Crawford, who was along as a scout, galloped up with orders for them to advance. Moving forward to a bluff, from which they saw the flashes of guns below, they met Grouard and a private who brought an order to send a courier back to Crook immediately. Two men rode off with the message.

In attacking the village, the mounted men had run off about two hundred ponies, sweeping them beyond reach of the bolting Indians. Then the dismounted cavalrymen advanced into the village. For the rest of the morning firing continued between the troops and the Indians secreted in a wooded gully. But the troops had possession of the village, made up of thirty-five tipis, in which they found stacks of dried meat, robes, agency cloth, corn, flour, arms, and ammunition. Some of the men carried a rifle in one hand and a chunk of dried meat in the other, gnawing at the meat during the brief fighting. The soldiers outnumbered the Indians, some of whom were captured.

Indian captives laughed when they saw the soldiers devouring the dried meat. When he asked them why they laughed, Grouard was in turn asked what kind of meat they thought they were eating. Grouard said they supposed it was buffalo and venison. No, an Indian replied, the pony soldiers had kept them too much on the run that summer for them to

274

hunt. Well, then, asked Grouard, what kind of meat was it? That, said a delighted savage, was the ponies that died.

Mills's couriers reached Crook, who then was about seventeen miles from the village. He pressed forward with that part of his command having the best horses. Finerty rode with him, "but my infernal beast broke down completely two or three miles from camp, and I had to lead him the rest of the way." The remainder of Crook's main column followed. Crook and the advance reached the village shortly before noon, the remainder in late afternoon, but the fighting was over by then.[25]

Captives told the officers that some Indians had escaped to carry the alarm to Crazy Horse, whose camp was near, and predicted that he would come to fight the soldiers. Crook then deployed his men around the village, concealing them to surprise any attack by Crazy Horse.

In late afternoon Crazy Horse counterattacked. Instead of finding Mills's small force, however, he ran head-on into Crook's entire force, deployed to meet him. The troops drove him away in brisk firing, during which an Irish soldier was heard to chuckle, when he had knocked an Indian from his horse, that he had "softened the wax in that boy's ears."[26]

The correspondents seem to have taken no part in the fighting after the first charge into the village, although they were active in gathering information during the fight, which came to be known as the Battle of Slim Buttes. When a small force of soldiers and scouts made the final charge on a cave in which Chief American Horse fought and in which he was mortally wounded, the correspondents came rushing up for information. During the afternoon fighting, Finerty was described as scurrying about along the firing line, gathering information for his story.

Evidence was found in the village that these warriors had

[25] Finerty, *War-Path and Bivouac*, 249–50; Secretary of War, *Report, 1876*, I, 511–12.
[26] King, *Campaigning with Crook*, 105–106; Sandoz, *Crazy Horse*, 339–41.

helped annihilate Custer's command. A Seventh Cavalry guidon, a glove marked with the name of Captain Miles Keogh, who died with Custer, a letter addressed to a private, and horses bearing the Seventh's brand were discovered. The Indians claimed later that American Horse (or Iron Plume, as the Indians knew him) had not been at the Little Big Horn, and that the Seventh Cavalry relics were brought to his camp by other warriors. Also found were letters of good conduct for that particular band, issued by Indian agents. The village was destroyed.

Fighting a brief rear-guard action against Crazy Horse, who appeared again the next morning, Crook left the village site on September 10. The Indian stores had given the troops some provisions, but not enough, and it became necessary once more to kill horses for food. The next day Crook again sent Mills on a rapid march to buy all the food in sight in the Black Hills settlements and rush it back to the troops. Strahorn and Davenport went along, the latter riding a recaptured Seventh Cavalry horse.

Strahorn had his mouth set for food, and satisfied his personal needs immediately after they arrived in Crook City in Whitewood Canyon on the evening of September 12. Painfully, he slipped out of his saddle in front of a restaurant in that mining camp, entered, and faintly asked the waiter, "Could you possibly serve a beefsteak and baked potato?" The waiter obliged. "With elbows on the counter and my head dropping down between my hands," he remembered, "I uttered a sigh of relief that meant so much it might well have echoed round the world."[27]

But Davenport had his mouth set for another *Herald* exclusive. Grouard carried dispatches from the correspondents as well as from General Crook, which he was to send on to Fort Laramie for telegraphing. He had all the dispatches, and Crook's orders to telegraph the official dispatches first. But Davenport had made a secret agreement with Captain Jack, to whom he had given a duplicate copy of his stories.

[27] Strahorn, Autobiography, 207.

Crawford was to slip away from the others and beat Grouard to the telegraph. If successful, he was to receive a large sum of money.[28]

When they had entered Whitewood Canyon, Crawford showed the route to Mills, and twice tried to get away with the dispatches, only to be thwarted by Mills and Bubb, the commissary officer. After they had arrived at Crook City and had eaten, Grouard told Crawford he should remain there and help buy supplies the next morning. With the excuse that he would spend the night with a friend, Crawford got away from the others.[29]

While the others slept, Crawford—who seems to have weathered the trip much better than most of the men, especially Strahorn—rode out of Crook City about 11:00 P.M. for Deadwood. In the darkness, his mule stumbled, and he had to walk almost all the way to Deadwood, where he arrived about 6:00 A.M. on the thirteenth. Obtaining a horse, he started for Custer City. When he was a few miles north of Custer City, he saw a horseman gaining on him from the rear.[30]

Meantime, Grouard had had a good night's sleep, and on the morning of the thirteenth set out for Deadwood. In the Deadwood livery stable he saw Crawford's mule, and when he learned that Crawford had obtained a horse and had ridden toward Custer City, he suspected for the first time that Crawford and Davenport had plotted a double-play. Grouard, who had originally planned to hire a courier, then determined to ride his dispatches through himself. After getting a fresh horse, he found a friend who went with him to the bank, where, with Crook's authorization, he drew $500 with which to buy other mounts along the way.

Knowing that he could reach a cavalry camp manned by Captain Egan of the Second Cavalry, Strahorn's comrade of the March village fight, who could send on a courier, Grouard set out on the first part of the two hundred-mile trip to Fort

[28] DeBarthe, *Grouard*, 159–61.
[29] *Ibid.*; a story by Crawford in *New York Herald,* September. 18, 1876.
[30] *New York Herald,* Sept. 18, 1876; *Alta California,* Sept. 12, 1876.

Laramie. He swung into the saddle at ten-thirty, and flogged his horse at such a clip that the animal played out after twenty-five miles, fortunately in sight of a road ranch, where he rented a fresh horse. He claimed to have ridden it and two other horses to death on that trip and to have ruined three others. He said he took his sixth horse from an unarmed German, forcing the latter to sell the animal. About five miles farther on, he overtook Crawford.[31]

Coming up with Crawford, Grouard asked him if he had not had orders to remain and help with the supplies. Upon Crawford's answer that he was carrying dispatches for the *Herald,* Grouard told him he was discharged as of the time he left the command. The half-blood then spurred his horse toward Custer City. He claimed that he rode 101 miles in four hours and ten minutes, and that he was so exhausted that friends had to take him out of the saddle. He hired another courier to take the dispatches to the army camp in Red Canyon, where they could be relayed by army riders to Fort Laramie.

Grouard went to his death thinking he had bested Crawford and that the *New York Herald* got its come-uppance that day, being thrown several days behind other newspapers because it had tried to crowd in ahead.

But Crawford stole a march on Grouard. In anger, Grouard had given Crawford the *Herald* dispatch in his pouch before he rode on. Thus two sets of dispatches for the world's greatest news-gathering newspaper were in the pouch of a bearded frontier scout, riding a winded horse, in the middle of nowhere, and several days from the Fort Laramie telegraph. On September 16, Crawford came to the Sage Creek camp, on the road between Cheyenne and the Black Hills, which had a telegraph operator. At the time, the wire was down between there and Laramie, but the operator thought the break would be repaired by mid-morning. Having two sets of dispatches, Crawford left one set with the operator at Sage Creek, instructing him to forward them as soon as the current

[31] DeBarthe, *Grouard,* 160–62.

was restored. With the other set Crawford rode to the next camp, where the telegraph operator told him the *Herald* dispatches were on the wire, and ahead of the others. He then rode on to Fort Laramie, arriving nine hours after the government courier but with mission accomplished. Davenport's stratagem had failed, but, despite Grouard's efforts, the *Herald* was in print with the story on the same day that the other papers had them. In fact, the *Herald* beat the opposition *Tribune* because the story came over the wires on the sixteenth, a Saturday, and the *Tribune* did not publish a Sunday morning paper. Claiming that he had beaten five men and seven horses [which would make a liar of Grouard, who claimed he rode six horses], Crawford wrote a story of his experiences for the *Herald*.[32]

Meanwhile, Finerty and Wasson struggled along with the main column on the last leg of the march. At first, Finerty hoofed it, having given up his scab-backed horse on the ninth, but then Crook gave him one of his own horses.

What was described as the worst day of the entire march came on September 12 as the men forced aching legs through the badlands. Not only were the men starving; they were by then reduced to absolute fatigue. Grown men flung themselves upon the ground and cried. Horses dropped. They struggled through boggy stream beds. Some mules hauling wounded on travois floundered in quicksand, plunged to escape the horror, and jolted screaming wounded from litters into the quicksand. But no one reported any deaths on the march, with the exception of a soldier who was scalped while hunting.

While eating pony steak on the thirteenth, Finerty heard the lowing of oxen. "Rations coming!" the shout went up. Oxen pulled in the wagons of food which Mills's detachment had sent back. The men slaughtered the oxen, roasting the meat on willow wands. They jerked boxes from the wagons, ripped them, and ate hungrily. Officers restored order at the

[32] *New York Herald*, Sept. 17, 18, 1876; *Chicago Tribune*, Sept. 17, 1876; *New York Tribune*, Sept. 18, 1876.

wagons, but in the trampling a lieutenant reached down and plucked three ginger snaps out of the mud and thought them the sweetest things he had tasted in years.

In the Black Hills, Crook received orders to meet Sheridan at Fort Laramie for a discussion of a new strategy. Because Crook and Terry had been drawn apart in their campaigns, Sheridan resumed his original plan of dismounting and disarming Indians at the agencies, over which the army then had control. Now that the summer's fighting was over, many of the hostile Sioux had slipped back into the agencies. Crook was to be given responsibility for disarming and dismounting the Indians at Red Cloud and Spotted Tail agencies in Nebraska.

All four correspondents left with Crook from Deadwood on September 16, making a party of thirteen or fourteen men who started for Camp Robinson, Nebraska, on the first leg of the trip to Fort Laramie. When they reached Camp Robinson, Strahorn went to sleep in front of the tent assigned to him, and awoke to find that someone had carried him inside and placed him on a cot. Eager to see the Centennial Exposition in Philadelphia, Strahorn left the party there, traveling to Sidney, where he took a train, but he would return to ride with Crook again during the winter. He seems to have let his reportorial responsibilities slide at that point. If he wrote a concluding story, it was crowded out of the *Rocky Mountain News* by the presidential campaign. The other three correspondents rode to Fort Laramie with Crook, and dispersed from there.

Wasson's movements are obscure, but he continued beating the drum for Crook to the last, and ultimately returned to California. In his story reporting the Slim Buttes fight, he described the march up to that point, and apparently had learned in conversation with Finerty that the *Chicago Times* man had likened it to Napoleon's retreat from Moscow. "It was not a Moscow affair, however, by any means," Wasson wrote. "Only about half a dozen men had to be carried on litters, and the infantry battalion under Col. Chambers showed remarkable endurance, and set an example that the United States army should profit by." He acknowledged that the campaign had not been the success hoped for, "but it has decided that it is only by such hard work and exposures that the hostile Sioux can be brought to terms; also that Gen. Crook has been on the right track ever since he left his wagons, and that his views as to their scattering were correct." The six hundred-mile march, he wrote, "should prove salutary to the whole army," and it had afforded "great knowledge" of the hostile country and its characteristics.[33]

By contrast with his delightful series of letters to the *Owyhee Avalanche* in 1867, Wasson's coverage of the Sioux campaign is disappointing. Possibly the scope and adversity of war with mounted Plains Indians left him a little stunned, just as it seems to have baffled Crook his first time out.

Finerty reached Fort Laramie on September 27 and in about a week reported at the *Times* office. His concluding stories appeared all in a bunch—his day by day "mailers," extending from August 24 through the end of the campaign, took up all four news columns on page one and ran two more columns on page two. A long final story appeared about a week later. He wrote his concluding paragraphs in Chicago on October 6:

> Since my return I have had to endure the usual boredom shoved upon an ephemeral human curiosity. One fellow says, "You're fat." The next man, "You're thin." Another fellow assures you that "You've not changed except for the better." An observing party discovers that your face, and especially your nose, is "awfully red." The constitutional, inevitable, universal "damphool" has asked me a dozen times: "You weren't in earnest when you said you lived on horse meat? Didn't you make that up?" This species of biped jackass flourishes in every community, and can hardly be expected to be absent from Chicago.
>
> In concluding the series of letters which I have written for *The Times*, in connection with the Sioux expedition, from May

[33] *New York Tribune*, Sept. 18, 1876.

6 to date, I have only to say that I have endeavored "naught to extenuate and naught to set down in malice." I despise the meanness of professional exaggeration, and, in the campaign just closed, there was nothing to exaggerate, the reality being of a character sufficiently sensational to satisfy the most morbid of imaginations.[34]

Ending a five months' war assignment, Finerty had little to say in criticism of Crook, good or bad, other than that he could look more to the comfort of his troops.

It remained for the disliked and disgruntled Davenport to stir things up. Davenport, who lay seriously ill in Cheyenne for a time as a result of his exertions on campaign, was a prodigious worker. He sent in two stories reporting the Battle of Slim Buttes and the next day's march, together running about twelve pages of double-spaced copy, and a third story in which he corrected the casualty list of that battle in which two soldiers were killed and fourteen wounded.[35] He wrote a valedictory of approximately 15,000 words, in which he charged that Crook should be court-martialed for his conduct of the campaign. The story filled a solid six-column page of the *Herald* and continued for almost another full column on a succeeding page.[36]

Davenport predicted the campaign would thereafter be likened to Napoleon's retreat from Moscow, and would have been just as disastrous had not "a freak of fortune" enabled the command to capture a small village in an "inglorious" action. The troops could not have failed to win that battle, he said, if properly led, for they greatly outnumbered the savages. Even so, he said, a reverse at one moment was imminent when Mills suddenly ordered his men to retreat, but the retreat was frustrated by a lieutenant who promised to shoot any man who tried to retreat, an accusation which the *Herald* was said to have retracted later.[37]

[34] *Chicago Times,* Sept. 30, Oct. 7, 1876.
[35] *New York Herald,* Sept. 17, 21, 1876.
[36] *Ibid.,* Oct. 2, 1876.
[37] King, *Campaigning with Crook,* 153–55.

282

Pointing out that the Shoshone and Ute scouts had turned their backs on the command on August 21 and 22, Davenport said: "The distrust of the aboriginal allies of the troops of the kind of generalship which has been displayed in the war has been reflected in the minds of every common soldier who marched from Fort Fetterman. The lack of respect for their commander has struck me many times."

Davenport also sneered at Crook's Spartan simplicity, causing a *Herald* editor to make "Crook's Sham Simplicity of Life" a deck in the headline. Even though the trooper was limited to one blanket, Davenport said, each night a mule packer moved over to Crook's headquarters with his arms full of hospital blankets and a tarpaulin "which contributed to the comfort of the terror of the Apaches."

He reported that the soldiers were limited to bacon, hardtack, coffee, and sugar, while the packers, "exercising a sort of usurped prerogative, winked at by the general commanding, was [*sic*] supplied with flour, beans, tea, rice, &c., on which they remained sleek, saucy and fat while the soldier dwindled." Sarcastically he added: "The reader has probably guessed that the spartan Indian fighter was often beholden to the civility of the packers for fare superior to that with which his military subordinates must be content. General Crook invariably established his headquarters near the pack-trains and lived a double life—one exhibited to the soldiers with calm vanity, but in which each one detected shams and flaws, and the other to his familiars and toadies, which was a consistent mirror of selfishness."[38]

Davenport was long gone when that copy of the *Herald* reached the men of the expedition who had been left in the Black Hills to recuperate in bivouac and to restore their animals. They were furious. All sorts of stories were told about Davenport, which reached the ears of King, who had not known the correspondent well. Those stories were repeated

[38] Although Bourke maintains that Crook fared as his men fared, he does furnish confirmation of better food in the packers' area. *On the Border with Crook*, 369, 357.

in an edition of King's book, *Campaigning with Crook*, in which the officer said Davenport was a "desperate coward" and had watched the Slim Buttes fight in "abject terror," statements which Davenport challenged. Threatening a libel suit, Davenport forced King to retract and revise. Out of King's investigation came an entirely different picture, and in the revision he wrote:

I since have had reason to regret this far more deeply than I can express. For ten years the statement went unchallenged. It was only last October [The book first came out in 1880, published by the *Milwaukee Sentinel*, and was issued by Harper's in 1890, the first edition of which seems to have been the one Davenport saw.] that the gentleman himself came upon the book and promptly demanded its withdrawal from sale, as it contained a libel that pointed directly to him. The investigation made by his efforts and by mine brought to light some curious facts which need not be detailed here, but I found enough to convince me that, in accusing him of cowardice, my numerous authorities had very flimsy ground to stand on. Captain Charles Morton, of the Third Cavalry, assured me that this very correspondent rode by his side on the fighting line at the Rosebud (June 17th), and bore himself with cool courage. Colonel Dodge, who commanded the expedition of '75, wrote me that he had to rebuke him for recklessness; and Colonel Anson Mills himself, who had most reason to feel aggrieved at this correspondent, wrote me finally that he thought the accusation of cowardice should be withdrawn. As complete a retraction and apology as lay in my power to write, was thereupon placed in the hands of Colonel W. C. Church, of the *Army and Navy Journal*, and it was accepted in a letter as courteous as could possibly be asked.

This practically closed the controversy, but I feel that it is due the gentleman referred to that these pages should contain a refutation of that charge of cowardice as positive as the original statement. We heard long after the campaign that he had been very ill at Cheyenne, but I, at least, did not know how ill and exhausted he was that wretched, dripping night before Mills's attack on the Indian village. There can be no further

284

doubt that any reflection on the courage of "Mr. D——," or on his conduct as a gentleman, was absolutely unjustifiable.[39]

Something more of the spirit of Crook's summer campaign is shown in the General's farewell to his troops. Indeed, it shows not only the spirit but the army—and white—point of view in Indian warfare. Breaking up the Big Horn and Yellowstone Expedition at Camp Robinson, Crook issued General Orders No. 8 on October 24, which read in part:

> Indian warfare is, of all warfare, the most dangerous, the most trying, and the most thankless. Not recognized by the high authority of the United States Senate as war, it still possesses for you the disadvantages of civilized warfare, with all the horrible accompaniments that barbarians can invent and savages execute. In it you are required to serve without the incentive to promotion or recognition; in truth, without favor or hope of reward.
>
> The people of our sparsely settled frontier, in whose defense this war is waged, have but little influence with the powerful communities in the East; their representatives have little voice in our national councils, while your savage foes are not only the wards of the nation, supported in idleness, but objects of sympathy with large numbers of people otherwise well-informed and discerning.
>
> You may, therefore, congratulate yourselves that, in the performance of your military duty, you have been on the side of the weak against the strong, and that the few people there are on the frontier will remember your efforts with gratitude.[40]

Phocion Howard became so disgusted with Terry's fizzling campaign that he went home in a rowboat. With Lathrop reporting that "a grumbling fever has become epidemic" in Terry's army, Diehl wrote that any hope of gaining an advantage over the Indians had been lost for the year, and he blamed the failure of the campaign on the lack of one general command. O'Kelly said Congress should investigate the whole

[39] King, *Campaigning with Crook*, 153–55.
[40] *Ibid.*, 166–67.

285

campaign, the failure of which he attributed to a lack of co-operation among the higher officers. "It is openly stated," O'Kelly wrote, "that rivalries and jealousies have in great part contributed to the want of success and have been directly the cause of the Little Big Horn massacre."[41]

After branching off from Crook, Terry scouted the Yellow-stone, taking his force across to the north bank for a short march there. But nowhere did he find Indians, even though some had fired at his infantry detachment at the mouth of Glendive Creek. By the end of August his campaign had come to a standstill. Under orders from Sheridan, he had to detach Miles's Fifth Infantry and part of the Twenty-second Infantry to build a cantonment at the mouth of the Tongue River. Fifteen hundred men were to be left in the field through the winter to continue the pressure upon the nomadic Sioux.

On August 31, or so he reported, Howard took advantage of a chance to go to Bismarck in a rowboat. He said the steamer *Benton* had burst a larboard cylinder in taking government supplies up the Yellowstone, and the captain had to send eight men in a metal lifeboat downriver to Bismarck to effect repairs. Howard went with them, reporting upon arrival at Bismarck on September 4: "Five hundred miles in a life-boat, with his life in his hands, running the gauntlet of murderously-hostile Sioux on the Yellowstone, and equally murderous and treacherous Indians on the Missouri, is the last foolish venture of your correspondent. It was not done out of any particular spirit of bravado, but because any chance of getting away from a sadly demoralized army was preferable to remaining with it and becoming demoralized one's self."[42]

On September 5 the news spread through Terry's camp at the mouth of Glendive Creek that the campaign was being abandoned, that some troops would remain in the field during the winter, that the remainder would go back to winter quarters. The "humiliation of defeat" permeated the com-

[41] *Chicago Tribune*, Sept. 5, 1876; *San Francisco Evening Bulletin*, Sept. 5, 1876; *Chicago Times*, Sept. 5, 1876; *New York Herald*, Sept. 12, 1876.
[42] *Chicago Tribune*, Sept. 5, 1876.

mand, which recognized the "utter failure" of their summer's labors, Diehl reported.[43]

But joy and gladness spread through the camp, too, and about nine o'clock that evening a hundred or so officers gathered around a fire near Terry's headquarters. For the next two hours they sang old campaign songs. But Terry did not take part. Instead, he paced the ground before his own campfire, stopping only to say farewell to those men who called on him.

Diehl strolled over to the General's tent to talk with him. He said Terry looked careworn and troubled. "Loth to enter the field," Diehl wrote, "and with a knowledge that his original plans were disarranged through a disobedience of orders, he has felt that whatever blame is attached to the failure of the troops will have to be borne by him. Gen. Terry is by nature one of the kindest of men, and has been willing to accept the odium of the campaign. This has been shown throughout his official reports, in none of which has he cast a reflection upon any of his subordinate officers."

In the interview with Diehl, Terry said he was compelled to abandon the campaign against his wishes and expectations, having hoped that he could scour the region north of the Little Missouri before winter, where the principal hostile bands could be expected. Instead, he had to provide supplies for 1,500 troops for the winter, which would mean that every exertion must be made to rush them through before low water and bad weather closed off the supply routes. "Under the circumstances," Terry was quoted as saying, "I cannot keep a consuming army in the field."

Naturally, Diehl wanted to know what Terry had to say at the conclusion of the campaign about the disaster of June 25, and about the plan he had evolved for combat on the Little Big Horn. "The plan of the fight was my own, and I considered it a good one," Diehl quoted him as saying. "It was the only one in which I could bring my infantry into action. As far as it was possible I felt assured the Indian village was on the Little Big Horn, and in my endeavor to co-operate with Gen.

[43] *Chicago Times*, Sept. 16, 1876.

287

Custer the troops made a most difficult march to reach the point selected for the junction of the troops."

And another question concerning Reno's disobedience on the reconnaissance in mid-June: "That is a matter of record," Terry was quoted as saying.

What of next year, General? "He felt confident," Diehl said, "that the campaign would have to be taken up again next year, at which time it would be necessary to place a sufficient number of troops in the field to allow five or six columns to operate independently."

The next day the command started breaking up. Diehl, Lathrop, Cody and a man named Talbot, identified as representing the *New York Graphic* and *Frank Leslie's Illustrated Newspaper*, went downriver on the *Josephine*, arriving in Bismarck during the week preceding Wednesday, September 13. O'Kelly came down on the *Chambers* with Terry, arriving in Bismarck by September 20.

In the final rush of getting ready for the trip home and to winter quarters, the ironic humor of the soldier cropped up again, as when a cavalry officer quipped that, since the Sioux had failed to find them, they were going home. "Well, Jack," an old veteran said to a buddy, "I'll see you in the spring."[44]

[44] *Chicago Times*, Sept. 16, 1876.

10. LATER AND LESSER CAMPAIGNS

*The noble red man is not a fool. He is
a cunning nomad, who hates civilization, and knows how to get all out of
it that pleases him—whiskey, tobacco,
rations and blankets, idleness in peace
and a rattling fight whenever he is
ready for it. And when he is beaten he
returns to the arms of his guardians on
the reservation, bringing his store of
white scalps with him as pleasing me-
morials of the good time he had.
     It is time to stop all that. The con-
tinent is getting too crowded.*
                    New York Herald[1]

THE ARMY BROKE THE BACK of organized Indian resistance on
the northern plains during the campaigns of 1876–77. Although the summer campaign had not brought a decision at
arms, it led to victory through logistics. Having used up most
of their ammunition on the Rosebud and the Little Big Horn,
having burned off much grass cover of their hunting range
in trying to stop the army, and having been harassed by the
army to such an extent that they could not hunt, the Indians
suffered a lessening of the food supply. During the succeeding
autumn, fall and spring, army columns—operating from
newly established bases in the former ranges of the hostile
Sioux—beat some Cheyenne and Sioux bands into submission,
and forced the rest into Canada. Miles garrisoned the cantonment at the mouth of the Tongue, from which he led a
column that fought through Sitting Bull's village in October;
the harassment forced Sitting Bull and his followers to find

[1] Editorial, Oct. 9, 1879.

sanctuary in Canada. Crook established an advance base on the site of old Fort Reno in Wyoming from which he also undertook winter operations.

After disarming the Indians at Red Cloud Agency in late October, Crook enlisted Sioux and Cheyennes to fight Sioux and Cheyennes, and took the field for a winter campaign on what was known as the Powder River Expedition, with a force of about 1,800 men organized at Fort Fetterman. On November 25, his cavalry, under Colonel Ranald S. Mackenzie of the Fourth Cavalry, struck and destroyed the Cheyenne village of Dull Knife, on what then was identified as the North Fork of the Powder River. The village contained about two hundred lodges and perhaps five hundred warriors.

Only one newspaper correspondent—Jerry Roche of the *New York Herald*—caught up with Crook's expedition before it left the railroad. Bourke remembered him as "a companionable, scholarly gentleman, who has since abandoned journalism and become possessed of considerable means in Texas." During the fighting at Dull Knife's village, Roche several times rode back and forth across the valley in which the village was situated, under a cross-fire from troops and Indians on either side. Indians on other occasions picked off some cavalrymen who made that same ride. Once Roche rode across the valley just to get something to eat, having heard that the pack train had come in with food and not having eaten since about the same hour the day before. After eating, he wrote a hurried story which went back with Indian couriers who also carried a message asking Crook to bring up the infantry. The soldiers camped there that night, and resumed their march the next morning after scattering the Indians.

That fight, which was a decided victory for troops who outnumbered the Indians and who were clothed and equipped for a winter campaign, was the only engagement of the Powder River Expedition, which remained in the field through most of December. Strahorn joined sometime during the remainder of the campaign.[2]

[2] Bourke, *On the Border with Crook*, 381–98; John G. Bourke, "Mackenzie's

By spring, Crazy Horse himself surrendered. Miles had struck his village on the headwaters of the Tongue in January, using artillery to gain a victory and forcing Crazy Horse to run again. Within a month the members of Crazy Horse's band, which also included some Cheyennes, had begun surrendering, some at Miles's cantonment and others at the agencies. Through the winter and spring Indians surrendered by the hundreds. By July, only a year after the Sioux and Northern Cheyennes had reached the high-water mark of their military glory at the Rosebud and Little Big Horn, that war power was gone. And General Sherman reported to the Secretary of War: "I now regard the Sioux Indian problem, as a war question, as solved."[3]

The northern plains were quiet. The mass of the hostile Sioux had either surrendered at the agencies or had fled across the border to join Sitting Bull in Canada.

But almost at once the northern plains became the decisive theater in the Nez Percé war which had begun in Idaho. Refusing to go on a reservation, the long peaceful Nez Percés fought off troops who tried to punish them for the murder of several whites and fled their Idaho homeland, trying to reach Sitting Bull. With never more than 250 warriors, they fought and maneuvered their way through enemy country. Warriors, women, children, and the aged, with all their remaining possessions in train, crossed the Rockies on the Lolo Trail, went south into Yellowstone National Park, and up through Montana, almost to the Canadian border. Nine times they whipped the troops of the one-armed Quaker general, O. O. Howard, in whose Department of the Columbia the outbreak occurred. After slipping through the Rockies, they by-passed a point which had been fortified by soldiers. In the Battle of the Big Hole in Montana, they soundly defeated Gibbon. Their war-

Last Fight with the Cheyennes: A Winter Campaign in Wyoming and Montana," *Journal of the Military Service Institution of the United States,* Vol. LIII (November-December, 1913), 345–49; *New York Herald,* Nov. 29, Dec. 1, 11, 1876; Robert Bruce, *The Fighting Norths and Pawnee Scouts,* 48, 49; Secretary of War, *Report, 1877,* I, 84.

[3] Nelson A. Miles, *Serving the Republic,* 154–60, 166.

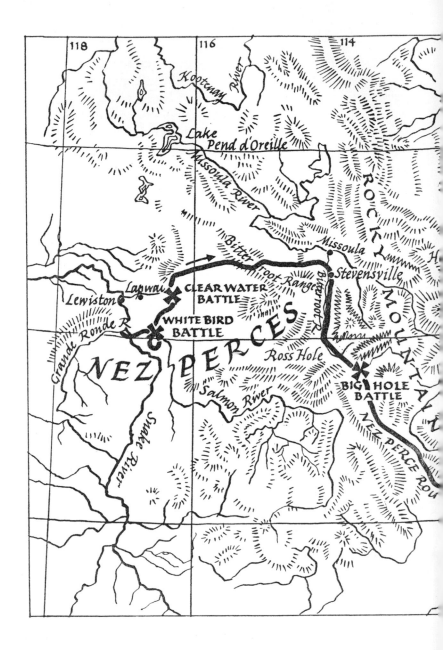

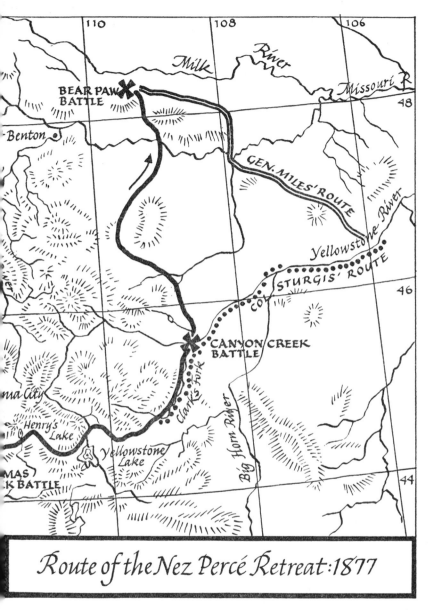

Route of the Nez Percé Retreat: 1877

From Francis Haines, *The Nez Percés: Tribesmen of the Columbia Plateau*

riors attacked two parties of tourists in Yellowstone, killing one man. Moving north, they defeated and eluded Colonel Sturgis and the Seventh Cavalry. Finally, utterly worn out, they were cornered in the Bear Paw Mountains by Miles, defeated in battle, and forced to surrender. But they had almost made it to Canada.

Apparently the only accredited newspaper correspondent in the Nez Percé campaign was Thomas A. Sutherland, of the *Portland Standard,* who also reported for the *New York Herald* and *San Francisco Chronicle,* although other newspaper reports seem to have been written by civilians, officers, and enlisted men. Twenty-seven years old at the time of the campaign, the California-born Sutherland had been educated at Harvard and had been an Oregon newspaperman for two years, having first worked with a foster brother who edited the *Oregon City Enterprise.*[4]

For Sutherland, who rode with Howard as a volunteer aide-de-camp, the campaign was just one continuous chase. He reported three battles, none of them decisive, and was with Howard when the General went forward with a small detachment to find Gibbon, who had been defeated at the Big Hole. Nothing in his dispatches or his book, *Howard's Campaign Against the Nez Perce Indians,* indicates any distinguishing activities. Sutherland presented a sympathetic picture of Howard, who often was belittled by other army officers, and never once did he criticize the General or his conduct of the campaign.

From his experience in that campaign, Sutherland did not think much of civilian Indian fighters. From time to time during the Western War, armchair strategists asserted that bands of armed frontiersmen could whip the Indians the army seemed unable to catch. That demand was voiced several times during the Modoc War, and the army had to beat off proffered volunteer held after the Custer defeat. Howard had

[4] Howard, *Nez Perce Joseph,* 177; Thomas A. Sutherland, *Howard's Campaign Against the Nez Perce Indians,* 3; *Portland Oregonian,* Aug. 21, 1891, excerpt furnished by Geneva Kershner, Library Association of Portland.

the "help" of such frontiersmen, causing Sutherland to write the following:

> To add to the bitterness of seeing the people and department commanders almost indifferent to our success, bands of armed men, styling themselves volunteers, have every now and then come in a cloud of dust to our assistance, and when assigned some position in the line not to their liking or promised that within two days we should overtake the Indians and they should have a chance to fight, they would play us the Arab trick of folding their tents and silently stealing away. Undoubtedly there were some intelligent and courageous men among these gangs—gangs which we sampled from three Territories—but, taken as a body, the frontiersman volunteer of to-day is an undoubted fraud, having almost as little pluck as principle and as meagre in conception of discipline as a backwoods schoolmaster. One band of men from Washington Territory, who represented themselves as thirsting for Nez Perce gore, turned out to be a gang of organized horse thieves. Another crowd of eighty, made up of Idaho and Washington Territory men, were across the Clearwater Creek the second day of our fight, in full view of our camp, and resolved to go back to Mount Idaho, instead of coming to our assistance, fearing that the Indians would overpower us. In Montana the volunteers join us merely to say they would like to fight, but their horses are worn out, and they can spare only one day, that they are subject to no commands and other similar absurdities. The frontiersman of my boyish fancy, the man who would fight Indians in Indian style and stand exposure as well as they and as cheerfully, is a thing of the past, dying out with such men as Kit Carson and Daniel Boone.[5]

The climax story of the Nez Percé campaign—Chief Joseph's surrender—was written by two correspondents who were there not even to cover a war. After Chief Joseph surrendered on October 5, only thirty miles from the Canadian sanctuary which some of the Nez Percé reached, Miles sent his report to Terry, then at Fort Benton on his way to Canada as head of

[5] *New York Herald*, Sept. 10, 1877.

a peace commission to treat with Sitting Bull. With him were two newspapermen—Diehl of the *Chicago Times* on his second plains assignment and Jerome B. Stillson of the *New York Herald*.

Then thirty-six years old, Stillson was a seasoned newspaperman. He had been a Civil War correspondent, Washington correspondent, and managing editor of the *New York World*. Giving up the managing editorship because he preferred reporting, he had joined the *Herald* in 1876.[6] Stillson taught young Diehl some important lessons that fall, lessons which were not only important to him personally but very probably important in the history of news reporting generally because of the invisible thread linking one generation with the next. At Fort Benton they first received word of Miles's fight, which lasted for four days. Since they were 120 miles from the nearest telegraph, Helena, it was necessary to hire a courier to take the dispatches. With Stillson leading, they hired, and shared the pay of, John Healy for a pony run to Helena, both with the story of the fighting and then with the story of the surrender. Diehl acknowledged his mentor, whom he remembered as "a strikingly handsome man":

> He accepted me as a tent companion, and I obtained from association with him, a broadened knowledge and daring in the handling of the news. It is only one phase to obtain an exciting budget of news. It is even more important, if you are remote from your newspaper, to arrange that the news gets through to the home office of the newspaper. Theoretically, I knew all of this, and yet, it was on this expedition, that I caught the vision that only by a possible degree of daring and tactical preparation, and by spending some of the office money freely, was I to be able to do what my newspaper had sent me for—to obtain and send through to it the news ahead of less enterprising journals. . . . My own reputation was as greatly enhanced in my newspaper office for having taken a plains courier into our service, as by my news narrative itself.[7]

[6] Louis M. Starr, *Bohemian Brigade,* 357; Andrews, *The North Reports the Civil War,* 525, 525 n.

Diehl and Stillson went into Canada with the Terry peace commission, which had been organized at the suggestion of the Canadian government. At the border they left their escort of two troops of the Second Cavalry and proceeded under escort by a troop of Mounted Police in red coats, white corduroys, helmets, and lances. They proceeded to Fort Walsh, near which Sitting Bull was camped.

The meeting with Sitting Bull proved fruitless for Terry but fruitful for Diehl and Stillson, who had the rare opportunity of interviewing the legendary Indian leader. Major James M. Walsh of the Mounted Police arranged the interview, at which the reporters had the service of an interpreter and a stenographer. The usual version is that Stillson telegraphed his Sitting Bull interview from Bismarck at a cost of $2,000, but the lapse of one month between the interview of October 17 and publication on November 16 would indicate otherwise. The *Herald* devoted page three, still the first news page, to the story and a two-column map of Custer's battlefield which Sitting Bull had partly corrected, and let the story run for more than two columns more on another page. Publication of the map with the story also belies the version of an expensive telegraphic transmission. Diehl's version of the interview was buried in a story that appeared on November 14, the absence of a date line suggesting it was written after his return to Chicago.[8]

After the Nez Percé campaign, Secretary of War George W. McCrary said the surrender of Chief Joseph "ended Indian hostilities for the present, and, let us hope, for the future as well."[9] But that was not to be, for the very next year the Bannocks went on the warpath in Idaho.

W. A. Goulder of the Boise *Idaho Statesman* covered the Bannock War of 1878, at least in its earlier stages. But the

[7] Diehl, *Staff Correspondent*, 118–21.

[8] *Chicago Times*, Nov. 14, 1877; *New York Herald*, Nov. 16, 1877; Diehl, *Staff Correspondent*, 129; Starr, *Bohemian Brigade*, 357; Paul F. Sharp, *Whoop-Up Country: The Canadian-American West, 1865–1885*, 272–78.

[9] Secretary of War, *Report*, 1877, I, xv.

war proved to be more of a scattered hunt than a contest of arms, for there were no major engagements.

The army continued to have trouble along the Canadian border, which gave Finerty a chance to see Sitting Bull in person.[10] Raiding parties from Sitting Bull's camp—said to harbor two thousand Indians—made sporadic incursions into Montana. In the summer of 1879 came the report that Sitting Bull was back on United States soil. Miles, who continued to direct military operations in the Yellowstone region, took the field.

Finerty was resting at Camp Sheridan, Nebraska, from a trip through Indian Territory and the Dakota badlands when a telegram sent him to Miles, whom he joined near old Fort Peck, Montana, in July. Miles went as far as the Canadian line without finding any Sioux other than a hunting party. Going into camp, the contingent awaited the arrival of Walsh, who agreed to take Finerty to see Sitting Bull. When Finerty told Miles where he was going, that officer burst out in a laugh, and sang this parody of a then popular song:

We're marching off for Sitting Bull!
And this is the way we go—
Forty miles a day, on beans and hay,
With the regular army, O!

Accompanied by Walsh, four Northwest police, and a Sioux, Finerty set out July 29 for Sitting Bull's camp. He was surprised at the size of the encampment twenty miles north of the border, reports of which he had thought had been exaggerated, and also learned immediately that the Sioux distrusted him as a "head soldier" because he was wearing the blue shirt and broad-brimmed white hat that many officers wore on campaign.

On July 30 he had the opportunity of observing a Sioux

[10] This account of Finerty's trip into Canada is based upon *Chicago Times,* Aug. 22, 1879; Finerty, *War-Path and Bivouac,* 311–22, 333, 353–83; Nelson A. Miles, *Personal Recollections,* 306–10; Secretary of War, *Report, 1876,* I, 483, *Report, 1879,* I, 61–63.

council which was conducted near Walsh's house. Sitting Bull was there, but refused to speak in council when Americans were present. During the council, Finerty saw an Indian on a cream-colored pony ride up in the rear and stare at him insolently. From another Indian the Irish reporter learned that he was Sitting Bull. The other Indians were reluctant to speak, not knowing who or what the reporter was, but Walsh convinced them that Finerty was his friend, and that was good enough for them. In fact, one brave sprang forward, shook Finerty's hand, and demanded that he speak in council.

Rising for "perhaps, the most singular experience of my life," Finerty addressed the Sioux, who looked upon all Americans as worse enemies than perhaps even the hated Crows. Several times, he said, the Indians broke in with "hows" as Finerty said he could not rival the eloquence of their chiefs, that he had not come to spy or fight, but to see how they lived, that his job was to hear what they said and write it so all Americans could then hear.

But Finerty did not get to interview Sitting Bull. Through an interpreter he learned that Sitting Bull had said he sought no one, least of all, Americans. Bull-headed, Finerty told the interpreter to tell the Indian leader that Finerty did not seek him, either. "I also learned," Finerty wrote in his memoirs, "that a certain high-flown interview, alleged to have been held with Sitting Bull, in which Custer is made to figure as the Long Hair—his hair, as already stated, was short at the time of his death—owed a great deal to the eccentrically brilliant imagination of the gentleman who wrote it." A slap at Diehl, who wrote for the same paper, or at Stillson? Probably Stillson.

Rawlins, Wyoming, became the date line on October 1, 1879. At midnight of September 30, Joe Rankin—former sheriff and a livery stable operator—completed a 160-mile ride to Rawlins in twenty-four hours, reporting that White River Utes in Colorado had ambushed and pinned down an army command of about 180 men, killing the commander, Major Thomas T. Thornburgh.

Thornburgh had been on his way to the White River

Agency to assist the agent, Nathan Meeker, who had called for troops because he feared for the lives of himself, his family, and white agency employees. Meeker—who has been pictured as an arbitrary, dictatorial, nonunderstanding Indian agent —had tried to force the Utes into agriculture. He had disturbed and threatened to disturb their normal ways so much that they were ready to kill. Meeker had been a Civil War correspondent for the *New York Tribune* and an unyielding idealistic collaborator of Horace Greeley in the Greeley Colony of Colorado. He was the father of the *New York Herald's* Ralph Meeker who had figured in the Sioux agency exposures. In response to Meeker's call for troops, Thornburgh's command had been dispatched from Fort Fred Steele near Rawlins. The Indians ambushed him in the Milk River country. When the story first broke, no one knew what had happened to Meeker and the others at agency.[11]

Before the sun was up on October 1, Merritt was assembling a relief force of his Fifth Cavalry at Fort D. A. Russell near Cheyenne, and on the next day left Rawlins, accompanied by John C. Dyer who had come up from Denver to represent the *New York World* and *Chicago Tribune*. He marched with four companies of cavalry and 150 infantry in wagons—"charioteers," the cavalry called them.[12]

When news of the outbreak reached the country, the closest *New York Herald* man was Stillson, then accompanying President Hayes on his western trip of 1879. The *Herald* picked him off at Indianapolis with orders to cover the Ute War. Going west, Stillson stopped in Chicago to talk with Sheridan, met Crook in Omaha, and rode with him on the train to Fort Fred Steele, where they arrived late on the night of October 5. The next morning, Crook and Stillson rode the caboose of a freight train into Rawlins, which was directly north of the trouble area in northwestern Colorado. Stillson—who suffered from neuritis and who died in Denver a few months

[11] Sprague, *Massacre; New York Herald*, Oct. 2, 1879; Wellman, *Death on Horseback*, 215–26.

[12] Sprague, *Massacre*, 216, 222; information supplied by Reta Ridings, head, Research Services, Wyoming State Archives and Historical Department.

later—seems to have made Rawlins his base, writing all his stories from there. His information came mostly from official reports and accounts sent in by officers such as Bourke of Crook's staff, although he seems to have engaged a leg-man to cover the story on the spot. The identity of the leg-man is not definitely established, but it may have been A. R. Johnson, a former Cheyenne newspaperman.[13]

On his fifth exciting assignment of the year, Finerty arrived in Rawlins. He had reported from Mexico, where Mexican troops escorted him from Vera Cruz to Mexico City; had toured Indian Territory; had explored the badlands; had covered Miles's abortive campaign, being escorted into Canada by scarlet-coated Mounties; and had seen the redoubtable Sitting Bull—all in the same year. He rode in with Colonel Guy Henry's battalion of the Third Cavalry, the same regiment with which he rode during the 1876 campaign.

Another newsman who went in with troops was W. P. Boardman of the *Denver Tribune*.

Finerty's experience on that campaign shows the privileged position to which the war correspondent rose during the Western War. Taking his place again with old friends of the Third Cavalry, Finerty found his horse cared for by an old veteran named McIntyre who insisted upon riding behind him like an orderly behind an officer. When Finerty told him he would prefer that the soldier keep his place in the column, McIntyre replied, "Oh, sure, our boys of the 3d Cavalry make no difference with you. You've been under fire with the regiment!"[14]

A thousand troops were on their way from Rawlins to the Ute country by October 6, but it was a dead story by the time the reporters got there. A company of Negro cavalrymen had reached the pinned-down Thornburgh force, Merritt freed them all, rode on to the agency, found Meeker and all his

[13] *New York Herald*, Oct. 5, 7, 1879, and later; *Indianapolis Journal*, Oct. 2, 1879; *Cheyenne Leader*, Nov. 4, 1879, quotation supplied by Miss Ridings; Diehl to Watson, letter of Oct. 30, 1937, Diehl Folder, Watson Papers; Starr, *Bohemian Brigade*, 357.
[14] Finerty, *War-Path and Bivouac*, 400–401.

white male employees killed and three white women in captivity. But before the troops could take vengeance, the government stepped in with a peace commission, assisted by the peaceful southern Utes, and the army marked time.

That is, it was a dead story from the standpoint of war coverage. Daily stories cleared the Rawlins telegraph office through practically all of October, reporting the early movements of troops, confirmation of the Meeker murder, and so on. Other stories came from Denver and Los Pinos Agency, reporting the negotiation for and final release of the white women captives. Interest in the affair ran high, but the war correspondents had no war to cover.

Scratching lice after almost a month in the field and certain there was nothing ahead for the troops except "inglorious activity, while some of the infernally idiotic or knavish benevolists [sic] who afflict America with their humane balderdash are trying to patch up an ignominious peace with the murderous Utes," Finerty decided to leave. He took advantage of an exploration by Henry for a better road from Rawlins to White River Agency, and left the field. At a ranch he met two other correspondents—the New York Herald leg-man and Boardman—with whom he rode into Rawlins.[15]

The best measure of how well the correspondents did their job came from Crook. When he wrote his annual report for the year, he said "the public journals gave such exhaustive and accurate narrations" that he considered it unnecessary to go into detail about the Ute outbreak.[16]

A major story appeared in the making when word was received that Sitting Bull had given in at last. Old "Slightly Recumbent Gentleman Cow," as some newspapermen called him, had finally decided to turn himself over to the United States government and become an agency Indian. For him that was the bitter end, for he had proudly told Miles in the fall of 1876 that the Great Spirit had made him an Indian but not an Agency Indian. Since 1879 his people had grad-

---

15 *Chicago Times*, Oct. 30, Nov. 6, 1879.
16 Secretary of War, *Report, 1880*, I, 79.

ually drifted away from him, with a great exodus coming in 1880. Hunger had done its work; that, and the realization that the Great Mother would not always shield him on her soil. To pleased Mounted Police, he said in the fall of 1880 that he would surrender to American authorities. In part, the final decision had been brought about by the Fort Buford interpreter, E. H. (Fish) Allison, who had been sent by the Fort Buford commander, Major H. D. Brotherton, to talk with the Sioux leader.

Receiving word that Sitting Bull would surrender at Fort Buford, the *Chicago Times* sent Diehl to cover the story, with orders to proceed to Bismarck by rail and then travel overland to Fort Buford the best way he could. That was a real order. Already it was December, the river closed, heavy snow on the ground, no road, and an uninhabited waste in western North Dakota, but Sheridan authorized army transportation for him.

Bundled in a buffalo coat and sealskin cap, Diehl made the trip—of about 175 miles, as the crow flies—by army sleigh and bobsled. By the time they reached Fort Buford, two soldier-drivers had had exposed flesh frozen, and Diehl had had to drive part of the way, following the hum of telegraph wires and watching for signs of the road, which was marked by weeds poking through the snow. Once he got lost, drifting away from the telegraph upon becoming snow-blind, but he worked his way back.

At Fort Buford, Diehl met Allison, who had escorted Sitting Bull south of the international boundary, and had then come in to the fort with Crow King, another Sioux chief. Crow King borrowed two dollars from Diehl to buy dolls for his daughters. With Allison and Crow King, Diehl rode to the Poplar River Agency in Montana, where Sitting Bull was expected to surrender, a distance of about fifty-five miles in a straight line.

By the time Diehl arrived at Camp Poplar the small garrison had been reinforced by Major Guido Ilges of the Fifth Infantry at the head of 180 troops, 6 Indian scouts, and twenty-four teamsters. Their presence had been considered necessary because the Indian camp there was that of Gall, a notorious Sioux war chief who had helped wipe out Custer.

Although the Sioux had come to surrender, they refused to move on to Fort Buford, and, at the expiration of an ultimatum, Ilges attacked their camp on January 2, 1881. With Diehl taking his place in the skirmish line, Ilges' troops moved across the Missouri River to the Indian camp—actually consisting of three separate camps—and found it vacated. A few artillery shells lobbed into the woods brought the Indians out of hiding, and the troops destroyed most of the lodges.

In his report of the action, Ilges said that Diehl and the scouts "behaved gallantly, and were of help to me." But Diehl wrote, "I have never understood how I could have done anything differently, as the march and short action were quietly performed." Diehl fired with the infantry when they had to riddle a lodge from which an Indian had fired at them. Even though the *Chicago Times* published Ilges' report in full, including the commendation of Diehl, the paper did not call attention to the honor bestowed upon its correspondent.[17]

The story Diehl had been sent out to cover did not materialize. Many other Indians surrendered that winter, but not until July 19 did Sitting Bull submit.

Colonel E. A. Carr, Sixth Cavalry, and his command wiped out by Apaches. Communications with Fort Apache cut off. So read the official army telegrams in early September, 1881. So reported the newspapers.

With an apparent small-scale Custer disaster shaping up, the *Chicago Times* and *New York Herald* had men on the ground for first-hand reporting. News of the outbreak came when Finerty was in San Francisco, and he hurried to Tucson by train. The *Herald* correspondent has been identified as Captain Jack Crawford, who had by then taken up a ranch in the Southwest, although he also maintained a home in Brooklyn.

[17] Secretary of War, *Report, 1881,* I, 101–105; Diehl, *Staff Correspondent,* 89, 153; *Chicago Times,* Mar. 6, 1881.

Not until September 5 did the truth come out, and then only when Carr sent a message by courier to Camp Thomas, Arizona, the next nearest post to the south. There had been a battle, there had been treachery, there had been an attack on Fort Apache, there had been casualties; but there had not been an annihilation of another army command.

The fight occurred when Carr took two companies of the Sixth Cavalry and a company of Indian scouts to arrest Nokay Delklinne, a medicine man who was responsible for a fanatic idea similar to the Ghost Dance which soon was to appear among the Plains Indians. As the necromancer, he was to re-populate the country with Apaches long since dead, and they would all unite to drive out the white men. Carr had received orders from the departmental commander to arrest Nokay Delklinne and a request from the Indian agent "to arrest or kill him, or both." The medicine man had promised to bring back to life two chiefs of whom the Apaches had been fond, and it was a tense situation when Carr arrived with eighty-five men and twenty-three Indian scouts to interrupt him—made all the more tense because for some time there had been indications of treachery among the usually reliable Apache scouts. When the troops reached Cibicu Creek, west of Fort Apache, on August 30, they found six hundred Indians en-camped. At first, however, things were not as bad as could have been expected. Nokay Delklinne went with Carr will-ingly, saying there would be no attack or any attempted escape. But as the troops went into camp a few miles west of the Indian encampment, Apaches began to appear on the surrounding bluffs.

Then the Apache scouts turned on their white comrades. An officer and several soldiers fell in the first fire. Other Apaches joined the scouts in attacking the soldiers. Someone shot Nokay Delklinne. With darkness the Apaches withdrew, and under cover of darkness Carr gathered up his command —which had lost eleven dead, three wounded, and many ani-mals—and headed back to Fort Apache, reaching there in late afternoon of August 31. In the meantime, wraith-like Apaches

305

had taken their vengeance on a few white men caught away from the fort, and on September 1 they attacked the fort itself. The telegraph line had been cut every few miles.

Carr's report, dated September 2, was taken to Camp Thomas and telegraphed to division headquarters in San Francisco, where it was made public in full on September 5. By then the trouble was all but over. Many Apaches had started to surrender, but some of the Apache prisoners had broken away and fled to the hostile Chiricahuas.[18]

As in the Ute War, it was a dead story from the standpoint of war coverage by the time the correspondents arrived and the military again took the field. Crawford remained at Camp Thomas, which had a telegraph operator, and did not bestir himself therefrom. But not Finerty. With his usual insistence upon being on the scene of a story, he rode with the troops, who searched the country from Fort Apache to no avail.

It was an unhappy assignment for Finerty, beset by frustration after frustration in what he called "this God-forsaken region." On the way from Los Angeles his train was detained in a desert ravine for eight hours because a long freight train had run off the track. "I never saw such another smash-up," he wrote. "The cars were chiefly freighted with groceries and liquors, the latter ranging from whiskey to champagne. About one hundred Chinamen were employed to clear the wreck, and they managed to get away with enough of the loose wine to become very imposingly drunk. Doubtless this circumstance accounted for our long detention." Near Tucson his train left the track, causing another delay, of three hours.[19] The Southern Pacific Railroad left him otherwise put out, too. He wrote:

> I was struck by the admirable consistency of the railroad authorities, who, having asked for arms from the government, for the use of their employees, allowed their baggage-man to

[18] Secretary of War, *Report, 1881*, I, 139–43; *Chicago Times*, Sept. 6, 1881; Wellman, *Death on Horseback*, 411–14.
[19] *Chicago Times*, Sept. 19, 1881.

take away such weapons as the passengers had with them. This seems to be an order on nearly all Pacific coast railroads, and appears very absurd on the face of it. The baggage-man charges for carrying the gun in his car, and, as the money goes into his own pocket, no Irish or Russian constable was ever sharper in spying out a firearm. As they are under orders to disarm passengers, nothing is left for the latter but submission. But is not the custom an infringement on the right of American citizens to have and to hold arms? Who gave the railroad people authority to override the constitution? Perhaps the railroad "kings,"—merry monarchs they are—feel themselves mightier than the constitution. If so, let us brag no more about "the best and freest government under the sun."[20]

Tucson only made him the more unhappy—an old Mexican town whose houses were mostly of "repulsive-looking adobe." He also said, "I met some very unpleasant people there. It seemed as if their whole business in life was to tax travelers heavily, and give as little as possible in return. There are many honorable exceptions to this rule, I suppose, but I failed to discover more than three or four during my stay."[21]

Moving eastward to Willcox he "found great difficulty in sending through my dispatches because of the official diarrhea which seemed to have seized upon department headquarters." The superintendent of the military telegraph had instructed operators not to send any newspaper dispatches unless they had been approved by the nearest commanding officer.[22]

That was the one and only instance of censorship during the Western War, and Finerty wrote an outraged story about it. The telegraphic limitation had cut off the right of free criticism by correspondents in the field, he said, adding:

The Times correspondent was never denied the right to criticize any military movements while on the campaigns of Gens. Crook, Miles, and Merritt. He does not know whether Supt. Ward's action has the sanction of Gen. Willcox, commanding

[20] *Ibid.*
[21] *Ibid.*
[22] *Ibid.*

this department. If it has the general will find that he has committed a gross blunder. This government is not Russian, and the submission of press telegrams to the supervision of military commanders who can not help being interested, is an outrage on journalistic freedom, against which *The Times* correspondent desires to enter protest. He does not desire to be acrimonious, but it is well that the country should learn that some military people at least are afraid of being criticized, and will permit nothing to go over the military wires that is unfavorable to the character of their operations, or that even presumes to question the wisdom of some particular commander. It is well that the people are not dependent on government telegraph offices for news. The attention of the people highest in power at Washington should be called to the insolent order referred to in this dispatch.[23]

It was a senseless restriction, as newspapermen have found many military press restrictions to be; for Finerty—who wrote that dispatch from Camp Thomas, which had a military telegraph line—easily evaded it by sending his story to Willcox, where Western Union had an office. Thus the order had the effect of delaying newspaper publication only one day.

On September 12, Finerty was at Camp Thomas en route to Fort Apache, ninety miles away by Indian trail, where he expected to join Carr's command in chasing Apaches. "It is singular, looking at the campaign from a business standpoint," he wrote, "that Carr was not heavily reinforced to start with, and a vigorous scout made after the revolted Apaches. But, then, there are things in the philosophy of military genius that civilians can not possibly undertake to understand."[24]

Finerty's outbursts were indicative of something more than the personal reaction of one reporter. The departmental commander, Brevet Major General O. B. Willcox, who commanded his troops from a telegraph office, upset his superiors as well as Finerty. The result was that Willcox was left in command of the department, but the field command of troops devolved upon Mackenzie.[25]

[23] *Ibid.*, Sept. 15, 1881.   [24] *Ibid.*, Sept. 19, 1881.

Finerty arrived in Fort Apache on September 17 and went into the field the next day with Carr, whom he had not seen since the Black Hills, at the head of a command consisting of 266 officers, soldiers, scouts, and packers. Two days later they reached the scene of the Cibicu Creek fight where they found, to their horror, that the Apaches had dug up and mutilated the remains of an officer and four soldiers killed there. The sight and stench caused some of the recruits to vomit, and Finerty, who said he thought he had become case-hardened to "many awful sights," found that that scene "capped the climax of my horrific experiences." Two days more and Carr learned he had only the mutinous scouts to hunt down, others having surrendered. He divided his command, and Finerty went with two companies of the Sixth Cavalry under Major T. C. Tupper and the scouts of Lieutenant Charles Gatewood to search the rough country between Cibicu and Carrizo creeks.[26]

The fruitless hunt that Finerty went on was typical of the uncounted, toilsome marches the army made in fighting the Apaches in a warfare as different unto itself as Plains warfare. Never had Apache warfare involved mass collisions such as those of the Plains. Rather, the Apaches attacked with precision in small war parties which laid waste everything in their paths. With imaginative cruelty they tortured captives. As much the master of their terrain as the Comanche of theirs, the Apaches moved swiftly, struck suddenly, and vanished. All the army could do was to hunt down the small bands patiently and inexorably. But it took hundreds of men divided into small parties, with Apache scouts as their eyes, ears, and scent. At one time in the summer of 1881 as many as one thousand United States troops, plus Texas Rangers, large groups of civilians, and Mexican forces kept on the jump in trying to intercept and defeat a band of not more than thirty to forty warriors led by a rheumatic, superannuated chief—Nana, who at the time was seventy or eighty years old.

[25] Secretary of War, *Report, 1881,* I, 139–142.
[26] *Chicago Times,* Oct. 4, 1881.

Probably it was because of the scattered nature of Apache warfare and the fact that the country was not in great demand that the newspapers did not direct their attention to it through staff coverage.

Finerty remained in the field until October 12, and then gave up, firing as his parting shot a story which said:

> The Apache war has, to all appearances, fizzled out rather ignominiously. . . .
>
> As a result of this outbreak the army is terribly out of humor, and no wonder. Gen. Willcox is mad over it. Gen. Carr is displeased with it. Col. [Reuben F.] Bernard swears over it. The staff quarrel about it. The line officers curse their luck, and the soldiers sulk, feeling more or less humiliated. . . .
>
> I desire to say a word about the regular army of the United States. I have a right to, as I have been out with it on several campaigns. . . . We want young, fresh blood in this army, more than dignity allied to servility, and we want to spare that young blood a sentiment of martial glory by abolishing, in service regiments—by which I mean all the cavalry and most of the infantry,—the moth-eaten, musty, demoralizing system of promotion by seniority. . . . If Congress will recognize Indian campaigning as legitimate warfare,—it is infinitely more dangerous than civilized warfare,—and promote an efficient young lieutenant who accomplishes a brilliant exploit over the head of some slow old captain, major or colonel who fails to accomplish anything, they will put into our army an esprit such as that which led the ragged Frenchmen, under republican generals, to drive the Austrian sharpshooters from the Alpine passes and achieve the conquest of Italy. . . . Under the slow-coach system our best Indian fighters remain lieutenants or captains. . . .
>
> . . . I don't believe a brevet gained in the civil war should entitle an officer who has no knowledge of Indian affairs, and who has never distinguished himself as an Indian campaigner, to override, or command, in the field an officer who knows Indian habits and who has proved his ability to deal with the savages in their peculiar mode of warfare.[27]

27 *Ibid.*, Oct. 21, 1881.

The Western War ended with the Wounded Knee affair in South Dakota in the winter of 1890–91, a tragic failure in Indian management, the newspaper coverage of which marks a sharp break in the handling of Indian war news. Finerty's Apache campaign assignment of 1881 ended a period of basically honest reporting of army campaigns against hostile Indians. During the succeeding decade, the so-called New Journalism developed. Spawned in the Middle West but more often symbolized by Joseph Pulitzer's *New York World,* the New Journalism rested upon a much stronger competition for circulation than had existed before, a much more energetic quest for news, an enlargement of the editorial staff and its news-gathering function, and a more deliberate and imitative use of reader-attracting devices in so-called human-interest writing, in which accuracy in principle was demanded, but in which accuracy in practice often gave way to distortion for effect. And it was under the spell of the New Journalism that correspondents gathered at Pine Ridge Agency to report a feared outbreak of the Sioux. Twenty-one correspondents were there—more than had covered all the preceding, and important, campaigns combined. The result of some of their work has been described as exaggerated, distorted, rumor-based, and even faked.

A mishandling of Indian administration had reduced the Sioux to starvation.[28] To them in their extremity came promise of a Messiah. There then developed among them the Ghost Dance religion, based upon a belief that the Indians would be restored to their inheritance and their long-dead brothers would come back to life and the white man would be driven from the land. To bring the Messiah, they must perform long hours of the Ghost Dance, a rite in a religion that was part-Christian, part-savage.

Because of their dancing and faith in their delivery, a jit-

[28] This account of Wounded Knee is based upon James Mooney, *The Ghost-Dance Religion and the Sioux Outbreak of 1890;* Downey, *Indian-Fighting Army,* 292–306; Wellman, *Death on Horseback,* 227–40; Muriel H. Wright, *A Guide to the Indian Tribes of Oklahoma,* 45, 174.

tery agent at the Pine Ridge Sioux Agency called for troops in November, 1890. The troops came, and large bands of Indians fled to the badlands. The growing ominousness caused the government to order the arrest of Sitting Bull, who had snapped his peace pipe at the Standing Rock Agency. But as Indian police took him from his cabin, he called for succor. His braves responded, cutting down the leader of the Indian police, who, dying, fired one of the shots that killed Sitting Bull on December 15.

On December 28 a force of the Seventh Cavalry intercepted a band of Sioux headed for the badlands and forced their surrender, placing them in camp on Wounded Knee Creek. Next morning, as the troops called for surrender of arms, a medicine man incited the warriors to their last desperate war whoop, telling them their bullets would find white targets but their ghost shirts would turn aside the soldiers' bullets. From under a blanket a warrior pulled a rifle, held it high in consecration, shouldered it, and pressed the trigger. The rest was slaughter. The Seventh Cavalry poured a deadly fire into the village. In the fight which lasted from mid-morning to mid-afternoon, counting the pursuit in which women and children were run down, the army lost 30 killed, 34 wounded; the Indians, 145 men, women, and children killed, 33 wounded.

Sounds of the firing carried to Pine Ridge Agency, which soon was invested by other Sioux, who were beaten off by Indian police. On the next day, December 30, the Seventh fought a battle at White Clay Creek from which it was extricated by the "buffalo soldiers" of the Ninth Cavalry, the Negro troopers who had a habit of arriving in the nick of time. A few more skirmishes occurred before all the Sioux were again rounded up and returned to the reservations that winter.

But to all intents and purposes the Western War ended at Wounded Knee, although a detachment of the Third Infantry had yet to quell a flare-up of the Chippewas in Minnesota in 1898, a show of force had yet to convince the Utes in 1906 and 1907, and quick action had yet to head off revolts by the Navajos in 1913 and the Paiutes in 1915.

312

Newspaper coverage of the Wounded Knee affair began with a repetition of the fraudulence of 1866 reporting.[29] At first, space-writers wrote reports foreshadowing the garish period to begin a few years later, to which the collision of Hearst and Pulitzer would give the name "yellow journalism." Unverified rumors became reports from reliable sources, idle gossip was reported as fact. As the distortion of an imminent Indian outbreak spread across the newspapers, terror in turn swept across Nebraska, the Dakotas, and even as far east as Iowa. Mass hysteria sent settlers flocking into the nearest railroad towns, telling stories—made of whole cloth—about murder, scalping, and desolation. The same sort of frontier terror, an example of mass psychology, had been observed at Yreka during the early part of the Modoc War and at Rawlins during the Ute outbreak of 1879. A South Dakota senator blamed it all on space-writers rather than accredited correspondents, saying they would send through three columns today and contradict themselves with three more the next day, their sole interest being money.

When the Indians fled to the badlands after the appearance of troops in November, newspapers started sending in "specials." The large press corps at Wounded Knee included Alfred H. Burkholder, Charles W. Allen, and Edgar F. Medary, all Nebraska and South Dakota newsmen representing the *New York Herald;* William F. Kelley, a business office employee with no previous reporting experience, for the Lincoln *State Journal;* Carl Smith and Thomas H. Tibbles, *Omaha World-Herald;* Will Cressey and Charles H. Coppenharve, *Omaha Bee;* Edward B. Clark and Irving Hawkins, *Chicago Tribune;* Charles G. Seymour, *Chicago Herald;* Edward A. O'Brien, Associated Press; John A. McDonough, *New York World;* Dent H. Robert, *St. Louis Post-Dispatch;* Guy Butler, *Duluth Tribune;* a man named Boylan for the *St. Paul Pioneer-Press;* Frederick Remington, *Harper's Weekly;* Warren K.

[29] This account of the newspaper coverage is based upon Elmo Scott Watson, "The Last Indian War, 1890–92—A Study of Newspaper Jingoism," *Journalism Quarterly,* Vol. XX (September, 1943), 205–19.

Moorehead, *Illustrated American* of New York; Gilbert F. Bailey, a civil engineer free-lancing for the *Chicago Inter-Ocean* and *Rocky Mountain News;* "Judge" Burns of Deadwood, free-lancing for the *Chicago Times;* and Mrs. Teresa Howard Dean of the *Chicago Herald,* who thereby laid claim to being the first woman war correspondent.

The composition of that press corps illustrates the growth of Middle Western journalism through the identity of the newspapers that had become strong enough to send staff men on a protracted assignment.

On the basis of information picked up from scouts, half-bloods and hangers-on, they filled their stories with rumors, half-truths, and lies. The inexperienced Kelley sent back stories that made a major war seem about to happen tomorrow. The *Omaha World-Herald* men were said by contemporaries to be particularly "reckless with the truth." In fact, the *World-Herald* had to recall Smith, who meddled in agency affairs and felt qualified as a military expert to tell the people how the army should handle that explosive situation.

The reporters converted the agency trading post into a press room at night where they swapped gossip, tried to sift fact from rumor, and wrote their stories, which were taken by courier to the Rushville, Nebraska, telegraph office thirty miles away. Whiling away the boredom of a waiting story, they created their own newspaper, the *Badlands Budget,* "a legendary publication dedicated to Rumor," and wrote a composite novelette entitled *Short Bull, the Brigand of the Bad Lands,* to which each reporter contributed a chapter burlesquing sentimental fiction and the dime-novel hair-raisers.

Only three correspondents—Kelley, Allen, and Cressey—were present at the Battle of Wounded Knee. All three were in the village when the firing started, Allen fleeing with Little Bat Garnier and getting caught in a cross-fire between troops and Indians before he could regain a position held by Cheyenne scouts. Kelley emptied his revolver at a brave who charged him, then picked up a rifle and continued firing, being credited by soldiers with killing at least three Indians. Cressey got away somehow.

Kelley, the business-office man without a shred of reporting experience, scored the only beat of the whole affair with his story of the battle. Because there was only one operator at Rushville, the correspondents had long since devised a rotation system for the sending of dispatches. On the day of the battle it was Kelley's turn to have his story go first. His story chattered into the *State Journal* office, where a bulletin was placed on the United Press wire. Later, Chicago called for a detailed story, whereupon Kelley's account was given general distribution. It was an earlier United Press, unrelated to the modern UPI.

After the solid budget of battle reporting, the reporters again fell back on rumor and think-pieces until Miles paraded his whole force in January to impress several thousand Indians who had moved in near the agency. Their reports of the surrender and the review were said to be both colorful and accurate.

A late arrival among the correspondents was George Harries of the *Washington Star,* a man who had spent several years on the frontier as soldier, scout, and newspaperman. He ridiculed the get-up of his colleagues, saying there were only two among them "who are not round-shouldered because of the weapons and missiles they have had to carry around."

With rumor, exaggeration, distortion, and falsifying, despite some accurate reporting, the reporters at Pine Ridge signed an unfitting "30" to newspaper coverage of the Western War.

Goodnight

11. CLOSING THE WIRE

[The newspaperman] works in the obscurity of his chambers, for the most part anonymously, and with the invisible forces latent in words. The effects he produces are like the insensible droppings of water upon granite, slow, minute and imperceptible—imperceptible in the details of the process, and known merely, if known at all, by the larger general results. They do not strike the multitude by their momentum, their volume, their mass or their brilliancy; they rather percolate society than fall upon it; and it is not strange that society should be insensible to the agents by whom these effects are wrought.

NEW YORK EVENING POST[1]

THE TWENTY IDENTIFIABLE accredited correspondents who reported the Western War during its important campaigns, from 1867 through 1881, stand apart from the mainstream of war correspondence development as distinctly as Indian fighting itself from other forms of war, as it was episodic rather than integral in American military history. Because of the nature of Indian warfare—a war that was not a war, a war that had no rear echelon—the correspondent traveled with the troops, lived with the troops, ate with the troops, fought with the troops, and shared the dangers of the troops. Since there was no need for military secrecy as there was in "civilized" warfare, but since there was a need to awaken awareness of what the army was doing, the correspondent was allowed to attach himself to Indian campaign expeditions without difficulty. Taking his place with the troops and sharing the tent

[1] Quoted in *San Francisco Evening Bulletin*, Dec. 13, 1872.

316

and mess of an officer, he at once acquired a status unknown to earlier correspondents as a group, a privileged status which has not since been granted routinely to all. His right to free criticism seems to have been respected by the soldiers with whom he served. Certainly it never brought punishment; the sight of Crook leaving the Black Hills with Davenport in his small company is evidence enough of that. Whether the forbearance of Crook and other commanders would have continued had they faced an indefinite campaign, as did Civil War commanders who expelled correspondents, is a matter of conjecture.

The role, status, and service of the Western War correspondents seem to have had no bearing upon subsequent press regulations of the army. After all, the United States Army in the twentieth century geared itself to the conditions of international war rather than the informal but disciplined camaraderie of the Indian fighters.

In serving on the front line in a workaday capacity, the Western War correspondents seem to have had greater kinship with the workaday men who covered World War II than with any other correspondents. They were equally distinct from the "romantic crisis-chasers"[2] like Richard Harding Davis and others who fragmentized war coverage into personal exploits and human interest stories. Western War correspondents reported the whole story.

They differed markedly from their nearest kin in time— the other war correspondents of the late nineteenth century, the men who covered the wars of Europe and the wars of Empire. Overseas, the war correspondent tended to be something of a professional, either a military man turned journalist (rare) or a journalist specializing as a military correspondent (more common).[3]

There was no professionalism among the men who re-

[2] Ralph O. Nafziger, "World War Correspondents and Censorship of the Belligerents," *Journalism Quarterly* Vol. XIV (September, 1937), 226.

[3] Joseph J. Mathews, "The Profession of War Correspondence," *Journalism Quarterly,* Vol. XXXIII (Winter, 1956), 23–34.

ported the Western War. Only one—Finerty—approached that status; although he identified himself as "war correspondent" on the title page of *War-Path and Bivouac,* he can be regarded more properly as a specialist in Indian campaign coverage rather than as a professional. None of these western reporters appear to have affected the garb and mannerism by which European professionals called attention to themselves; for example, the Englishman who fired blank cartridges and an air rifle from his window. Because of their status with the troops, they did not have to write extensively about their personal preparations for the field or use servants as literary foils, as did the men overseas.[4]

The subsequent careers of the newspapermen who covered the important campaigns—Wounded Knee can be regarded as the death quiver—show them to have been, on the whole, a substantial group. Most of them had many years in which to develop their careers, for they were young men—the majority in their late twenties—when they rode with the Old Army. Seven, or better than one-third, were college trained, although only three were college graduates.

In their later careers, one served in Congress, two in Parliament, and two in state legislatures; one helped open Africa, another helped open the West, another was interested in Australian development; two represented the United States abroad; two became newspaper publishers; one wrote the legislation creating the California Mining and Mineral Bureau; one became a lay leader in his church; and one became a philanthropist who brought to America many valuable foreign plants. Some duplications appear in such a synopsis, because some of the men recorded achievements in more than one area, as can be seen in the following listing:

H. Wallace Atwell, who covered the Modoc War, continued in California journalism until his death in 1888. He edited the *Visalia Delta* and the *Sunset Route,* the latter describing the towns and country along the Southern Pacific Railroad from New Orleans to California.[5]

[4] *Ibid.,* 30.

318

Robert D. Bogart, who also covered the Modoc War and then escaped from a navy brig, left little trace behind him, but he at least remained in San Francisco and under his own name, for in 1878 he wrote for the *San Francisco Daily Stock Report* and was correspondent for the *Boston Commercial Bulletin.*[6]

William Mitchell Bunker, also of the Modoc War, likewise remained in San Francisco journalism. Two years after the Modoc War, having risen to city editor and news editor of the *Bulletin,* Bunker acquired his own newspaper, the *Daily Evening Report,* which he built into a lucrative property.[7]

Reuben Briggs Davenport, the goshawk about Crook's head, was with the *Herald* until 1882, when he established the *Morning News* in New Haven. Two years later he became associate editor of the *Morning News* in Paris. In 1886 he edited the *Star and Herald* in Panama City while en route to San Francisco, where he wrote editorials for the *Chronicle,* from which he returned east as managing editor of the *New Haven Morning News* in 1890. In 1895 he became literary editor of the *New York Commercial Advertiser,* leaving that paper to become an Associated Press correspondent during the Spanish-American War in Haiti, Jamaica, and Cuba. Early in the twentieth century he served as foreign correspondent for the *New York Times* and *Philadelphia Public Ledger,* ultimately becoming chief editorial writer of the *New York Herald's* Paris edition in 1920, a position he retained until his death in 1932.[8]

Charles Sanford Diehl remained with the *Chicago Times* for several years and later became general manager of the Associated Press. While heading the AP, which has had its effect upon news-gathering methods and philosophy in this

[5] *Visalia Weekly Delta,* Jan. 5, Feb. 23, 1888, photostatic copy from California State Library.

[6] *Pacific Coast Annual Mining Review,* 1878, p. 65, photostatic copy from California State Library.

[7] *The Californian Illustrated Magazine* (May, 1892), 536, photostatic copy from California State Library.

[8] Eric Hawkins, managing editor of European Edition, *New York Herald-Tribune,* to author, Dec. 22, 1958; Davenport Folder, Watson Papers.

country, he drew upon the lessons learned from Stillson and others while covering Indian negotiations and Indian fighting on the plains. Later he bought the *San Antonio Light,* remaining in charge of it until his death.[9]

John F. Finerty remained at the head of the column. From 1879 to 1881 he was Washington correspondent of the *Chicago Times.* From 1883 to 1885 he represented a Chicago district in Congress. Throughout, he remained a radical advocate of Irish independence, elected seven times president of the United Irish Societies of Chicago and in 1905 president of the United Irish League of America. An accomplished orator, he was invited to Montana as principal speaker at the dedication in 1905 of a statue to General Thomas F. Meagher, who had organized the New York Irish Brigade in the Civil War and who had later served as acting governor of Montana Territory. When Finerty died in Chicago in 1908, the G.A.R. took charge of the funeral, several hundred veterans accompanying the body from the Finerty home to Holy Angels Church in a mile-long procession headed by a platoon of police. Trailing the G.A.R. came members of the United Irish Society, the Irish Fellowship Club, and other organizations. His honorary pallbearers included the Mayor of Chicago and six judges.[10]

Edward Fox, of the Modoc War, continued on the *New York Herald* for some years, went into business in Wall Street unsuccessfully, and returned to England. During his time with the *Herald,* he helped expose corruption in Indian management with stories from Red Cloud Agency in 1874, and he testified before a Congressional investigating commission in New York in 1875. After returning to England, he became involved in two duels—first as a second in a proposed duel, and then, after a dispute with his principal, they slipped into Belgium and fought a duel, in which Fox was slightly wounded. In England he became interested in Australian de-

9 Diehl, *Staff Correspondent,* 118–21, 293–95.
10 Quaife, "Historical Introduction to Lakeside Classics edition of Finerty's *War-Path and Bivouac* (see n. 21, chap. 5 above), *xl, xliii–xlv.*

velopment and was credited with being instrumental in establishment of an Anglo-Colonial newspaper, *The British Australian*. In 1894 he went to West Australia as a broker and mining agent, associated with the West Australian Exploring and Finance Corp. He lost his life in a yachting accident on March 4, 1895, near Perth.[11]

James William (Phocion) Howard continued in Illinois journalism, editing the *Tuscola Review* for a short time, but specializing in political writing. He made his home in Danville, dying in 1893.

DeBenneville Randolph Keim, who reported the Washita campaign of 1868, might have been the man to find Livingstone had not a letter from Bennett to him in Ceylon miscarried, so that the publisher picked Stanley for the assignment. After his Western War assignment, Keim was a Washington correspondent of the *New York Herald* and other papers, his position there solidified by a confidential relationship which he had established with Grant in the West during the Civil War. He was said to have been the only reporter who had access to the White House during the Grant administration, interviewing the President on Sundays. In 1870, Grant sent him to examine United States consulates and make a personal report on certain diplomatic missions. He also carried out foreign assignments for the *Herald*.[12]

Barbour Lathrop, who covered part of the 1876 Sioux campaign, inherited a fortune and became a world traveler. As a philanthropist he was the prime mover of an extensive, practical plant importation program in the United States. It was he who turned David Fairchild from entomology to a career which made Fairchild foremost among American plant explorers. He took Fairchild on a trip around the world once, and then—after Fairchild had set up the Section of Seed and Plant Introduction in the Department of Agriculture—Lath-

---

[11] *The Western Mail* of Perth, West Australia, March 9, 1895; *New York Herald*, July 23, 1875, March 19, 1895; *New York Tribune*, March 20, 1895.
[12] Andrews, *The North Reports the Civil War*, 62, 67, 67 n.; *American Biographical Directories, District of Columbia* (Washington, 1908), excerpt supplied by Washington, D. C., Public Library.

rop financed his travels to other countries. As a result of the trips, the United States obtained a seedless raisin grape from Italy, a Chilean avocado, Japanese bamboos, a Japanese lawn grass which became popular in Florida, the nectarine, a Nile onion which came to be grown extensively in Texas, berseem clover for desert areas, the hairy Peruvian alfalfa which came to be the most productive variety for irrigated lands of the Southwest, and an Austrian horseradish which took root in New Jersey, as well as varieties of okra, red pepper, vegetable marrow, pumpkin, cucumber, and peanuts.[13]

T. C. MacMillan, who covered the Crook 1876 campaign at the Battle of the Rosebud, remained in Chicago, working for the *Inter-Ocean* until 1895, and then served a long term as clerk of the federal district court. He was a member of the Illinois House of Representatives from 1885 to 1889 and of the state Senate for the next two years. He was a member of the Cook County Board of Education, a director of the Chicago Public Library, a member of the commission which drafted the Chicago Sanitary District Act and chairman of the Senate Committee on Waterways which secured its passage; chairman of the Senate Committee on the World's Fair; author of the first woman's school suffrage act in Illinois; member of the Board of Managers of the Illinois State Reformatory in Pontiac; president of the LaGrange, Ill., school board; a trustee of Illinois College in Jacksonville; president of the Illinois Congregational Home Missionaries Society for ten years; president of the Chicago Congregational Club; first president of the American Congregational Deaconess Association; first vice-president of the Third International Congregational Council in Edinburgh, 1908; and moderator of the National Council of Congregational Churches, 1907–10.[14]

James J. O'Kelly, who reported the Terry campaign after the Custer defeat, returned to Ireland and spent the rest of his life, except for one short interlude, in Irish politics. Taking

[13] David Fairchild, *The World Was My Garden*, 84 ff.; Klose, *America's Crop Heritage*, 113–14.
[14] MacMillan Folder, Watson Papers.

his place beside Parnell as an Irish nationalist, he was elected to Parliament in 1880, where he was more noted for his impetuous outbursts than for debate. In fact, one outburst led to his challenging another Irish member to a duel, which did not come off, but at the time of his death in 1916 it had been the last challenge offered in Parliament. In 1885 he went to the Sudan for the *London Daily News*, becoming lost for some months in the desert and being given up for dead, but at length turned up on the Nile, not far from Khartoum. In 1881 he had shared prison with Parnell, and was described as the one Nationalist member with whom Parnell had a close personal relationship. O'Kelly remained steadfast to Parnell even when the latter's political influence suffered sharply as the result of scandal. He lost his seat in 1892 but regained it in 1895, continuing in Commons, but passively, for the remainder of his life.[15]

Henry Morton Stanley, who began his professional newspaper career with the Hancock expedition of 1867, is best remembered in his connection with Africa. His catch-phrase, "Dr. Livingstone, I presume?" dogged him to his death, because many people did not believe he had really said any such thing. Finally, the sensitive Stanley was cornered and asked why he used those words. He replied that he could think of nothing else to say at the moment. When he knelt to receive an honorary degree from Oxford, some prankish student called out, "Dr. Stanley, I presume?" He made other trips to Africa, helping to unlock its secrets for white eyes, and credited his success in dealing with African primitives to the lessons he learned observing Sherman, Harney, Hancock, and others deal with Indian primitives in the West. He, too, was elected to Parliament.[16]

Robert E. Strahorn, who was with Crook in 1876 and 1877, became a new type of explorer in the American West, a type whose contributions in frontier history have not yet been

[15] *The Times*, London, Dec. 23, 1916; Thomas Power O'Connor and Robert McWade, *Gladstone-Parnell and the Great Irish Struggle*, 410–16.

[16] Stanley, *Autobiography*, 225–28; Anstruther, *I Presume*, vii, 190–91; A. J. A. Symons, *H. M. Stanley*, 120.

assessed. Immediately after leaving the Indian campaign of 1877, he wrote a guidebook to Wyoming, which has been termed excellent. The book caught the fancy of Jay Gould, directing genius of the Union Pacific, who engaged Strahorn to organize and conduct the railroad's publicity bureau. He was not, however, the ordinary "press release" type of publicity man. Rather, his job was to penetrate into the farthest reaches of the West and write newspaper articles and books about the western states and territories which could be expected to encourage more western migration, hence, more passenger revenue. He also gathered economic intelligence for railroad executives—possibilities for railroad extensions, tonnage that might develop, tillable acres, scenic attractions, and all the inducements that could be offered homeseekers.

For six years, beginning in 1877 when he took his bride into the West, Strahorn toured the West. In their life together during those first years, she recalled, they went the length of almost every stage road across the frontier, reaching into remote districts, mountain areas, and secluded valleys, visiting hundreds of mines, computing millions of feet of timber, estimating the number of cattle and sheep, studying prairie and hillside in assessing their adaptability to cereal and fruit production, examining streams and drainage—all the many facts a prospective homeseeker would want to know.

Later, Strahorn engaged in irrigation, power, and townsite enterprises in Idaho, Oregon, and Washington. He also built and was president of the North Coast Railroad and of the Portland, Eugene and Eastern Railway. Making his home in Spokane, he also was at the head of other railroads and utilities in the Pacific Northwest.[17] He outlived all the other Western War correspondents, dying in 1944.

Thomas A. Sutherland, who covered the Nez Percé war, was a Portland newspaperman for the rest of his life, except for the years 1879–81 when he was clerk of the House Committee on Manufactures in Washington, D. C. Returning to

[17] Who's Who (1916–17); C. A. Strahorn, *Fifteen Thousand Miles by Stage*, v–vii, 91; Struthers Burt, *Powder River*, 11.

Portland, he acquired control of *The Sunday Welcome,* which he published until his death in 1891.

Joe Wasson, who was with Crook in both Oregon and the Sioux country, finally struck it rich—according to one account —in the California mines, after making several trips to Europe as a newspaperman. Settling down in California, he was elected to represent Mono County in the state legislature, where he introduced and guided to passage the legislation creating the California Mining and Mineral Bureau. In failing health, he went to San Blas, Mexico, as United States consul in 1883, dying there about two months later.[18]

The later careers of Alex McKay, who covered the Modoc War, and Jerry Roche, who reported the Dull Knife fight, are not known. Jerome Stillson died the year after the Ute uprising. Kellogg was the twentieth reporter.

By comparison with the approximately three hundred reporters in the Civil War and five hundred in the Spanish-American War, the number of Western War correspondents shrinks to insignificance. Their number shows that only a few of the more energetic newspapers turned their resources to first-hand coverage of Indian fighting in the West. Of these, only the *Chicago Times* and *New York Herald* consistently reported from the western army, and only the *Herald* reported every major campaign from 1868 through 1881. Both the *Herald* and the *Times* profited from experience gained during the Civil War, building postwar reputations upon the latest telegraphic advices. Only once did other newspapers emulate them in enterprise, as it was proudly called—the *Bulletin* and *Chronicle* of San Francisco, in reporting the Modoc War. Others had staff men on rare occasions, others used free-lance correspondents like Wasson, and others received reports from army officers in the field, such reporting providing an important source of income to officers serving a government which failed to pay their salaries in 1877, the year after the

[18] C. A. Strahorn, *Fifteen Thousand Miles by Stage,* 411; Rockwell D. Hunt (ed.), *California and Californians,* V, 225, and other photostatic material supplied from files of California State Library.

Custer disaster. All of which means, in turn, that the Western War was reported largely by Middle Western and Far Western papers, except for the *New York Herald*, with other New York papers paying attention to it only occasionally.

No attempt has been made to assess over-all press performance in chronicling the frontier war, but the conclusion is at once obvious: The United States press generally, in reporting Indian warfare, had to rely upon second-hand sources if it used anything at all—clippings from the newspapers having staff correspondents or receiving letters from officers and soldiers, Associated Press and general press dispatches based upon those same dispatches and placed on the wire, and official announcements from Washington and divisional and departmental headquarters in various cities. Telegraphic and local stories found in the newspapers which staffed the Indian campaigns show that army headquarters regularly made public the full text of reports, letters, and telegrams from commanders in the field. The fact that certain newspapers did not send out staff men is no indication of relative attention to the Western War, because the availability of these army dispatches made possible the reporting of important events by any newspaper interested in doing so.

Only on two occasions during the entire twenty-five-year period did press relations with the military reflect anything other than co-operation and a cordial reception of the press. One instance occurred during the Modoc War, the only time the army encountered a problem in keeping military information from the enemy. At that time, the tone of the dispatches showed the reporters co-operative and understanding. The other instance was the ill-considered attempt at press censorship through military telegraph control.

Reporting of the Western War came during what is known as the period of the independent press in United States journalism history. It encompassed the years intervening between the personal journalism characteristic of the antebellum and Civil War periods at one end and the strident New Journalism at the other.

Although the period gained its name from the political stand of the newspapers, the term "independent" certainly is applicable to the reporting done by the men in the field. On the whole, their reporting was both responsible and accurate —as accurate, that is, as it is possible for one human being to be in reporting the activities and behavior of other human beings. The initial approach to the problem of accuracy in this account was based upon the premise that the best that could be hoped for would be a determination of the degree of variance, if any, between the newspaper report and the official report, since neither could be assumed to be completely accurate. The agreement of the two on essential points, in most instances, leads to the conclusion that most of the reporting was reliable.

The Western War correspondent reported the story in detail, but did not have and could not have had the Indian side of the story. Often, however, the reporter did reveal the Indian side when he sought to explain the cause of a conflict, not in terms of Indian interpretation, but in terms of criminal mismanagement of Indian affairs by civilians. In that connection, the reporter generally reflected the feelings, attitudes, and thoughts of the military, as demonstrated in annual reports, periodical articles, and books in later years. Many of the contemporary accounts of Indian warfare have been modified by the later accounts of Indians, which provide, however, a body of literature that is as treacherous as it is valuable to the historian who seeks a balanced view. These modifications have not been fully utilized in this volume because they more properly belong in a history of the Western War in perspective—which still needs to be written—than to an examination of newspaper coverage in which the most important element is the reporter's knowledge of events within his perception.

The fidelity of Western War reporting is shown in another way. All first-hand accounts of Indian campaigning in the West reveal one characteristic distinctly—Indian warfare meant long and weary hours, days, weeks, and even months searching for the enemy, and the resulting fight when they were found was quickly over. The periodic reports sent in by correspondents in the field give, when taken as a whole, a faithful picture of that aspect of an Indian campaign. Most of the accounts are valuable, too, in presenting the thoughts and feelings of the soldier, along with his day-by-day living and marching conditions. That picture was not drawn in terms of individual personal experience, but in general experience from which the individual can be deduced.

In contrast to their Civil War colleagues, the Western War correspondents often had the advantage of being eyewitnesses of the scenes and events which they recorded. This, undoubtedly, is the key factor that distinguishes the accuracy and general reliability of the campaign reporting from that of 1866 and that of Wounded Knee, where the correspondents did not have the advantage of personal observation. Rather than trust wholly to second-hand reports, the Modoc War correspondents devised a pooling system, in which one man reported for all papers from a given point.

Usually, the Western War report took the form of a straightforward account without adornment, except in such instances as the indignation of Howard and Davenport, which, one suspects, might have been more rebellion at the indignity of personal discomfort than considered criticism, and the playfulness of Wasson during inactivity in 1867. Nevertheless, the reporters of 1867–81 wrote about what they witnessed, calling the shots as they saw them, describing them with aptness and detail.

In that respect, the reporting of the latter nineteenth century can be considered superior to most modern news writing. The correspondent reported the facts as he saw them and then placed them in context with the interpretation and opinion which his own intelligence allowed him to exercise. But that was before the great god of mass technique castrated American reporting by clamping the spurious doctrine of objectivity upon American newspapers and forcing the news story into a formula pattern.

The stories were straightforward in the sense that they reported what the reporter saw happen or what he thought he saw happen. Further, the Western War reporter was a nineteenth-century man, and he wrote with the characteristic prolixity of his century. Differing from modern news writing which presents the most recent event first, the Western War correspondent's story was most often written chronologically. Even when a batch of stories arrived together, his paper usually printed them in the order in which they were written, instead of placing the most recent one first.

The correspondent also often wrote two stories about the same event—sending the first story by wire, and then elaborating in a later "letter," which, of course, was just that. An interesting element of these letters, as they were called, is the point of view which repeatedly illustrates that the reporter wrote as though to his editor and not to a general public through the paper.

The stories also included, invariably, the personal experiences of the reporters, usually of their hardships or presumed hardships. Sometimes these appear to be in the sentimental vein of self-sacrifice; at other times, self-pity, braggadocio, and occasionally plain shock.

Throughout the correspondence appears one consistent element: geographical description. That it should appear, in considerable detail, is not surprising. Even though the general outlines of the continental nation were known, there still existed much ignorance regarding locality. The reports of the war correspondents helped to dissipate some of that ignorance—that is, for those who read—not in precise geographical terms but in general descriptive terms: good grazing land, land fit for nothing, well-watered, and so forth. How much the reporters knew what they were talking about is another matter.

There was no fine writing in the Western War dispatches, no brilliantly lathed phrases. The stories were clear, they were understandable, they were often exciting. They were not, however, sensationalized, except perhaps in the case of some

329

of Bogart's reporting in the Modoc War. On occasion the correspondent included some gruesome detail with the names of the victims, such as Keim's reporting the condition in which the body of Major Elliott and his men were found, which would be too repulsive for today's sensibilities, but those details without exception appeared in the stories in perspective. What Keim reported, for example, was exactly what the surgeon reported. In short, the Western War correspondents were simply reporters doing a job.

They did it well.

BIBLIOGRAPHY

MANUSCRIPTS

National Archives, Civil War Branch, Adjutant General's Office, Letters Received.
Strahorn, Robert E. Ninety Years of Boyhood. Unpublished autobiography in typescript, Strahorn Memorial Library, The College of Idaho, Caldwell.
Elmo Scott Watson Papers, Newberry Library, Chicago.

DOCUMENTS

Chronological List of Actions, &c., with Indians, from January 1, 1866, to January, 1881. Office Memoranda, Adjutant General's Office, n. p., n. d.
Compilation of General Orders, Circulars, and Bulletins of the War Department, Issued between February 15, 1881, and December 31, 1915. Washington, Government Printing Office, 1916.
43 Cong., 1 sess., House Executive Document 122. Message from the President of the United States transmitting copies of the correspondence and papers relative to the war with the Modoc Indians in southern Oregon and northern California, during the years 1872 and 1873. Washington, Government Printing Office, 1874.
44 Cong., 1 sess., House Executive Document 184. Papers and correspondence relative to the Sioux War of 1876. Washington, Government Printing Office, 1876.
Mooney, James. The Ghost-Dance Religion and the Sioux Outbreak of 1890. Fourteenth Annual Report of the Bureau of American Ethnology (1892–93), Part 2. Washington, Government Printing Office, 1896.
Secretary of War. Reports. [For each of the years from 1866 through 1886.] Washington, Government Printing Office, 1866–86.

NEWSPAPERS

Bismarck Tribune.
Chicago Inter-Ocean.
Chicago Times.
Chicago Tribune.
Hot Springs (S. D.) *Times Herald.*
New York Herald.
New York Recorder.
New York Tribune.
Owyhee Avalanche, Silver City, Idaho.
Rocky Mountain News, Denver.
San Francisco *Alta California.*
San Francisco Chronicle.
San Francisco Evening Bulletin.
Yreka Journal.
Yreka Union.

BOOKS

Andrews, J. Cutler. *The North Reports the Civil War.* Pittsburgh, University of Pittsburgh Press, 1955.
Anon. *The San Francisco Chronicle and Its History.* San Francisco, 1879.
Anstruther, Ian. *I Presume: Stanley's Triumph and Disaster.* London, Geoffrey Bles, 1956.
Athearn, Robert G. *William Tecumseh Sherman and the Settlement of the West.* Norman, University of Oklahoma Press, 1956.
Bancroft, Hubert Howe, *History of Oregon.* 2 vols. San Francisco, The History Company, 1888.
Bates, Col. Charles Francis. *Custer's Indian Battles.* Bronxville, 1936.
Beers, Henry Putney. *The Western Military Frontier, 1815–1846.* Philadelphia, published by the author, 1935.
Bourke, John G. *On the Border with Crook.* New York, Charles Scribner's Sons, 1891; reprinted by Long's College Book Co., Columbus, Ohio, 1950.
Brady, Cyrus Townsend. *Northwestern Fights and Fighters.* New York, 1909.
Brill, Charles J. *Conquest of the Southern Plains: Uncensored Narrative of the Battle of the Washita and Custer's Southern Cam-*

paign. Oklahoma City, Golden Saga Publishers, 1938. Leaning toward the Indians both in sources and in treatment, this volume —which is highly critical of Custer—is a good counterweight to official and army views.

Brininstool, E. A. *Troopers with Custer*. Harrisburg, Stackpole Co., 1952.

Bruce, Robert. *The Fighting Norths and Pawnee Scouts*. Lincoln, Nebraska State Historical Society, 1932.

Burdick, Usher L. *The Last Battle of the Sioux Nation*. Stevens Point, Wis., published for the author, 1929.

Burt Struthers. *Powder River, Let 'er Buck*. New York, Farrar & Rinehart, 1938.

Carrington, Col. Henry B. *Ab-sa-ra-ka, Land of Massacre: Being the Experience of an Officer's Wife on the Plains, with an Outline of Indian Operations and Conferences from 1868 to 1878.* (Fifth Edition of Mrs. [Margaret Irvin] Carrington's Narrative.) Philadelphia, J. B. Lippincott & Co., 1879. To avoid confusion, it should be noted that Mrs. Carrington usually is listed as the author of this book, but her husband appears as the author of this edition because of the appended material.

Carter, Capt. R. G. *On the Border with Mackenzie*. Washington, Eynon Printing Co., 1935.

Cortissoz, Royal. *The Life of Whitelaw Reid*. 2 vols. London, Thornton Butterworth, Ltd., 1921.

Crawford, Lewis F. *Rekindling Camp Fires: The Exploits of Ben Arnold (Connor)*. Bismarck, Capital Book Co., 1926. This account is written mostly in the first person, as though from Arnold.

Crook, Gen. George. *General George Crook: His Autobiography*. Ed. by Martin F. Schmitt. Norman, University of Oklahoma Press, 1946.

Custer, Elizabeth B. *"Boots and Saddles"; or Life in Dakota with General Custer*. New York, Harper & Brothers, 1885. The appendix is valuable for several letters written by General Custer to Mrs. Custer while he was on campaign.

Custer, Gen. George Armstrong. *My Life on the Plains*. The Lakeside Classics. Ed. by Milo Milton Quaife. Chicago, The Lakeside Press, R. R. Donnelley & Sons Co., 1952. Capt. Frederick Benteen, Custer's inveterate enemy, called this book "My Lie on the Plains."

DeBarthe, Joe. *Life and Adventures of Frank Grouard*. Ed. by Edgar I. Stewart. Norman, University of Oklahoma Press, 1958.

Diehl, Charles Sanford. *The Staff Correspondent*. San Antonio, Clegg Co., 1931.

Dodge, Col. Richard Irving. *Our Wild Indians: Thirty-Three Years' Personal Experience Among the Red Men of the Great West*. Hartford, A. D. Worthington & Co., 1883.

———. *The Plains of the Great West and Their Inhabitants*. New York, G. P. Putnam's Sons, 1877.

Downey, Fairfax. *Indian-Fighting Army*. New York, Charles Scribner's Sons, 1941.

Fairchild, David. *The World Was My Garden: Travels of a Plant Explorer*. New York, Charles Scribner's Sons, 1939.

Finerty, John F. *War-Path and Bivouac*. Second Edition. Chicago, no publisher, c.1890. [Also published by M. A. Donoghue & Co., Chicago, 1890.]

Fiske, Frank. *The Taming of the Sioux*. Bismarck, Bismarck Tribune, 1917.

Forsyth, George A. *The Story of the Soldier*. The Story of the West Series, ed. by Ripley Hitchcock. New York, D. Appleton & Co., 1900.

———. *Thrilling Days in Army Life*. New York, Harper & Brothers, 1900.

Godfrey, Lt. Edward Settle. *The Field Diary of Lt. Edward Settle Godfrey . . . May 17, 1876 . . . September 24, 1876*. Ed. by Edgar I. and Jane R. Stewart. Portland, Oregon, Champoeg Press, 1957.

Graham, Col. W. A. *The Custer Myth: A Source Book of Custeriana*. Harrisburg, Stackpole Co., 1953. For the historian, this volume is the most valuable of all the many things that have been written about the Battle of the Little Big Horn. An officer in the Judge Advocate General's Department, Colonel Graham is the only investigator who brought historical method to the much-disputed and overly romanticized battle. As a lawyer, he collected evidence, and—even though a junior officer—not only interviewed but seems to have cross-examined general officers of his day who were subalterns in 1876. Through his efforts of more than thirty years, much primary source material has come to light. Like almost everyone else who has written about the Little Big Horn, Colonel Graham formed his own opinion of Custer, but unlike the others, his opinion is neither dogmatic nor intrusive.

———. *The Story of the Little Big Horn.* Harrisburg, Military Service Publishing Co., 1952.

———. *Abstract of the Official Record of Proceedings of the Reno Court of Inquiry Convened at Chicago, Illinois, 13 January 1879, by the President of the United States upon the request of Major Marcus A. Reno, 7th Cavalry, to Investigate his conduct at the Battle of the Little Big Horn, 25–26 June 1876.* Harrisburg, Stackpole Co., 1954.

Grinnell, George Bird. *The Fighting Cheyennes.* Norman, University of Oklahoma Press, 1956.

———. *Two Great Scouts and Their Pawnee Battalion.* Cleveland, Arthur H. Clark Co., 1928.

Hancock, Major. Gen. W. S. *Reports of Major General W. S. Hancock upon Indian Affairs, with Accompanying Exhibits.* Washington, McGill and Witherow, c.1867.

Hanson, Joseph Mills. *The Conquest of the Missouri: Being the Story of the Life and Exploits of Captain Grant Marsh.* New York, Rinehart & Co., 1946.

Herr, Maj. Gen. John K., and Edward S. Wallace. *The Story of the U. S. Cavalry, 1775–1942.* Boston, Little, Brown & Co., 1953. General Herr was the last Chief of Cavalry.

Howard, O. O. *Nez Perce Joseph.* Boston, Lee & Shepard, 1881.

Hunt, Rockwell D., ed. *California and Californians.* 5 vols. Chicago, 1926.

Keim, DeBenneville Randolph. *Sheridan's Troopers on the Borders.* Philadelphia, Claxton, Remsen & Haffelfinger, 1870. The book gives more of Keim's personal experiences than did his dispatches written from the field during the Washita campaign.

King, Charles A. *Campaigning with Crook and Stories of Army Life.* New York, Harper & Brothers, 1890.

Klose, Nelson. *America's Crop Heritage.* Ames, Iowa State College Press, 1950.

Lounsberry, Col. Clement A. *Early History of North Dakota.* Washington, Liberty Press, 1919.

Mathews, Joseph J. *Reporting the Wars.* Minneapolis, University of Minnesota Press, 1957.

Meacham, A. B. *Wigwam and War-Path; or the Royal Chief in Chains.* Boston, John P. Dale & Co., 1875.

335

————. *Wi-ne-ma and Her People*. Hartford, American Publishing Co., 1876.

Miles, Nelson A. *Serving the Republic*. New York, Harper & Brothers, 1911.

Mills, Anson. *My Story*. Ed. by C. H. Claudy. Washington, published by the author, 1918.

O'Conner, Thomas Power, and Robert McWade. *Gladstone-Parnell and the Great Irish Struggle*. N. p., Edgewood Publishing Co., 1886.

Pelzer, Louis. *Marches of the Dragoons in the Mississippi Valley*. Iowa City, State Historical Society of Iowa, 1917.

Rister, Carl Coke. *Border Command: General Phil Sheridan in the West*. Norman, University of Oklahoma Press, 1944.

Sandoz, Mari, *Crazy Horse, the Strange Man of the Oglalas*. New York, Alfred A. Knopf, 1942.

Sharp, Paul F. *Whoop-Up Country: The Canadian-American West, 1865–1885*. Minneapolis, University of Minnesota Press, 1955.

Sheridan, P. H. *Personal Memoirs*. 2 vols. New York, Charles L. Webster & Co., 1888.

Simpson, William. *Meeting the Sun: A Journey All Round the World*. London, 1874.

Sprague, Marshall. *Massacre: The Tragedy at White River*. Boston Little, Brown & Co., 1957.

Stanley, Henry Morton. *The Autobiography of Sir Henry Morton Stanley*. Ed. by Dorothy Stanley. Boston and New York, Houghton Mifflin, 1909.

————. *My Early Travels and Adventures in America*. 2 vols. New York, Charles Scribner's Sons, 1895.

Starr, Louis M. *Bohemian Brigade*. New York, Alfred A. Knopf, 1954.

Stewart, Edgar I. *Custer's Luck*. Norman, University of Oklahoma Press, 1955.

Strahorn, Carrie Adell. *Fifteen Thousand Miles by Stage*. New York, G. P. Putnam's Sons, 1911.

Sutherland, Thomas A. *Howard's Campaign Against the Nez Perce Indians, 1877*. Portland, Oregon, A. G. Walling, 1878.

Symons, A. J. A. *H. M. Stanley*. New York, Macmillan, 1933.

Vaughn, J. W. *With Crook at the Rosebud*. Harrisburg, Stackpole

Co., 1956. This volume contains the official reports of the Battle of the Rosebud, plus rosters of the various units in Crook's force.

Vestal, Stanley. *New Sources of Indian History, 1850–1891.* Norman, University of Oklahoma Press, 1934.

Villard, Oswald Garrison. *Some Newspapers and Newspaper-men.* New York, Alfred A. Knopf, 1923.

Webb, Walter Prescott. *The Great Plains.* New York, Ginn & Co., 1931.

Wellman, Paul I. *Death on Horseback.* Philadelphia, J. B. Lippincott Co., 1947.

Wilkie, Franc B. *Personal Reminiscences of Thirty-five Years of Journalism.* Chicago, F. J. Schulte & Co., 1891.

Wright, Muriel H. *A Guide to the Indian Tribes of Oklahoma.* Norman, University of Oklahoma Press, 1951.

ARTICLES

Anon. "Hugh McQuaid Told World of the Custer Massacre," *Contributions to the Historical Society of Montana,* Vol. IV. Helena, Historical Society of Montana, 1903.

Bourke, John G. "Mackenzie's Last Fight with the Cheyennes: A Winter Campaign in Wyoming and Montana," *Journal of the Military Service Institution of the United States.* Vol. LIII (November-December, 1913). Reprinted from the same journal of 1890.

Bradley, James H. "Journal of James H. Bradley: The Sioux Campaign of 1876 under the Command of General John Gibbon," *Contributions to the Historical Society of Montana,* Vol. II. Helena, 1896.

DeLand, Charles E. "The Sioux Wars," *South Dakota Historical Collections,* Vol. XV. Pierre, State Department of History, 1930.

Gibbon, Gen. John. "Hunting Sitting Bull," *American Catholic Quarterly Review,* Vol. II (October, 1877).

Hixon, John C. "Custer's 'Mysterious' Mr. Kellogg," *North Dakota History,* Vol. XVII (July, 1950).

Hughes, Col. Robert P. "The Campaign Against the Sioux in 1876," *Journal of the Military Service Institution of the United States,* Vol. XVIII (January, 1896). Text in Graham, *Story of the Little Big Horn.*

Kellogg, Mark. "Mark Kellogg's Diary," *North Dakota History*, Vol. XVII (July, 1950).

Mathews, Joseph J. "The Profession of War Correspondence," *Journalism Quarterly*, Vol. XXXIII (Winter, 1956).

Nafziger, Ralph O. "World War Correspondents and Censorship of the Belligerents," *Journalism Quarterly*, Vol. XIV (September, 1937).

Partoll, Albert J. "After the Custer Battle," *Frontier and Midland*, Vol. XIX (Summer, 1939).

Watson, Elmo Scott. "A Check-List of Indian War Correspondents, 1866–1891," *Journalism Quarterly*, Vol. XVII (December, 1940).

———. "The Indian Wars and the Press, 1866–1867," *Journalism Quarterly*, Vol. XVII (December, 1940).

———. "The Last Indian War, 1890–91—A Study of Newspaper Jingoism," *Journalism Quarterly*, Vol. XX (September, 1943).

INDEX

Boardman, W. P.: 301, 302
Bogart, Robert D.: 113, 130, 135, 136, 156, 157, 330; reports early stage of Modoc War, 106 f.; returns to front, 108; visits Captain Jack, 127–29; leaves field, 137; court-martialed, 138; later life, 319
Bogus Charley: 121–22, 123, 124, 131
Bordeaux, Louis: 173
Boston Charley: 133, 154
Bourke, Lt. John G.: 169, 180, 193, 243, 245, 248, 251, 255, 290, 301
Bozeman, Mont.: 213, 261
Bozeman Trail: 9, 30, 175
Box Family, James: 67–68
Boylan, ——: 313
Brewster, Capt. Charles: 98
Bridger, Jim: 82
Brisbin, Maj. James: 206, 214, 216
Brotherton, Maj. H. D.: 303
Bubb, Lt. J. W.: 168, 277
Buffalo: 8, 70–71
Bunker, William Mitchell: 150–56, 319
Burkholder, Alfred H.: 313
Burns, "Judge": 314
Burt, Capt. A. S.: 171, 188
Butler, Guy: 313

Cabaniss, Dr. T. T.: 140, 143
"California Joe": see Milner, Moses E.
Calamity Jane: 245
Calamity Jim: 261
Calhoun, Lt. James: 211
Camas Prairie: 49–50
Camp Cloud Peak: 193 f., 233 f.
Camp Lyon, Ore.: 34
Camp Robinson, Neb.: 285
Camp Sheridan, Neb.: 298
Camp C. F. Smith, Ore.: 34, 36, 38
Camp Steele, Ore.: 45
Camp Supply, Okla.: 25, 83, 89
Camp Thomas, Ariz.: 305 f.
Camp Warner, Ore.: 34, 42
Campaigns: recognized, 11; winter, 20, 72, 82, 303–304
Campaigns, individual: Modoc, 11, 104–58; Powder River Expedition (Connor), 16; Oregon-Idaho-California, 33–57; Hancock Expedition, 57–68; Washita, 82–103; Sioux-Cheyenne (1876), 160–288;

Sioux-Cheyenne (1876–81), 289–91, 298, 302–304; Nez Percé, 291–95; Bannock, 297–98; Ute, 299 f.; Wounded Knee, 311 f.
Canby, Gen. E. R. S.: 108, 112, 114, 118, 129, 131, 133, 139; quarters, 115; suggests Rosborough, 127; offers amnesty, 130; superiors' confidence in, 136–37; interviews Captain Jack, 140–41; assassinated, 142–43, 157
Captain Jack: 104, 107, 109, 121, 123, 124, 128, 129, 131, 133, 139; meets Canby, 140–41; captured, 152; executed, 154–55
Carland, Lt. John: 215
Carnahan, J. M: 195, 196, 215
Carpenter, Lt. Col. L. H.: 82
Carr, Col. E. A.: 82, 304 f.
Carrington, Col. Henry B.: 30 f., 176
Carroll: 224
Carroll, Matthew: 214
Case, Samuel: 112, 114, 133, 137
Casualties: 11–13; see also under battles and wounded, transportation of
Cavalry: 174, 249, 253–54, 259, 300; horses, 63, 258–59; "troop," 247; see also regiments
Censorship: 307–308
Centennial Exposition: 194
Chambers (boat): 288
Chambers, Col. Alexander: 174, 175, 176, 280
Cheyenne Indians: 9, 10, 59, 60, 62, 71, 78, 86, 89 f., 92, 95, 98, 99, 102, 103, 162, 185 f., 207 f., 231, 236, 241, 289, 290, 291, 314
Cheyenne, Wyo.: 164
Chippewa Indians: 312
Chivington, J. M.: 9
Clark, Edward B.: 313
Clarke, S. A.: 151
Cody, William H. ("Buffalo Bill"): 253, 257, 264, 288
Columbia, Dept. of: 108, 291
Comanche Indians: 9, 14, 19, 65, 71, 78, 99, 103
Competition, newspapers: 108, 129, 178, 189
Connor, Patrick: 23–24
Cook, Lt. Col. W. W.: 98
Cooke, Maj. Philip St. George: 14

Coppenharve, Charles H.: 313
Correspondents, free-lance: 30 f.,
198, 215, 313
Correspondents, war: *vii*, 4–5; early
wars, 27; Civil War, 28, 29, 296,
300, 325; Spanish-American War,
319, 325
Correspondents, Western War: 5;
accreditation of, 6; accuracy of,
31–32, 66, 77, 94, 101, 106–107,
138, 144–45, 150, 156–57, 204,
223, 230–31, 302, 311, 313, 327;
status in field, 36, 175, 301, 317;
assessed, 316 f.; professionalism,
317; writing of, 328
Countryman, Horace: 213
Couriers: 38, 109, 146, 148, 154–55,
178–79, 192–93, 201, 213, 234,
246, 250–51, 253, 261, 269, 296
Crawford, Capt. Jack: 253 f., 274 f.,
276 f., 279, 304 f.
Crawford, Gov. S. J.: 82
Crazy Horse: 161, 170, 180, 181,
185, 191, 231, 266, 275 f., 291
Cressey, Will: 313 f.
Crook, Gen. George: 43, 44, 55, 162,
175–77, 180–91, 193, 198, 233–34,
249, 251 f., 262, 264; on weapons,
18; northwestern campaign, 32 f.;
Sioux campaign, 160 f.; favors pack
trains, 174; at Goose Creek camp,
178–79; reinforcements for, 224;
learns of Custer defeat, 240; hears
from Terry, 241; joins Terry, 257 f.;
separates, 266; on Starvation
March, 267 f.; at Slim Buttes,
275 f.; ends Sioux campaign, 280;
"sham simplicity" of, 283; farewell
to troops, 285; on Powder River
Expedition, 290; in Ute campaign,
300–302
Crook's Peak (or Mountain): 44, 49
Crosby, Lt. Col. J. Schuyler: 98, 100
Crow Indians: 175, 177, 180, 181,
183, 184, 241
Crow King: 303
Custer, Boston: 203, 211
Custer, Mrs. Elizabeth: 200, 201
Custer, Gen. George A.: 64, 100–102,
161, 194, 200, 217, 226, 228, 250;
alleged corruption of, 25; on Hancock expedition, 63; in Washita
campaign, 86 f.; at Battle of Wash-

ita, 88–89, 92–95; finds Elliott's
remains, 98; encourages reporters,
196; deprived of command,
197–98; on Sioux campaign, 201,
202, 204, 225; at Little Big Horn,
205, 206 f., 227; appraised, 218–19

Dakota, Dept. of: 60, 161, 224
Darragh, Capt. John: 37, 42–43, 51
Davenport, Reuben B.: 172, 181,
182, 191, 192, 233, 244, 249, 258,
282–83; joins Crook expedition,
165; begins campaign, 167; on
march, 175; methods of, 178; at
Battle of Rosebud, 187–88; in Big
Horns, 234; criticizes Crook, 241,
260; criticized, 243–45, 247–48;
remains with Crook, 261; appearance of, 265; to Black Hills,
269–70; at Slim Buttes, 271 f.;
attempted coup, 276 f.; leaves
with Crook, 280–81; charged with
cowardice, 284; later life, 319
Davis, Maj. Gen. Jefferson C.: 150,
151
Davis, Theodore R.: *viii*, 62, 63
Day, Benjamin: 28
Dean, Mrs. Teresa Howard: 314
Delano, Columbus: 110, 112, 136,
137, 197
Diamond R Transportation Co.: 214
Diehl, Charles Sanford: 257, 265,
286; assigned to Terry, 220–21;
earlier life, 222; replaces Kellogg,
223; goes to front, 231; on Yellow-
stone, 261; interviews Terry,
287–88; goes home, 288; and
Sitting Bull interview, 296–97, 299;
at Poplar River fight, 303–304;
later life, 319–20
Dispatches: 329
Dodge, Col. Richard I.: 19–21, 21–22
Dorris, P. A.: 109, 110
Dull Knife: 290
Dunn, J. P.: 212
Dyar, L. S.: 139, 141, 142–43, 157
Dyer, John C.: 300

Egan, Capt. Teddy: 170, 277
Eighth Infantry: 23
Elliott, Maj. Joel: 93, 95–96, 97–98,
102, 200, 210
"Epizootic": 148

Grant, U. S.: 25, 70, 100, 197, 321
Great Plains: 3, 7f., 60, 145
Greeley Colony: 300
Greeley, Horace: 28, 300
Green, Maj. John: 112
Gridley, William H.: 216
Grinnell, George Bird: 200
Grouard, Frank: 177, 180, 181, 183,
  234–40, 244, 264, 272 f., 276–79
Grover, Gov. L. F.: 114
Grover, Sharp: 76 f.
Gruneison, Charles L.: 28

Hale, Lt. Owen: 98
Hamilton, Capt. Louis M.: 96
Hancock, Gen. W. S.: 57–68, 71
Harney-Sanborn treaty: 30, 59
Harries, George: 315
Harris, Capt. Moses: 46
Hasbrouck, Capt. H. C.: 152
Hawker Jim: see Hooker Jim
Hawkins, Irving: 313
Hays City, Kan.: 71
Healy, John: 296
Heard, E. H. ("Lige"): 107
Hector, Mrs. Annie French: 225 n.
Henry, Capt. Guy V.: 183, 301–302
Herendeen, George: 264
Hickok, "Wild Bill": 64
Hill, W. J.: 48
Holtes, Charles: 252
Hooker Jim: 105, 119, 126
Howard, James William ("Phocion"):
  223, 230–31, 258, 259, 264–65,
  286; assigned to Terry, 220; earlier
  life, 222; reaches Terry's camp,
  224; goes home, 285; later life, 321
Howard, Gen. O. O.: 18, 291 f.
Hovey, Eugene: 146–47
Hughes, Charles E.: 216
"Humble John": see Smith, John
  Simpson

Idaho: 32–33
Ilges, Maj. Guido: 303–304
Indian Affairs, Bureau of: 14, 21,
  184, 191
Indian agents: 21, 24–24, 105
Indian Campaign Badge: 11
Indian fighting: 5, 71; nature of,
  15–16, 285; as frontier terror, 313;
  see also tactics
Indan scouts: 37 n., 37 f., 92 f., 148,

152, 175, 180, 182, 184, 199, 241,
  247, 253, 254, 256, 283, 305 f.
Indian wars: see Western War and
  under names of tribes
Infantry: 174, 175, 182, 249, 250,
  253, 259, 290, 300; see also names
  of regiments
Inman, Maj. Henry: 97
Iron Plume: see American Horse

Jackson, Capt. James: 105, 152
Jarboe, John R.: 144
Johnson, A. R.: 301
Joseph, Chief: 295, 297
Josephine (boat): 231, 288

Kansas Pacific Railroad: 60, 73–74,
  78, 224
Keim, DeBenneville Randolph: 73,
  79, 83, 84, 85, 91–93, 103; earlier
  life, 69–70; on buffalo hunt, 74;
  interviews Forsyth, 75–77; learns
  of battle, 89–90; on Battle of
  Washita, 94; in Benteen-Custer
  controversy, 95–96; finds Elliott's
  remains, 97–98; explores Wichita
  Mountains, 99; appraised, 100–
  101; on Custer, 102; later life, 321
Kelley, William F.: 313f.
Kellogg, Mark: 194, 199, 200, 202,
  203–204, 206; earlier life, 195 f.;
  assigned, 196; joins Terry, 198;
  "Frontier," 201; on Far West, 205;
  at Little Big Horn, 210; fate of,
  211–12; eulogized, 216–17
Kelly (Crook's scout): 241
Kendall, George Wilkins: 28
Keogh, Capt. Miles: 276
Key West (boat): 231
Kientpoos: see Captain Jack
Kill Eagle: 242
King, Lt. Charles: 258, 283–84
Kiowa Indians: 9, 59, 71, 78, 98, 99,
  103
Klamath Indians: 104
Knapp, Capt. O. C.: 136

Lathrop, Barbour: with Crook, 251 f.,
  258; with Terry, 261 f.; stories,
  265, 285; goes home, 288; later
  life, 321–22
Lawson, Lt. Joseph: 268
Lava Bed: 119, 120, 121, 140, 141

Wallace, Kan.: 73
Walsh, Maj. James M.: 297, 298
Warm Springs Indians: 37 f., 148 f., 152
Wasco Indians: 37 f.
Washakie: 241
Wasson, Joe: 30, 34, 38, 180, 190, 191, 192, 233, 243, 244, 249–50; 255, 261, 266–68; covers Crook's northwestern campaign, 32 f.; fights Indians, 42; learns *Avalanche* sold, 47–48; at Infernal Caverns, 53–56; leaves Silver City, 57; joins Crook's 1876 expedition, 168; appraised, 169; on march, 175; at Battle of Rosebud, 187, 189; in Big Horns, 234; criticizes Terry, 263–64; to Black Hills, 279; leaves with Crook, 280–81; later life, 325
Wasson, John: 32, 48, 57, 168
Watson, Elmo Scott: x
Watson, Sam: 146
Weapons: 14, 18, 47, 76, 148, 187, 199, 242
Weir, Capt. Thomas: 229
Wells, Capt. Elijah: 165
Western Associated Press: 197
Western War: 4; causes, 6–7; prelude to, 8–9; phases of, 10–11;

cost of, 13; territory, 14; command, 15; mobility, 16–17; government's dual role in, 21; *see also* U. S. army, battles, campaigns, casualties, tactics, weapons
Weston, Capt. John F.: 231
Wheaton, Lt. Col. Frank: 107, 108
Whittle, Matilda: 116, 118, 121, 122, 124
Whittle, Robert: 116, 117, 118, 119, 122
Wichita Mountains: 99
Wilber, J. H.: 112
Wild Gal: 122, 124, 128, 131, 132
Willcox, Gen. O. B.: 307, 308
Williams, George H.: 110
Wilson, Dad: 51–52
Wi-ne-ma: *see* Riddle, Tobey
Woods, Gov. George L.: 43
Wounded, transportation of: 190, 213, 230, 279
Wynkoop, Col. E. W.: 62 f.

Yellow Hand: 253
Yellow Journalism: 313
Yellowstone Expedition: *see* Terry, Sioux campaign
Yellowstone National Park: 291, 294
Yreka, Calif.: 104, 105, 106, 108, 109, 143, 146, 150, 158

Following the Indian Wars has been set in 11-point Caledonia, with two points of leading between the lines. Caledonia is an original design by W. A. Dwiggins for the Linotype. While it is suggestive of Scotch Roman and other British modern faces of around 1800, it is distinctly a contemporary type adapted to modern tastes and printing conditions.

UNIVERSITY OF OKLAHOMA PRESS : NORMAN